FOUNDATIONS OF ACCOUNTING

Edited by
RICHARD P. BRIEF
New York University

A GARLAND SERIES

Accounting in Eighteenth Century Scotland

MICHAEL J. MEPHAM

GARLAND PUBLISHING, INC.

NEW YORK & LONDON 1988

For a list of Garland's publications in accounting,
see the final pages of this volume.

Library of Congress Cataloging-in-Publication Data

Mepham, Michael J.
Accounting in eighteenth-century Scotland.
(Foundations of accounting)
Bibliography: p.
Includes index.
1. Accounting—Scotland—History—18th Century. I. Title.
II. Series.
HF5616.G72S375 1988 657'.09411 88-24497
ISBN 0-8240-6117-9 (alk. paper)

Design by Renata Gomes

The volumes in this series are printed on
acid-free, 250-year-life paper.

Printed in the United States of America

Acknowledgements

This book has been published on behalf of the Scottish Committee on Accounting History of the Institute of Chartered Accountants of Scotland.

Some of the material in this book previously appeared in "John Mair, M. A.: Author of the First Classic Bookkeeping Series" (co-authored with Willard Stone), in *Accounting and Business Research* (Spring, 1977); "Robert Hamilton's Contribution to Accounting," in *The Accounting Review* (January, 1983); "Eighteenth Century Origins of Cost Accounting," in *Abacus* (March, 1988). The author's thanks are extended to the editors of these journals for permission to reproduce this material.

The title pages of a number of eighteenth century texts are reproduced, with permission, from texts held in the antiquarian collection of the Institute of Chartered Accountants of Scotland

ACCOUNTING IN EIGHTEENTH CENTURY SCOTLAND

CONTENTS

Contents (continued)

CHAPTER 1

THE ECONOMIC, SOCIAL AND CULTURAL BACKGROUND OF EIGHTEENTH CENTURY SCOTLAND

1.1 Accounting Textbooks

This is a study of the development of accounting in 18th century Scotland. The investigation is organised around a survey of 18th century Scottish accounting texts, an analysis of their exposition of the Italian Method of Book-keeping(1) and their treatment of certain selected topics.

J Crawford has written: "The first Scottish book on accounting was published in 1683. That book heralded a century during which Scotland established its reputation as a land of accountants: a steady stream of textbooks, including some which ran to so many editions that they could be called classics, appeared from Scottish presses."(2)

The view expressed in this comment has received considerable support and is the main motivation for this study. The aim is to evaluate the contribution that these 18th century Scottish writers made and the significance of any improvements that they suggested.

All the 18th century Scottish publications were reviewed and from this it was possible to identify certain topics as being appropriate for more detailed consideration. The review also suggested that the emphasis should be placed on an impressive series of texts produced by four of the writers. These are:

Alexander Malcolm	1685-1763
John Mair	1702 (or 1703)-1769
William Gordon	1720 (or 1721)-1793
Robert Hamilton	1743-1829.

In 1813 James Morrison, accountant, textbook writer and Master of the Mercantile Academy at Glasgow, characterised the last three of these as: " ... the elaborate Mair, the ingenious Gordon and the judicious Hamilton".(3)

The importance of the texts must be stressed. Although many accountants and bookkeepers learned their craft solely by experience gained from working in the counting houses of merchants and manufacturers, the formal teaching of the subject in schools and mercantile academies expanded considerably during the century and the writings of Malcolm, Mair, Gordon and Hamilton played a major part in spreading a knowledge of the 'Italian Method of Book-keeping' throughout Scotland and beyond.(4) By disseminating knowledge of the Italian system, the books gave valuable support to the developing economy which was growing rapidly from 1750.(5)

As trading conditions changed and business methods and structures became more complex, the techniques that the text books discussed adjusted in response. The manner in which the books developed will be considered. It is not the purpose of this study to research 18th century accounting practices, as evidenced by surviving records, but, where convenient and relevant, an attempt will be made to compare the textbook methods and theory with contemporary accounting records. This point is important because, although much can be learned from a study of the textbooks, it cannot be assumed that these always described the contemporary 'state of the art'. The textbooks did adapt but there was a time lag and it seems likely that accounting theory (as presented in the texts) was often well behind practice. Even as early as the 1680's the New Mills Cloth Manufactory of Haddington had developed a management accounting system(6) which was more sophisticated than anything described by the textbook writers until Robert Hamilton's book one hundred years later.(7) It follows that it is not possible to assume that successful textbooks mirrored the best (or even the most common) practice.(8)

The 18th century saw the origins of the Scottish accountancy profession and relevant features of this development will also be considered where appropriate.

1.2 The Economic, Social and Cultural Background of Scotland in 1700

This first chapter describes the economic and social background of Scotland in the 18th century and suggests some reasons for her accounting progress in this period.

At the end of 17th century Scotland had been hit by successive failures of the harvest, there was the aftermath of the Darien disaster,(9) the effect of internal conflict(10) and commercial repercussions from the English wars with Holland (in the reign of Charles II) and with France (in the reigns of William and Anne). Apart from the sale of cattle and linen,(11) trade between Scotland and England was minimal. In 1700 Scotland was poor in comparison with its southern neighbour and it has been suggested that fully 300 years of economic development separated the two countries.(12)

Although it is right to emphasise the economic poverty of Scotland at this time, Smout considers the 1690's as the period when the " ... Scots first began to consider economic growth as an objective at which society should aim"(13) and Sombart(14) claims that the change in the attitude of Scots at the end of the 17th century was dramatic. He says: "Nowhere else in the world did the birth of capitalism come about in so curious a fashion as in Scotland. Nothing is more surprising than the suddenness of its appearance. It is as though a pistol-shot had given the signal for the capitalist spirit, fully grown, to come into the land and dominate it ... Everywhere you might have observed an unbridled desire for gain and undertakings innumerable."(15)

Clearly there can be debate about the definitions of the 'capitalist spirit' and 'capitalism' and whether, with any given definitions, Sombart is correct(16) but contemporary support for the view that some Scots believed that an important change was taking place in economic attitudes, is provided by Colinson. In 1683 Colinson, in the first Scottish book on book-keeping, expressed his view that the number of new Scottish manufacturing ventures was increasing and that there was optimism that trade would grow and flourish. He said: " ... Manufacturies are erected, and a hopeful appearance of their encreasse and continuance, doeth every day encourage the Nation to Traffique ... ".(17)

Marshall provides a list of manufacturing enterprises founded in Scotland from 1560 to 1707.(18) This list can be summarised as follows:

Date of Foundation	Number of Enterprises
1581-1590	2
1591-1600	1
1601-1610	2
1611-1620	10
1621-1630	3
1631-1640	5
1641-1650	4
1651-1660	2
1661-1670	9
1671-1680	6
1681-1690	18
1691-1700	36
1701-1707	8

This might be regarded as corroborative evidence for

Colinson's statement but the numbers are small and it is appropriate to use Weber's distinction between the appearance of the 'capitalist spirit' and the arrival of 'capitalism', the former being a contributory factor to the latter.(19)

1.3 The Religious Background and the Capitalist Spirit

The increasing number of manufacturing enterprises can certainly be regarded as evidence of the appearance of the 'capitalist spirit' in Scotland. Weber(20) used the term 'capitalist spirit' in his thesis that 'the origins of the modern capitalist mentality may be located in the neo-Calvinist ethic of the seventeenth century'.(21) Weber argued that profit maximising economic man is not a universal type. In earlier times, he would have been viewed as unethical aberrant but Calvinism led to a mode of everyday conduct which fostered the spirit of capitalism and gave it moral legitimacy. Weber considered that this 'spirit' was an important feature in the initial stages of the development of the modern capitalist form of economic organisation but that, once the system 'took off', it became self supporting without the need for religious sanctions.

Calvinism encouraged the believer to adopt a certain ethical posture of 'inner-worldly asceticism'. The Calvinist 'inner-worldly' ascetic engaged in strenuous, protracted effort as God's servant and on behalf of God's purpose. This 'calling' was to be exercised within his immediate social environment and in pursuit of his mundane calling at his work place. For those involved in business as traders or manufacturers this developed into an occupational ethic (Weber's 'spirit of capitalism').(22)

In short, Calvinism taught that a secular life could be a holy life.(23) The importance that was attached to being 'called' and providing visible proof of this, led to exhortations to diligence in following ones calling and an emphasis on such virtues as thrift, education, prudence, sobriety and self control. Weber believed that this ethical posture legitimated the capitalistic search for profit.

Marshall sets out to test the applicability of Weber's theory to Scotland and he believes that his study supports the thesis in so far as it deals with "the psychological consequences of the Calvinist ethic for the development of modern capitalist activity as far as the behaviour of Scots capitalists is concerned".(24) In the course of his study Marshall devotes some time to a consideration of a 'case study' of the use of accounting controls by a Scottish 'manufactory' at the end of the 17th century(25) and he regards this as evidence of a capitalistic approach to trade. He provides evidence to show that the accounting system was providing information useful for profit maximisers. Starting with Colinson, the contemporary authors, did recognise this as an accounting objective but they also emphasised another feature, this is accounting's role in the maintenance of justice(26) which was essential for the promotion of commerce. In this connection Colinson described book-keeping as 'the very Scale of Commerce'.(27)

Marshall does not consider the need for justice in the economic system although the capitalistic search for business profit would only have been regarded as legitimate by Calvin if it took place within a framework that ensured justice, albeit a less restrictive form of morality than that obtaining in the middle ages which required merchants to charge a 'just price'.(28) "Calvinism ... was the first of the Reformation movements to recognise the existence of a new economic society characterized by the commercial rather than the mediaeval agrarian viewpoint" but "In no sense did he (Calvin) encourage moral laxity in economic relations. On the contrary, he tried to moralize as never before all phases of social life."(29)

The law might provide the required framework but the regularity of the merchant's books and their completeness, when maintained under the 'Italian Method', were the instruments of ensuring justice in detail. Although traders might view their book-keeping systems as aids in the pursuit of profit, the textbook authors(30) emphasised that double entry was also a 'Regular and Ingenious form' designed to prevent 'all disorder in the Common wealth of Traffique'.(31)

1.4 Accounting Developments and the Emergence of Capitalism

In addition to accounting's roles of ensuring morality in a capitalist system and providing information for profit maximising decision makers, Sombart has argued that the double entry book-keeping technique was, in general, a prerequisite for the development of a capitalist system. To successfully pursue the goal of profit maximisation, the capitalist must have a method of quantifying his profit and gauging the effect of his actions on this profit.

"The idea of creation of wealth is developed in double-entry bookkeeping to the point where the 'wealth producing sum,' that is, the amount invested for the purpose of obtaining profits, is separated from all natural objectives of human welfare. In double-entry bookkeeping there is only one objective: the increase of a sum of money, expressed in purely quantitative terms. He who buries himself in double-entry bookkeeping forgets all quantities of goods and work, forgets all the organic limitations of the necessity to satisfy human wants, and satisfies himself solely with the idea of wealth: he cannot do otherwise if he is to understand this system ... As double-entry bookkeeping first created the concept of capital, so it simultaneously created the concept of the capitalistic enterprise as that economic organization, that institution, whose object is the evaluation of a particular capital ... We have established that the essence of the capitalistic enterprise as an assemblage of property must be seen to lie in the separation of the business from its owners.(32) The bookkeeping system substantially aids this separation of the business."(33)

This theory has been disputed by Yamey(34) and the question will not be considered in detail here. For our purposes it is sufficient to note that the century which saw the development of capitalism in Scotland also saw the development of accounting and to recognise that there were important interactions between the two.

1.5 Changes in the First Half of the Eighteenth Century

It can be argued that the emergence of the capitalist spirit interacted with other changes that were taking place at the turn of the century to form a basis for economic advancement within a capitalist system. A crucial development was the Treaty of Union of 1707 (35) but the short term economic effects of this were not all good for Scotland. New taxes placed additional burdens on the economy.(36) The Anglo-Scottish Common Market created by the Union did not lead to an instantaneous growth of trade with England but there was a steady improvement in this and overseas trade.(37)

In 1700 Scotland's trading partners were the countries of northern Europe, the Hanse towns,(38) Scandinavia, northern France and even Russia. The trade with the Netherlands was particularly important so that the English commercial writer Sir Josiah Childs (1630-1699) complained that "The trades of Scotland and Ireland, two of our own Kingdoms, the Dutch have bereaved us of, and in effect wholly engrossed to themselves."(39) At the end of the 17th century the Scottish Staple at Veere(40) had been in decline, opening up the possibility of an expansion of trade with other major Dutch cities. Rotterdam became the real centre for Scottish trade.(41) At the Scottish end of this trade the east coast had an advantage. This led to the development of trading activity in the East of Scotland and Edinburgh, whereas Glasgow and the West were at a distict disadvantage. The linen trade, which developed early on in the 18th century, was also strongest on the east coast (Angus, Fife, Perth and Edinburgh) which was well placed for importing flax from the Baltic countries.

During the first half of the century, however, the balance shifted. Article 4 of the 1707 Treaty gave Scottish traders entry to England's jealously guarded colonial markets, without payment of customs duties, and article 5 gave Scottish owned ships the protection and privileges afforded by the Navigation Acts. John Gibson, an 18th century Glasgow accountant who wrote a book on the history of Glasgow, explains Glasgow's commercial development as follows: "The Union with England opened a field of trade, for which the situation of Glasgow was greatly to her advantage; the commerce of the east coast, since that period, has declined: that of the west has increased to an amazing degree."(42)

The 15th article of the Treaty of Union included a provision " ... that Two Thousand Pounds per annum, for the space of seven Years shall be applyed towards Encouraging and promoting the Manufacture of coarse wool ... And afterwards the same shall be applyed towards the Encouraging and promoting the Fisheries and such other Manufactures and Improvements in Scotland as may most conduce to the general Good of the United Kingdom." Nothing was done with this fund until 1727 when Parliament passed 'An Act for Encouraging and Promoting Fisheries and Other Manufactures and Improvements in Scotland' and 'An Act for the Better

Regulation of the Linen and Hempen Manufactures in Scotland'. The Board of Trustees for Manufactures, established under the first of these Acts, started with an accumulated fund of £30,000.

At the time of the Union, linen manufacture was Scotland's most important industry. This trade had received benefits from the Union with England, in the form of export bounties and tariff protection from the competition of Dutch and German manufacturers but the general standard of Scottish linen was poor. The trade received considerable assistance from the formation of the Board for Manufactures. In 1728 the output was 2,200,000 yards; in 1742, 4,500,000 yards and in 1750, 7,575,000 yards.(43)

In agriculture there was also progress and significant change(44) although there was nothing that could be called an agricultural revolution before 1750. Farmers were producing grain surpluses in most years between 1680 and 1740 (apart from a disastrous period at the end of the century) and the extension of the grain bounty to Scotland in 1709 stimulated the export of grain. The major trade with England in 1700 was, however, in livestock and this trade increased considerably. The number of beasts exported south rose from 14,000 in 1701 to 30,000 in 1709 (45) and prices were rising. Adam Smith claimed that: "Of all the commercial advantages ... which Scotland has derived from the union with England, this rise in the price of cattle is, perhaps the greatest. It has not only raised the value of all highland estates, but it has, perhaps, been the principal cause of the improvement of the low country."(46)

The 1715 and 1745 Jacobite risings were worrying interludes for those who were benefiting from the changes in the economic and social conditions but, when these were passed, the ensuing period of political stability enabled the pace of change to quicken. There were extensive road building programmes in the Highlands following the rebellions.

1.6 Changes in the Second Half of the Century

Any estimate of Scotland's population at the start of the 18th century is inevitably dubious and largely calculated guesswork, but a review of the estimates that have been made suggests that a figure of 1,000,000 may be a reasonable guess.(47) By 1755 this had grown to 1,265,000.(48) An analysis of the total is interesting since it shows that the majority lived in the Highlands (652,000) against 464,000 in the central district and 149,000 in the Lowlands. The first official census took place in 1801 and this showed a growth to 1,599,000. Although population increased in all regions, the largest increase was in the central district and by 1820 almost half the Scots lived in the central belt.

Seventy years after the Treaty of Union, James Scruton, of the Academy in Glasgow, in the introduction to his accounting text, asked the rhetorical question "what was Scotland before its union with England?"(49) By that time the economic advantages of the union were clear, particularly to someone living in Glasgow. In writing this, Scruton would have had in mind Glasgow's flourishing trade with the West Indies and North America - a trade which was only possible after the Treaty of 1707 had permitted Scotland to trade with the English overseas possessions. The tobacco trade was the outstanding feature; by 1762, tobacco comprised 40% of all Scotland's imports from overseas and accounted for 52% of all her exports.(50) The funds generated by the tobacco trade found their way into other trades and helped to stimulate the economy.

Although the tobacco trade(51) collapsed with the American War of Independence (1776-1783), just as Scruton was writing, Scotland consolidated its industrial success in the second half of the century and started a period of economic expansion which lasted until the 1870's. The sugar trade(52) with the West Indies, which had been in existence since the beginning of the century, developed rapidly, partially filling the gap caused by the demise of the tobacco trade.

At the beginning of the 19th century Macpherson described these and other developments: "The merchants of Glasgow, when their American trade was interrupted by the war, extended the West-Indian branch of their commerce, and resumed, or enlarged, their trade with the continent of Europe, which their convenient situation for the trade with America had made them in some degree overlook for many years bypast. A considerable number of them withdrew their capitals from foreign trade and shipping, in order to employ them in manufactures, the improvements of which, and the establishment of new ones, were with good reason thought to afford a prospect of more permanent, as well as more solid, prosperity than foreign trade ... from about this time the quantity of manufactured goods, sent from Glasgow to London and other parts of England, was greatly increased ... ".(53)

Linen manufacture, was one industry which benefited from the funds generated by the tobacco trade. This industry experienced an era of rapid growth in the period from 1740 to 1780 and the profits earned from it, in turn, became an important additional source of capital for the developing manufacture of cotton yarn and cloth. This new branch of the textile industry, which was centred on Glasgow and Paisley, was soon making use of spinning machines driven by water power.(54) In another major development, the first important iron works was built at Carron near Falkirk in 1759.(55)

The improvements in agriculture continued in the second

half of the century. There was an expansion of sheep farming in the Highlands and this was accompanied by considerable consolidation of land holdings because sheep farming was less labour intensive than raising cattle.(56) Swarms of destitute Highlanders made their way to the Lowlands or emigrated to America. The Clan System, which had been weakened by the '15 and '45 rebellions, collapsed in this period.

1.7 The Scottish Enlightenment

In addition to the major economic and social changes that took place during the lifetimes of Malcolm, Mair, Gordon and Hamilton, the age in which they wrote their accounting texts is distinguished in other respects. In recent years the period has become known as the Scottish Enlightenment. It is the remarkable epoch which Dugald Stewart described as a "sudden burst of genius".(57) To put the four into context it is useful to list dates for, and to outline the achievements of, three of their more famous contemporaries who are regarded as leaders of the movement:

David Hume 1711-1776 Philosopher and Historian
Adam Smith 1723-1790 Political Economist
Lord Kames (Henry Home) 1696-1782 Lawyer and Philosopher

In philosophy, Hume must be ranked as one of the great writers. His 'Treatise of Human Nature' (1739/40) contains the most complete exposition of his theories. He tried to remove metaphysical speculation from philosophy and to separate religion from the discussion of moral and social conduct. The Treatise was considered to be antireligious but a sceptical approach to religion was not uncommon among the leaders of the Enlightenment. Hume's 'History of England' went beyond the conventional political treatment and dealt with the cultural dimension of history.

In law, MacCormick lists ten notable Scottish texts in the period from 1681, when James Dalrymple, first Viscount Stair, transformed the existing chaotic collection of court decisions into a complete and coherent legal system in his "Institutions", to 1810. He comments: "By contrast, in England over the whole period only one work appeared which in any way aspired to the same general standard, Blackstone's Commentaries on the Laws of England (1st ed 1756-9). Blackstone himself notes with regret the extent to which contemporary English legal writing lags behind Scottish."(58)

Henry Home, Lord Kames, has been described as a 'philosopher-judge'.(59) He wrote on both law and philosophy and 'contributed prolifically to both disciplines'.(60) His approach was often historical and this was particularly relevant for his treatment of commercial law where he emphasised that changing commercial conditions required appropriate modifications to the Scottish legal system. The law and philosophy did not exhaust his talents and energy and he was also active as an agricultural improver in Berwickshire and Perthshire and as an important propagandist for this movement.(61)

In the field of political economy Sir James Steuart (1712-1780) " ... was the author of the first comprehensive treatise in English entitled Political Oeconomy, one of the first to introduce a rigorous scientific methodology, deductive as well as inductive, into economic enquiries ... ".(62) 'An Inquiry into the Principles of Political Oeconomy' was published in 1767 by A. Millar and T. Cadell, London but it was Adam Smith's 'The Wealth of Nations' that overshadowed all other contemporary writings. When it was published in 1776 it immediately became the most influential economic work. Fox praised it in the House of Commons, Lord

North and the Younger Pitt consulted both it and its author on their economic policy, and Smith was commissioned to make a number of economic studies for the Government of the day. Chitnis has even suggested that " ... political economy, was a new discipline produced by the Scottish Enlightenment".(63) Others, while not going as far as Chitnis, fully recognise the importance of the Scottish contribution.

"Although Adam Smith did not create the study of political economy, The Wealth of Nations, coming at a point when 'natural liberty' was being widely debated, had a decisive influence both on the study of national economy and on the freeing of economic policy from the artificial restraint of the mercantilist system. Smith's statement that labour is the source of a nation's commodities and that the variations in 'stock' values are due to the interaction of wages, profits, and rent, formulated the doctrine of the classic school of economic thought, and round it all modern economic discussion has revolved."(64)

Adam Smith, David Hume and Lord Kames are recognised as leading figures in this extraordinary development of philosophy, law and economics, but the Enlightenment was not restricted to a small group working in a narrow range of subjects. There were many other important advances in a wide range of disciplines such as medicine, mathematics, agriculture, chemistry, geology, sociology, anthropology and psychology. The roll call of luminaries would include such people as: William Hunter, Andrew Duncan, William Cullen, Colin Maclaurin, James Hutton, Joseph Black, William Robertson, Adam Ferguson and John Millar. The Enlightenment also saw a flowering of the arts so that there were great architects (such as Robert Adam), a noteable literary revival (Sir Walter Scott, Tobias Smollet etc.) and the poetry of Robert Burns.

1.8 Accounting and the Enlightenment

David Hume emphasised the catalytic effect of the 'spirit of the age': "The same age which produces great philosophers and politicians, renowned generals and poets, usually abounds with skilful weavers, and ship-carpenters. We cannot reasonably expect, that a piece of woollen cloth will be wrought to perfection in a nation which is ignorant of astronomy, or where ethics are neglected. The spirit of the age affects all the arts; and the minds of men, being once roused from their lethargy, and put into a fermentation, turn themselves on all sides, and carry improvements into every art and science."(65)

The effect of the Enlightenment on the intellectual and cultural life of Scotland was dramatic but, as Hume suggested, there were also substantial improvements in the practical arts. Douglas Young considers that " ... the Scots thinkers of the Enlightenment not merely refused to recognize any distinction between the pure and applied sciences, but were prepared to treat the practical applicability of their speculations as a yardstick of their merits".(66) Examples of this emphasis on the practical are: Francis Home (Professor of Materia Medica at the University of Edinburgh) whc undertook experiments in bleaching to improve Scottish linen, William Cullen (Professor of Chemistry at the same university) who was a pioneer in the chemistry of soils and manures (a study with obvious applicability to the improvement of farmland and estates) and Profesor Black (Professor of Chemistry at the University of Glasgow) who cooperated with James Watt's steam engine experiments. It is likely that the Scottish accounting authors were encouraged by this enlightened attitude to the practical arts.

The Enlightenment also fostered a belief in the printed word as an instrument in the advancement of society and it gave encouragement to the publication of 'academic' texts of all kinds. This was assisted by the strength of the printing industry in Edinburgh. These factors also helped the accounting authors and a majority of their texts were published in Edinburgh. Arnot states that in 1739 there were only 4 printers in that city but 40 years later the number had risen to 29.(67) In part the large number was sustained by reprinting English books which were not protected by the English copyright restrictions (68) but there were, in addition, substantial numbers of Scottish works. From the 1730's the Edinburgh firms produced cheaper texts than the London printers.(69) Towards the end of the century it even seemed possible that Edinburgh might supplant London as the main centre of publishing in Britain and in 1869, when its best days were gone, Bremner could still describe printing as "the staple industry of Edinburgh"(70)

Authors frequently published their own works but there were also important publishing houses and Hamilton had family connections with the major publishing firm of Hamilton, Balfour and Neill. This firm alone published 400 titles between 1750 and 1762.(71) Publishing was profitable and publishers and booksellers were able "to offer substantial advances for their works".(72)

It seems clear that the 'Scottish Ascendancy'(73) in accounting texts was facilitated by the Scottish Enlightenment but it does not necessarily follow that it is appropriate to consider Alexander Malcolm, John Mair, William Gordon and Robert Hamilton as <u>part</u> of the Enlightenment. The following chapters will provide evidence that is proper to consider their achievements in this way.

1.9 Summary

This chapter has argued that the emergence of the

capitalist spirit in Scotland and the country's economic progress during the 18th century created a need for a wider knowledge of accounting to enable the new capitalists to manage their enterprises profitably whilst reassuring them that they were operating within a just framework. Reciprocally, whether or not Sombart's thesis is accepted, it is clear that the more widespread knowledge of sound accounting practices helped capitalism to develop.

If the 'Spirit of Capitalism' created a demand for accounting texts, it was the 'Spirit of the Enlightenment' which provided an environment conducive to the creation of 'improving' texts such as the series of important Scottish accounting texts that will be reviewed in this study. Without the combination of factors that have been considered in this chapter, it is difficult to believe that this period of 'Scottish Ascendancy' would have occurred when the conditions for advance might have seemed to be so much more propitious in England.

In the 18th century Scottish writers did much to popularise the Italian Method and to develop it from the 200-year tradition that Pacioli had initiated with his 'Summa de Arithmetica, Geometria, Proportioni et Proportionalita' in 1494.(74) Some of the writings demonstrate significant advances in accounting thought and the development of some important ideas and techniques which remain relevant more than 200 years later. This book will consider whether this series of Scottish 18th century book-keeping texts (which culminated in Hamilton's 'Introduction to Merchandize') established the basis for a new discipline of Accounting from the old 'Bookkeeping after the Italian Method.'

CHAPTER 2

AUTHORS, TEACHERS AND PRACTITIONERS

2.1 The Dutch Contribution to Scottish Accounting

The economic importance of Scottish trading connections with Holland has been emphasised in chapter one, but there is another sense in which these links were relevant. Italy's earlier leadership in book-keeping had passed, by the 17th century, to the Dutch. Sir Josiah Childs (a contemporary English writer on commerce) suggests that one reason for the the commercial success of the Netherlands was the emphasis that the Dutch placed on "The Education of their Children, as well Daughters as Sons, all which be they never so great Quality or Estate, they always take care ... to have the full knowledge of Arithemetic and Merchants-Accounts"(1) and Sombart points out that in the 17th century " ... more than 60 books on accounting were published in the Dutch language".(2) Scotland's trade links with Holland, thus, contributed to the wider knowledge of the Italian Method of Book-keeping among Scottish merchants.

Colinson, who had lived and traded in Holland,(3) provides contemporary confirmation of the important part that the Dutch played in the dissemination of the knowledge of book-keeping. He says "Amsterdam hath been a great nurserie of this Science" (ie book-keeping). 'Nurserie' is a particularly appropriate metaphor since, increasingly training in Holland was an alternative to apprenticeship at home, which had been the major form of mercantile education throughout the 17th century. Apprenticeship involved a lengthy and costly training period. Its normal duration was seven years although this had begun to fall even during the course of the 17th century and, by the 1720's three year apprenticeships had become the norm in Dundee and

Aberdeen.(4)

For young Scots with business ambitions, money and the right connections, the advantages of training in Holland were attractive. "In the later seventeenth century Scots enrolled in mercantile 'schools' in the great Dutch commercial centres of Amsterdam, Rotterdam and Dort where the arts of cyphering,(5) accounting and languages were taught. When William Dunlop of Glasgow was in Dort in 1681 there were five fellow Scots from Edinburgh in his class and a much larger number under instruction in Rotterdam."(6) An example of an accountant who gained his experience by this route is George Watson (1644-1723) who Richard Brown has identified as "the first professional accountant in Scotland".(7) Watson followed three years apprenticeship in an Edinburgh merchant house with study in Rotterdam, from 1672 to 1675, to improve his arithmetic, book-keeping and knowledge of Dutch.(8)

2.2 Scottish Accounting Education

Although many Scots went to Holland for their mercantile education, provision for such studies at home was improving at the beginning of the 18th century. In the first decade of the century both Glasgow and Edinburgh Councils established the official post of teacher of book-keeping and there were other developments.

In 1696 the Scottish Parliament had passed an Act for the Settling of Schools which decreed that "there be a School Settled and Established, and a School-Master appointed in every Paroch, not already provided ... And for that effect, That the Heretors in every Paroch meet, and provide a commodious House for a School, and Settle and Modifie a Sallary to a School-Master, which shall not be under one hundred Merks, nor above two hundred Merks ... ". This act had a marked effect on the provision of educational facilities throughout Scotland. Although the parish school system did not apply in the burghs, there were primary and grammar schools in all towns of any size and there were also 'sessional schools' funded and managed by the Kirk.

Although a grammar school education, in the first half of the century, was almost entirely devoted to Latin and the classics,(9) by 1750 changes in the curriculum were taking place and mathematics, science and book-keeping were finding a place.(10)

Scotland's first professional accountant, George Watson, demonstrated his conviction that book-keeping should have a place in the school curriculum when, in leaving instructions in his will for the establishment of a school, he provided that the scholars should be instructed in accounting and book-keeping - "res praesertim arithmetica et rationaria".(11) Watson died in 1723; his school, George Watson's Hospital, opened in 1741.

Five years later, in 1746, the curriculum at Ayr Grammar School was broadened to include mathematics, navigation, natural philosophy, surveying and book-keeping. This development took place under the able direction of John Mair, whose achievements will be outlined in chapter 4 and whose accounting texts will be considered throughout this study. Mair was later chosen to head the new Academy in Perth which was opened in 1761. This was founded to provide a new style of curriculum with an emphasis on Science, English, Civil History, Mathematics, Book-keeping, Religion and (later) Drawing and Painting. On Mair's death, in 1769, another noteable accounting writer, Robert Hamilton, whose career is considered in chapter 6, took over the rectorship. The achievements of Perth Academy under the leadership of Mair and Hamilton soon led to the foundation of similar academies in Dundee, Inverness, Elgin, Fortrose, Ayr and Dumfries.(12)

The new academies typically included mercantile studies as an important part of the syllabus. Alongside these developments, as the century passed, there was a rapid growth in the number of private educational establishments run by writing masters and book-keeping teachers.

2.3 The Background of the Educators

It is probably true that most teachers of accounting in the first half of the 18th century had practical accounting experience and that they used their expertise to assist local merchants.

One Edinburgh teacher at the beginning of the century makes this clear in advertising his services:

> That Alexander Heriot, now Book-keeper to New - Milns - Manufactury at Edinburgh, who hath these many Years Taught Book-keeping, still continues to do the same: so that any who desire to Learn, may Speak with him at his own House, in the Turnpike at the East-Entry of the Meal-Mercat in the Cowgate, or at the foresaid New - Milns - Manufactory Hall below the Trone-Church.(13)

Heriot's post as book-keeper to the New Mills Cloth Manufactury (the manufactury used by Marshall as a case study of early capitalism in Scotland)(14) seems to have been a professional appointment rather than a full-time job(15) and it is possible that he was primarily a practitioner who did some teaching rather than the reverse.

The New Mills copartnery seem to have made a considerable effort to develop the control features of its accounting system. Soon after its formation in 1681 it had obtained specialist advice from a Mr Collison (or Collineson) to bring " ... John Raes bookes in some good method and particularly to putt Mr Rae upon keeping a memoriall book of every dayes proceedings as its really acted and done quhich the master is to take inspection of soe often as he pleases ... ".(16) Bywater and Yamey suggest that this consultant may have been Robert Colinson the author of the first Scottish book on book-keeping.(17)

About the same time that Heriot was working for the New Mills Manufactury, another accountant John Dickson, 'Book-keeper and Accomptant to the Good Town of Edinburgh' was appointed by Edinburgh Town Council to be a master and Professor of Book-keeping.(18) He advertised his appointment as follows:

> The Council of Edinburgh considering how necessary the Science of Book-holding is for the Advantage of Trade and Commerce, especially when the same is carried on in Co-partnery, have therefore thought it convenient to establish a publick Profession of the said Science within this City; And having several Years Experience of the Ability and Capacity of John Dickson Merchant (present Book-keeper and Accomptant to the Good Town of Edinburgh) to teach the said Science: Do therefore Nominat and Authorize the said John Dickson to be Master and Professor thereof within this City, Extracted by Adam Watt Clerk
>
> The said John Dickson having finished his two Setts of Book-holding, as a Form and Rule to teach the said Science in a clear compendious Method, conform to the Italian Rule, wherein is included a Stated Accompt of a Fisherie in Company, with a Stated Ac-

compt of a Draw-back, conform to the late Act of Parliament: Any who desires to be taught the said Science of Book-holding, they may apply themselves to the said John Dickson, at his Lodgings in the Parliament Clos the Entry to the Meal-Mercat, where he will agree with the Persons. (19)

Some fifty years later the post of 'Master and Professor of Book-keeping' seems to have lapsed since William Stevenson, a teacher of book-keeping who described himself as "some time Merchant in Rotterdam ",(20) proposes such an appointment in his book "A Serious Advice to Tradesmen shewing them the Inconveniencies they lye under ... by not learning book-keeping: with a proposal for having that art more universally well taught, under the Authority and Inspection of the Magistrates ... " (1756). At page three he emphasises his practical experience: " ... I have been frequently employed in revising books of all kinds, and regulating Accompts which were confused and out of order; upon which occasions I always observed, that the reason of the confusion proceeded either from the persons concerned not having been taught BOOK-KEEPING at all, or their being taught it in such an indistinct manner, that neither they, (and I'm afraid I may say) nor their Teachers, know much about the affair."(21)

This last comment may indicate that book-keeping teachers in the second half of the century were less likely to have had a practical accounting background. William Gordon, of the Glasgow Mercantile Academy, also comments on the need for improvement in commercial education in the introductory essay to Volume I of his Universal Accountant (1763). He proffers the view that: " ... there is not another class of men, in the British community, who labour under greater disadvantage, in point of education, than that of the commercial profession." Echoing Stevenson, he laments the fact that the time spent at grammar school and university studies are not geared to providing a relevant education. He also comments on " ... the low opinion that is generally entertained of the use of those studies among men of business ... "(22) and he gives suggestions for an appropriate curriculum.

The supply, if not the quality, of commercial teachers increased dramatically in the second half of the century. Most of the teaching was carried out by private teachers with many of these coming from England.(23) In 1768 Stevenson was experiencing the effect of this increase in competition as is shown by the following advertisement in the Caledonian Mercury:

> William Stevenson, who has taught Book-keeping upwards of forty years in Edinburgh, finding the city now over stocked with young teachers of that branch of education, has thought proper to move to the Canongate, both for the benefit of a free air, and that he expects to have as good a chance of getting a few scholars - His house is over against Mr Crichton's Coach and harness manufactory, where he now teaches as well as ever, notwithstanding of its having been falsely reported, that he is superannuated and ab agendo, and therefore hopes, that his well-wishers and old scholars will not forget him, but continue to recommend as formerly. - He will also, when employed, balance books or accounts that have fallen into disorder, and translate Dutch or French papers into English upon very reasonable terms.(24)

Figure 1 shows the growth in the number of book-keeping teachers in Edinburgh during the century. This might be compared with the increase in the city's population from about 25,000 in 1700, to 50,000 in 1750 and about 100,000 in 1800.(25) The graph is based on the details in Appendix 1 (Edinburgh Teachers of Book-keeping) which was prepared from information gleaned from a variety of sources.(26)

Where there is information that a book-keeping teacher was operating in a given decade it has been assumed, for the purposes of the graph, that he was active throughout that decade. The dramatic increase in the number of teachers in the last 30 years of the century is undoubtedly exaggerated because much of the information comes from street directories which are absent for the earlier period. The reduction in the last decade of the century might suggest that the boom of the 70's and 80's had resulted in an oversupply of teachers in that period.

There is some doubt about the teaching specialisms of some teachers listed; the details given in contemporary newspaper advertisements is helpful but many teachers did not advertise their services in this way. From the advertisements it seems that the link between mathematics and accounting was strong enough to allow the assumption that most teachers of mathematics also taught book-keeping. Similarly it is probable that most 'writing masters' were also book-keeping teachers. There are fewer street directories available for Glasgow but it seems likely that the picture there would have been similar to that in Edinburgh. In 1776 John Anderson, Professor of Natural Philosophy at the University of Glasgow, claimed that there were 500 persons in Glasgow who had studied the double entry system and were well enough versed in the art to be able to manage the university's accounts.(27)

All four of the authors that will be considered in some

FIGURE 1

EDINBURGH TEACHERS OF BOOK-KEEPING

AND ACCOUNTS IN THE EIGHTEENTH CENTURY

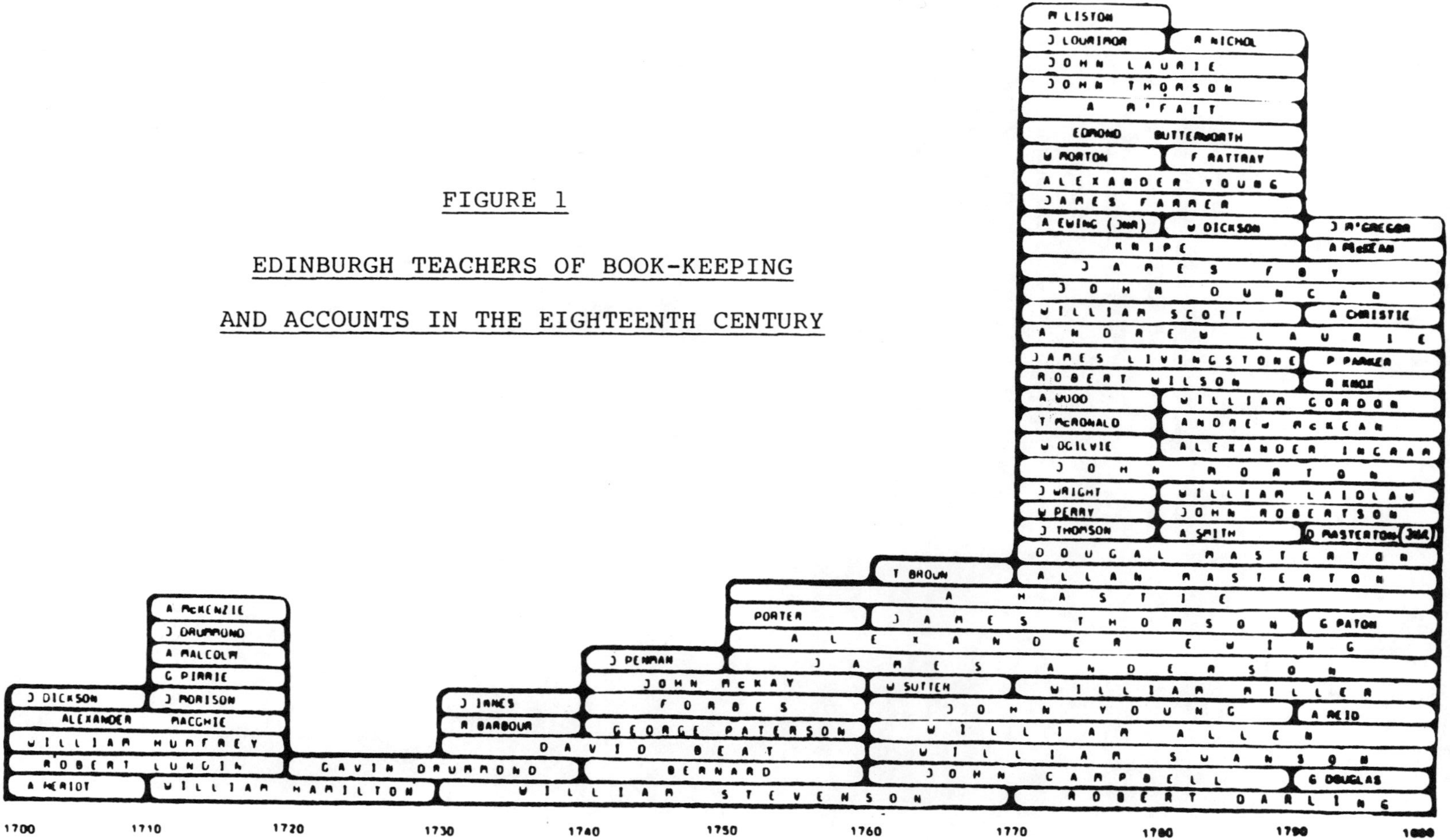

detail in this study, were teachers in Scotland. Malcolm taught in both Edinburgh and Aberdeen before emigrating to America. Gordon, after teaching at Fochabers and Stirling, opened his own Mercantile Academy in Glasgow and later taught at a similar establishment in Edinburgh. Mair held the post of rector at both Ayr Grammar School and Perth Academy and supervised the important curriculum developments that took place in these institutions. Hamilton followed Mair as rector of Perth Academy and then moved to a chair at Marischal College, one of the two universities in Aberdeen. All four were themselves products of the Scottish university system. They were all well educated and the brief biographies (given in chapters 3 to 6) will show that they all wrote on other topics beyond that of accounting. Some of these other books can be regarded as important contributions to such disciplines as Music, Economics, Mathematics and Social Studies.

Hamilton had practical experience of business and finance and his family had extensive business interests. Gordon dabbled (unwisely) in bill discounting. Mair's father was a manufacturer and his detailed treatment of some technical topics suggests that he may have had some practical experience of them. There is no direct evidence that Malcolm had a business background.

2.4 Accountants as Teachers

It has been emphasised that it was quite common for teachers of book-keeping to undertake professional accountancy work. Conversely it was not unusual for accountants to do some teaching. This latter point is illustrated by the following account(28) rendered by James Ewart, Accomptant in Edinburgh to The British Linen Company:

The British Linen Company
To
James Ewart Accomptant in Edin. Dr

1746	To Planing the Companys Books	£31 10 -
	To Acting the part of Chief Accomptant for 1 1/4 years from Oct. 1746 To Jany 1748 both incl @ £60 per Ann	75 - -
	To Instructing their Accomptant and one of his Clerks in the Art of Book-keeping	10 10 -
	To A Written Table Book for Calculating of Interest at 4 and 5 per Cent per Ann	3 3 -
		£120 3 -

Edin. 22nd December 1748

I hereby referr the Determination of the above Acco to the Right Honourable The Lord Milton

James Ewart

Ewart was one of a growing number of book-keepers and accountants employed by merchants and manufacturers as the century passed.

2.5 University Education

Although one of our authors (Robert Hamilton) was a university professor, accounting was not a university subject until the 20th century. Its inclusion in the syllabus was, however, advocated by William Gordon. In addition to the advances taking place in the nation's school system, 18th century Scotland had a strong, well established university sector(29) and, during the century, important reforms were taking place in the methods of teaching and the educational programmes provided by the universities. In 1783, when Gordon moved to Edinburgh, the University had chairs in: Medicine (5), Divinity (3), Law (3), Oriental Languages, Civil History, Botany, Chemistry, Greek, Humanity, Mathematicks and Astronomy, Moral Philosophy, Natural History, Natural Philosophy, Logic and Rhetorick.(30) Three years later (1786) the Edinburgh Chamber of Commerce was established by Royal Charter.(31) These developments together with the progressive and innovative atmosphere of the 'Enlightenment' and the character of Scottish universities,(32) led Gordon to include in the New Modelled fifth edition of his Universal Accountant (1787) a strong plea for the creation of Chairs in Accounting at all universities.

Gordon argues that a university course in accounting and commerce would be of much more public utility than the established classes of logic and metaphysics. He writes: "The ideas to which a young mind hath been early accustomed, generally make the most lasting impression, wherefore it would tend much to the prosperity of trade, that not only such as are intended for the commercial line, but that all youth of distinction also, should be early introduced to the knowledge of figures and accounts, and of commercial affairs, as far at least as they are connected with the public revenue and police. For this purpose, it is to be regretted, that a proper Professor is not appointed in every University in Britain, where a commercial class would, perhaps, be of more public utility than all the logic and metaphysics that have ever been devised; were this the case, we should not only have more intelligent merchants, but the members of both Houses of Parliament, would thereby become better judges of political economy ... ".(33)

2.6 Accountants and Lawyers

Accounting had to wait 150 years before it was to be fully recognised as a university subject but Law was an established academic discipline in the 18th century and in the second half of that century some lawyers began to move into accounting.

Although much of the business development was based on Glasgow and the West, the mercantile law business of Edinburgh lawyers expanded along with Glasgow's growing prosperity. Lockhart pointed out that " ... the more the commercial towns thrive, the more business is created for this legal one ... every great merchant in Glasgow pays large salaries to some two or three members of the law in Edinburgh, who conduct the numerous litigations, that arise out of a flourishing business with great civility".(34) In addition the Jacobite Rebellions created much work for the lawyers although this work was mainly concerned with the forfeiture of estates.

Edinburgh was well supplied (perhaps oversupplied) with writers (ie law agents) but the term 'writer' was used in a vague sense. The membership of the elite group of 'Writers to His Majesty's Signet' was small and the majority of those who described themselves as 'writers' did not join the Society of Solicitors to the Court of Session and other Supreme Courts of Scotland (the SSC) which was founded in 1784.(35) In the second half of the century, some of these 'unattached' writers began to practise as accountants and to regard this as a valid legal specialism.

The 18th century Book-keeping authors, however, did not view accountancy as a profession. Although there were a few accountants practising as such before 1750, it is clear that Mair, for example, uses the description 'accomptant' to mean a merchant skilled in book-keeping and his 'Book-keeping Methodiz'd' was primarily written for "the young merchant" to help him to become such an accomptant.(36) The textbook authors were, however, convinced of the universal usefulness of the new art and Stevenson, in the 1730's, specifically noted its relevance for the legal profession: "How often are the Lawiers themselves puzzled in carrying on their Clients Processes, by their not being thoroughly acquainted with Numbers, and the Nature of stating Accounts as they ought? For which Reason they are frequently obliged to employ Accomptants to regulate the Accounts, and give them due information for the Managing their Pleadings."(37)

There was economic sense for lawyers to take this advice and to develop accounting as a specialism because " ... the Scottish Courts were more willing to recognise the standing of the independent accountant than were Courts in England".(38) In England matters of accounting were dealt with by Masters in Chancery whereas in Scotland such matters were often remitted to an accountant (not a court official) for investigation and a report.

It might be noted that, in addition to serving as 'a great nurserie' for accounting, Holland also trained many Scots lawyers throughout the 18th century.(39) Stevenson's 'Kidnapped' has David Balfour seeking instruction in Holland.

2.7 Bankruptcy Work

Lockhart, whose comments on the work provided for Edinburgh lawyers by the Glasgow merchants has already been quoted, went on to say that still more work was generated by "the more numerous litigations which attend the untwisting of the Gordian knot of mercantile difficulties and embarrassments".(40) In a similar way the emerging accountancy profession was stimulated both by commercial advance and the growth of capitalism and, paradoxically, by the business failures and the bankruptcies which followed the loss of the American colonies and the French Revolution. Accountants in Edinburgh had much bankruptcy work despite the fact that they were not mentioned in the Bankruptcy Act of 1696. This Act sought to prevent the bankrupt favouring certain of his creditors to the prejudice of the remainder.(41) Murray comments on the position as follows: "During the later years of the seventeenth century, and the early part of the eighteenth, many complicated questions ... arose for judicial determination amongst creditors ... In settling the various claims which were presented, it became the practice of the court to remit to an accountant to prepare a scheme."(42)

The use of accountants in bankruptcy increased substantially following an act of 1772. This statute " ... was the first to provide a judicial process of sequestration by which the bankrupt's estate was transferred to a trustee for the benefit of creditors as a whole, thereby preventing a creditor from acquiring a preference by the use of diligence."(43)

The act provided that: "A two-thirds majority of the creditors might demand that the sequestration should be carried through not by a factor but by a trustee or trustees of their own choice."(44) In 1783 another act restricted sequestration to traders but extended its scope to cover heritable property.(45)

2.8 Estate Accounting

Helped by their strong links with the legal profession, some of the early professional accountants in Edinburgh became heavily involved in accountancy and audit work for the large estate owners. A good example of the manner in which such a practice arose is afforded by the estate of the Duke of Gordon. Cosmo George, 3rd Duke of Gordon, inherited his estate whilst a minor so that the estate was managed by trustees. These trustees instituted a system of regular audits by professional accountants(46) and, in similar circumstances, other trustees did the same.(47)

An additional factor was that owners of large estates were frequently in need of financial assistance. Many estates were being improved and reorganised in the second half of the century. Although there were commercial benefits to be gained from such improvements, they required considerable investment by the landowner.

Chapter 14 discusses the role of accountants as financial advisors to the large estates. In this connection, Grant says: "To a considerable degree accountants came to be employed as trustees or judicial factors on estates where the owners were in financial difficulties ... reference might be made to William Keith, trustee for James Drummond, Lord Perth (CS 18/714, no 17), Samuel Clerk, Trustee on Clanranald, (GD 201/5/769 etc), James Brown, trustee of Lord MacDonald's estates (GD 221/153/6) and Patrick Cockburn (GD 46/1/92) and Thomas Mansfield, (GD 46/1/106) trustees on the Seaforth estates".(48)

Accountants were also employed to deal with the substantial amount of accounting work which was required in connection with the estates forfeited after the 1745 rebellion.

2.9 Municipal Accounting

Francis Farquharson, the auditor of the estate of the Duke of Gordon, also acted for Edinburgh town council. In early January 1758 he and Alexander Chalmers, another Edinburgh accountant, were appointed to examine the books of the Charity-Workhouse. Money had been provided for the Workhouse six years earlier and " ... in order to satisfy the Inhabitants, that the Sum raised by voluntary contribution in the year 1752 had been truly expended in the Service of the House, and that the Contribution they now ask for is necessary for the Support of it; that some Persons of Judgement and Skill in these matters, should be appointed to examine the Books which relate to the Affairs of the House, from the Time the foresaid Contribution was made to this Time, and that their Opinion thereof should be reported, before another Contribution was authorised".(49)

Farquharson and Chalmers (described as 'Accountants') were included in this committee and it was agreed to ask them " ... to examine by themselves these Books and Accounts, with such Vouchers as they find necessary for their Inspection, and they to report their Opinion on the whole."

The 'Act' continues: " ... pursuant to the foresaid Remit, the said Mr Francis Farquharson and Mr Alexander Chalmers having accordingly (upon the 9th January current) met, and examined the Books of the Affairs of the Charity-Workhouse, from January 1752, when the last voluntary Contribution was made within the City, down to 30th day of September last, did find that Contribution (which amounted to L.1626 : 18 : 2), and interest arising from the interim Loans thereof, fairly entered and accounted for, except L.200, which has been uplifted and applied since the said 30th of September last; and find, that the Books are balanced, examined, and docketted by a Quorum of the weekly managers, and the whole drawn into a general Abstract yearly; and having compared the yearly Accounts with the general Abstract referred to in the Representation, and marked by them as relative hereto, did find the same agree with the Books; and having summed up the particular and general Accounts before mentioned, find them rightly summed, and the Balances rightly carried forward: And, upon the Whole, so far as they could judge from the said Examination, they were humbly of Opinion, that the Books are kept in as regular and distinct a Method as the Variety of Circumstances attending so extensive a Management can admit".(50)

Two years later Francis Farquharson and Thomas Boswell, accountants, were appointed members of a committee to consider a scheme for a new water supply that was proposed for Edinburgh.(51) It seems that the town council recognised the relevance and value of financial and accounting expertise for municipal projects.

2.10 The Expanding Profession

Figure 2 shows the increasing numbers of Edinburgh accountants during the century. This chart has been prepared from the details in Appendix 2 which is derived from a variety of sources, including information in Williamson's Edinburgh Directories and supporting evidence provided by Murray(52) and Brown.(53) The table and the chart are intended to relate to professional accountants but there is often considerable uncertainty as to the exact nature of the work that was undertaken by someone who is described, in these 18th century street directories, as an 'accomptant'. It has been assumed, however, that someone who so described himself is likely to have been offering professional accountancy services to the business community. If there is evidence that an individual was operating as an accountant in a particular decade it has been assumed for the purposes of the chart that he was active throughout the decade. Another difficulty experienced in the preparation of the chart is the fact that much more information is available for the last 30 years of the century, than for the first 70 years. It seems unreasonable to assume that there was no growth in the number of accountants in the middle years of the century.

2.11 Merchants and Accountants

From a perusal of the few 18th century Glasgow Directories that were published, it seems that most accountants in that city, were employed in merchants' Counting Houses. There are fewer references to practising accountants than in the Edinburgh directories. For example, John Tait's Directory for the City of Glasgow, 1783-1784, lists five accountants. Although not so evident, the profession was also emerging in Glasgow. In 1778 John Gibson of Glasgow, announced the commencement of his accountancy practice in The Glasgow Mercury.(54) This advertisement was as follows:

JOHN GIBSON

Who has been regularly bred to business, offers his services to the Public, as an ACCOUNTANT in EXAMINING and ADJUSTING of BOOKS and ACCOUNTS; SETTLING OF COPARTNERY or OTHER DISPUTES, MAKING OUT ACCOUNTS of the RANKING of CREDITORS, and the DIVISIONS of SUBJECTS, and ACCOUNTS of EVERY KIND, and in transacting every other species of business, as practised by the most approved Accountants in Edinburgh.

Gentlemen of the Law, or others, who shall be pleased to favour him with their business, may depend upon having it executed with the utmost fidelity and dispatch."(55)

In this advertisement it should be noted that Edinburgh practice is acknowledged as constituting a model for emulation but it should also be recognised that the backgrounds of the Glasgow practitioners tended to differ from that of Edinburgh accountants. In Edinburgh there was the strong connection with the legal profession. Glasgow

FIGURE 2

EDINBURGH ACCOUNTANTS

IN THE EIGHTEENTH CENTURY

Those accountants shown below the heavy line seem to have had a legal background.

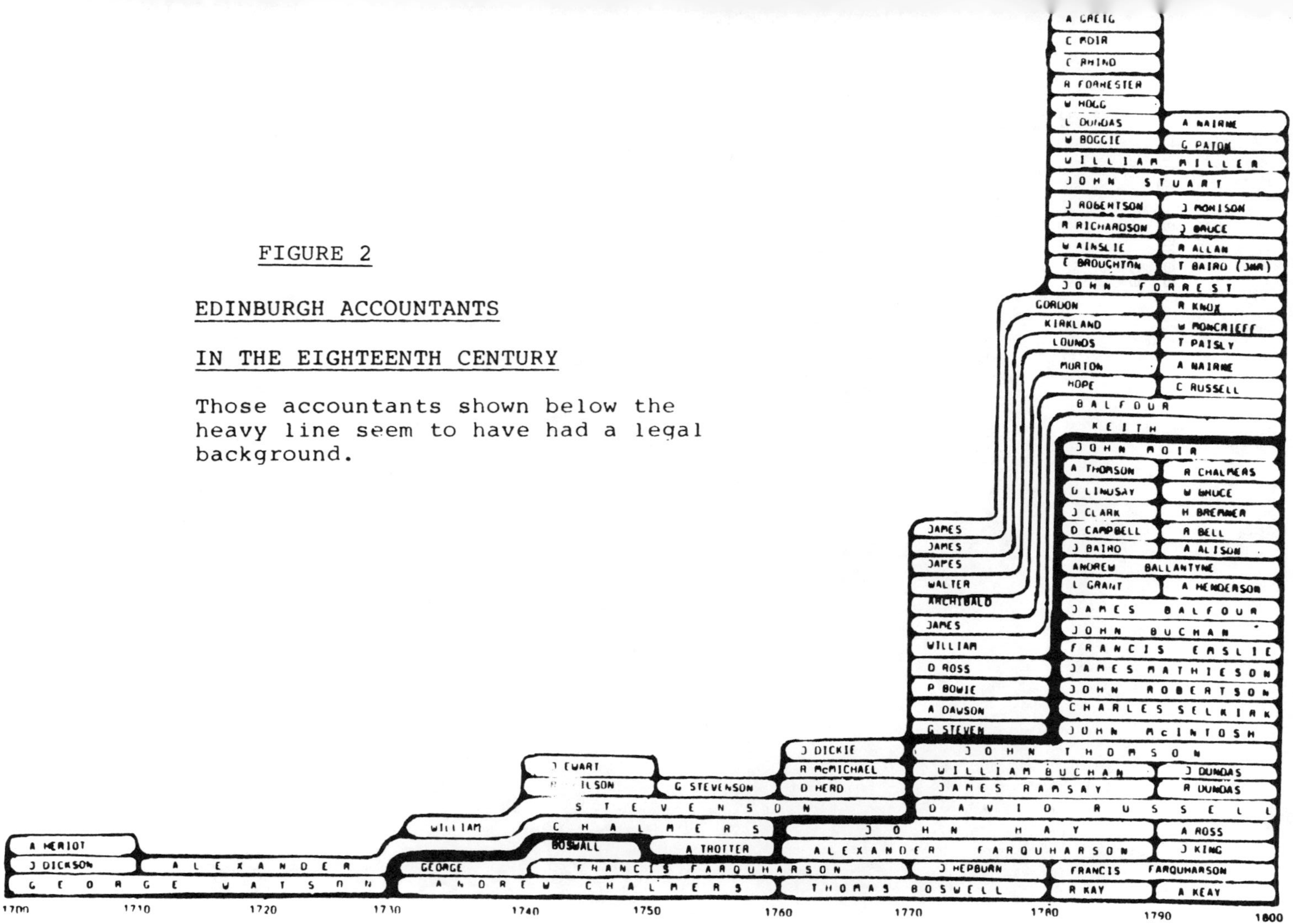

accountants had more commonly been merchants although they also were involved in bankruptcy work. In the year following the Bankruptcy Act of 1783, Gibson (by then in partnership with Richard Smellie) extended the range of services proffered, to include acting as "Factors on Estates and Subjects, under the management of Executors or Creditors".(56)

2.12 Summary

In the early 18th century the teachers of accounting and the authors of book-keeping texts usually had practical business experience. There was some overlap so that accountants might do some teaching and teachers might write up a local merchant's books. Commonly accountants and book-keeping teachers received their commercial education abroad (in Holland) but the provision of book-keeping as a formal part of the school curriculum in Scotland increased substantially in the second half of the century. As the century passed, in both Glasgow and Edinburgh, private teachers of writing, book-keeping and mathematics flourished and their numbers increased despite complaints that the quality of the tuition was falling as teachers no longer had practical experience to reinforce their book knowledge. In 1756 Stevenson deprecated the fact that " ... some of those who pretend to teach ... have never seen or written books in real business ... "(57) and " ... know little or nothing about it ... ".(58)

Pedagogically there was a strong connection between book-keeping and mathematics.(59) Mathematical works were written by Malcolm, Gordon, Mair and Hamilton and often textbooks embraced both mathematics and book-keeping.(60) Gordon preferred to call himself a mathematician and Hamilton was ultimately to become Professor of Mathematics at Marischal College. Although the textbook writers considered book-keeping to be a branch of business mathematics, they were also aware of the importance of the law (particularly the law concerning bills of exchange) and they included relevant information on commercial law and practice in their texts. This legal link was more important as the embryonic profession of accountancy began to develop from merchant book-keeping in the second half of the century. This development had its roots in the legal profession.(61)

The origins of the Scottish accountancy profession can be clearly seen in the 18th century movement of some Edinburgh lawyers towards a specialisation in accountancy which began a hundred years before the profession was formally established in the second half of the 19th century.(62) There was a similar development in Glasgow but there the accountants were more likely to have a merchant background in one of the many counting houses of Glasgow or the West of Scotland.

CHAPTER 2

APPENDIX 1

EDINBURGH TEACHERS OF BOOK-KEEPING AND ACCOUNTS

The following listing of 18th century Edinburgh teachers of book-keeping has been derived from a variety of sources. The basic list is that given by Law (Law, A, 'Teachers in Edinburgh in the Eighteenth Century', Book of the Old Edinburgh Club, Vol XXXII, 1966) but this has been supplemented by detail obtained from street directories.

Key to References

AD = Thomas Aitchison's Edinburgh Directory.

WD = Peter Williamson's Edinburgh Directory.

Law = Law, A - 'Teachers in Edinburgh in the Eighteenth Century', Book of the Old Edinburgh Club, Vol XXXII, 1966.

ALLEN, William
Teacher of writing, arithmetic, book-keeping, navigation (Law), Luckenbooths (Edinburgh Courant, 11 November 1767; 16 August 1783; WD 1773/74-76/77, 80/81-84/85); Fleshmarket Close, Scale Stairs (WD 1788/90, 90/92, 94/96).

ANDERSON, James
Master SSPCK Charity Working School (Law; Caledonian Mercury, 3 September 1759); Teacher of writing, arithmetic, accounts, book-keeping in the Italian Method, shorthand, French (Law); Writing master, foot of Forrester's Wynd (WD 1773/74); head of Blackfriars Wynd (WD 1773/74-76/77); Marlin's Wynd (Edinburgh Courant, 26 Ocober 1785); Writing master, Advocates Close (WD 1790/92, 94/96).

BARBOUR, Robert
Teacher of mathematics and book-keeping (Law); Horse Wynd (Caledonian Mercury, 11 October, 1736).

BEAT, David
Writing master (Law); Carrubers Close (Caledonian Mercury, 21 September, 1730; Edinburgh Courant, 5 March, 1756).

BERNARD
Teacher of French, Italian, Latin; also taught: writing, book-keeping, arithmetic and geography through the medium of French (Law); Niddry's Wynd (Caledonian Mercury, 6

September, 1743); Bull's land over against Tron Church (Edinburgh Courant, 30 January, 1755).

BROWN, Thomas
Teacher of writing, arithmetic and book-keeping (Law); Upper Common Close, Head of Cannongate (Edinburgh Courant, 31 May, 1766).

BUTTERWORTH, Edmond (Edward)
Writing Master at High School (Law); Horse Wynd (appointed 23 August, 1780) also taught privately at house in Brown Square (Edinburgh Courant, 22 November, 1780; Caledonian Mercury, 31 July, 1784; WD 1786/88). Niddery's Wynd (WD 1783/84). At one time partner to Andrew McKean.

CAMPBELL, John
Writing Master, Old Assembly Close (WD 1774/75, 75/76); Milne's Square (WD 1780/81); opposite the Linen Hall (WD 1780/81); Canongate Head (WD 1782/83); Milne's Square (WD 1782/83, 83/84) Subscriber to Stevenson's 'Bookkeeping by Double Entry', 1762 (described as Writing master); described by Law as teacher of English, writing and singing. Entries in Williamson's Directory commence in 1774/75 but there is a John Campbell who is described as 'merchant - Writers Court' in WD for 1773/74.

CHRISTIE, Adam
Writing master, 5 South Bridge (WD 1790/92), Christie's Writing School, 5 South Bridge (AD 1793/94, WD 94/96); Morison's Close (AD 1797/98).

DARLING, Robert
Teacher of mathematics, geography, writing, book-keeping (Law); Gosford's Close (WD 1774/75, 75/76); Ramsay's Land, opposite City Guard (Caledonian Mercury, 1 June, 1776); Warriston's Close (WD 1780/81, 83/84, 84/85); Luckenbooths (WD 1788/90, 90/92, 94/96) Warriston's Close (AD 1793/94, 97/98).

DICKSON, John
Teacher of book-keeping (Law); appointed by Town Council (Minutes of Town Council 15 June 1705; Edinburgh Courant, 15 October, 1705).

DICKSON, W
Teacher of writing, arithmetic, book-keeping (Law); South Bridge Street (Caledonian Mercury, 25 April, 1789).

DOUGLAS, George
Teacher of mathematics (Law); Lady Stairs Close (AD 1793/94).

DRUMMOND, Gavin
Teacher of arithmetic, book-keeping, navigation (Law); Dickson's Close (Caledonian Mercury, 29 August, 1728; 17 October, 1737).

DRUMMOND, John
Merchant and Teacher of book-keeping, author of 'Accomptant's Pocket Companion', Edinburgh, 1718 (Murray; Law).

DUNCAN, John
School-master, Libberton's Wynd (WD 1773/74); Canongate-head (WD 1774/75-78/79); Lawnmarket (WD 1788/90); Libberton's Wynd (WD 1790/92); Teacher of Mathematics, Libberton's Wynd (AD 1793/94, 97/98).

EWAN (or EWING), Alexander
Teacher of mathematics, writing, book-keeping etc (Law); Horse Wynd (Edinburgh Courant, 10 February, 1756); School-master, Cowgate (WD 1773/74); Teacher of Mathematics, Bishop's Land (WD 1774/75-78/79); Bishop's Close (WD 1780/81-83/84); Bishop's Land (1784/85-90/92, AD 93/94, WD 94/96, AD 97/98; Edinburgh Courant, 17 April, 1790); Ewan was the author of 'Institutes of Arithmetic'; he was a subscriber to Stevenson's 'Bookkeeping by Double Entry', 1762, and was there described as 'teacher of mathematics'.

EWING, Alexander (Junior)
Son of above, teacher of writing, arithmetic, book-keeping (Law); St Anne Street (Caledonian Mercury, 28 November, 1778; 17 November 1779).

FARMER, James
Partner of Dougal Masterton (Law); Bell's Wynd (WD 1780/81-84/85; Edinburgh Courant, 8 March, 1775; Caledonian Mercury, 22 December, 1784).

FORBES
Teacher of French, Italian, Latin; also taught: writing, book-keeping, arithmetic and geography through the medium of French (Law); Niddry's Wynd (Caledonian Mercury, 6 September, 1743, 3 March 1752); Bull's land over against Tron Church (Edinburgh Courant, 30 January, 1755).

FOY, James
Writing master, Skinners Close (WD 1774/75-90/92).

GORDON, William (1720/21-1793)
Teacher of arithmetic, book-keeping and Latin (Law); Mercantile Academy in the Scale Stairs, Head of Blackfriar's Wynd (Caledonian Mercury, 30 September, 1786; 24 October, 1789). Moved to Edinburgh from Glasgow in 1783. Teacher of

Mathematics, Allan's Close (WD 1788/90); Chalmers Close (WD 1790/92); Carruber's Close (AD 1793/94, WD 1794/96); Paton and Gordon, Commercial Academy, South Bridge (WD 1794/96). Author of 'The Universal Accountant and Complete Merchant' (1763/65) and 'The General Counting-House and Man of Business' (1770). Died 12 December, 1793 (Scot's Magazine, 1793, p 621).

HAMILTON, William
Teacher of book-keeping (Law) (Edinburgh Courant, 24 September, 1718; Caledonian Mercury, 23 December, 1740); Author of 'Bookkeeping New Modelled' (1735) (published after he had moved to Perth).

HASTIE, A
Teacher at George Watson's Hospital 1757-1760 (Law); Commercial Academy, 37 North Bridge (AD 1797/98).

HERIOT, Alexander
Teacher of book-keeping, Meal Market, Cowgate (Edinburgh Courant, 14 August, 1706). Book-keeper to New Mills Factory at Haddington.

HUMFREY, William
Teacher of book-keeping, Partner of Robert Lundin (Edinburgh Courant, 31 March - 2 April, 1708); Hand and Pen, Opposite the Cross, South Side (Scots Courant, 6 June, 1716); Middle of Cant's Close (advertisement in Lundin's pamphlet 'A Reason of Accompting by Debitor and Creditor', 1718).

INGRAM, Alexander
Appointed teacher of writing, arithmetic, mathematics in town of Leith in 1783, also taught shorthand and book-keeping, Niddry's Wynd (Law); later Kirkgate, Leith (AD 1797/98).

INNES, John
Teacher of mathematics, geography (Law); Stewart's Close (Caledonian Mercury, 19 November, 1730; 17 November, 1737). Before 1727 he taught mathematics at the University of Saint Andrews. Author of 'A Dissertation Concerning the Arithmetick of Annuities', Edinburgh, 1741.

KNIPE
Teacher of writing, accounts at Academy (Law); Riddle's Close (Caledonian Mercury, 13 November, 1784). Perhaps this is Rev Knipe.

KNOX, Robert
Teacher, Baxter's Close, House Bristo Street (WD 1794/96); Mathematician, North Richmond's Street and Todrick's Wynd (AD 1797/98); practising as an accountant, 1793 (Brown).

LAIDLAW, William
Teacher of mathematics, accounts, book-keeping, practical mathematics for the marine and military professions (Law); Bishops Land (Caledonian Mercury, 24 October, 1789; WD 1790/92, AD 93/94); head of Stevenlaw's Close (WD 1794/96, AD 97/98).

LAURIE (or LOWRIE or LAWRIE), Andrew (died 1794)
Writing master, Campbell's Close, Cowgate (WD 1774/75-88/90, 94/96). Died August 1, 1794 (Scot's Magazine, 1794, p 512).

LAURIE, John (died 1791)
Mathematician (Law); Anchor Close (WD 1775/76-77/78); author of a book of interest tables, 1776. Scot's Magazine, 1791 notes death at Leith of Mr John Laurie, Land Waiter formerly teacher of mathematics (p 155).

LISTON, Matthew
Teacher of mathematics, Hammermen's Land, Cowgate (WD 1774/75-78/79).

LIVINGSTONE, James
Writing master (Law), West Bow, (WD 1774/75-78/79, 82/83, 83/84); Brodie's Close (WD 1784/85, 86/88).

LOURIMOR (or LORIMER), James
Mathematician, Teacher at Heriot's Hospital 1773-1775 (Law); Anchor Close (WD 1775/76).

LUNDIN, Robert
Teacher of writing, arithmetic, book-keeping (Law); Hand and Pen, Opposite the Cross, South Side (Scots Courant, 6 June, 1716); Author of 'The Reason for Accompting by Debitor and Creditor', 1718; there is an advertisement for his school in this book, giving the address as Middle of Cant's Closs; Partner of William Humfrey.

M'FAIT, Dr Ebenezer
Mathematician (Law), Merlin's Wynd, Leith (WD 1773/74); foot of Horse Wynd (WD 1778/79, 80/81-86/87); in the directories from 1774/75 to 1777/78 M'Fait is described as a 'musician'.

MacGHIE, Alexander (died 1715)
Author of 'The Principles of bookkeeping Explain'd', Edinburgh, 1718; (Edinburgh Courant, 18 February, 1715).

M'GREGOR, John
Teacher of Mathematics, Parliament C (WD 1794/96).

McKAY, John
Teacher of writing, arithmetic, book-keeping; Master at

George Watson's Hospital 1746-175?, (George Watson's College - History and Record - 1724-1970).

McKEAN (or McKAIN), Alexander
Writing master, 35 South Bridge, East Side (WD 1790/92, AD 93/94, WD 94/96, AD 97/98).

McKEAN, Andrew
Teacher of writing with book-keeping (Caledonian Mercury, 30 May, 1789; WD 1793/94). At one time partner to Edward Butterworth.

McKENZIE, Alexander,
Teacher of mathematics (Law) (Edinburgh Courant, 23 May, 1715; 21 October, 1715).

McRONALD, Theodore
Teacher of writing, arithmetic, book-keeping, mathematics (Law); Baron Maule's Close (Caledonian Mercury, 10 November, 1779).

MALCOLM, Alexander
Teacher of Book-keeping (Law); Cowgate, opposite Burnet's Close (Edinburgh Courant, 18 February, 1715); Author of 'A New Treatise of Arithmetic and Bookkeeping', Edinburgh, 1718 and 'A Treatise of Book-keeping', London, 1731; moved to Aberdeen in early 1720's, then to America.

MASTERTON, Allan (died 1799)
Writing master, Old Assembly Close (WD 1774/75, 75/76), School-master (WD 1776/77); Stonelaws Close (1777/78); Writing master (WD 1778/79); Stevenlaw's Close (WD 1780/81-84/85, 86/88); High School writing master from 1795 (Law); Carruber's Close (WD 1788/90, 90/92, 94/96, AD 97/98). Friend of Burns featuring in his poem 'Willie Brew'd a Peck o'Maut' (Scot's Magazine, September 1824, p 337).

MASTERTON, Dougal (or Dugald) (Senior)
Writing master, Opposite the Guard (WD 1774/75, 75/76, 78/79, 80/81, 82/83-84/85, 86/88, 88/90; Edinburgh Courant, 8 March 1775); writing master to High School (Law); High School Yards (WD 1790/92, 94/96, AD 97/98).

MASTERTON, Dugald (Junior)
Writing master at High School with his father (Law), presumably in the 1790's.

MILLER (or MILLAR), William
Writing master, Cannongate, later Niddry's Wynd (Law; Caledonian Mercury, 29 May, 1779; Edinburgh Courant, 24 November, 1781); Accomptant, Back of the Guard (WD 1783/84); Writing master (WD 1784/85, 86/88, 88/90); Writing master

and Accountant, Blackfriar's Wynd (WD 1790/92, AD 93/94); described only as 'Writing master' in WD 1794/96; Strichen's Close (AD 1797/98).

MORISON, John
Teacher of mathematics, astronomy, dialling and the Italian method of book-keeping, Peebles Wynd (Scots Courant, 16 March, 1716).

MORTON, John
Writing master, teacher of writing, arithmetic, book-keeping, geography (Law); School-master, Merlin's Wynd (WD 1773/74); Writing master (1774/75-76/77); Opposite the Guard (WD 1777/78); Cant's Close (Caledonian Mercury, 24 November, 1784; WD 1778/79, 80/81, 84/85, 86/88, 90/92); Carubber's Close (WD 1788/90); 32 George's Street (WD 1794/96); Milne's Square and 32 George's Street (AD 1797/98).

MORTON, Walter
Accomptant, Opposite the Guard (WD 1774/75, 75/76); Writing master and Accomptant of Excise, Opposite the Guard (WD 1778/79); practising as accountant 1774-1780 (Brown).

NICHOL, Robert
Teacher of Arithmetic, writing, book-keeping, mathematics, geography, Dicksons Close (Caledonian Mercury, 6 May 1786 - 9 December, 1786).

OGILVIE, William
Teaching English, Latin, arithmetic, writing, book-keeping (Law); Vinegar Close, Leith (Caledonian Mercury, 6 May 1776; 21 April, 1777).

PARKER, P
Teacher of mathematics, head of North Bridge (AD 1797/98).

PATERSON, George
Teacher of arithmetic, book-keeping (Law), Horse, Wynd (Edinburgh Courant, 21 October, 1746; 6 November, 1753).

PATON, George
There is a George Paton described as 'of the customs, Castle Hill' in WD from 1774/75-1778/79; Writing master to the High School, appointed 10 November 1790, jointly with Edward Butterworth; Writing master, 16 South Bridge (WD 1790/92); dismissed from High School position, 26 August 1793 but described as 'Writing master and Accomptant, Commercial Academy of High School, House 10 George's Street' in AD 1793/94; opened a Commercial Academy (with William Gordon) Paton and Gordon, Commercial Academy, 50 South Bridge, East Side (WD 1794/96, Minutes of Town Council, AD 1797/98, 98/99).

PENMAN, John
Teacher of English, Latin, writing, arithmetic, book-keeping and church music at George Watson's Hospital 1741-1746 (George Watson's College - History and Record - 1724-1970).

PERRY, William
Teacher of English, French, writing, accounts, mathematics (Law), Tailor's Hall (Edinburgh Courant, 22 April, 1775; Caledonian Mercury, 8 April, 1778); author of 'The Young Man of Business', 1774; described as Master of the Academy, Edinburgh on title page of another of his books, 'The Only Sure Guide to the English Tongue', 1776.

PIRRIE, George
Teacher of mathematical sciences and the Italian method of book-keeping, next stair above the sign of the Red Lyon, opposite the Luckenbooths, formerly teacher in London and Dundee (Scots Courant, 4 June, 1716).

PORTER, Rev
Teacher English, mathematics, book-keeping, arithmetic (Law) (Caledonian Mercury, 23 November, 1752; Edinburgh Courant, 23 October, 1755).

RATTRAY, Francis
Teacher Greek, Latin, English, writing, arithmetic, book-keeping (Law); Libberton's Wynd, Cowgate (Caledonian Mercury, 12 June, 1782).

REID, Andrew
Teacher of English, writing and accomptant, Bristo Street (AD 1797/98).

ROBERTSON, John
Taught English, writing, arithmetic, book-keeping (Law); Mercantile Academy, South Bridge Street (Caledonian Mercury, 31 October, 1789); described as 'writing master and accomptant' in WD 1788/90; Mercantile Academy, 23 South Bridge (AD 1793/94); Milne's Square (AD 1797/98).

SCOTT, William
Writing master (Law), Niddry's Wynd (WD 1775/76, 76/77); Carruber's Close (WD 1777/78); Dickson's Close (WD 1778/79, 80/81); Trunk Close (WD 1782/83, 83/84); Bailie Fife's Close (WD 1784/85).

SMITH, A
Teacher arithmetic, bookkeeping, mensuration, navigation, astronomy, Vinegar Close, Leith (Edinburgh Courant, 16 June, 1783).

STEVENSON, William
Licenced as teacher of bookkeeping by town council 1730 or 1731 (Caledonian Mercury, 22 October 1731; 2 July 1768); Brownhill's Land, Blackfriar's Wynd, 1732 (address given in his pamphlet 'A General Discourse shewing the Usefulness of the Italian method of bookkeeping'); Author of 'Book-keeping by Double Entry', 1762; Cannongate (The Caledonian Mercury, 2 July, 1768). Stevenson was previously' a merchant in Rotterdam.

SUTTER, William
Teacher of writing, arithmetic, book-keeping (Law); Niddry's Wynd (Caledonian Mercury, 12 December, 1761).

SWANSON (or SWANSTON), William
Writing master (Law) (Edinburgh Courant, 1 October, 1763; 23 October, 1765), "The Great hand-spoiler" (Cockburn's Memorials, 1856). Subscriber to Stevenson's 'Book-keeping by Double Entry', 1762; Writing master, Back of the Guard (WD 1774/75 (where Christian name is given as John), 75/76); New Bank Close (WD 1777/78, 78/79); South Side of the Cross (WD 1780/81-83/84); New Bank Close (WD 1786/88, 97/98); described as 'Writer, Back of the Guard' in WD 1776/77.

THOMSON, James
Writing master (Law), subscriber to Stevenson's 'Book-keeping by Double Entry', 1762; Writing master, Anchor Close (WD 1773/74); Niddery's Wynd (WD 1774/75-78/79, 80/81, 84/85).

THOMSON, John
Mathematician, Skinner's Close (WD 1773/74-78/79); Subscriber to Stevenson's 'Book-keeping by Double Entry', 1762; possibly practising as an accountant, see p 59.

WILSON, Robert
Writing master, teacher of writing, accounts (Law), Bell's Wynd (Edinburgh Courant, 30 October, 1773), Niddery's Wynd (WD 1774/75-77/78, 80/81, 82/83-84/85, 86/88).

WOOD, Alexander
Mathematician, Riddel's Close (WD 1773/74-78/79).

WRIGHT, John
Teacher of mathematics (Law), Brown's Close, Luckenbooths (WD 1773/74-76/77, 77/78); Kennedy's Close (WD 1778/79).

YOUNG, Alexander
Writing master, Blackfriar's Wynd (WD 1778/79, 80/81).

YOUNG, John
Writing master, teaching writing, arithmetic, book-keeping,

mathematics (Law); Luckenbooths (Edinburgh Courant, 27 April, 1765), Dickson's Close (WD 1774/5-76/77), Niddry's Wynd (WD 1780/81, 84/85, 85/86; Caledonian Mercury, 9 February, 1782).

CHAPTER 2

APPENDIX 2

EDINBURGH ACCOUNTANTS

An attempt has been made to restrict the following list of 18th century accountants to accountants who were offering professional services to merchants, manufacturers or municipal bodies, but there is insufficient information to be sure that all those listed were practising. Some of the difficulties involved in the preparation of the list have been outlined in the chapter. Where there is evidence that an accountant had a legal background this has been noted.

Key to References

AD = Thomas Aitchison's Edinburgh Directory.

WD = Peter Williamson's Edinburgh Directory.

BROWN = Brown, R, 'A History of Accounting and Accountants', 1905, pp 361-381.

GRANT = Grant, I D, 'Landlords and Land Management in North East Scotland 1750 - 1850', Ph D Thesis, University of Edinburgh, 1978.

LAW = Law, A, 'Teachers in Edinburgh in the Eighteenth Century', Book of the Old Edinburgh Club, Vol 32, 1966.

MURRAY = Murray, D, 'Chapters in the History of Bookkeeping, Accountancy and Commercial Arithmetic', 1930.

AINSLIE, Walter (died c 1787)
(Brown)

ALISON, Alexander (died 1805)
Writer, Milne's Court (WD 1780/81-84/85); George's Square, (WD 1788/90); 3 North St James's Street (WD 1794/96); Accomptant, 2 St James's Street (AD 1797/98) (Brown) LEGAL BACKGROUND.

ALLAN, Robert
Sun Fire Office, New Bank Close (WD 1776/77); Writers Court (WD 1778/79, 80/81); Banker, 17 St Andrews Square (WD 1782/83, 83/84); described as 'merchant' when his appointment as constable is listed in WD 1778/79; practising as accountant 1797 (Murray p 91).

BAIRD, James
Accomptant, Niddery's Wynd (WD 1782/83, 83/84). There are two writers with the name James Baird in WD 1780/81, ASSUMED LEGAL BACKGROUND.

BAIRD, James (junior)
Accomptant, Gavinlock's Land, Leith (WD 1793).

BALFOUR, James (c 1735-1795)
Accomptant, Old Custom House Stairs (WD 1776/77); Writer, Advocates Close (WD 1777/78-80/81); Accomptant, Advocates Close (WD 1782/83, 83/84, 86/88); Accountant, Advocates Close, 1786 (Brown); Accomptant, Advocate's Close (WD 1788/90). Old Posthouse Close, 1794 (Brown); Accomptant, Old Post House Close (WD 1794/96); Scots Magazine (October 1795) records death, Brown pp 188-193. LEGAL BACKGROUND.

BALFOUR, James
Accountant, Charles Street (WD 1784/85, 86/88, 90/92); Accomptant of Bank of Scotland, Charles's Street (WD 1788/89, AD 97/98); Writer, Charles's Street (WD 1794/96). This may be the same James Balfour as in the previous entry. LEGAL BACKGROUND.

BALLANTYNE (or BANNATYNE), Andrew (died 1804)
In Ramsay's bank for 38 years (Brown); Writer, Society Port (WD 1774/75); Bankers clerk, Society Port (WD 1775/76-77/78), Bankers clerk Caltonhill (WD 1778/79, 80/81), Writer, Caltonhill (WD 1782/83-83/84, 86/88), Accomptant, Calton Hill (WD 1788/90), Writer (AD 1790/92, 94/96, 97/98). LEGAL BACKGROUND.

BELL, Robert (died 1816)
Practising 1797-1805 (Brown); Writer to the Signet, George Street (WD 1788/90, 90/92); 59 Queen's Street (WD 1794/96, AD 97/98); listed in the Register of Society of Writers to the Signet, admitted 1784. LEGAL BACKGROUND.

BOGGIE, William
Accountant, Fountainbridge (WD 1786/88); Brown gives 'Walter' as Christian name.

BOSWALL, George (died 1761)
Practising 1736, 1747 (Murray pp 68, 69, 96, 97). Murray states that Boswall was a writer. LEGAL BACKGROUND.

BOSWELL (or BOSWALL or BOSWALT), Thomas (died c 1778)
Son of George Boswall, Accomptant, Custom-House Stairs (WD 1773/74); Old Custom-House Stairs (WD 1774/75, 75/76), deputy secretary of Friendly Insurance against fire; described by Murray as 'accountant' 1760, 1768 (pp 72, 97) but Murray also indicates that Boswell was a 'writer'

(p 72). LEGAL BACKGROUND.

BOWIE, Peter
Accomptant, Castlehill (WD 1774/75-76/77) (Brown).

BREMNER, Hugh (died 1804)
Writer, Hunters Close, Grassmarket (WD 1775/76-78/79, 80/81, 82/83-83/84, 84/85); Corner of South Bridge, 1790 (Brown and WD 1790/92); Accomptant, 5 South St David's Street (WD 1793, 94/96, AD 97/98); Bremner trained an apprentice of the Farquharsons (Grant, p 215), (Murray, p 90). LEGAL BACKGROUND.

BROUGHTON (or BROUGHAM), Edward
Accomptant of excise, Fountainbridge (WD 1775/76-78/79); Accomptant, Crighton Street (WD 1780/81, 82/83-83/84); accomptant of excise, Fountainbridge (WD 1784/85, 86/88, 88/90, AD 93/94, 97/98); no job description WD 1794/96.

BRUCE, James
7 York Place, practising 1796-1825; accountant to City of Edinburgh 1796-1820 (Brown); Described as 'of excise' or 'accomptant of excise' Panmure's Close, Canongate (WD 1788/90, 90/92), Society (AD 1793/94), Merchant Street (AD 1797/98).

BRUCE, William
Writer, 3 St James's Street (WD 1790/92, AD 93/94); Accomptant, 3 St James's Street (AD 1797/98). LEGAL BACKGROUND.

BUCHAN, John (1756-1808)
Positive identification is difficult in early directories; there is a writer with this name in WD 1775/76, there are two in WD 1776/77 and three in WD 1777/78 and 78/79, all are described as writers; accomptant, Foulis's Close (WD 1780/81, 82/83, 83/84); Caltonhill (WD 1786/88); Writer to Signet, James's Square (WD 1788/90, 90/92, AD 93/94, WD 94/96, AD 97/98); Accountant, St Patrick's Street (WD 1790/92); Accomptant to Post Office, St Patrick's Square (AD 1793/94, WD 94/96, AD 97/98); (Brown). Practising as accountant "for about twenty years prior to his death in 1782" (Murray, p 102). LEGAL BACKGROUND.

BUCHAN, William
Goodwin's Lane, West-bow (WD 1778/79); Writer, West-bow (WD 1780/81). LEGAL BACKGROUND.

CAMPBELL, Duncan
Writer, Back Stairs (WD 1775/76-80/81); Accomptant, Niddery's Wynd (WD 1782/83, 83/84). LEGAL BACKGROUND.

CHALMERS, Alexander (died 1760)
Accountant General to Board of Excise in Scotland; Accountant to City of Edinburgh 1717-1759 (Brown); undertook audit of Edinburgh Charity Workhouse 1758.

CHALMERS, Andrew (died 1765)
In practice 1736, 1738 (Murray, p 70); described in 1753 legal action as 'Writer and Accomptant' (Murray, p 97). LEGAL BACKGROUND.

CHALMERS, Robert
Writer, foot of Niddery's Wynd (WD 1773/74), Adam's Square (WD 1776/77-78/79, 80/81); General Accomptant Excise, Adams' Square (WD 1782/83, 83/84, 88/90, 90/92, 94/96); Accountant to City of Edinburgh for some time prior to 1796 (Brown). LEGAL BACKGROUND.

CLARK (or CLERK), John
Practising in 1783 (Murray p 87); Advocate, Princes Street (WD 1786/88); Advocate, Frederick Street (WD 1790/92); Advocate, Princes Street (WD 1794/96). ASSUMED LEGAL BACKGROUND.

DAWSON, Alexander
Accomptant, Cowgate-Head (WD 1774/75, 76/77); Wrights Houses (WD 1775/76); teller in the new bank, near Grange Toll (WD 1780/81).

DICKIE, John (1678/79-1766)
Accountant-General Excise Office, death recorded in Scots Magazine as being in 1766 but Brown (p 365) gives death as c 1775.

DICKSON, John
'Merchant' and 'Book-keeper and Accomptant to the Good Town of Edinburgh', South Bridge Street (Minutes of Town Council, 15 June, 1705; Edinburgh Courant, 15 October, 1705).

DUNDAS, James of Ochtertyre (1752-1831)
In practice from 1794 (Brown); Listed in Register of Society of Writers to the Signet. Writer, Alison's Square (WD 1788/90), Writer to Signet, Nicolson's Street (AD 1793/94, WD 94/96), St Andrew's Square (AD 1797/98). LEGAL BACKGROUND.

DUNDAS, Laurence
Keeper of the excise, Chessels' Court (WD 1774/75, 75/76, 76/77, 77/78, 78/79); Accomptant, Chessels' Court (WD 1780/81); Accomptant of Excise, Chessels Buildings (WD 1782/83, 83/84); Excise Office, St Andrew's Square (WD 1788/90).

DUNDAS, Robert
Writer to the Signet, James's Square (WD 1788/90); Acccountant, Excise Office (WD 1790/92); Writer to the Signet, 4 North James's Street (AD 1793/94, WD 94/96, 97/98). LEGAL BACKGROUND.

EMSLIE (or ELMSLEY), Francis
Writer, Thomson's land, Cowgate (WD 1774/75-76/77); Todderick's Wynd (WD 1782/83, 83/84, 86/88); 'writer at Mr Farquharson's, Adam Square (WD 1784/85); Lochend's Close, Canongate (WD 1788/90); Nicholson's Street (WD 1790/92); St Patrick's Square (AD 1793/94, 97/98); trained as an apprentice to one of the Farquharsons (Grant p 215). LEGAL BACKGROUND.

EWART, James
Practising 1746-48 (Saltoun MSS 17594, item 89, NLS)

FARQUHARSON, Alexander Ogilvie (died 1788)
Nephew of Francis Farquharson. In practice 1764 (Brown); Accountant, Opposite the Cross, (WD 1773/74); Above Balfour's Coffee House (WD 1774/75); at the Cross (WD 1775/76, 76/77); Adam's Square (WD 1777/78, 78/79, 80/81, 82/83-84/85, 86/88). Court of Session Minute Book 1782 pp 78, 259, 387. There was a writing master of this name in Grants Close (WD 1778/79) (Murray pp 74, 85, 87, 96), ASSUMED LEGAL BACKGROUND.

FARQUHARSON, Francis of Haughton (died 1767 (Murray) or 1770 (Brown))
In practice 1746, 1747, 1748, 1760 (Murray pp 68, 69, 85, 96, 97), ASSUMED LEGAL BACKGROUND.

FARQUHARSON, Francis of Haughton (c 1772-1808)
Son of Alexander Farquharson (Brown), (Murray p 96); Accountant, Adam's Square (WD 1790/92), South St David's Street (WD 1793); listed in AD 1797/98 at 78 Prince's Street but no job description given. ASSUMED LEGAL BACKGROUND.

FORREST, John
In practice from 1793 (Brown); Merchant, Old Assembly Close (WD 1786/88); Accomptant, Old Assembly Close (WD 1788/90); Accountant, 32 Prince's Street(WD 1790/92, AD 93/94); Writer (WD 1794/96); Accountant (AD 1797/98).

FORRESTER, Robert of Comiston
George's Square, no job description (WD 1780/81); accomptant, George's Square (WD 1782/83, 83/84, 84/85); banker, George's Square (WD 1786/88, 90/92, 94/96, AD 97/98).

GORDON, James
Accomptant, Horn's Building, Calton Hill (WD 1773/74); Dickson's Close (WD 1774/75-78/79); Accomptant to British Linen Hall, Calton Hill (WD 1775/76-78/79); accomptant, opposite Milton's Lodgings (WD 1780/81); Linen Office, no job description, Head of Bull's Close, Cannongate (WD 1784/85, 86/88); Accomptant, opposite British linen office (WD 1788/90); in practice 1773-1780 (Brown). Two entries in Williamson's Directories for 1775/76 - 78/79 but assumed to be two references to the one person.

GRANT, Ludovic (or Lewis) (died 1792)
Writer, Covenant Close (WD 1774/75); Head of Brodie'S Close (WD 1775/76); Thistle Court (WD 1776/77-78/79) Horse Wynd (WD 1780/81-86/88) (Court of Session Minute Book, 1782, p 28), (Murray pp 71, 86, 100); in practice 1780 (Brown); died 1792 (Scots Magazine, 1792, p 623). There are two Ludovic Grants, both writers, in early directories (WD 1775/76 - 78/79), WD for 1780/81 identifies Ludovic Grant Senior (Covenant Close, Brodie's Close, Horse Wynde) as the writer who became an accountant. LEGAL BACKGROUND.

GREIG, Alexander
Trained as an apprentice with one of the Farquharsons (Grant p 215).

HAY, John (died 1790)
Practising in 1769 (Murray p 86); Blackfriars Wynd (WD 1773/74-84/85) in entry for 1773/74 Hay is described as 'accomptant' but he is listed in the section for 'writers'); Strichan's Close (WD 1786/88). Court of Session Minute Book 1783 p 273. Hay trained as an apprentice with one of the Farquharsons (Grant p 215). LEGAL BACKGROUND.

HENDERSON, Alexander
Described as 'Accountant in Edinburgh (marriage noted in Scots Magazine, October 1797, p 782).

HEPBURN, John (died 1800)
Castle Hill (WD 1773/74, 74/75); in entry for 1773/74 Hepburn is described as 'accomptant' but listed in the section for 'writers'; Milln's Court (WD 1775/76-80/81); Excise officer, Milne's Court (WD 1782/83, 83/84); Writer, Castle Hill (WD 1784/85); Writer to the Signet, James's Court (WD 1786/88); Accountant of Excise, Milne's Court (WD 1788/90, 90/92, AD 93/94, 97/98); Writer, Milne's Court (WD 1794/96). Accountant General of Excise (Brown). LEGAL BACKGROUND.

HERD, David (1732-1810)
Practising from c. 1760, chief clerk to David Russell (Brown).

HERIOT, Alexander
Cowgate. A teacher of accounting who was also a practitioner; book-keeper to New Milns Manufactory, 1706 (Edinburgh Evening Courant, 28 - 30 August 1706).

HOGG, Walter
Assistant Manager of Linen Company, Abbey Hill (WD 1773/74-78/79); Assistant in the Linen Hall, Abbey Hill (WD 1780/81); close to the British Linen Company, Abbey Hill (WD 1782/83, 83/84); Secretary to the British Linen Company (WD 1784/85); (Court of Session Minute Book 1782, p 234); (Murray pp 87, 102).

HOPE, Archibald of Craigie Hall (died 1790)
Sometime accountant in Edinburgh (Brown); Cashier of Royal Bank (WD 1774/75-77/78); Secretary of Royal Bank, Newtown (WD 1778/79); St. David's Street, no job description (WD 1780/81); Secretary Royal Bank, St. Andrew's Square (WD 1784/85, 86/88, 88/90).

KAY, Robert
Writer, Robertson's Close, Cowgate (WD 1774/75-78/79); Accomptant, Sandiland's Close (WD 1786/88). LEGAL BACKGROUND.

KEAY (or KAY), Alexander (died 1804)
Writer, Robertson's Close, Cowgate (WD 1774/75-78/79); Writer, Potterrow (WD 1782/83-83/84); Accountant, 5 George's Street, South Side (WD 1793, 94/96, AD 97/98) (Brown). LEGAL BACKGROUND.

KEITH, William (1748-1803)
Accomptant, Head of Blackfriar's Wynd (WD 1777/78-78/79); Head of the College Wynd (WD 1780/81, 82/83-83/84); St Andrew's Street (WD 1783/84); St Andrew Square (WD 1786/88-88/90); 6 St Andrew's Street (WD 1790/92, 94/96, AD 97/98). Son of Alexander Keith of Ravelstone and Dunnottar (Brown), (Murray pp 72, 87). William's son, Alexander, may also have practiced as an accountant before 1800 (Murray, p 87).

KING, John
Writer, Prince's Street (WD 1775/76-76/77; Shakespeare Square (WD 1777/78); Hanover Street (WD 1778/79, 80/81); 5 North St David's Street (WD 1782/83-90/92); Accomptant, 9 North St David's Street (WD 1794/96); practising 1793 (Brown). LEGAL BACKGROUND.

KIRKLAND, James
Accomptant, Laurieston (WD 1774/75-78/79, 80/81); practising 1774-1780 (Brown).

KNOX, Robert
Teacher, Baxter's Close, Bristo Street (WD 1794/96); Mathematician, North Richmond Street and Todrick's Wynd (AD 1797/98); Practising 1793 (Brown).

LINDSAY, David (died 1786)
Writer, above the weigh house (WD 1773/74); Castlehill (1774/75-83/84); Accountant, Castlehill (WD 1784/85, 86/88); appears on list of Agents and Solicitors admitted and enrolled by the Court of Session, 1755. LEGAL BACKGROUND.

LOUNDS (or LOWNES or LOWNDES), James (died 1797)
Accomptant, Morocco's Close (WD 1774/75); Morisons Close (WD 1775/76-76/77); Rea's Close, Canongate (WD 1777/78); Accomptant of Excise (WD 1780/81); Excise Officer (WD 1782/83-83/84); Accountant, Barrenger's Close (WD 1784/85); (Brown); Accomptant of Excise, Barrenger's Close (WD 1786/88-88/90); death recorded in Scots Magazine, June 1797, p 432.

McINTOSH, John
Clerk to the New Bank, Crichton Street (WD 1780/81); Accomptant, Nicolson's Street (WD 1782/83-83/84); Accomptant to the New Bank, 64 Chapel Street (WD 1784/85, 86/88-88/90); Accomptant, Hanover Street (WD 1790/92); 8 George's Street, no job description (AD 1793/94); Writer, 8 George's Street (WD 1794/96). LEGAL BACKGROUND.

McMICHAEL, Robert
Described as 'Accomptant, Edinburgh' in List of Subscribers to Stevenson's 'Bookkeeping by Double Entry', 1762.

MATHIESON, James
Opposite Queensberry Lodging, no job description (WD 1776/77); Writer, Opposite Queensberry Lodging, Canongate (WD 1777/78-86/88); Accompant, Cooper's Land (WD 1788/90); Cooper's Land, Canongate (AD 1797/98); practising as accountant 1780-1803 (Brown). LEGAL BACKGROUND.

MILLER (or MILLAR), William
Writing master, Cannongate, later Niddry's Wynd (Law) (Caledonian Mercury, 29 May 1779, Edinburgh Courant, 24 November 1781); Accomptant, back of the Guard (WD 1783/84); writing master (WD 1784/85, 86/88-88/90); Writing master and Accountant, Blackfriar's Wynd (WD 1790/92, AD 93/94); described only as 'Writing master' in WD 1794/96; Strichen's Close (AD 1797/98).

MOIR, Charles
Royal Bank, Mint Close, no job description (WD 1783/84); Accomptant, Windmill Street (WD 1784/85).

MOIR (or MORE), John
Accountant, Brown's Close (WD 1783/84), Royal Bank, Caltonhill (WD 1784/85); Accomptant to the Royal Bank, Leith Walk (WD 1786/88-88/90). In WD 1790/92 there are two entries (i) Royal Bank, Sciennes, (ii) Accountant, Causewayside; described as Accomptant in the Royal Bank, Sciennes (AD 1793/94); Accomptant, Causeway Side (WD 1794/96); Accomptant to the Royal Bank, St. Leonard's Hill (AD 1797/98) Practising 1797 (Murray p 91). Two John Moirs are listed in Register of Society of Writers to the Signet. ASSUMED LEGAL BACKGROUND.

MONCRIEFF, William Scott of Newhalls (1766-1846)
Practising in Edinburgh from 1799 but Brown gives starting date as 1800.

MORISON, John
Described as Accountant, Edinburgh on title page of his book of 'Tables of Interest', W. Creech, Edinburgh, 1790.

MORTON, Walter
Accomptant, Opposite the Guard (WD 1774/75-75/76); Writing master (WD 1776/77-77/78); Writing master and Accomptant of Excise (WD 1778/79-83/84); practising 1774-1780 (Brown).

NAIRNE, Alexander
Described as Accountant in the report of his wedding in Edinburgh (Scots Magazine, October 1794, p 655).

NEILSON, Robert
Accomptant in Edinburgh 1743 (Murray, p 84).

PAISLY, Thomas
Accomptant, St David's Street (WD 1790/92).

PATON, George
Writing master and Accomptant, Commercial Academy of High School, House 10 George's Street (AD 1793/94); appointed Writing master to the High School in 1790, Writing master, 16 South Bridge (WD 1790/92); in partnership with William Gordon, Commercial Academy, 5 South Bridge (WD 1794/96); Rector of Commercial Academy, 50 South Bridge (AD 1797/98).

RAMSAY, James
Accomptant, West End of Laurieston (WD 1774/75-83/84); practising 1774-1784 (Brown); James Ramsay of excise, Lauriston (WD 1784/85, 86/88); James Ramsay, Accomptant of Excise appears in the list of subscribers to Stevenson's 'Book-keeping by Double Entry' (1762). There is a James Ramsay (died 1798) listed in the Register of the Society of Writers to H M Signet (this was an apprentice of Walter Scott, the novelist's father) but The Scots Magazine

(December 1796, p 865) records death of James Ramsey, General Accountant of the Excise for Scotland in 1796. ASSUMED LEGAL BACKGROUND.

RHIND, Charles
East End of Cross Causey, no job description (WD 1777/78, 78/79); writer (WD 1780/81, 82/83-83/84, 84/85); Accomptant, Lady Stair's Close (WD 1786/88); Dean of Guild Officer, Lady Stair's Close (WD 1788/90); practising 1780-1788 (Brown).

RICHARDSON, Robert
Accomptant, Air Bank Close (WD 1780/81); Accomptant, Air Bank (WD 1782/83-83/84); Practising in 1782 (Court of Session Minute Book, pp 33, 70); Manager, British Linen Office, Cannongate (WD 1788/90-90/92); Secretary to British Linen Co, Netherbow (AD 1793/94); Foulis Close (WD 1794/96); Netherbow (AD 1797/98).

ROBERTSON, John
Writer, Chalmers Close (WD 1780/81); Accomptant (WD 1782/83-84/85); Head of Todrick's Wynd (WD 1786/88); Accountant, 13 George's Street, South Side (WD 1788/90, AD 1793/94, WD 94/96, AD 97/98). Appears on list of Agents and Solicitors admitted and enrolled by the Court of Session 1772; also became a member of S S C. LEGAL BACKGROUND.

ROBERTSON, John
Writing master and accomptant, head Wardrop's Court (WD 1788/90).

ROSS, Alexander
Practising 1791 (Murray, p 72). There is an Alexander Ross, Depute Clerk of the Court of Session, Castlehill (WD 1788/90-90/92); 19 Queen Street (AD 1793/94, WD 94/96, AD 97/98). LEGAL BACKGROUND.

ROSS, David (died 1789)
Accomptant, Crighton Street (WD 1773/74); Gabriel's Road (WD 1774/75-76/77); Bull Turnpike (WD 1777/78-78/79); Secretary to the Post Office, 1780 (Brown), (Murray, pp 72, 101).

RUSSELL, Claud (1769-1846)
Brown's Square (AD 1797/98); Brown identifies Claud Russell as the son of John Russell of Roseburne, W.S. and nephew of David Russell.

RUSSELL, David (born 1722)
Gosford's Close (WD 1773/74-78/79); in entry for 1773/74 Russell is described as 'accomptant' but he is listed in the section for 'writers'; Society (WD 1780/81-86/88); Accomptant, Argyle's Square (WD 1788/90); Brown's Square (AD 1797/98); Court of Session Minute Book 1782 (p 205);

(Murray, pp 81, 86, 87, 100). Brown identifies David Russell as the son of John Russell of Braidshaw, W S , but there may have been two David Russells as both Brown and Murray give his date of death as 1782. David Russell is on the list of Agents and Solicitors admitted and enrolled by the Court of Session, 1755 and is so described in WD 1773/74. LEGAL BACKGROUND.

SELKIRK (or SELKRIG), Charles
Grassmarket, described as a writer (WD 1776/77); Accomptant, St. Ann Street (WD 1786/88); Jame's Square (WD 1788/90); No. 29 North Frederick Street, East Side (AD 1797/98); Selkrig was also a notary public; in practice from 1786 (Brown), (Murray, p 91). LEGAL BACKGROUND.

STEVEN, George
Accomptant, Baxters Close, Lawn Market (WD 1774/75-78/79) (Brown).

STEVENSON, George
Merchant Accountant, description of witness to an Edinburgh marriage in 1751 (Marshall, J S (editor), 'Calendar of Irregular Marriages', Scottish Record Society, Edinburgh, Vol 95, 1968, reference 869).

STEVENSON, William
Merchant and then book-keeping teacher and author of 'Book-keeping by Double Entry' (1762) etc. His books indicate that he was in practice. Blackfriar's Wynde, 1732; Cannongate, 1768 (The Caledonian Mercury, 2 July 1768).

STUART, John (died c.1837)
In practice from 1784 (Brown); there are several John Stewarts in WD, some of them lawyers.

THOMSON, Alexander (died 1806)
Clerk to the Excise, Potter Row (WD 1776/77); of Customs, back of Weigh House (WD 1777/78-78/79);Accomptant, Potter Row (WD 1780/81); of customs, back of Weigh House (WD 1782/83-83/84); of excise. Potter Row (WD 1782/83-83/84); Accomptant, Bristo Street (WD 1786/88); Deputy Cashier of Excise (Brown). An Alexander Thomson is on the list of Agents and Solicitors admitted and enrolled by the Court of Session, 1772. ASSUMED LEGAL BACKGROUND.

THOMSON, John (c.1733-1807)
Author of several Ready Reckoners and Interest Tables. In 1761 and 1777 he is described on title page as 'Writer in Edinburgh' but from 1776 in his book of Interest Tables he is described as 'Accomptant in Edinburgh.' John Thomson, Accomptant of Excise, was a subscriber to Stevenson's 'Book-keeping by Double Entry' (1762). ASSUMED LEGAL BACKGROUND.

TROTTER, Archibald of the Bush, Edinburgh (died 1784)
In practice from c 1753 to 1760 (Brown), (Murray, pp 98-100); Heriot's Close, no job description (WD 1777/78-1778/79); High School, Canongate (WD 1780/81); Canongate head (WD 1782/83-84/85).

WATSON, George (1645-1723)
Identified by Brown as the first professional accountant in Scotland (Brown, p 183).

CHAPTER 3

ALEXANDER MALCOLM (1685-1763)

'Philo Dogmaticus' (1)

3.1 Edinburgh

Alexander Malcolm was born in Edinburgh in 1685.(2) His father, also named Alexander, was minister of the Greyfriars Kirk,(3) and his mother was Jean Reith.(4) On the re-establishment of Presbyterianism in Scotland in 1689, his father declined to accept the authority of the General Assembly and was consequentially 'deprived' of his post. In the following year he left Edinburgh to seek the help and advice of Bishop Burnet(5) who had previously assisted other Episcopally minded Scots clergy to find positions in England.

It is not known what happened to the family after this; they may have spent some time in London,(6) but Alexander (junior) at some stage returned to Edinburgh and it is assumed that he obtained his university education and his Master of Arts degree from the University there.(7) In Edinburgh he was a member of one of the early literary societies, the Athenian Society,(8) which included James Thomson(9) and David Mallet(10) among its members, and it is known that he was interested in music and that he played both the flute and the violin.

At some time prior to 1718 Malcolm became a teacher of mathematics in Edinburgh and in 1718 he published 'A New Treatise of Arithmetick and Book-keeping'. His treatment of bookkeeping in this, and a subsequent work, was imaginative and innovative and this suggests that he had a scholarly approach to teaching. The three authorities (Robert Wightman, George Drummond and David Spence) who favourably reviewed the work in an endorsement following the Dedication, did perhaps suspect that it might be a little too scholarly for general use by merchants when they emphasised that the work would be " ... particularly pleasing to any ingenious Gentlemen, who for real Use or Curiosity, are inclined to study either of the two Sciences."

This work includes a reference to Roger North's book, 'The Gentleman Accomptant', which had been published two years earlier, and it is clear that Malcolm was influenced by this although 'The New Treatise' is in no sense a copy of North's text.(11)

Three years later, while he was living "in the Cowgate opposite Burnet's Close",(12) Malcolm published another major book, this time on the theory of Music.(13) This text, 'The Treatise of Musick' (1721), is noteworthy in that it was the first important book on the theory of music to be published in Scotland.(14) "Relying on the writings of Descartes, Kircher, Mersenne and others, Malcolm's object was to 'gather together in one system what lay scattered in several treatises'."(15) Sir John Hawkins (1719-1789), the music historian, described this book as "one of the most valuable treatises on the subject of theoretical and practical music to be found in any of the modern languages". Ten years later a second edition was published in London and in 1776 the work appeared again, now 'corrected and abridged, by an eminent musician'. On this last claim there is a note on the title page of the copy held by the Library of Congress, that it is "neither corrected, abridged nor improved" but that it is made up of "entire chapters taken verbatim from the original, omitting only the most useful".

3.2 Aberdeen

It seems that by the time Alexander had written his

'Treatise of Musick' he was married (to Mary Neilson) and that there was a son, John. At some date between 1721 and 1724 the family moved to Aberdeen and Alexander took up a teaching post there.(16) Four other children were born between 1724 and 1731.(17) In 1730 and 1731 he published separate books on mathematics and book-keeping. These were based on, but not direct copies of, the relevant sections of his 1718 book.

In 'A New System of Arithmetick, Theoretical and Practical ... ' (London, 1730) Malcolm continues his proclaimed approach of combining practice and theory. The book is one of the few works giving a description of Neper's (ie Napier's) rods. The section on proportion (ie on progressions) deals with arithmetic, geometric and harmonic series and it is more advanced than any earlier arithmetic book. The chapter on Harmonic Proportion (Chapter 6 of Book IV) shows the author's interest in its application to Music. Augustus De Morgan called this text "One of the most extensive and erudite books of the last (ie the 18th) century".(18) Malcolm's stated aim was to produce "a complete system of theory for the purposes of men of science; and of practice, for men of business" but De Morgan says "Probably the union of such masses of scientific and commercial arithmetic made the book unusable for either purpose."(19)

The 'Treatise of Book-keeping' (1731) is perhaps better organised than the book-keeping section of 'A New Treatise of Arithmetick and Book-keeping' but the material in both is very similar and the appendices are almost identical. A second edition of the 'Treatise of Book-keeping' appeared in 1743 and this was cited by Professor Anderson in the long running dispute over the accounting methods used by the University of Glasgow.(20)

3.3 America

Soon after the appearance of the first edition of the 'Treatise of Book-keeping' Malcolm emigrated to America. The reason for this move is unclear but it is possible that Mary, his wife, may have died.(21) It seems that at least two of his sons accompanied him. The family first settled in New York where Alexander taught privately for a time until an Act of the General Assembly of the Province appointed him as the master of a public (grammar) school in 1732 for a fixed term to 1737.(22) The school was established to teach Latin, Greek and Mathematics but the curriculum was advertised as including 'Merchants Book-keeping after the most Perfect Manner'.

There was some difficulty with Malcolm's reappointment at the end of 1737 and the uncertainty of his position left him disallusioned and regretful of his decision to move to America. In 1738 he writes, in a letter to his friend Charles Macky,(23) that he feels "Damned alas to the Slavery of Teaching Latin and Greek to the Cubs of a Stupid ungrateful purse proud race of Dutchmen. I shall say no more on this Subject But that Learning is the Very worst Cargo can be brought to America."(24)

Malcolm seems to have remained in his post until 1740 when he became rector of St Michael's Church at Marblehead, Boston, having received a licence from the Society for the Propagation of the Gospel in Foreign Parts (for Massachusetts Bay).(25) This was both a change of vocation and a change of religious allegiance but in the second respect he was following his father. Malcolm explains his liberal views in a letter to Macky: "I had considered the thing Long and Carefully; & Even Long before any thoughts of Engaging in or once thinking of this way of Life, I had gott a quite different View of the controversy Betwixt the 2 Neighbouring Churches; So as to think that if Ever I had any call that way I might honestly & with good conscience serve the Cause of Vertue and Religion in Either of ye Schemes, upon whose Slender difference The Bigots on both Sides lay too great a Load."(26)

In 1748, at Marblehead, Malcolm married Mary Reed and twins (Mary and Hannah) were born in the following year.(27) Whilst he was rector, Malcolm became friendly with Dr Alexander Hamilton (1712-1756), a fellow Scot who had emigrated from Edinburgh to Annapolis in 1738/39. Dr Hamilton, a physician and social historian,(28) was also an uncle of Robert Hamilton(29) whose important accounting text will be considered at various points in this book and whose biography is given in Chapter 6. Alexander Hamilton was a vestryman at St Anne's, Annapolis and his friendship with Malcolm probably had a part to play in the latter's move to become rector of that parish in 1749. Malcolm had been suffering from ill health so that the move to Annapolis, where the climate was warmer than that of Marblehead, was attractive. From 1749 to 1754-55 he may have also taught at King William's School, Annapolis(30) and this could have helped with his finances as he had been finding his the St Michael's church stipend insufficient for his family's needs.

In 1753 Malcolm was made Chaplain in Ordinary to the Assembly of Maryland and in 1754 he became rector of St Paul's in Queen Anne's County. From 1755 he was also master of the county Free School but at 70 this was too arduous a position. His failure to attract scholars, his insistence on too elaborate a curriculum and the behaviour of one of his sons (who he frequently left in charge of the school) led to an acrimonious dispute and his eventual dismissal although he retained his position as rector of St Paul's until his death on 15 June 1763.

The announcement of his death in the Maryland Gazette

(June 30, 1763) was as follows: "A few Days ago Died, in an advanced Age, in Queen-Anne's County, the Reverend Alexander Malcolm, A M Rector of St Paul's Parish in that County: A Gentle man who has obliged the World with several learned Performances on the Mathematics, Music and Grammar."

CHAPTER 3

APPENDIX

BOOKS WRITTEN BY ALEXANDER MALCOLM (1685-1763)

'A New Treatise of Arithmetick and Book-keeping'
Edinburgh: printed by John Mosman and William Brown for John Paton — 1718

'A New System of Arithmetick, Theoretical and Practical. Wherein the Science of Numbers is Demonstrated ... ' London: J Osborn and T Longman, F Fayram and E Symon — 1730

'A Treatise of Book-keeping, or, Merchants Accounts; in the Italian Method of Debtor and Creditor'

- 1st edition, London: printed for J Osborn and T Longman — 1731
- (facsimile reprint as vol 11 of 'Historic Accounting Literature', London: Scolar Press, 1979; facsimile reprint, New York: Garland Publishing, 1986)
- 2nd edition, London: printed by Dan Browne for D Browne 1743

'A Treatise of Musick, Speculative, Practical and Historical'

- 1st Edition, Edinburgh: printed for the Author — 1721
- 2nd Edition, London: J Osborn and T Longman — 1730
- London: J Osborn — 1731
- 'Malcolm's Treatise of Music ... corrected and abridged by an emminent musician' London: printed for J French — 1776
- 2nd Edition, London: printed for J French — 1778
- 2nd Edition, London: printed for J Murray — 1779

CHAPTER 4

JOHN MAIR (1702/3-1769)

'The Elaborate Mair' (1)

4.1 Background and Education

John Mair was born in 1702 or 1703, the son of William Mair of Burnside, Strathmiglo, Fife. His father " ... was a portioner or small proprietor in that parish, and also carried on business as a manufacturer, to a considerable extent".(2) John received his early education in the neighbouring parish school of Portmoak in the county of Kinross.(3) There was an older brother, William, a younger brother, Alexander,(4) and two sisters. William became a manufacturer in Perth but John and Alexander both entered the University of Saint Andrews in 1722, when John was aged about 20, then a late age to start university studies.(5) The two brothers graduated together with MA degrees in 1726 having "completed the usual course of studies prescribed to candidates for the Ministry in the Church of Scotland".(6)

Alexander was licenced as a preacher in the Church of Scotland in 1733 and was ordained minister at Forteviot parish church in 1736.(7) John enrolled as a first year divinity student at Saint Andrews in 1726/27 but he had doubts about the church as a vocation and in 1727 he applied for the post of 'doctor' (assistant master) in the Grammar School at Ayr.

4.2 Ayr Grammar School

For the position at the Ayr Grammar School, John was in competition with John Hall, student of the University of Edinburgh. During a three-day examination, the two young men were examined in Greek, Latin, book-keeping, arithmetic and navigation; Mair excelled in navigation but Hall had better handwriting. By the tie-breaking vote of the chairman of the eleven man committee, Hall received the appointment and Mair, instead, took up the post of "Governor to Mr Charles Cathcart, son to the Honourable Collonell Chas. Cathcart".(8) A few months later, however, John Hall resigned and Mair, "his handwriting having improved", was appointed to the post at a salary of 200 merks.(9)

Teachers' salaries were low. The minimum annual salary authorised by the 1696 Act was 100 merks.(10) A Scottish merk was two thirds of a Scottish pound which in turn was one twelfth of an English pound so that an annual salary of 100 Scots merks was equivalent to £5.55 sterling. Mair, at a salary of twice this, still seems to have found it necessary to supplement it by undertaking private teaching. In the Edinburgh Evening Courant for 4 May 1730 (11) he advertises: "That Gentlemen may have their Children instructed at reasonable Rates, in Writing, Vulgar and Decimal Arithmetic, Algebra, the Italian Method of Book-keeping, plain and spherical Trigonometry, Land surveying, Geography, Navigation, the Use of both Globes, Dialing, and other Parts of the Mathematics, by John Mair A M Ordinary Teacher of the said Sciences at Air."

Mair remained teacher in this post for 19 years during which time he was active initiating and implementing important curriculum developments in addition to carrying out his regular teaching duties and engaging in an extensive writing programme. In 1746 the First Master, James Ferguson, retired after 50 years of service, " ... aged, valetudinary, tender and much afflicted with the gout and gravel"(12) and Mair became Rector and First Master and teacher of Arithmetic, Bookkeeping and other Sciences, with his salary increased to 400 merks per annum.(13)

4.3 Developing the Curriculum

When Mair was first appointed as assistant master, economic conditions in Ayr were at a low ebb. Ayr Council Minutes for 4 August 1724 quoted the following 'findings' from a report from the Commissioners appointed by the Convention of the Royal Burghs:

"Find the trade of the said burgh very low and much decayed, and that there is only two barques, one of about thretty tons, and the other of about twenty, belonging thereto.

"That many of the houses on the fore street of the said burgh are ruinous and waste ...

"That the bridge of the said burgh needs to be calseyed of new, which will cost considerable charges."(14)

There was, however, a changing attitude to education which gave Mair the opportunity to introduce changes. Boyd gives the following description of the educational environment at the time: "The progress made in the sciences in the 17th century and the general acceptance of the Newtonian philosophy had altered men's ideas of culture. Practical people like these Ayrshire business men wanted schools that gave a training for life and work and they found in the mathematical studies a basis not only for work in shipping and agriculture but also for mental cultivation. 'As the world now goes', said the school doctor (ie Mair) in 1729, 'the mathematical part of learning is a principal part of a man's education'."(15)

By the time that Mair assumed the Rectorship in 1746, there was a new vitality in the economic life of Scotland, particularly in the West where the trade with North America had expanded. There were also changes in the country's intellectual and cultural life, as the Enlightenment got underway.

Both developments contributed to a climate which

supported educational reform and the time was now right for Mair to introduce radical reforms. The Ayr Council was supportive and set itself to plan for a new kind of school and "after much deliberation adopted a method that appeared to them most proper for promoting the purposes of education, that is, the training up of youth in the knowledge of literature and preparing them for business in the most expeditious way possible".(16) The remodelled school, based on plans drawn up by Mair, had three masters, one teaching English, another teaching Latin and Greek, and Mair who taught mathematics, including book-keeping,(17) mathematical sciences and the highest Latin class.(18) The school was converted into a "sort of Academy where almost every sort of the more useful kinds of Literature will be taught, and the want of College Education will in great measure be supplied to boys whose parents cannot well afford to maintain them at Universities. Gentlemen also in the County will be encouraged to send their children to Ayr, considering that the school will by this means have no rival, there being no such fund for education anywhere in the neighbourhood."(19)

In this book Mair's contribution to accounting education will be considered, in some detail, but it is appropriate to note that his educational vision and the innovations that he introduced at Ayr, qualify him for a much wider recognition. In the history of Scottish Education he was a pioneer in science, mathematics and business education.(20)

4.4 Perth Academy and Mair's Last Years

John Mair remained at Ayr until 1761 but, in that year, his reputation, led to an invitation to become Rector at a newly founded Academy at Perth, nearer his birth place. He accepted this at a salary of £50 per year(21) for life. At Perth he taught arithmetic, book-keeping, mathematics and a course in natural philosophy illustrated by experiments. Both Ayr Grammar School and Perth Academy continue to operate today.

Mair died in February 1769 at 66 years of age. The epitaph on his tombstone in Greyfriars Burying Ground, Perth read: "Here lies Mr. John Mair, late Master of the Academy at Perth. His eminently distinguished abilities and successful labours as a public teacher of the liberal sciences, in a course of many years; and the clear vein of solid and accurate judgement, joined to an extensive knowledge of various branches of polite literature, apparent in his publications, have raised a lasting monument to his memory. He died the 10 of February, 1769, in the 66th year of his age. Mark the perfect man, and behold the upright, for the end of that man is peace. Psa xxxvii."(22) His son Alexander completed the term and his widow and children were awarded £25 for this and for removal expenses.

4.5 Mair - the Textbook Author

During his career Mair was a prolific textbook author who produced a wide range of books covering history, geography, mathematics, Latin and book-keeping. A list of his works is given in the Appendix to this chapter. It will be noted, from this, that many of the texts continued to appear in new editions long after his death.

Here we will concentrate on Mair's works on bookkeeping and accounting which are characterised by a very detailed treatment of technical material. Mair wrote two books on this subject. His 'Book-keeping Methodiz'd' was first published in Edinburgh in 1736. This book went through nine editions (eighteen printings) in the years to 1772, with the successive editions mirroring the economic and trading changes that were occurring in Scotland. Thus the third edition (1749) includes new material on the tobacco trade and the fifth Edinburgh edition (1757) introduces a chapter on the sugar industry.

In 1773 the first edition of Mair's 'Book-keeping Moderniz'd' appeared (published posthumously). The preface gives the reason for the new work as follows: " ... as forms and fashions in accountantship, as well as in other things, are in a potential flux, and continually changing, I resolved once more to turn my thoughts on this useful and important topic with a view to expunge whatever might appear less modish or obsolete, and give the whole a higher degree of perfection and consequently be a better title to public approbation". The new book went through nine editions (ten printings) over 35 years, the last appearing in 1807, 38 years after Mair's death.

The various editions of 'Book-keeping Methodiz'd' had been published in Edinburgh and Dublin but all editions of 'Book-keeping Moderniz'd' were published in Edinburgh alone. The final edition of 'Book-keeping Moderniz'd' appeared in 1807 but it continued to be used for many more years.

4.6 The Popularity and Influence of Mair's Accounting Series

Of the four accounting authors that we are considering, Mair was the most influential. The use of his texts was not restricted to Great Britain, they were also accepted and popular in the United States (George Washington possessed a copy of 'Book-keeping Moderniz'd' in his private library at Mount Vernon) but they were not reprinted there as his Latin grammar was. Holmes, in his study of accounting in early Massachusetts, attests to the popularity of Mair's writings: "Several private schools of 18th century Boston advertised the teaching of 'Book-keeping After the Italian Method' and one such school, ran an advertisement on October 10th, 17th, and 24th, 1763, stating that he taught 'Mair's Italian Method of Book-keeping'."(23) Sheldahl's inspection of some

160 eighteenth century library, retail and auction book listings enables him to state that "Contemporary sales listings and library catalogs imply that 'Mair's book-keeping' was easily the most popular accounting text in the major American cities during the latter half of the eighteenth century."(24)

Yamey, Edey and Thomson note that Mair's book was not only popular with the public, but also with his fellow-authors.(25) They quote from the anonymous author who had edited the first Glasgow book-keeping text in 1758. This 'Teacher of Book-keeping' wrote: "It must be confessed, that Mr. Mair's treatise on Book-keeping is the most perfect of its kind, it particularly merits the attention of every man of business."(26) This praise is sincere as the book ('Essays on Book-keeping') is largely made up of material taken from 'Book-keeping Methodiz'd', most of the remainder being the complete text of William Webster's 'An Essay on Book-keeping'.(27)

Yamey, Edey and Thompson also cite Cronhelm: "Writing in 1818, Cronhelm, himself a writer on accounting, could say: 'In 1736, Scotland had the honour of producing, in the Book-keeping Methodiz'd of John Mair, the most complete and Elaborate exposition of the old Italian Method, ever published'."(28)

4.7 Translation and Adaptations of Mair's Books

Mair's popularity and influence extended beyond Britain to North America but he was also the first book-keeping author to be translated from English to a foreign language and thus to achieve influence beyond the English speaking nations. This occurred when the 6th edition of 'Book-keeping Methodiz'd' was translated into Norwegian in 1775 by Jasper Vande Velde de Fine. It was the first book-keeping text to be printed in that language.

The anonymous Glasgow 'Teacher of Book-keeping' who

included a large section of 'Book-keeping Methodiz'd' in his 'Essays on Book-keeping', was one of several writers who based their texts on Mair's works. In 1776 Richard Roose, who described himself as 'late accountant in Chesterfield' reprinted "The Six Questions in Company Accompts, first published by Mair in his Book-keeping Methodized, in the year 1742, in order to be stated in separate books, and compleat the Accomptant" in his 'Essay to make a Complete Accomptant'.(29)

In 1794 'Book-keeping Moderniz'd' was summarised by the Rev John Shaw (Head Master of the Free Grammar School at Rochdale) and published as 'Book-keeping Epitomized, or, a Compendium of Mair's methodical treatise of Merchant's-accompts, according to the Italian form, for the use of schools'.(30)

In 1808 'Book-keeping Methodiz'd' became the basis for a book published by R Langford, 'Merchants' Accounts; or Book-keeping according to the Italian Method of Double Entry', which ran through several editions to 1853. Langford makes no claim to be the author of this and specifically notes that: "The Treatise here presented is Mair's Book-keeping Methodized, with some Corrections and Additions ... I claim no Merit from the Performance; but that of being an Advocate for the original Work, the Sale of which is discontinued to give the Preference to another published by the same Author, more elaborate and complete, but not calculated for the Comprehension of Youth."

In fact whilst Langford's specimen accounts are based on Mair's, the commentary bears little resemblance to Mair's work. The 'more elaborate and complete' work is 'Book-keeping Moderniz'd'.

4.8 Criticism and Appraisal

During his lifetime Mair always attempted to update his

text regularly and in 'Bookkeeping Moderniz'd' he expressly set out to "expunge whatever might appear less modish or obsolete, and give the whole a higher degree of perfection". Inevitably as time passed after his death, his books became dated and, because of their erstwhile popularity, they were open to criticism. It is surprising, however, how little criticism there was.

William Mitchell, who published one of the first American Book-keeping texts in 1796, (31) refers to the length of time that Mair's system had been established but he is critical of the elaborate and detailed nature of the exposition. "It appears to me that this is the general fault of those other Systems, particularly that of Mairs, which is so overburthened with rules, problems, sections, cases, &c. that the young Book-Keeper, instead of deriving a benefit from them, gets bewildered and lost."

Fifteen years later Kelly, wrote of 'Book-keeping Moderniz'd': "... if this improved edition was modelled after the real practice of the time, the forms and fashions of Merchants' Accounts must have since undergone great changes also; for persons at present instructed in Mair's Book-keeping only, are, when placed in a Counting-house, generally found ignorant of what is going forward in every department."

Even this criticism is muted since Kelly goes on to say: "In Mair's Book-keeping, however, the principles of Double Entry are explained with great perspicuity and correctness; but the system is too elaborate and verbose for school practice ...".(32)

This judgement (which continues in subsequent editions of Kelly's book) does not seem to have been taken up by other writers until 1861 when F Hayne Carter described 'Book-keeping Moderniz'd' as: "... a work elaborate, and now almost unintelligible. Such are the changes effected by time and the course of events. Who could wade through 600 pages of small print to acquire a knowledge of 'Debitor and Creditor' ?"(33)

This critical view should not be permitted to cloud our assessment of Mair's outstanding achievement. His books were established standard book-keeping texts for over 100 years in Britain and North America. There was no real competitor for much of this period and they did much to spread the knowledge of this "beautiful and curious" art.(34)

CHAPTER 4

APPENDIX

BOOKS AND ARTICLES WRITTEN (OR EDITED) BY JOHN MAIR (1702/3-1769)

BOOKS

'Book-keeping Methodiz'd'

1st ed, Edinburgh: T and W Ruddimans for the Author (facsimile reprint as vol 12 of 'Historic Accounting Literature', London: Scolar Press, 1979)	1736
1st ed, Edinburgh: W Sands, Brymer et al	1736
2nd ed, with Additions and Improvements, Dublin: printed by Mary Fuller,	1737
2nd ed, Edinburgh: printed by W Sands, Brymer et al	1741
2nd ed, Edinburgh: printed for, and sold by W Sands ... and by Midwinter, Innys et al, London	1741
2nd ed, Dublin: printed by Isaac Jackson	1742
2nd ed, Dublin: printed by Isaac Jackson	1748
3rd ed, with Additions and Improvements, Edinburgh: printed by Sands, Murray, and Cochran	1749
'the Last Edition, with Additions and Improvements', Dublin: printed and Sold by Isaac Jackson,	1750
4th ed, Edinburgh: printed by Sands, Murray et al	1752
3rd ed, Dublin	1754
4th ed, Dublin	1754
5th ed, with Additions and Improvements, Dublin: printed and Sold by I Jackson	1754
5th ed, Edinburgh: printed by Sands, Donaldson et al	1757
6th ed, Edinburgh: printed by Sands, Donaldson et al	1760
7th ed, Edinburgh: printed by Sands, Murray et al	1763
7th ed, Dublin: printed by H Saunders	1763
'From the last edition printed at Edinburgh and revised', Dublin: printed by I Jackson	1764
8th ed, Edinburgh: W Sands, A Murray et al	1765
8th ed, Dublin: printed by H Saunders	1767
9th ed, Dublin: printed by H Saunders	1772
'From the last edition printed at Edinburgh and revised ... ', Dublin: R Jackson	1773
Norwegian translation by Jasper Vande Velde de Fine, Norway	1775

'Book-keeping Moderniz'd'

1st ed, Edinburgh: A Kincaid, W Creech and J Bell	1773
2nd ed, Edinburgh: John Bell and William Creech	1778
3rd ed, Edinburgh: J Bell et al	1784
4th ed, Edinburgh: John Bell and William Creech	1786
5th ed, Edinburgh: Bell & Bradfute and Wm Creech	1789
6th ed, Edinburgh: Bell & Bradfute and Wm Creech	1793

7th ed, Edinburgh: Bell & Bradfute and Wm Creech	1797
8th ed, Edinburgh: Bell & Bradfute	1800
9th ed, Edinburgh: Bell & Bradfute	1807

'Arithmetic, Rational and Practical'

1st ed, Edinburgh: A Kincaid and J Bell	1766
2nd ed, Edinburgh: A Kincaid and Wm Creech	1772
3rd ed, Edinburgh: John Bell and Wm Creech	1777
4th ed, Edinburgh: John Bell and Wm Creech	1786
5th ed, Edinburgh: Bell & Bradfute and Wm Creech	1794
6th ed, Edinburgh: Bell & Bradfute and Wm Creech	1799

'Ancient History Epitomized'

Edinburgh: T and W Ruddimans 1750

Also published as part of 'An Introduction to Latin Syntax' (next item)

'An Introduction to Latin Syntax ... to which is subjoined, An Epitome of Ancient History ... '

1st ed, Edinburgh, 1750; 2nd ed, Edinburgh, 1755; 3rd ed, Edinburgh, 1760; 4th ed; 5th ed; 6th ed, Edinburgh, 1770; 7th ed; 8th ed, Edinburgh, 1777; 8th ed, 1779; 9th ed, 1786; another ed, Dublin, 1790; another ed, Glasgow, 1790; 11th ed, Kilmarnock, 1790; 10th ed, Glasgow, 1797; another ed, Edinburgh, 1797; 1st American ed, Philadelphia, 1799; 11th ed, Dublin, 1800; 12th ed, Edinburgh, 1793; another ed, New York, 1804; 12th ed, Edinburgh, 1805; 13th ed; another ed, New York, 1807; another ed, Baltimore, 1811; another ed, New York, 1811; 15th ed, Edinburgh, 1811; another ed, New York, 1813; 17th ed, Edinburgh, 1815; 18th ed, Edinburgh, 1816; another ed, New York, 1817; stereotype ed, Edinburgh, 1818; another ed, Baltimore, 1820; stereotype ed, Edinburgh, 1821; another ed, New York, 1821; stereotype ed, Edinburgh, 1823; another ed, Baltimore, 1824; stereotype ed, Edinburgh, 1826; another ed, Edinburgh, 1827; another ed, New York, 1830; another ed, Edinburgh, 1831; another ed, New York, 1833; another ed, New York, 1836; another ed, New York, 1838; another ed, New York, 1839; another ed, New York, 1843; another ed, New York, 1846; another ed, New York, 1848; another ed, New York, 1853; another ed, Philadelphia, 1857; revised, Edinburgh, 1860; another ed, Philadelphia, 1861.

'The Tyro's Dictionary, Latin and English'

1st ed, Edinburgh, 1760; 2nd ed, Edinburgh, 1763; 3rd ed, Edinburgh, 1778; 4th ed, Edinburgh, 1785; 5th ed, Edinburgh, 1793; 6th ed, Edinburgh, 1801; 7th ed; another ed, New York, 1809; 8th ed, Edinburgh, 1812; 9th ed, Edinburgh, 1817; 10th ed, Edinburgh, 1822; revised by Ferguson, Edinburgh, 1846.

'A Radical Vocabulary, Latin and English'

1st ed; 2nd ed; 3rd ed, Edinburgh, 1772; 4th ed; 5th ed, Edinburgh, 1779; 6th ed, Edinburgh, 1785; 7th ed, Edinburgh,

1791; 8th ed, Edinburgh, 1799; 9th ed, Edinburgh, 1803; American ed, New York, 1809.

'The first four books of C. Julius Caesar's Commentaries of his Wars in Gaul, with an English Translation'
1st ed; 2nd ed; Edinburgh, 1757; another printing, Edinburgh, 1769; 3rd ed, Edinburgh, 1770; 4th ed, Edinburgh, 1770; 5th ed; 6th ed, Edinburgh, 1792; another printing, Edinburgh, 1793; 7th ed, Edinburgh, 1808.

'Sallust's History of Catiline's Conspiracy, and the War with Jugurtha'
1st ed, 1741; 2nd ed; 3rd ed, Edinburgh, 1770; 4th ed, Edinburgh, 1774; 5th ed; 6th ed, Edinburgh, 1793; another printing, 1822; another printing, 1831; another printing, 1847.

'A Brief Survey of the Terraqueous Globe'
Edinburgh and Perth, 1762; republished "with great additions, amendments and improvements", Edinburgh, 1775; another printing, Edinburgh, 1789; another printing, London, 1795; 2nd ed, London, 1802.

'A Select Century of M. Cordery's Colloquies'
Glasgow, 1775; another printing, 1786; another printing, 1788; 7th ed, Dundee, 1792; another printing, 1797.

ARTICLES

'Arithmetick' section in Encyclopaedia Britannica
1st ed, Edinburgh: Bell & Macfarquhar,
pp 365-423. 1771

'Bookkeeping' section in Encyclopaedia Britannica
1st ed, Edinburgh: Bell & Macfarquhar,
pp 582-620. 1771

BOOKS EDITED AND/OR REVISED BY MAIR

'Cocker's Arithmetic', revised by Mair

Edinburgh: Sands, Murray and Cochran	1751
51st ed	1756
Edinburgh	1760
A new ed, Edinburgh: Alexander Donaldson	1762
a new ed, Edinburgh: A McCaslan	1765
another ed, Glasgow: James Brown	1771
another ed, Edinburgh	1771
another ed, Edinburgh	1780
another ed, Glasgow	1787

'Wilson's Introduction to Arithmetic', edited and revised by Mair, 2nd ed, Edinburgh: W Sands et al (1st ed, which was not edited by Mair, was 1741). 1752

ADAPTATIONS OF MAIR'S WORKS

'Essays on Book-keeping wherein the Art is fully explained, To which is added a Large Appendix containing a Variety of Specimens in Company Accounts ... ' by 'a Teacher of Bookkeeping' Glasgow: printed for John Orr 1758
(The major part of the contents of this book comes from Mair's 'Bookkeeping Methodiz'd', the remainder is Webster's 'An Essay on Book-keeping').

'An Essay to Make A Compleat Accomptant ... ' by Richard Roose, London: for Hannah Roose 1760
(contains 'The Six Questions in Company Accompts' from Mair's 'Book-keeping Methodiz'd).

'Book-keeping Epitomized or a Compendium of Mair's Methodical Treatise of Merchants-Accompts'
by the Rev John Shaw, Leeds: J Binns and London: J Johnson, Ogilvy and Speare, and Vernor and Hood 1794

'Merchants' Accounts; or Book-keeping according to the Italian Method of Double Entry'
London: Published by R Langford 1808
(preface describes the book as "Mair's Book-keeping Methodized, with some corrections and additions")
'another ed' 1822
'another ed' 1824
'another ed' 1826
'another ed' 1828
'another ed' 1830
'another ed' 1835
'another ed' 1843
'another ed' 1853

'Clavis Mairiana, or a Key to Mair's Introduction to Latin Syntax', by 'a young gentleman' 1st ed, New York: J Seymour, 1809; 2nd ed, revised by Muirhead, Edinburgh: Wallace & Co, 1814; Another ed by John Black, Edinburgh: University Press, 1818; Another printing, Edinburgh, 1822.

CHAPTER 5

WILLIAM GORDON (1720/1-1793)

'The Ingenious Gordon' (1)

5.1 The Ducal Connection

William Gordon is reputed to have been the son of Cosmo George, the Third Duke of Gordon, by an early marriage to a French lady in Tours. The legend is that the marriage was not recognised in Scotland, the mother died young of a 'broken heart' and William did not succeed to the Dukedom.(2) William's reputed father later married Lady Catherine Gordon and the eldest son of this marriage, Alexander, inherited the estate and title to become the Fourth Duke of Gordon. If this story were true then William would have been the half brother of Lord George Gordon, the colourful eccentric, who played a key roll in the Gordon Riots of 1780 which are so graphically described in Dickens' Barnaby Rudge. This episode led Walpole to say of the Gordons in general, "They were, and are, all mad".(3)

Two critical birth dates, however, suggest that the story of William's parentage cannot be true. Cosmo George, the third Duke of Gordon, was born about 1720 (he died in 1752 "in the 33rd year of his age") and yet William must have been born at a similar date since he died on 12 December 1793 "in the 73d year of his age".(4) Although the romantic legend must be rejected, it does seems likely that there is an underlying element of truth in the claimed connection to the ducal line even allowing for the fact that "There was a distinct tendency to allot stray Gordons to various Dukes, whose magnificence made them such desirable relations."(5)

William did receive considerable help from Alexander, the Fourth Duke, and dedicated several of his books to him (eg 'The General Counting-House and Man of Business', 1766 and the fourth and later editions of 'The Universal Accountant and Complete Merchant', 1777, 1787), referring to Alexander as his "illustrious patron and Generous benefactor". The Fourth Duke of Gordon, was considered to be the greatest public figure at that time in Scotland. In 1766 he married Lady Jane Maxwell who sponsored Burns and became the most spectacular Duchess of the era whose prestige was enormous in Scotland, London and beyond.

In 1767 the Duke provided a loan of £300 to help with the purchase of William's Glasgow house.(6) This loan was made soon after the Duke attained his majority, and thus obtained control of his estate from his 'Tutors and Curators'.(7) Later there was a suggestion that the loan might have been intended as a gift, as a matter of "generosity to a man of genius of the clan struggling with a large family".(8) The facts do seem to point to the existence of some close family relationship.(9)

5.2 Education and Early Career

Moving, momentarily, to a more solid factual basis it is known that William studied at Marischal College, Aberdeen from 1732 to 1736 and that he graduated, Master of Arts, in 1736.(10)

His activities in the 15 years following his graduation are unknown. It is tempting to suggest that he might have been involved in the Forty Five Rebellion as many Gordons were Jacobites (including Lord Lewis Gordon, a brother of the third Duke) although the Duke himself was loyal to the Crown.(11) About 1750 William became schoolmaster at Fochabers which is adjacent to Gordon Castle. This school received financial support from the Dukes of Gordon(12) and

William's appointment may indicate the exercise of some influence by the Duke.

In 1773, James Boswell in his Journal of a Tour to the Hebrides with Samuel Johnson noted that "Fochabers ... is a poor place, many of the houses being ruinous". This sorry state of affairs may have been part of a deliberate policy of running down the village as the Fourth Duke of Gordon, who established a reputation as an improver, required room to build his new Gordon Castle on land occupied by the village. The village was moved to a new site in the last quarter of the century. The whole area was Gordon country and at the end of the century the Rev Mr James Gordon's comments on the Parish of Bellie were that "The Duke of Gordon is our only residing heritor, and, indeed, sole proprietor of the parish, except of one farm belonging to the Earl of Findlater."(13) The same source indicates that in 1795 the school master taught: English, Latin, writing, arithmetic and book-keeping and that his salary was 14 bols(14) of meal augmented by the school dues, a small fee for acting as session clerk and payments for the registration of baptisms and marriages.(15)

William Gordon left his teaching post at Fochabers in 1753, just after the death of the Third Duke, to take up an appointment as writing and mathematical master at the High School, Stirling. In Stirling, Gordon married Elizabeth Christie (b 1737), daughter of James Christie, Town Provost and woollen manufacturer.(16) In 1755 William was suspended from his church precentorship (leader of the congregation's singing) because of some domestic scandal but he was eventually reponed.(17) This incident presumably affected his teaching post as, in 1757, he applied to be put on the same footing with the record of the Grammar School and he was, accordingly, installed anew. In the following year, however, there was another complaint that he was not taking proper care of the boys under his charge and not giving due attention to his work at the Grammar School. The Magistrates admonished him and shortly after this he resigned from the post, leaving the town on May 1, 1759.(18) It should be noted that Gordon's successor, James Innes, lasted less than two years before he too was charged with "being negligent of his duty, and otherwise deficient with respect to his office as a teacher of youth".(19)

5.3 The Glasgow Academy

Gordon next moved to Glasgow where, in 1759, he founded and ran a Mercantile Academy with James Scruton(20) and Robert Dobson (and later Alexander Jack). The Academy was originally in the Trongate at the head of the Stockwell gate (the commercial centre of Glasgow). In 1767 William received the loan of £300 (referred to earlier) from the Fourth Duke of Gordon to purchase the part of the premises that he occupied. Later the school moved to a building behind Mr Scruton's house in Candleriggs.(21) At Stirling, William had written his first book, 'Every Young Man's Companion',(22) but his period in Glasgow saw the appearance of his major works, 'The Universal Accountant and Complete Merchant' and 'The General Counting-House and Man of Business'. While these were not so influential as Mair's texts they were well regarded and, as with Mair's, their worth was recognised in America. Thomas Jefferson kept a copy of the 'General Counting-House' in his library and Chauncey Lee, an early American book-keeping author, used Gordon's writings in preparing the book-keeping section of his book, 'The American Accomptant' (Lansinburgh, 1797).(23) One of Gordon's partners in the Mercantile Academy, James Scruton, also wrote a book-keeping text.(24)

The Academy continued until 1783 but latterly it does not seem to have been successful. James Scruton, was ill(25) and Gordon himself was in perpetual financial difficulties because of his propensity for ill-advised business ventures. Thomas Grahame, a neighbour, writing in 1781 says "They have lost almost all their boarders but I see the Girls (William's daughters) very commendably busy in sewing."(26)

5.4 Gordon's Business Misfortunes and Imprisonment

Thomas Grahame's letter was to Charles Gordon of Braid (who acted for the Duke) and the correspondence was concerned with the loan of £300 that the Duke had made to William. This loan was still outstanding and Grahame's letters were pleas on his friend's behalf. He goes on to say: "William Gordon is a man of knowledge and abilities as a Teacher and might have acquired both fame and money in that line but coming to a mercantile place and piqueing himself on his knowledge in business and imagining he might make money out of his own line his head went wrong with projects which brought him difficulties that he never extracted himself from. For many years he has been so harassed with diligence that it is astonishing he could keep up his head and teach thro distraction of mind."

Because of these 'projects' and the resultant difficulties he had resorted to, "... bad temporary expedients of borrowing from hand to hand and drawing bills. His connections with bills and business were disreputable as generally happens in such cases and he is suspected and ill looked upon on this account."

On 17 September 1782 Gordon was imprisoned in Glasgow's Tolbooth(27) for non payment of outstanding debts.(28) A standard legal text sets out the position as follows: "In the earlier history of the Law of Scotland there was no provision whereby a person who had become insolvent might obtain a discharge from his debts unless by full payment or the favour of his creditors. He was liable to imprisonment and could escape it only by taking refuge in the Abbey of Holyrood. Where a debtor was imprisoned release was obtainable by the process of cessio bonorum, whereby the debtor, on giving up all his property, was released and could not be afterwards imprisoned for pre-existing debts. He did not, however, obtain a discharge, and any property he might afterward acquire could be attached by his creditors for even pre-existing debts by appropriate diligence ... The process of cessio bonorum was abolished by the Bankruptcy (Scotland) Act of 1913."(29)

Gordon obtained a cessio bonorum in December 1782 and then was released from jail. The papers in the Scottish Record Office(30) show that he had a deficiency of £618.9.0. His position was blamed on his "engaging in a bill of exchange Trade at the solicitation of Thomas Johnston merchant in Glasgow who married Mrs Gordon's sister". The statement of losses are mostly concerned with the bill trade but he may earlier have been involved in the sugar trade since in 1764 he (together with three others) had advertised in the Glasgow Journal for a carpenter and a piper for the West Indies.(31)

5.5 The Edinburgh Mercantile Academy

In May 1783 the Glasgow Candleriggs premises of Gordon and Scruton were taken over by Robert Nichol who was already running a Commercial Academy in Glasgow.(32) Scruton "fitted up a Room in his own house in Candleriggs for the accommodation of a few Pupils"(33) and Gordon moved to Edinburgh to become "Master of the Mercantile Academy" there.(34) He had been considering making the move some years earlier in 1771 but his decision seems to have been made to obtain some respite from the attentions of his Glasgow creditors. He established his new Mercantile

Academy in the Scale Stairs at the head of Blackfriars' Wynd(35) but, in the early 1790's, he went into partnership with George Paton at the Commercial Academy, South Bridge, Edinburgh.(36)

In Edinburgh, Gordon continued his writing, including a major revision of 'The Universal Accountant'. This book he seems to regard as his most prestigious contribution since the title pages of his other books often refer to him as the "Author of The Universal Accountant".

5.6 Gordon's Death

Gordon died in Edinburgh on 12 December, 1793 and the notices of his death in the Scot's Magazine and the Edinburgh Magazine also record that he was the author of 'The Universal Accountant'.(37) His will, proved on 10th September 1794 (Edinburgh Commissariot), clearly shows that he was not wealthy, the total value of his goods and chattels amounted to only £76 3s 3 3/4d and there was still the matter of the £300 loan from the Duke that he had not repaid and which the Duke did not regard as a gift.(38)

Scottish Notes and Queries reports that William Gordon had two sons and two daughters but a letter in the Gordon Castle Muniments refers to him as "struggling with a large family".(39) His eldest son was General Gabriel Gordon (1762-1855) who had an adventurous life in the West Indies.(40) Another son, Captain James Gordon, died in the American War of Independence.(41) A third son, William, was midshipman on board the Queen's Armed Sloop in 1794.(42) There seem to have been three daughters: Catherine (who married a Glasgow merchant and agent of the Sun Fire Office), Mrs Maxwell Gordon (who married Mr Thomson, a 'medical man') (43) and Margaret (who married William Laing).(44)

CHAPTER 5

APPENDIX

BOOKS WRITTEN BY WILLIAM GORDON (1720/1-1793)

'Every Young Man's Companion'

1st ed	
2nd ed, London: J Hodges	1757
3rd ed, 4th ed, London: J Rivington, H Woodfall et al	1765
5th ed, London: H Woodfall	1769
6th ed, London and Salisbury: H Woodfall, J Rivington et al	1777

'The Universal Accountant and Complete Merchant' (2 Vols)

1st ed, Edinburgh: printed for the author and A Donaldson	1763/65
(facsimile reprint of Vol II, New York: Garland Publishing, 1986)	
2nd ed, Edinburgh: printed for Alexander Donaldson	1765
3rd ed, corrected, and revised by the Author, Edinburgh: printed for Alexander Donaldson	1770
4th ed, Edinburgh: A Donaldson	1777
5th ed (New Modelled), 2 Vols, Edinburgh: printed for A & J Donaldson & C Elliott	1787
6th ed, Dublin: printed by T Henshall	1796

'The General Counting-House and Man of Business'

1st ed, Edinburgh: printed for A Donaldson	1766
2nd ed, Edinburgh: A Donaldson & S Crowder	1770
Glasgow	1770

'The Elements, Analysis and Practice of Arithmetic'

1st ed (written with Robert Dobson), Volume 1 of 3 (according to title page), Glasgow: printed by R Urie for the Authors	1771
2nd ed (NOT with Robert Dobson), Glasgow	1775

'Institutes of Arithmetic, elementary and practical'

Edinburgh: W Creech	1779
Edinburgh: W Creech	1789

'Revision of Hayes' translation of Livy'

(8 Vols), Edinburgh	1761

'Titus Livius' Roman History, translated into English'

Edinburgh: W Smith	1783
Edinburgh,	1809
Edinburgh: Bell & Bradfute	1813

'<u>Cornelius Nepos</u>, Vitae Excellentium Imperatorum ...
with an English translation'
Edinburgh 1790

'<u>A New Geographical Grammar and Complete Gazetteer</u>'
Edinburgh: Alexander Guthrie, 1789
Another Issue, Edinburgh: Martin, McDowall, and Co 1789
(This book seems to have been initially issued in parts)

CHAPTER 6

ROBERT HAMILTON (1743-1829)

'The Judicious Hamilton' (1)

6.1 Childhood and Education

Robert Hamilton was born at Pilrig(2) in Edinburgh on 11 June 1743, into an influential family with strong kirk and university connections and important business interests. He was the eighth child of a noted Edinburgh publisher, bookseller and paper maker, Gavin Hamilton,(3) a bailie of the burgh who, two years after Robert's birth, distinguished himself by his courageous loyalty to the British crown when, during the 1745 Rebellion, Bonnie Prince Charlie's father was proclaimed King James VIII of Scotland in Edinburgh.(4) Although not wealthy Gavin Hamilton had considerable influence which he skilfully used. A family tree which illustrates the place of the family in the Scottish 'Establishment' is given as an appendix to this chapter.

After a youth plagued by illness, Robert became a student at the University of Edinburgh (where in 1732 his grandfather had been Principal and where two uncles were currently professors). University records show that he studied Greek, logic and metaphysics in 1758/59/60 and law in 1763 and 1764. He must also have attended the classes in mathematics given by Professor Matthew Stewart since he is reported to have shown a special aptitude in this subject.(5)

6.2 Banking and Manufacturing Experience

On leaving university, he spent some time in the banking-office of William Hogg and Son(6) with the reluctant aim of making a career in banking or becoming a general merchant. His real interests are shown by his membership of two literary and debating clubs (the Speculative Society(7) and the Newtonian Club(8)) and his friendship with Lord Kames, a leading figure in the Enlightenment. Hamilton clearly wished for an academic life and in 1766, at the age of 22, he was persuaded to apply for the Chair of Mathematics at Marischal College, Aberdeen.(9) He was not selected for this post, but the decision was a close one.

After the failure to secure the Aberdeen chair Robert became involved in the management of his father's paper mill at Bogsmill, on the Water of Leith at Colinton, Edinburgh.(10) This was an important manufacturing enterprise. The Hamiltons lived in Millbank House overlooking the Mill, in a lovely setting which gave Hamilton senior the opportunity to indulge his talent for gardening and landscaping.(11) This house is still standing. In 1767, his father died and the whole responsibility of the day-to-day management fell on Robert, but he soon took the opportunity to divest himself of these irksome obligations. A manager was hired, although Robert continued to oversee the business for several years until it was eventually sold.

6.3 Perth Academy

In 1769, the Rectorship of the Perth Academy became vacant on the death of John Mair and Hamilton was appointed to the position. An Act of the Council of Perth in that year records: "Considering that the office of Master of the Academy of Perth has become vacant by the Death of Mr John Mair, and being well Informed of the fitness and Sufficiency of Mr Robert Hamilton Son of the Deceased Mr Gavin Hamilton late Bailie in Edinburgh for Discharging that Office, Have Nominated Elected and Chosen ... the said Mr Robert Hamilton".(12) The annual salary was £50 plus fees.

At that time Perthshire had the largest population of

ROBERT HAMILTON

any of the Scottish counties, 120,116 compared with 81,726 for Lanarkshire, 90,412 for Midlothian and 116,168 for Aberdeen.(13)

In 1777/79, Hamilton published his main accounting work, 'An Introduction to Merchandize', suggesting that he was not altogether happy with his predecessor's accounting texts.(14) In 1778, he contributed the section on book-keeping to the second edition of the 'Encyclopaedia Brittanica' replacing the section, in the first edition of that work, which had been based on Mair's writings. Hamilton's article is essentially chapter I of part IV of 'Merchandize'. This section continued in later editions up to and including the 6th edition of 1823.

In 1775, Hamilton was awarded an LL D by the University of Edinburgh. In 1771, he had married Anne Mitchell of Ladath, but she died in 1778, leaving him with three daughters. In 1782, Hamilton was remarried to Jane Morison. There were no children by this second marriage and Jane died in 1825.

6.4 Marischal College

In 1779, Hamilton was appointed to the Chair of Natural Philosophy (not of Mathematics - his first love) at Marischal College, Aberdeen. This chair was in the gift of the crown. University regulations were not so rigid at that time, so that after one session of teaching natural philosophy, during which time he "broke much of the apparatus",(15) Hamilton came to an amicable agreement with the professor of mathematics to exchange classes. Thus, although he remained officially (until 1817) professor of natural philosophy, he in fact taught the mathematics classes. In 1817, he officially transferred to the Chair of Mathematics.

One of his students later described him as "learned and

excellent, but most eccentric". This student, Donald Sage, relates an anecdote which shows that Hamilton's teaching performance did not match his scholarship. "When he entered the class, it was with the bustle of one who felt he was too late, and had kept people waiting for him. With this impression, he would walk up to his desk with his hat on; after jumping about here and there, and handling this thing and the other, it would at last occur to him that his hat should be taken off; but, in the hurry of the removal, both hat and wig would come off at once, exposing his bald pate, and setting the class in a roar. Stunned by the noise, he would clap his wig on the nail and his hat on his head; and then, on discovering his mistake, would make the hat and wig immediately exchange places."(16)

In 1788, an abbreviated version of his 'Introduction to Merchandize' was published.(17) This was reprinted eight times during the following 38 years and a 'Key' to the arithmetic questions was prepared by R Thomson and published in 1811.(18) In 1790 he published, anonymously, an anti-war essay entitled 'Reflections on Peace and War'(19) but his next important work did not appear until he was 70. This was 'An Inquiry Concerning the Rise and Progress, the Redemption and Present State, and the Management of the National Debt of Great Britain'.(20) It is this book, demonstrating the fallacy of attempts to painlessly redeem the National Debt by means of a sinking fund, which has always been regarded as Hamilton's main claim to fame. In 1820 David Ricardo contributed an 'Essay on the Funding System' to the Supplement of the Encyclopaedia Britannica (6th edition). The historical section of this was based on Hamilton's work on the National Debt.

Throughout his life, Robert Hamilton was very active in humanitarian, religious, civic and philanthropic activities. He was, for example, involved in work for the Aberdeen

Infirmary,(21) the Church's Widows' Fund and the Antislavery Society of Aberdeen. In 1792 he was admitted to be a 'Free Burgess of Guild of the city' of Aberdeen in recognition of his work in connection with the town's water courses.

He wrote several essays on social problems and some of these were published posthumously in two books. One, on 'The Progress of Society' (1830), contains an early estimate of the amount and distribution of the national income of Britain.(22) The other, entitled 'Essays' (1831) contains three articles, the first, 'On Peace and War', was previously published anonymously in 1790, the second, 'On the Management of the Poor', was written in 1822 when there was a proposal to establish Poor Rates in Aberdeen and the last, an unfinished essay 'On Government', was written at some time during the French Revolution. These writings show Hamilton to have an enlightened concern for the social problems of his day and views which were in advance of many of his contemporaries. Of the four writers who are considered in this study, Hamilton is the one who is most in tune with the Scottish Enlightenment. In Camic's work on the Enlightenment both Robert Hamilton and his father, Gavin, are listed among 375 Scottish 'intellectual achievers' of the 18th century.(23)

Hamilton died in 1829 and there is a massive Grecian memorial to him within the pillared facade of St Nicholas' churchyard in Union Street, Aberdeen. He was not rich at his death but much more comfortably placed than Gordon.(24)

6.5 'An Introduction to Merchandize'

Hamilton's contribution to the development of accounting is contained in his book, 'An Introduction to Merchandize', which can now be recognised as the most important accounting text of the 18th century. The book ran through five editions from 1777 to 1820 but the accounting section of the last edition was drastically rewritten by Elias Johnston. Although the reviser claims that the "new modelled" book is issued with Hamilton's approbation, it not only fails to develop (or even to recognise) Hamilton's pioneering work, but it completely deletes it and substitutes a method based on Cronhelm's system.(25) The explanation of this method is very inadequate since there are only 4 1/3 pages of explanatory text followed by over 100 pages giving three lengthy worked examples.

That so much valuable material should be replaced, without explanation, by such a poor exposition of Cronhelm's system, can only be described as a disaster. It is difficult to see how a student could use this edition of the book to learn accounting unless he had considerable assistance, and it seems right to regard it as being Hamilton's in name only.

Hamilton's appearance in the 'Dictionary of National Biography' is by virtue of his work on the national debt, while his accounting writings are described as "unpretending but useful and well-written".(26) This condescending description is unfortunate, and a reappraisal is long overdue since the book (and in particular Part V) introduced and developed a number of important ideas on such topics as residual income and deprival value, which have currently reappeared as important issues in accounting. Furthermore, with his emphasis on the need for accounts to be relevant for decision making, he was the precursor of management accounting, and his chapter on cost accounting is clearly the most important piece of work on this topic in the 18th century and, arguably, for much of the 19th. Although essentially a scholar and a theorist, the sound knowledge of business practice acquired in his youth ensured that he kept practicalities in view when advancing his theories.

With the foregoing in mind, it is difficult to

understand why his ideas were so generally ignored by his contemporaries. In 1813 James Morrison wrote that Hamilton "has explained the principles of Dr. and Cr. with unusual perspecuity",(27) and he demonstrates the sincerity of his opinion by basing (without acknowledgement) significant sections of his two books(28) on Hamilton's work. He makes no use, however, of any of Hamilton's innovative ideas.

It may be that Johnston's revision became accepted as the "authorised version" of the text, thus spoiling any chance of contemporary recognition, or it may be that, despite his efforts to emphasize the practicality of his methods, Hamilton was just too far ahead of his time. In any case, 100 years after Hamilton first set down his accounting theories, the 'Encyclopaedia Britannica', could say of his writings, "some minor works of a practical character (Introduction to Merchandize, 1778; Essay on War and Peace, 1790) are now forgotten".(29) Now more than 100 years later, it is time to attempt a reassessment of the importance of Hamilton's 'Merchandize', since his writings can now be appraised in the context of the subsequent development of accounting theory and practice, and this juxtaposition provides a new perspective on their value. We can now appreciate that Hamilton's approach to accounting is the approach that accountants currently wish to stress and that the topics that he considered are still alive today and continue to engage the attention of accountants. Furthermore, what he said on these topics remains relevant.

CHAPTER 6

APPENDIX I

BOOKS AND ARTICLES WRITTEN BY ROBERT HAMILTON (1743-1829)

BOOKS

'An Introduction to Merchandize'
1st ed, 2 volumes, printed for the Author; sold by T Cadell, London and John Balfour, Edinburgh 1777/79
2nd ed, Corrected and Revised, Edinburgh and London: Charles Elliot, (this and later editions were 1 vol) 1788
(facsimile reprint as vol 15 of 'Historic Accounting Literature, London: Scolar Press, 1979)
3rd ed, Edinburgh, Glasgow, Aberdeen, Perth and Leith: J Hunter; Bell & Bradfute et al 1797
4th ed, Corrected and Revised, Edinburgh, London, Glasgow, Aberdeen, Perth and Leith: Hunter, Robinson et al 1799
5th ed, Edinburgh 1802
'New-modelled' edition revised by Elias Johnston, Edinburgh, Aberdeen and London: Archibald Constable and Co and Fairbairn & Anderson et al 1820

'A Short System of Arithmetic and Bookkeeping'
1st ed, London and Edinburgh: C Elliott & T Kay 1788
2nd ed 1796
3rd ed, Edinburgh, Glasgow, Perth and Leith: J Hunter, Bell & Bradfute et al 1798
4th ed
5th ed, Edinburgh 1802
6th ed
7th ed, Edinburgh 1810
8th ed, Edinburgh 1815
Another ed "Enlarged and Improved" by James Welsh, Aberdeen and Edinburgh: A Constable and Co et al 1826

'An Essay on Peace and War ... '
published anonymously, London: G G J and J Robinson 1790

'Heads of a Course of Lectures on Mathematics'
Aberdeen: A Brown and Edinburgh: W Creech 1800

'An Inquiry concerning the Rise and Progress, The Redemption and Present State, and the Management of the National Debt of Great Britain'
1st ed 1813
2nd ed, Enlarged, Edinburgh: Oliphant, Waugh & Innes 1814
American ed, 'From the 2d London ed', Philadelphia: M Carey 1816
French Translation by J Henri La Salle, 'Recherches

sur l'origine, les progres, le rechat, l'etat actuel et la regie de la dette nationale de la Grande-Bretagne', Paris: Gide fils 1817
3rd ed, Enlarged (title extended by the addition of the words "and Ireland"), Edinburgh: Oliphant, Waugh, and Innes 1818
Part reprinted in J R McCulloch (editor), 'A Select Collection of Scarce and Valuable Tracts and other Publications on the National Debt and Sinking Fund', London 1857
(reprinted New York: Augustus M Kelly, 1966)

'An Adress to the inhabitants of Aberdeen on the Management of the Poor'
Aberdeen 1822

'Observations upon the causes of distress in the country, and proposals of a plan for ameliorating the condition of the poor ... '
Glasgow: printed by J Curll 1822

'The Progress of Society'
London: John Murray, Albemarle-Street 1830
(reprinted New York: Augustus M Kelly, 1969)

'Essays'
Aberdeen: printed by D Chalmers and Co 1831

'Mathematical Tables: containing logarithms of numbers ... also, Tables of Compound interest, probabilities of life, and annuities for years and lives'
1st ed, Edinburgh: printed for William Creech 1790
2nd ed with several additional tables, Aberdeen: printed by Chalmers for William Creech, Edinburgh 1807
2nd ed, Edinburgh: J Fairbairn 1816

A book entitled 'Remarks on the Necessity and the Means of Extinguishing a large portion of the National Debt' (1818) has been attributed both to Hamilton and Thomas Bunn (Halkett, S and J Laing, 'Dictionary of Anonymous and Pseudonymous English Literature', Edinburgh: Oliver and Boyd, 1929, Vol 5, p 75).

ARTICLES

'Book-keeping' section of 'Encyclopaedia Britannica'
2nd ed, Vol 2, Edinburgh: J Balfour et al 1778
3rd ed, Vol 3, Edinburgh: Bell and Macfarquhar 1797
4th ed, Edinburgh: A Bell 1801

5th ed, Edinburgh 1810
6th ed, Vol IV, Edinburgh: Constable & Co 1823
(an additional section is appended on a 'New Method of Book-keeping by Mr Jones, ie 'Jones's English System of Book-keeping', 2nd ed, 1796)
7th ed, Edinburgh: Black (includes a reference to Cronhelm, F W, 'Double Entry by Single', 1818) 1842

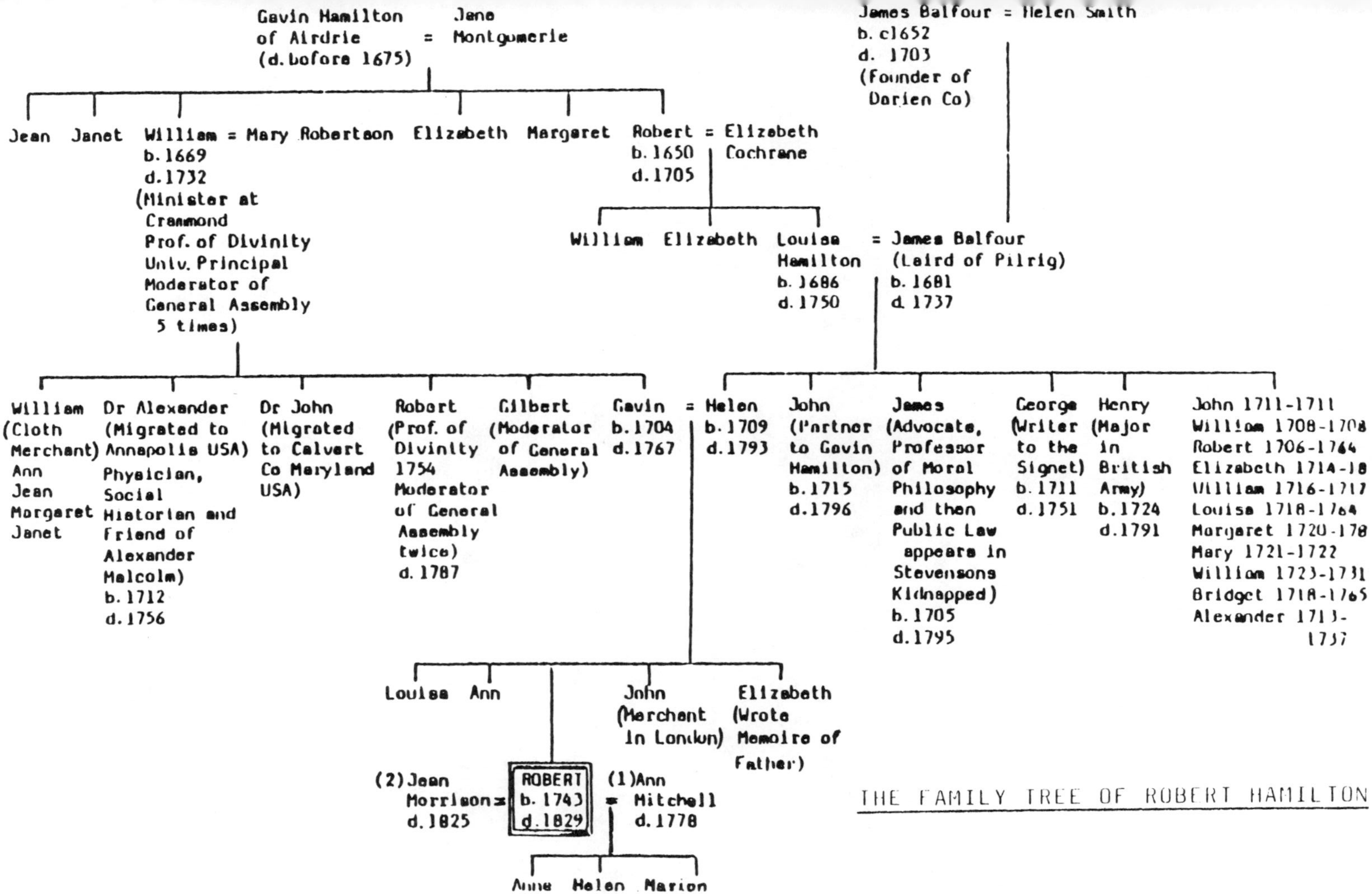

THE FAMILY TREE OF ROBERT HAMILTON

CHAPTER 7

A SURVEY OF SCOTTISH ACCOUNTING TEXTS UP TO THE END OF THE EIGHTEENTH CENTURY

7.1 Introduction

This chapter is a survey of the 18th century Scottish accounting texts. There is room for differences of opinion both as to what constitutes a Scottish text and as to whether a particular book can properly be regarded as an accounting text. The book's authorship has been used to determine whether or not it is 'Scottish' for the purposes of this study. Although this approach differs from the 'place of publication' approach used by Pryce-Jones and Parker,(1) considerable use has been made of their bibliography in the preparation of this chapter.

A book has been regarded as an accounting text if it contains an explanation of the double entry system (ie Italian Method of Bookkeeping). Two books with titles suggestive of a book-keeping or accounting content have, however, been included although they do not meet this criterion.(2) With one exception, ready reckoners and books of interest tables have been excluded from the survey, although they have connections with accounting and might be written by self-styled accountants.(3) Some of the texts include material on commercial mathematics but books wholly concerned with this topic have been excluded.

For the first edition of each text considered, the title page is provided. This is followed by a brief description and assessment of the contents of the book and any other information that is relevant for the purposes of this study.

7.2 Idea Rationaria - Robert Colinson - 1683

This is the first Scottish book on bookkeeping. It appeared 140 years after the first English book on the subject(1) and Parker suggests that "The long delay reflects the relatively under-developed state of the Scottish economy and the ready availability of textbooks from south of the Border."(2) Robert Colinson, the author, had been a merchant who had lived and traded in Holland(3) and, because of this connection, the book is dedicated "To Mr James Kennedy, Lord Conservator of the Priviledges of the Scots Nation in the 17 Provinces of the Netherlands, and his Majesties Resident there, for all affaires of his Majesties ancient Kingdom of Scotland" for his endeavours in restoring the prosperity of the Staple at Campheer.(4)

The Introduction, which is addressed to the Merchants of Edinburgh,(5) outlines the role that book-keeping plays in the maintenance of justice. Although Colinson emphasises that no one should call himself a merchant unless he is proficient in the art, he is clearly aware of its wider application, beyond its use by merchants. He says: "Nor is this Art of Book-keeping circumscrib'd within the limits of Merchant-commerce only, but doth really extend to all Commutative Traffique in the World, and is most useful for all men, who have any dealings or business, from the Prince to the Peasant. By this all great designes are mannag'd, whylst Princes yearly Revenues, Taxes, Gabels, and Subsidies reduc'd to a Capital, and brought upon the square, are layed in Ballance with their necessare disbursements: And accordingly issued in proportion with their incomes; which if not punctually observed, would occasion bad Success in their interprizes, disturbances in their Government, and mutinies in their Armies. By this the Nobility and Gentry become great Proficients in the Art of oeconomy; and by

IDEA RATIONARIA,

OR

THE PERFECT ACCOMPTANT,

Necessary for all Merchants and Trafficquers;

CONTAINING

THE TRUE FORME OF *BOOK-KEEPING*,

According to the *Italian* Methode:

Wherein is First,

The Introduction to the Forme,

244. *Queries* and *Answers*, with Instructions how to Ballance the *Leger*, two *Waste-Books* transported in two *Journals*, out of which are transported 2. *Legers* both Ballanced.

After which followes

A MONETH-BOOK,
INVOYS-BOOK,
FACTOR-BOOK,
SPECIE or CASH-BOOK;
Instructions how to keep a Book of Petty-Charges *or* Pocket-Book.

By ROBERT COLINSON.

EDINBURGH,

Printed by DAVID LINDSAY, Mr. JAMES KNIBLO, JOSUA van SOLINGEN and JOHN COLMAR, in the Year 1683.

recording their Receipts, and expences in a just accompt, keep such proportion in their way of living, as they transmit their Estates entire to their Successors ... ".

In discussing the nature of the trader's stock (capital) Colinson introduces the metaphor of a tree: "Now let us begin our Books, and place down the Estate wee have; which is our stock, and is like the Trunk of a tree, it hath many Branches proceeding from one Center."(6) The comparison was a natural one in that the word stock originally had the meaning of 'tree trunk'. The origin of the commercial use of the word branch can be seen in the quotation. Although 'branch' did not acquire the meaning of 'a geographically separated commercial sub-unit' until later, 18th century accounting authors frequently referred to a merchant's ventures, voyages and projects as 'branches of trade' or 'accomptable branches'. Malcolm and Mair later adopted and developed the tree metaphor in their texts.

In common with most other contemporary book-keeping texts, the main part of the book is made up of specimen accounts, the explanatory text being only 31 pages long. These specimen accounts deal with the affairs of a merchant trading in such commodities as: wine, cloth, hides, wheat, tallow, fish etc and they are kept in £'s sterling <u>not</u> £'s Scots.(7) The transactions are for a year's trading (1682) and the books are closed and the trading results ascertained both at the end of the first six months and at the end of the year. It is interesting that the accounting periods are each of six months as the practice of closing the books at regular intervals was not commonly adopted at the time that the book was written. Parker notes that Colinson avoids dealing with the valuation of unsold merchandise by assuming that all goods are sold within the accounting period.(8)

The illustrative material covers a wide range of transactions.(9) Much of the explanatory text is made up of a series of short questions on the debit and credit entries required to record the trader's dealings. There are 244 of these questions with answers supplied.

Colinson uses the traditional three books introduced by Pacioli: waste book, journal and ledger, together with six supplementary books: the invoice (invoyes) book (to record goods sent to factors), a factor book (to record goods received as a factor), a book of petty charges, a cash book (specie book), a month (moneth) book (for a cash budget) and a copy book of letters.

THE MERCHANT's COMPANION

Being a more

Exact, *Quick* and *Easy*

Way for making up of

ACCOMPTS

In Shops, Faires &c. betwixt Buyer and Seller, than any heretofore

Wherein is reduced Sterling to Scotish, and Scotish to English Coin - Fit for all degrees of Trade whether by Weight or Measure, Liquid or Dry, Yard or Ell from 1 d. to 20 d. and upwards. And may be said, to be an infallible Guide in the height of a Market.

By W. NEWALL

A New EDITION,

To which is added the Fairs of both Kingdoms with Mr STREET'S Memorial Verses. &c. Carefully Corrected by

P. B. M.

GLASGOW.

PRINTED by DONALD GOVAN and Sold by Andrew Wales at his Shop at the Cross. M.DCC.XV

7.3 The Merchant's Companion - W Newall - 1715

Although the long title of this book states that it is "a more Exact, Quick and Easy Way, for making up of Accompts", it is not an accounting text but rather a book of tables designed to give the total value for a quantity of merchandise for any unit price specified in Scots money. "The Price is in Scotish Money, beginning at one Shilling Scots, and rising gradually by a Bodle, (which is the sixth Part of one Penny Sterling) till it amounts to one Pound Scots." The total value is given in both Scottish currency and Sterling, a Scottish pound being one twelfth of an English pound. The author points out that the tables can also be used to find the total value in Sterling when the unit price is also quoted in Sterling. The Treaty of Union (1707) had provided that " ... the Coyn shall be of the same Standart and Value throughout the United Kingdom, as now in England ... ",(1) but the publication of this book shows that prices were being commonly quoted in Scots money in 1715. It was, in fact, many years before the Scots pound completely disappeared.(2)

Newall says in the preface that he originally prepared the tables for his own use but that he had transcribed them so many times, at the request of business associates, that he has now decided to print them. The title page calls this as 'New Edition' but no earlier printing has been located.

The author makes the following claim: "to the World I may boldly say this, it has made the Dull quick, the Weak resolve weighty Questions, and the Illiterate run parallel with him of great learning in managing of his Markets."

A list of "The Names of the Principal Fairs in Scotland, England and Wales" is given (pp 232-247) and the book concludes with "Mr Street's Memorial Verses for the Ecclesiastical and Civil Kalender" (pp 247-248).

7.4 The Accomptant's Pocket-Companion - John Drummond - 1718

This peculiar book-keeping text, with its supplementary 'Essay Towards the METHOD of Curing Cod and Ling Fish', is dedicated to "The Right Honourable The Governour, The Honourable The Deputy-Governour, And the Directors of the Bank of Scotland".

Although describing himself as a 'Merchant' on the title page, the preface shows that Drummond was also (or perhaps mainly) a teacher. He says: "The following Sheets were only designed for the Heads of my Discourses, to these Noblemen and Gentlemen whom I instruct in Merchant-Accompts." The title's description of the book as a 'pocket-companion' is very appropriate as it is more a notebook, or checklist, of topics that the student should understand, rather than a comprehensive text.

The book-keeping section of the text is short and the usual extended numerical examples are missing. It seems that Drummond intended to publish such examples separately since he takes the " ... Opportunity to apologize to all who have done me the Favour to subscribe for my Sett of Books; and promise, tho' the day appointed has been put off, I shall publish them with all possible Dispatch." Later he gives the title of this proposed publication as 'Merchants Accompts made easy' but no information is available which would suggest that the promised 'Sett of Books' was ever published.

In the 21 pages of text Drummond covers much ground and discusses: the opening Inventory, journalising the opening entries, the Warehouse Book, the Book of Incident Charges, the Memorial or Waste-Book, Proper Accompts, Estate Accompts, Voyage Accompts and Partnership Accompts.

In line with other contemporary authors he explains the

THE

ACCOMPTANT'S Pocket-Companion:

A

MANUAL,

Instructing Merchants, Gentlemen of Estates and others to begin their Books, carry on their Business, and make a Ballance; where nothing is omitted which can occur in the Course of Trade.

To which is added,

The Method of catching and curing *Cod-Fish*, *Ling*, *Tusk*, *Seath* and *White Herrings*, with TABLES shewing the CHARGES and PROFITS on FISHING, and DIRECTIONS about boyling OYL.

By *John Drummond* Merchant.

EDINBURGH, Printed in the YEAR M. DCC. XVIII.

(Price stitcht 2 Shill. *Sterl.*)

origin of the word 'cash': "Ready Money is commonly exprest by the Word 'CASH' which is derived ... from the Italian Word 'CASSA'; whence we make that Chest in which our Money is, Debtor for what Sums we receive and put into it; and Creditor, by what Sums we take out, and pay from it".(1)

The book-keeping section of the text is followed by the 38 page 'Essay Towards the METHOD of Curing Cod and Ling Fish, Dry and Mud, White Herrings and Seath-Fish, and some short Directions about boyling Oyl.' Drummond says that this is appended "to encourage all our Country-men in the Application and Improvement of the most beneficial Branch of our Product".(2)

The essay is mainly technical material on the tackle required, the process of curing etc but it also includes an appraisal of the financial benefits obtainable from taking advantage of the Crown Bounty (or Debenture) for the various types of fish and the profitability of the curing process. For curing 120 Mud Cod of 24 inches his calculations are as follows:

	L.	sh.	d.
Salt		4	-
Custom and Excise		13	6
Value of 120 Cod		16	8
Total Charge	1	14	2
Debenture	2	10	-
Profit by Debenture over the Charge of the Fish		15	9

7.5 The Reason of Accompting by Debitor and Creditor - Robert Lundin - 1718

This is a brief 20 page pamphlet (numbered as 14 pages) by an Edinburgh teacher of bookkeeping. It commences by emphasising the importance of the ledger and relating the purpose of accounting to a proper understanding of that book. "The whole Art of Accompting consists in a perfect Knowledge of a Book called the LEGER, whose Name implies its Use and Design, viz by it any that accompts this Way, may at any Time, at a View, without Trouble, be informed into any, or all the Circumstances of his Business; since in it Accompts are so clearly stated that it answers all that can be wish'd for, or expected from accompting in any Business whatsoever."(1)

It is interesting that, although it is sometimes claimed that it was rare for the ledger to be emphasised in the textbooks until the 19th century,(2) two of the Scottish texts published in 1718 (those by Lundin and Malcolm) did have an emphasis on the ledger.

Lundin relates 'Accompting by Debitor and Creditor' to the account charge and discharge system. "To begin; Book-keeping is nothing but the Opposition of Sums in Accompts, which differs from Charge and Discharge in this, that there is no Article in any Accompt, but what has reference to one, or more Accompts, and that all proceed from, and tend to one Accompt, viz from Stock to Ballance."(3)

In common with the majority of the 18th century book-keeping writers, Lundin concentrates his attention on Merchants Accompts (or business accounts). The pamphlet is divided into: Without Company (ie Sole Trader) and Company (ie Partnership).

There are 7 pages of text and 11 pages of specimen accounts. In addition to ledger accounts, the illustrative

THE

REASON

OF

ACCOMPTING

BY

Debitor and Creditor,

With General Rules for attaining to that Way of Accompting.

By ROBERT LUNDIN, (Teacher of that Art) for the Use of his SCHOOL.

EDINBURGH: Printed in the YEAR M. DCC. XVIII.

material shows a day book and a journal but the purpose and use of these are not adequately explained in the text.

The pamphlet finishes with an advertisement for the author's school.(4)

7.6 A New Treatise of Arithmetick and Book-keeping - Alexander Malcolm - 1st Edition - 1718

This scholarly text on arithmetic and accounting is dedicated to the Lord Provost, Baillies,(1) Dean of Guild, Treasurer, Deacon Conveener and the other members of the Honourable Council of the City of Edinburgh. The detailed description of contents on the title page sets the tone for the work.(2)

The 'arithmetick' section includes commercially relevant material on such topics as barter, alligation, fellowship, foreign exchange, equation of payments, tare and trett and interest (simple and compound) but the treatment of compound interest is very rudimentary.(3) Malcolm acknowledges this and explains that a proper treatment of the subject requires a study of algebra.

For both Arithmetic and Bookkeeping, Malcolm's objective is to combine Theory and Practice. He dislikes the idea of practitioners slavishly following rules and "forced to work like Machines" without understanding the underlying theory. He thus sets out " ... to explain and clear the Foundation, and give such Rules and Directions as might make the Practice a Work of Judgement rather than of Memory" since "every Thing in this excellent Art has a Reason which may and ought to be shown".(4)

He proposes to establish the "few fundamental Principles" and then to show their application.(5) Whereas the majority of his contemporaries emphasised the practice by providing page upon page of illustrative material, but little in the way of supporting text, Malcolm gives a full explanation of principles involved in the points under discussion. He argues that: " ... it is not an infinite Variety of Application which is necessary to illustrate the general Theory; a few Cases well chosen (especially if you

A NEW TREATISE OF ARITHMETICK AND *BOOK-KEEPING.*

CONTAINING

I. ARITHMETICK: Wherein the Theory and Practice are mixt together after a New Method. The *Practical Part* is largely insisted upon; no Instance of ordinary Use being omitted, and many Things delivered, both Useful and Curious, particularly upon the Subject of Interest *Simple* and *Compound*; the Value and Purchase of Annuities and Leases, and the Calculation of Foreign Exchanges, *&c.* which have either not been handled at all, or not so fully in practical Books. The THEORY is carried on with the PRACTICE in a regular Manner; wherein the *fundamental Principles* of the *Science* are plainly exposed, and the true *natural Reason* of every *Practice* clearly *demonstrated*, and set within their Reach who are Strangers to the *Mathematicks*.

II. BOOK-KEEPING: In which the *first Principles*, and *fundamental general Notions* and *Rules* of that admirable *Method* of *Accompts* by Debtor and Creditor, are fully explained; and from these are deduced the particular *Rules* in Application to *Merchants Accompts*, both great and small Traders, whether they act for themselves, for others as their Factor, or for themselves and Company; and this last explained with a great and useful Variety.

THE whole illustrated with Two Set of Books filled with *Examples* of *fictitious Trade*, such as may, and does most ordinarly occur. The *Instructions* are delivered in a Method *perfectly New*, and such as may make the Thing plain and easy to enter the Conception of Persons of any Thought, and enable them to apply it to any other Subject; and to put them in the *Way* of this *Application*, there is a large *Instruction* for *Gentlemen* of *Land-Estates*, and their *Stewards* or *Factors*; how the *First* may keep their own *Accompts*, and how the *Latter* may be able to make a fair *Accompt* to their *Employer*.

See the Scheme *of this Work more largely in the Preface*

By ALEXANDER MALCOLM Teacher of the said Arts in *Edinburgh*.

Recommended by the most famed Accomptants *in* North-Britain.

EDINBURGH:

Printed by John Mosman and William Brown, for JOHN PATON Bookseller and are to be sold at his Shop in the *Parliament-Close*. M.DCC.XVIII.

see practical Examples thereof duly stated in Form ...), will fix the Notion of this Method, and open all the Nature of it ... ".(6)

On the first page of the preface Malcolm quotes from 'The Gentleman Accomptant' by Roger North(7) which was published four years earlier and he is clearly influenced by this 'amusing and perceptive' work.(8) Although North used a different vehicle (ie estate accounting) to introducing the subject, he had similarly rejected the idea of writing a text which emphasised rote learning.(9)

Malcolm introduces the subject of accounting by stressing the fundamental importance of commerce to society and the role of justice in promoting commerce: " ... Societies are supported by Commerce, by which I mean, not only Merchandize in a strict and proper Sense, but where-ever there is giving and receiving, there is Commerce; we cannot otherwise live, but by mutual giving and receiving, either the Labour and Service of our Body or Mind, or something else we are possessed of ...".(10)

This "mutual giving and receiving" requires the support of 'justice' and it can be disrupted and destroyed by injustice. Malcolm points out that injustice does not only arise from malice, it can also follow from a lack of method. He considers that it is a "plain necessity" that the transactions involved in human affairs should be "orderly and distinctly recorded". This he perceives to be the task of accounting. Colinson had also emphasised this point.

Malcolm takes 'Merchants Accompts' as the vehicle for explaining the 'Method of Accompts by Debtor and Creditor' since the method " ... was invented and improven, for the sake of Merchants Accompts" and "It is here we have the greatest Variety of Occurrences." He starts by arguing that: "Men, Goods and Money, are the essential Subjects of Merchants Accompts."(11)

Using this approach he analyses accounts into: "Personal Accompts such are Mens-Accompts",(12) "Real Accompts as Accompts of Goods, and Cash",(13) and Imaginary (or Mediate) Accompts. Examples given for this last category are accounts for Wagers, Bottomry and Voyages (ie goods in transit).(14) This group is described as imaginary because of uncertainty as to the nature of the transactions at the time the records are made.(15) A liability may arise from a wager but this is contingent on losing the bet. A loss may arise from a loan secured on a ship (bottomry) but there may be a substantial profit. Today's 'prudence' concept might suggest that the appropriate assumption is that luck is malevolent but even with the 'prudence' concept contingent liabilities are excluded from the accounts. Malcolm would include them as Imaginary (or Mediate) accounts. Today's accountant would probably regard them as a form of suspense account.

Malcolm proposes the conventional books: Wastebook, Journal and Ledger but he emphasises that the Ledger is the "principal Book of Accompts".(16) This concentration on the ledger is relatively unusual. He states that the Journal "is only the Waste-Book in another Stile"(17) and he describes a combined Waste-book/Journal. Malcolm was the first to describe the 'marginal journal' (Rule off a margin of one third of the page in the waste book and use this for noting the debit and credit entries for adjacent transactions). Malcolm does not illustrate the 'marginal journal' in 'A New Treatise' but he does so in his second book-keeping text (1731).

Malcolm analyses Proper Trade(18) or Accompts into: 'proper Domestick Accompts' and 'proper Foreign Accompts'. He deals with 'company accompts'(19) in some detail and this section of his book(20) is discussed in chapter 11.

In opening the ledger to deal with Proper Accompts, an

account called Stock (ie Capital) is required "which in a Manner personates the Owner in this Case".(21) "The Stock you are to look upon as the Root, from which all the other Accompts in the Book (as far as they are for the Owner's Behoof) do flow; for whether there be Encrease or Decrease, or Equality, by the various changing of some Things for others (in which trading does entirely consist) it is the capital Stock that is affected, and either raised or diminished in Value, or simply changed in its constituent Parts, retaining the same Value ... but to prevent Confusion in this Accompt, it is more convenient and agreeable to the Nature of regular Accompting, to have a separate Accompt of Profit and Loss, which is mediate betwixt the capital Stock and the Traffick, in which the Gains are set upon the Creditor, and the Losses upon the Debtor Side, and there a State of the Encrease or Decrease may be made, and from thence carried to the Stock in Totals."(22)

Malcolm's description of the capital account as a root (or as 'trunk' in his second book) to which all other accounts are branches, is similar to the metaphor used previously by Colinson and North and subsequently by Mair.(23)

Although there is a concentration on Merchants Accompts, Malcolm also discusses 'private accompts' and, in some detail, estate accounts.(24) North's book had an emphasis on estate accounting.

7.7 The Principles of Book-keeping Explain'd - Alexander Macghie - 1718

Macghie's book is published by his widow. Brown and Murray both state that the book was first published in 1715 but no copy of this earlier edition has been traced.(1) Although Macghie is described as an Edinburgh merchant on the title page, the dedication indicates that he was, for several years, a teacher of arithmetic and book-keeping in Edinburgh. The book is dedicated to the Lord Provost of Edinburgh, the Baillies, Dean of Guild, Treasurer, Deacon Convener and members of the City Council. Macghie's widow claims that her deceased husband " ... was esteemed the First who brought the Teaching of these Valuable Sciences, which are so universally useful, into some Measure of Reputation amongst us, and contributed to the more general Knowledge of these Arts, which had then made less Progress in Scotland than in other Places and could not be with so much Advantage learned in our own Country". The book is certainly one of the more important of the 18th century texts.

The first 66 pages give the Principles of Bookkeeping. Like Lundin, in his explanation of the double entry system Macghie makes a comparison with the established 'charge-discharge' system. He says: "By Debitor, is understood the Charging of Things as well as Persons, with that which they are answerable for; or owe to some other Person or Thing. And again, by making a Thing Creditor, is meant either the discharging of such an Accompt of what is owed; or, the giving the same a Title or Right to what it never possessed before, in so much as it gets Credit for."(2)

Following the section on 'principles' there is an extended example of 'supposed Trade' for two accounting periods. The period from January 1 to May 17, 1705 is dealt

THE

PRINCIPLES OF *BOOK-KEEPING* EXPLAIN'D,

With the Chief CASES thereof STATED and RESOLVED.

To which are annexed,

Two *Setts* of *Books* of Fictitious Trade, Wherein the WHOLE is reduced to PRACTICE.

By Mr. ALEXANDER MACGHIE Merchant in *Edinburgh*.

EDINBURGH:

Printed by *James Watson* One of His Majesty's Printers, for the AUTHOR'S Relict; and to be Sold at her Shop, a little above *Black-Friar*-Wynd, and at most Booksellers Shops in Town. 1718.

with in 63 pages and the period from May 17 to September 7, 1705 takes up 52 pages. The accounts are kept in Scots money(3) and the contemporary complications that occurred with a mixture of currencies are well illustrated. In the inventory at 1 January 1705 (required to establish the opening capital or stock) some details are given in merks (1 merk = 2/3 Scots £). Some are given in Sterling (£ Scots = 1/12 £ Sterling) and one debtor owes in a Lisbon currency, Milrees (6s 8 1/2d Sterling = 1 milree). The relevant items in the Waste-Book are shown as follows:

	lib	sh	d
I have a house in Smith's new Land, in the High-Street of Edinburgh, being the Third Story of Ditto Land, which with all Charges cost me 8000 Merks, is	5333	6	8
I have 1000 Elns fine Linen at 2sh 6d Ster per Eln is	1500	0	0
One of debtors owes 154 1/2 Milrees converted at 6sh 8 1/2d Sterl. for each Milree	621	17	3

Book-keeping is introduced and illustrated in the traditional manner via the waste book (or memorial), the journal and the ledger.

"The Waste-book is the Foundation ... wherein is contained a plain ... Narrative ... of each Bargain, Transaction, or Business ... in the Order of Time, as they succeed one another." Macghie opens his specimen Waste-book with the prayer: "Deus Opt. Max. mihi meisq; benedicat, per

& propter Jesum Christum."

"The Journal takes the Business out of this plain Dress, by assigning each Parcel of the Waste Book, a true Debitor and Creditor ... ".

"The Leger is the Perfection of all the other Books ... all the Parcels that are dispersed in the Journal, are here brought upon their respective Accompts ... ".(4)

Three 'subservient' books are introduced. These are: (1) a Cash Book perhaps with a Book of Proper (ie personal) Expenses and a Book of Household Expenses, (2) a 'Factor Book for goods received to sell for another' and (3) an 'Invoyce Book'.

The subservient books are regarded as being subservient to the Waste-book into which their totals are periodically transcribed. The intention is to ensure that the Waste-book does "not swell too big".

In common with his contemporaries there is no emphasis on the annual calculation of profit in the section dealing with the closing of the books but Macghie does point out that some merchants close their books at regular intervals (either annually or 6 monthly).(5)

A
New and Easy Method
OF
Book-keeping
OR
Instructions for a Methodical keeping
OF
Merchants Accompts

by Way of Debtor and Creditor
after the Italian Manner
Distributed into three Parts

BY

Alexander Brodie

George Bickham
Sculpsit

7.8 A New an Easy Method of Book-keeping - Alexander Brodie - 1722

Alexander Brodie was a Scot who worked in England in the Customs Service. At the time when he was writing this text, he was dissatisfied with his position as, in the dedication to the second part of the book, he comments on " ... the various Turns of Fortune, and the many tedious Days spent in Expectation of my own Employment in the Custom-House ... ". Because of his background, there is some interesting information on accounting for duties and subsidies in his book.(1)

The printed (type set) title page of the book is preceded by an attractive engraved title page.(2) There are two dedications. The first part of the text is dedicated "To the Honourable Alexander Brodie of Brodie Esq; Member of Parliament for the County of Murray, North Britain". Parts II and III, which have a separate title page, are dedicated "To John Forbes of Culloden, Esq. Member of Parliament, and present PROVEST" of the town of Inverness and to the magistrates and council of that town. One of the long list of subscribers is Charles Snell(3) who commends the book in a letter which Brodie reproduces (although the commendation does not seem over-enthusiastic). The subscription list includes many Scots.

In Part I the main books of account are introduced in pages 1 to 4. Although Brodie considers the Waste-Book to be important, he does allow that some traders might find it superfluous and manage without it. He says " ... the old Practitioner and advanced Trader may easily enough comprise his Books in this Manner, ... ".(4)

The Journal is described as the book in which " ... the Debtor and Creditor of every Parcel is declared, the Sum and Substance of the Transaction expressed, and the whole Skill of an Accomptant employ'd in making proper Entries, ... the main Study of every Accomptant ought to be on the right ordering his Journal, that his Accompts may be render'd Authentick, in case of any Controversy before a Judge or Magistrate."(5)

Brodie describes the ledger as the 'principal Book of Accompts'(6) and he discusses the posting of items from the journal to the ledger and the process of balancing the ledger. He advocates the use of a Trial Ballance. The correction of ledger errors is discussed as follows: " ... if by Mistake you place a Debtor for a Creditor; or if you make any wrong Accompt, you must never rase or blot it out, but instead thereof write Error, expressing the Value in its proper Place, and then enter the same Parcel or Thing on the Creditor-side, as if no Mistake had been made ... ".(7)

An illustrative set of accounting records for an Inverness merchant is the major content of parts I and II. Three pages entitled 'Rules for Book-keeping Explained, &c." set out certain general points and then detail 18 representative transactions for the merchant. The transactions are described on the right hand pages with the left hand pages showing appropriate records in the Waste Book. In part I the accounts are engraved copper plate script " ... so that they become a written Pattern to be followed by all Beginners, whereby this Advantage will accrue to them, that as they are done with the Hands proper for Business ... so those who have not had the Advantage of being taught by able Masters, may at the same Time perfect themselves in the true Art of Writing, while they are engag'd in the Study of Book-Keeping."(8)

The example used in part I continues for a subsequent period in part II (9) but the specimen accounts in part II are now type set. It is interesting that the example illustrates trading with Aberdeen, Forres, Holland, France

(Bordeaux), Italy (Leghorn), Sweden (Stockholm) and the South Seas but NOT England. A similar pattern applies in other Scottish texts. Insurance transactions are illustrated and the trader is shown receiving premiums for providing cover on ships and goods bound for Barbados and the 'Maderas' and paying premiums to the London Insurance Company for a consignment of Herrings and Salmon bound for Leghorn.(10)

Included in the illustrative transactions are some dealings in South Sea Company stock. Brodie's book was published just at the time that the South Sea Bubble Act was passed (after the bubble had burst) and the illustrative transactions are " ... set down to shew the great Advantages were got by that Way of Dealing, while the South-Sea Company, and other Stocks were on the rising Credit; and the vast Losses many sustained by grasping too eagerly without a thorough Knowledge in such Affairs: for some gained more in a few Days, than many honest and considerable Merchants were able to acquire in an Age, in their way of Trade; whereas the Loss of others was in a manner, altogether irrecoverable."(11)

An example of company (ie partnership) accounts is provided. There is a section on 'A Method for Shop-Keepers, and other Dealers, to keep their Business in a Retailing Trade' and a section headed 'To the Nobility and Gentry' which deals with estate accounts and accounts charge and discharge.

7.9 Rental Accounts made easy - Robert Hamilton - 1727

Pryce-Jones and Parker(1) give the title of this text as 'Rental Accounts made easy, or, A Clear and Distinct Method by which Persons of Estates, ... may ... see what they have received ... and what is yet due ... '. The book was published "for the author" at Edinburgh. No copy has been located. The copy that was held by the Edinburgh City Library cannot be traced by the library staff. The author should not be confused with the author of the same name who wrote 'An Introduction to Merchandize' (1777-79).

A TREATISE OF BOOK-KEEPING, OR, Merchants Accounts; IN THE *Italian* METHOD of *Debtor* and *Creditor*.

WHEREIN

The Fundamental Principles of that curious and approved Method are clearly and fully explained and demonſtrated, from the Nature and Reaſon of Things: From which again is deduced a complete Syſtem of particular Rules, and Inſtructions for their Application to a Merchant's Buſineſs, conſidered as acting either for his own proper Account; or in Commiſſion, as Factor for another; or, as concerned in Company. The whole illuſtrated and exemplified with two Sets of Books, containing great Variety of Practice in all thoſe Branches of Buſineſs.

To which are added,

Inſtructions for Gentlemen of Land Eſtates, and their Stewards or Factors: With Directions alſo for Retailers, and other more private Perſons.

By *ALEXANDER MALCOLM*, A. M.

Teacher of the Mathematicks at Aberdeen.

LONDON,

Printed for J. OSBORN *and* T. LONGMAN, *in* Pater-noſter-Row; F. FAYRAM *and* E. SYMON, *at the* Royal Exchange. M.DCC.XXXI.

7.10 A Treatise of Book-keeping - Alexander Malcolm - 1731

Malcolm's earlier work(1) covered both accounting and arithmetic. In 1730 and 1731 he produced separate books on these subjects. The 1730 book was 'A New System of Arithmetick, Theoretical and Practical' and the 1731 book was 'A Treatise of Book-keeping or, Merchants Accounts in the Italian Method of Debtor and Creditor'. The preface to this latter book indicates it is based on " ... the System or Course of Lessons, which I have, for many Years, read to Students, very successfully ... ".

Chapter I (Containing the fundamental Principles, and general Rules - pp 1-33) has four sections. All Malcolm's books are scholarly texts and section I of chapter I of the book-keeping work starts characteristically with a definition of the subject: "BOOK-KEEPING is the Art of keeping Accounts (ie recording the Transactions) of one's Affairs, in such a Manner, that the true State of any Part, or of the Whole, may be thereby known with the greatest Clearness and Dispatch."(2) The stress on accounting's role in the maintenance of justice, which was evident in his earlier text, is absent in this book.

The second section describes the books of account. In his earlier text he had given the conventional three 'chief books of record', ie the waste book, the journal and the 'leger'. He now states that only the waste book and the 'leger' are principal books; the journal he classifies as a 'subservient' book. As in his earlier book, he continues to emphasise the importance of the 'leger'.(3) The third section gives four fundamental rules and the fourth section elaborates on these and recapitulates some of the earlier material.

Chapter II 'Containing more particular Instructions for the Formation and Use of Accounts in the Leger' covers pages

33 to 77. Section I analyses accounts into three classes (personal, real and imaginary) and divides trade into three branches: proper trade (trading on one's own account), factorage and company (or partnership); these distinctions were made in Malcolm's earlier book. Malcolm again emphasises that he is not going to explain the ledger by giving a detailed list of instructions but that he is concerned with general rules based on principles. For those who prefer 'the Catechetical Way'(4) he does, however, provide a five-page index of all the "Variety of Cases or Examples" after his worked illustrations.(5)

Sections II to IV deal respectively with accounting for each of the 3 branches.(6) In the section on 'Accounts for Proper Trade' he develops the idea of the stock account as being a tree: " ... the Stock-Account ... may be considered as a Root or Trunk to which all the other Accounts in the Leger-Book, do, in some Sense, belong, as Branches. As to those that originally belong to it in the Inventory, the Notion is plain enough; and for others that arise in the Course of Business, they may be said to grow upon it ... in all the Transactions of our Trade, whether there is Increase or Decrease, or simply a Changing of Things of equal Value, or putting one Account in the Place of another, the Capital-Stock is always affected, being either raised or diminished in its Value, or simply changed in its constituent Parts; some of the old Branches remaining but altered in their State; some lopt off, by being finished and cleared, and new ones grown up."(7)

Chapter III is entitled 'Of the Closing and Balancing of Accounts; with the Method of comparing the Books, and correcting of Errors'.(8) The chapter demonstrates how "... the whole Accounts are closed, and terminated in one General Account or Inventory, of the present total State of your Affairs; upon which a new Leger, and Course of Accounts may be begun".(9)

Two worked examples follow the textual material. These examples both deal with the accounts of A M Merchant in Aberdeen. The first set of books concerns trading for the period from 1 May 1729 to 7 October 1729. The waste book, the journal book and the ledger are given.(10) The books are closed and profit and loss and balance accounts are prepared. The second set of books deals with the period from 8 October 1729 to 30 December 1729. A combined waste book and journal is illustrated and the ledger is given.(11) The books are again closed at 30 December 1729.

The book finishes with an "APPENDIX CONTAINING, INSTRUCTIONS for the APPLICATION of the preceeding ART, to the Business of RETAILERS, and PRIVATE CONCERNS, more especially for Gentlemen of LAND ESTATES, and their STEWARDS or FACTORS".(12) This material is reproduced from chapter II of the Appendix from Malcolm's 1718 book.

7.11 A General Discourse Shewing the Usefulness of the Italian Method of Book-keeping - William Stevenson - 1732

This is a 28-page pamphlet which gives the text of a public lecture given by William Stevenson on the Italian Method of Bookkeeping. There is no attempt to explain the system but rather the lecture is designed to explain the importance of a more widespread knowledge of accounting methods. The enthusiasm of the speaker for this 'universally necessary' art is very apparent. This enthusiasm, and perhaps the fact that he is delivering his address in a church, leads him to some extravagent philosophical/religious observations on the 'true Nature of Debitor and Creditor': " ... we shall find, that according to this Method, not any one Accident can happen in a Man's Affairs, but what is regularly recorded and turned into the Shape of an Accompt by Way of Debitor and Creditor every one of which so regularly succeeds and discharges another, by moving in a continual Circle, that a Man would almost be tempted to imagine, the first Inventer had been well skilled in natural Philosophy, by which he had acquired a perfect Comprehension of the entire Fulness of the Universe, and that there is nothing lost of created Beings; but only, that by a continual Moving according to the General Laws of the Great Creator, every Part only makes Change of its Forms and Places. Now if we carefully consider the true Nature of Debitor and Creditor, we shall find this to be no unfit Comparison, if we take the Debitor on the one Hand for the new Form into which the Thing is changed, and on the other Hand the Creditor for the Form and Place, from which the Thing has been moved and drawn by an Equivalent, in order to be transformed from thence to the Debitor, whether entirely or in Part."

Stevenson uses a striking (if eccentric) simile when he

A GENERAL DISCOURSE

Shewing the Usefulness of the

ITALIAN Method OF BOOK-KEEPING, AND THE Practise of Exchange,

By WILLIAM STEVENSON

Teacher of BOOK-KEEPING.

Publickly delivered by him in St. Mary's *Chapel,* Niddry's *Wynd,* Edinburgh, *upon* Monday *the* 8*th* November. 1731.

EDINBURGH:

Printed by R. FLEMING and COMPANY, and sold at Mr. *James Mc Euen's* Shop, MDCCXXXII.

Price Six Pence.

describes the profit earning process as follows: " ... let us make one Remark with Relation to the Gain and Loss upon Trade or Commerce, upon which Point a Man must have an Eye to his whole Stock or Capital, as a round and massy Object, rolling and moving upon the Universe, (because unless it be kept always in Motion, it will be like the hidden Talent;) now this Object I say, rolling upon a fat and clay Ground, always carries some Part of that fat Ground along with it, and thereby increases its Weight and Bulk, which being the Case with a Man's Stock, that Increase is called Gain or Profit. But on the other Hand, that same Capital, or round Mass rolling and moving upon a dry, parched, sharp and stony Ground, must of Necessity, by its continual Motion and rubbing, wear off and leave behind it some of its parts, which is called Loss ... ".(1)

On a less elevated but more practical plane, part of the discourse is concerned with the need for merchants to have an understanding of Exchange and the use of Bills of Exchange.

7.12 Book-keeping New Modelled - William Hamilton - 1735

Before taking up his career as a teacher of book-keeping, William Hamilton had been "employed as Factor in the most considerable places of trade in Europe".(1) The title of his book makes use of the modern spelling 'accounts' rather than 'accompts' and this form is also used throughout the text.

The book's dedication to "His Grace James Duke of Hamilton, Brandon and Chattlerault, Marquis of Clydsdale, Earl of Arran, Lanerk and Cambridge, Lord Avan, Polmont, Machanshire and Innerdale, Barron of Dutton", reads as if it were a roll call of the nobility but these titles are all held by the one person. The dedication is followed by a preface which claims that no other book " ... has either shown such a plain and convincing Method of teaching, or yet discovered so many various Methods of framing the Journal ... ".

Hamilton echoes Colinson in his views on the importance of accounting, when he stresses on the first page "Let no Man assume the Name of Merchant unless he understand Merchant-accounts ... ".(2) In company with some other eighteenth century authors he exhibits the optimistic zeal of a missionary when he claims that the science of book-keeping is " ... not only necessary, but yields a great Deal of Pleasure and Satisfaction ... ".(3)

The objectives of accounting are stated as being to provide the merchant with information on "...what Effects he has, what Debts he owes, and what he has gained or lost by every Subject, and what his gross or free Estate is; and when any Person is desirous to clear with him, or know how Matters stand betwixt them, he may always find his Account ready, and in such Order, that he may at the first View see all the different Subjects of Trade that has past betwixt

BOOK-KEEPING New Modelled:

OR, A

TREATISE

OF

Merchants Accounts.

According to the

True *Italian* METHOD of *Debitor* and *Creditor*;

Wherein that Excellent and Curious METHOD is clearly laid down, in a plain and convincing Manner; the Whole being altogether new and concise, and illustrated with three Set of Books.

To which are added

A SPECIMEN of a *Factor-Book*, a *Ware-house Book*, and an *Invoice-Book*: With Directions how to frame a Book of *Charges of Merchandize*, and a Book of *Personal and Household Expences*.

By WILLIAM HAMILTON *M. M. P.* and Teacher of *BOOK-KEEPING*.

EDINBURGH,
Printed for the AUTHOR by R. FLEMING. M.DCCXXXV.

them, be they never so numerous or various, with the Quantity and Value of every one of them, and the Balance due by either of the Parties to the other."

Although the need to establish the gain or loss "by every Subject" is recognised the preparation of regular statements of profit and loss is not proposed as an objective.

The introduction briefly explains the use of the waste book, the journal and the ledger. The book then deals with: 'Proper Domestick Accounts' (opening the books, writing up the transactions (4) and closing and balancing the accounts), Factor Accounts 'Domestick and Foreign' (both when acting as a factor and when employing a factor) and Company Accounts and Exchange. Some General Rules are given and a substantial part of the text gives: " ... three Sets of Books, each Set consisting of Waste-book, Journal and Leger. And, for the Sake of the Learner that may happen to go abroad into other Countries, that they may not be surprised with any Method of journalizing Accounts, I have in the first Set of Books made two Waste-books and two Journals, that they may see how the very same Accounts in the Waste-books may be journalized either of the Ways."(5)

Three methods of keeping the waste book and journal are illustrated: (a) Two separate books are kept with the Journal being written up from the waste book. (b) Only one book is kept and the " ... Journal is upon the Margin of its Waste-book." This method was an innovation introduced by Malcolm in 1718 and illustrated by him in his 1731 text. (c) Again only one book is kept but now " ... the right Debitor and Creditor (which is the Journal) is set down at the Foot of every Account of the Waste-books". This is virtually the modern style of journal with the waste book entry for each transaction becoming the narrative supporting the journal entry. Malcolm had illustrated this format in his 1718 book.

The illustrations demonstrate how the account books are closed and balanced(6) and the book concludes with 'Directions how to frame a Book of Personal and Household Expenses' and 'Directions how to frame a Book of Charges of Merchandize'.

Book-keeping Methodiz'd.

OR,

A Methodical TREATISE

OF

Merchant-Accompts,

According to

The *Italian* Form.

WHEREIN,

The THEORY of the ART is fully Explained, and reduced to PRACTICE, by Variety of suitable EXAMPLES in all the Branches of Trade.

To which is added,

A Large APPENDIX,

CONTAINING,

I. Descriptions and Specimens of the *Subsidiary Books* used by Merchants.

II. An Explication of the Nature of *Bills of Exchange*, *Promissory Notes*, and *Bills of Parcels*.

III. Precedents of Merchants *Writings*, peculiar to *England*, *Scotland*, and common to both.

IV. The *Commission*, *Duty*, and *Power* of Factors.

V. A short History of the trading Companies in *Great Britain*, with an Account of her Exports and Imports.

VI. A Dictionary, explaining the *abstruse Words* and *Terms* that occur in Merchandize.

By JOHN MAIR, *A. M.*

EDINBURGH:

Printed by T. and W. RUDDIMANS for the AUTHOR, and sold by most Booksellers in Town and Country.

M DCC XXXVI.

7.13 Book-keeping Methodiz'd - John Mair - 1st Edition - 1736

The popularity of Mair's works has been considered in chapter 4. That chapter emphasised that this and Mair's later book(1) were the most successful book-keeping texts of the century and that they played a major part in spreading a knowledge of the Italian Method in Scotland, England, Ireland, North America and Norway.

Mair attempted to make 'Book-keeping Methodiz'd' a comprehensive treatise and it was augmented steadily with new material as successive editions were published. In the second edition (1741), Part I was expanded to include a section on Monies and Exchanges. The third edition (1749) introduced 38 pages on 'The Produce and Commerce of the Tobacco Colonies; with a Specimen of the Accompts usually kept by the Storekeepers'.(2) This additional material was particularly appropriate in view of the extensive Scottish Tobacco Trade and it will be considered in chapter 12.

In the fifth edition (1757) two new sections were added: (i) 96 pages on 'The produce and commerce of the Sugar Colonies; with a specimen of the accompts kept by the factors and store-keepers; and an explication of wharf and plantation accompts.'(3) and (ii) 29 pages on 'The method of keeping accompts proper for Shopkeepers or Retailers'.(4) Accounting for the Sugar Trade is considered in chapter 13 of this study.

These additions meant that the 251 pages of the first edition (1736) had swollen to 416 pages by the fifth Edinburgh edition (1757). This size remained constant up to the Edinburgh eighth edition (1765). This was the last edition.

The first edition is dedicated to the Rt Hon Charles, the 8th Lord Cathcart who was Governor of Duncannon Fort in the Kingdom of Ireland. The second edition records Mair's "Joy, upon your Lordship's Promotion to be Commander in Chief in an expedition against the Spaniards, for vindicating our Rights of Trade and Navigation". These congratulations were ill timed as Lord Cathcart died at sea in 1740 before the second edition appeared. In chapter four it was noted that Mair had been "Governor" to Lord Cathcart's son for a few months in 1727. This son now became the 9th Baron Cathcart and subsequent editions of Book-keeping Methodiz'd were dedicated to him. The 9th Baron Cathcart is said to have befriended James Watt and Adam Smith(5) in addition to his friendship with John Mair.

The book's preface extols the usefulness of the Italian Method and conveys the enthusiasm that Mair had for accounting. He says: "the theory of this art or science is beautiful and curious, very fit for improving the minds of youth, exercising their wit and invention, and disposing them to a close and accurate way of thinking. On this account several gentlemen, after having got acquainted with it themselves, have been induced, from the satisfaction and entertainment they found, to recommend it to others, as a valuable piece of human literature, proper to be studied and understood by everyone who pretends to liberal education."

This section is similar to a passage in Malcolm where he instances the work of Roger North.(6) The repetition of such sentiments may be regarded as evidence in support of Yamey's thesis that the double entry system became accepted as the standard system (in part at least) because its symmetry, completeness and elegance appealed to the scholarly authors who first described it and extolled its virtues.(7)

It is evident from this, and other passages, that Mair was familiar with, and influenced by, Malcolm's work but, whereas, Malcolm uses a ledger based approach to introduce the Italian System, Mair adheres to the more conventional form of exposition based on the waste-book and journal. Although Mair recognises that 'Italian Book-keeping' is applicable to a wide range of situations, he uses the familiar example of 'Merchants Accompts' as the vehicle for explaining the method because this area is so important and because it is "the fittest for exemplifying the several parts of this method".(8)

'Book-keeping Methodiz'd' appeared in a number of Irish editions; these may well have been unauthorised publications. There were a few minor differences between the Edinburgh and Dublin printings and the latter were not always based on the most recent Edinburgh versions.(9)

The 1764 Dublin edition does not include the new material added by Mair to his fifth (Edinburgh) edition but its contents are described as follows on the title page: "From the last EDITION printed at EDINBURGH and revised BY JOHN MAIR, A. M. with many ADDITIONS and IMPROVEMENTS. In the New Edition is added a SUPPLEMENT, Containing a Specimen of some Entries new modelled, and carried from the WASTE-BOOK into the JOURNAL and LEDGER, in a Manner agreeable to the present practice of MERCHANTS."

Mair is not the author of this 17-page supplement.(10) The additional material is introduced by the following note: "The following Entries are taken from the Author's preceding Waste-Book (the dates referring to the Cases therein,) and offer'd to the Perusal of the Public, in a new Dress. By W. J.". The author is almost certainly William Jackson, a Dublin teacher of book-keeping and accounts, who 21 years later wrote his own text 'Book-keeping in the true Italian Form of Debtor and Creditor'.(11)

By 1765 the structure of 'Book-keeping Methodiz'd' was as follows:

1. An Introduction describing the general nature of book-

keeping and the principal books involved.

2. Book I describing the nature and use of the waste book.

3. Book II describing the journal, the use of the terms debtor and creditor, some rules for determining debits and credits under the Italian Method and records appropriate for proper domestic trade, proper foreign trade, factorage and partnership.

4. Book III describing the ledger, posting transactions to the ledger and balancing the ledger.

5. A comprehensive 67-page example of a year's trading described in the pages of the waste book, journal and ledger.

6. Six questions on company (partnership) accompts.

7. An appendix comprising 9 chapters; the use of the word 'appendix', to describe this material, is something of a misnomer as these chapters account for well over half the book.(12)

The appendix covers: a description of various subsidiary books, foreign currency and bills of exchange etc, legal precedents in commerce (specimen commercial documents), the legal position of factors, a history of the major British trading companies, the sugar trade and the tobacco trade (with illustrative sets of accounting records), shopkeeper's accounts and a mercantile dictionary.

Mair had just completed a major revision of 'Book-keeping Methodiz'd' when he died in 1769. 'Book-keeping Moderniz'd', which appeared in 1773, is discussed at 7.20.

A SERIOUS ADVICE TO TRADESMEN.

SHEWING THEM

The INCONVENIENCIES they lye under, and NEEDLESS EXPENCE they are put to, by not learning BOOK-KEEPING:

WITH A

PROPOSAL

For having that ART more univerſally well taught, under Authority and Inſpection of the MAGISTRATES;

And alſo,

For eſtabliſhing an AUTHORISED BROKER, for the Eaſe and Conveniency of COMMERCE.

By WILLIAM STEVENSON,
Teacher of BOOK-KEEPING.

EDINBURGH:
Printed by R. FLEMING. MDCCLVI.

7.14 A Serious Advice to Tradesmen - William Stevenson - 1756

This is a short book of 29 pages (excluding the preliminary pages) in which William Stevenson makes a case for more official support for the teaching of book-keeping in Edinburgh. On page 3 he refers to an earlier publication. He says: "About twenty five years ago I delivered a discourse in Mary's Chapel, and the year after published it; in which discourse I shewed the usefulness of BOOK-KEEPING to all ranks of persons, from the highest to the lowest, so that I never intended to appear again in public upon that subject; but many reasons having prompted me, I have resolved at last to trouble the public once more with this small essay, in which I shall not resume any thing I have said in my above mentioned discourse, but only add such observations as have occurred by practice and experience since that time ... ". The publication referred to is 'A General Discourse Shewing the Usefulness of the Italian Method of Book-keeping - 1731.' This has been discussed earlier at 7.11.

Stevenson indicates that he regards book-keeping as part of mathematics. He complains that, whereas all tradesmen recognise the value of mathematics in their specialist trades, the value of book-keeping in managing the business itself is too often dismissed. He says that he has had extensive practical experience " ... in revising books of all kinds, and regulating Accompts which were confused and out of order".(1) He considers that the general level of accounting expertise is poor and that this calls for an examination of the provision for accounting education.

Stevenson considers the poor state of accounting education in Edinburgh can be attributed to four factors:

(i) Parents and tutors "... hurry on their Children and

Pupils to business very young ... before thay have got other education proper to qualify them for that study ... ". He particularly complains of the poor understanding of English grammar and Arithmetic.

(ii) Pupils frequently do not finish a proper course of study but leave "... before they have gone through one half or one third of their course ... thinking they have got enough of it ... ".(2)

(iii) Parents and tutors often choose the cheapest teachers rather than the best. Here Stevenson complains of " ... writing masters, who, perhaps, have thirty, forty, or more scholars; and when he gets one or two for BOOK-KEEPING, he sets them in a corner, with a book before them to copy, without ever regarding them, explaining the principles or answering their difficulties ... ". (3)

(iv) The fourth reason is lack of practical experience on the part of some teachers. Some teachers have "... only read a book or two upon the subject, by which they have pickt up a little of the science of Debitor and Creditor, but they know nothing of the Art of applying them". He complains of the standard of the accounting textbooks and says that few of the writers " ... know more of it, than what they have copied from one another ... some of the old Authors are the best, and most substantial, as having been either Traders themselves, or taken their books from those of real Trade ... ".(4)

He then proceeds to make a case for official support for accounting education. "Every body knows, that in this city there are public establishments for Teachers and Professors of all or most parts of human literature: such as languages and all the arts and sciences, all of which were erected long ago, and before trade and manufactures were come to such a heighth ... but now that these are become more in esteem ... is it not reasonable that there should be an establishment at least for one who is qualified to teach the traders and manufacturers to carry on their business with regularity? and that one should be recommended by public authority ... ".(5)

Stevenson proposes that the city magistrates (to whom the book is dedicated) should appoint a Teacher of Book-keeping. This teacher should teach both book-keeping and arithmetic, " ... the last being indispensibly necessary to qualify the learner for the first ... ", but he should not teach writing and the whole range of mathematics. Stevenson emphasises that this teacher should be someone " ... who has been at least some years in real business, and knows both Theory and Practice ... ". The teacher should have a small salary from the city to augment his income and other benefits " ... such as giving him the freedom of the city ... he might also have the privilege of teaching Watson's and other hospitals, when they have scholars fit for that piece of education".(6)

Stevenson quite openly admits that he would wish himself to be appointed to the proposed official post and, in fact, he was later to become 'teacher of book-keeping authorised by act of council of the city of Edinburgh'.(7)

The book also discusses the need in Edinburgh for "... a Broker or Agent for Merchants: such as are established in all the trading cities, both in England, and upon the whole Continent". Such a broker would keep a register of all goods offered for sale or required, he would note and witness bargains entered into and would provide information on insurance, currency exchange, the discounting of bills and shipping details and charges.

7.15 Essays on Book-keeping - William Webster - with a Large Appendix by 'A Teacher of Book-keeping' - 1758

This book is the first Glasgow publication on book-keeping. There are two versions of the title page, one printed in red and black(1) and the other printed in black.(2) There are also variations in the number of pages. David Murray(3) states that the book has 228 pages but in some versions there are 250 pages. The difference is accounted for by 2 unnumbered pages (the preface which appears in all versions) and 20 unnumbered pages that appear in some copies but are missing from other copies.(4) It is assumed that these 20 pages, which deal with accounting for the tobacco trade, are intended to be part of the text.

The preface comments on the works of Mair and Webster: "It must be confessed, that Mr. Mair's treatise of Book-keeping is the most perfect of the kind, it particularly merits the attention of every man of business, but without derogating from his merit, it must be owned that the subject is still capable of further improvement.

"This treatise begins with Mr Webster's system of Book-keeping, which is a neat, easy, and elegant enough essay, and very well calculated to initiate the reader, or learner, in the science: He is too sparing of his rules, and leaves the reader intirely ignorant how to manage many of the common occurrences in business. His examples are perfectly well explained, and adjusted to the level of the meanest capacity. Had he not stopped short, but pursued the design, with the same perspicuity, thro' all the different branches of Book-keeping, he would have left little work for others, and done a mighty service to mankind."

The anonymous editor then proceeds by reprinting Webster's short text and adding to it, without acknowledgement, more advanced material from Mair. He calls

ESSAYS

ON

BOOK-KEEPING

WHEREIN

The ART is fully explained, and reduced to Practice, by a Variety of pertinent Examples, in all its different Branches.

By *WILLIAM WEBSTER*

To which is added,

A Large APPENDIX,

CONTAINING,

A VARIETY of SPECIMENS in COMPANY ACCOMPTS, both in the common Method, and in a new One: Together with FACTORAGE ACCOMPTS, and a Method of keeping Accompts proper for SHOP-KEEPERS or RETAILERS.

By a TEACHER of BOOK-KEEPING

GLASGOW,

Printed for JOHN ORR Bookseller.

MDCCLVIII.

the compilation 'Essays on Book-keeping.' William Webster's book was first published in London in 1719 with the title 'An Essay on Book-keeping'.(5)

Murray correctly states that "the Essay is given verbatim and page for page as in the London edition of 1740." but he assumes that the remainder of the book "pp 73-216, and the introductory chapter, pp i-xii are by the Glasgow editor".(6)

The editor reproduces questions III, IV and VI from the 'Six Specimens of Company-accompts in 'Book-keeping Methodiz'd'(6) and gives solutions for the first two which are not provided by Mair.(7) This is followed by "A Specimen of the Accompts kept by the Factors in the Sugar Colonies", "A Specimen of the Accompts usually kept by the Merchants or Storekeepers in Virginia and Maryland" and "Of the Method of Keeping Accompts Proper for Shopkeepers or Retailers". This material is, respectively, from chapter VI (section II), chapter VII (section II) and chapter VIII of Mair's 'Book-keeping Methodiz'd.' Of the book's 250 pages, 72 are by Webster, 14 (the introduction and preface) are by the unknown editor and 164 are either directly taken from Mair or substantially based on his work.

7.16 Book-keeping by Double Entry - William Stevenson - 1762

This book is dedicated to the Lord Provost and members of Edinburgh city council in gratitude for the author's appointment as teacher of Book-keeping in the city, the post for which he had campaigned in his earlier publication (discussed at 7.14).

Stevenson says that he is hesitant about publishing the book "... being a Scots Man born, and not Master of the English Idiom, which now prevails over the whole Island of Britain"(1) but he sets against this 'disadvantage' the fact that " ... I have been bred to the Practice of Business for most Part of my Life, and by some Misfortunes in Trade not being able to carry it on with any Advantage, I betook myself to teaching, for which I presumed I might be qualified, considering the Experience I had pick'd up by my long Practice in real Business."

The Introduction(2) describes the double entry system. The General Rule, that he proposes, uses the terminolgy of accounts charge and discharge: "WHATEVER is received, or ought in Reason to be charged, must be made the Dr. And WHATEVER is delivered away, or ought in Reason to be discharged, must be made Cr".(3) The application of this rule is demonstrated by the illustrative material.

Stevenson insisted that the book should be printed as a large folio volume rather than as a more convenient smaller book "1st, Because I think all Books on that Subject ought to be printed precisely in the same Manner and Volume in which they are written. 2dly. Because there are many Parts of the Legers, (especially those for Gentlemen and Farmers) which are made up of so many different Columns in the same Accot. that a less Volume than that in which they are published could not have contained them." He emphasises that his approach is a practical one.

BOOK-KEEPING

BY

DOUBLE ENTRY;

REDUCED,

In its THEORY, to one Simple Rule;

AND APPLIED,

In its PRACTICE, to all the Variety of Accompts

Necessary to be kept by

The SHOP-KEEPER, MERCHANT, BANKER, LANDED GENTLEMAN, STEWARD or FACTOR upon a Landed Gentleman's Estate, and FARMER: All exemplified in Sets of Books adapted to each Kind of Business; with Specimens of the most necessary Subsidiary Books in Business.

By WILLIAM STEVENSON some Time Merchant in Rotterdam,

And present Teacher of Book keeping, authorised by Act of Council of the City of Edinburgh.

EDINBURGH:

Printed by R. STIRLING for the AUTHOR.

M. DCC. LXXI.

Stevenson writes from the solid base of practical experience. He is obviously a traditionalist so that in his example of an estate memorial and journal he begins the specimen books with the traditional phrase "In Nomine Domini : Amen" which is similar to the heading used by Pacioli two and a half centuries earlier.(4)

7.17 The Universal Accountant and Complete Merchant - William Gordon - 1st edition - 1763

This is Gordon's most well known work published soon after his move from Stirling to his own Mercantile Academy in Glasgow. Volume 1, published in 1763, commences with an 'Essay on the Education of a Young Gentleman intended for the Counting-House'. In this he extols the benefits that society obtains from 'the judicious and industrious merchant'. "It is he who employs the poor, rewards the ingenious, encourages the industrious, interchanges the produce and manufactures of one country for those of another; binds, and links together in one chain of interest, the universality of the human species, and thus becomes a blessing to mankind, a credit to his country, a source of affluence to all around him, his family, and himself."(1) He laments the lack of an appropriate system of education for the 'commercial profession' and complains that often during the student's work experience in the counting house " ... he will be employed, during the time of his apprenticeship, in copying letters, going messages, and waiting on the post-office".(2) He argues for "academies for training up youth to business, especially in trading cities ... " to be established and financed from public funds.(3) In volume II of the 'New Modelled' 5th edition he extends this proposal by making a case for the teaching of accounting in the universities.(4)

The material in volume I is organised in four parts: part I which deals with the elements of arithmetic, part II which is concerned with fractions, part III on the elements of algebra and part IV which deals with 'The Application of Arithmetic to the Business of the Merchant, the Banker, Custom-house, Insurance-office, etc.'(5)

Gordon had emphasised in his preface that his objective

THE
UNIVERSAL ACCOUNTANT
AND
COMPLETE MERCHANT.

IN TWO VOLUMES.

By WILLIAM GORDON,
of the ACADEMY, GLASGOW.

VOLUME I.

Quid munus reipublicæ majus meliusve afferre possumus, quam si juventutem bene erudiamus? CICERO.

EDINBURGH:
Printed for the AUTHOR, and A. DONALDSON.
Sold by the said A. DONALDSON at his shops in EDINBURGH, and the Strand, LONDON.
MDCCLXIII.

in Volume I is to go beyond the proof of the arithmetical processes that he introduces and to demonstrate the uses of the techniques in real practice. More than half of volume I is devoted to this under the main title 'Varieties in Proportion.'(6) This title is not very helpful, but the list of topics that Gordon covers is impressive. These are: Tare and Trett calculations (ie the calculation of allowable deductions (for packing and waste) from the gross weight of produce); Computation of Customs, Bounties etc; Rule of Mixtures (cost and price calculations when various types of produce are mixed); Warehouse and Shop Computations (calculation of gross profit percentages and pricing to achieve given mark-up); Computations in Barter; Computations in Partnership; Bankruptcy and Computations relating to Compositions; Stock Jobbing; Factorage; Insurance; Computations in Exchange; Arbitration of Exchanges; Comparisons of Weights and Measures (with two fold-out tables); Simple Interest; Compound Interest; Purchasing Freehold or Real Estates (with tables of Terminal Value, Present Value, Annuity Terminal Value, Annuity Present Value, Annuity Purchaseable for £1; for rates of interest of 3, 3 1/2, 4, 4 1/2 and 5% and from 1 to 40 years); Annuities on Lives; Mensuration of Surfaces and Solids.(7)

Much of the material in the section on Stock Jobbing seems to come from Thomas Mortimer's 'Every Man his Own Broker or a Guide to Exchange-Alley' which was first published in 1761, two years before 'The Universal Accountant'.(8)

Volume II, which was published two years later in 1765, commences with a 'Dissertation on the Business of the Counting-House'(pp 1-14). The volume continues with: the elements of mercantile accountantship (pp 15-58), specimens of account books (pp 59-350), a section on bills of exchange (pp 351-390 and a view of the British customs (pp 391-466).

A major revision was undertaken for the 5th edition which was published in 1787.

The material on pages 60-62, 'The method of collecting the balances, closing the books, and raising new ones therefrom' (art IV) has clearly been adapted from Mair's 'Book-keeping Methodiz'd'.(9)

A

FULL AND PRACTICAL

TREATISE

UPON

BILLS OF EXCHANGE.

TOGETHER WITH

An ACCOUNT of the NATURE of the

BANK of AMSTERDAM,

And how PAYMENTS are made and received in it, *&c.*

BY

WILLIAM STEVENSON,

Some time merchant in *Rotterdam,*

And present teacher of book-keeping, authorised by act of council of the city of *Edinburgh.*

EDINBURGH:

Printed by JOHN ROBERTSON,

And sold by him and other booksellers.

MDCCLXIV.

7.18 A Full and Practical Treatise upon Bills of Exchange - William Stevenson - 1764

This, the fourth of Stevenson's publications, is not a book on book-keeping, but Stevenson makes it clear that it is based on material that he included in his book-keeping course. He says in the preface "When I first set about teaching book-keeping, I found the greatest difficulty I had was, to make my scholars understand the nature of bills of exchange; and consequently, when transactions occurred in which bills were introduced, they were at a loss to find proper debitor and creditor ... ". He states that his original intention was to include the material on bills of exchange as an appendix to his book-keeping text but this, for unspecified reasons, was not possible.(1)

The book is intended to be a practical work based, primarily, on Stevenson's own experience but the last 19 pages(2) deal with the history and operations of the Bank of Amsterdam. Stevenson explains that, before the foundation of the Bank of Amsterdam, Dutch merchants had experienced considerable difficulties, because most of the coins circulating had a low value. Traders with large sums to pay or receive " ... found it both inconvenient and chargeable, by reason of the time it employed, as well as the extraordinary expences of servants, porters, with wheelbarrows, and even frequently horses with sledges, to transport their money from place to place ... ".(3)

The Bank of Amsterdam was established to remove this difficulty. " ... the magistracy of the city of Amsterdam, in the year 1609, proposes to the merchants to take in their money, and secure it in strong vaults ... The merchants ... soon brought in vast sums of money ... every one got credit in the bank books for his particular sum; and thus, by circulating payment from one to another, they could pay millions in a moment, by subscribing their names."(4) So convenient did this bank money become that it soon stood at a premium over coins. This difference in value was termed 'agio' or 'exchange'.

Some of the bank's accounting procedures are described in this section of the book. "When any merchant or banker hath a demand made upon him, he goes along with the person, who is to receive the payment to the bank, and there fills up the blanks in the billet(5) with the person's name to whose credit it is to go, and the sum to be paid; which billet he then signs in presence of the book-keepers, two of whom sit together at bank hours, the one writing in the journal, and the other at his hand in the ledger. The person who signs the billet having delivered it over to these book-keepers, he is immediately debited, and the other person whose name is inserted gets credit for the same sum, by which means their journal and ledger are continually kept up equal; so that, at all bank hours, any one who has an accompt hath access to see how it stands, upon paying a small perquisite to the book-keepers.

"It is necessary to observe, that the person who makes the payment must always be present, and sign the billet at the sight of the book-keepers, to whom he delivers it out of his own hand: but then, there is no necessity for the person in whose favour the transfer is made to be present; for he may get credit for many thousands in his absence, and may be informed at any time what sums are put to his credit, which again he may immediately write off (6) to others, in the manner above prescribed."(7)

Stevenson notes that the Bank of Rotterdam is very similar to the Bank of Amsterdam but that it will also keep "an account in current money with those who chuse it, which is a great conveniency to the inhabitants".(8)

THE GENERAL COUNTING-HOUSE, AND MAN OF BUSINESS.

CALCULATED

To promote FACILITY and ACCURACY in Accounts of Busineſs, relative to the MERCHANT, the BANKER, UNDERWRITER, BROKER, FACTOR, EMPLOYER, DRAWER, REMITTER, PARTNER, TRUSTEE, MANUFACTURER, WAREHOUSE-KEEPER, SHOPKEEPER, STOREKEEPER, LANDED GENTLEMAN, CHAMBERLAIN, FARMER, &c.

WITH THE

Method of negotiating BILLS of EXCHANGE, in all the trading Countries in EUROPE.

BY WILLIAM GORDON,
Author of the UNIVERSAL ACCOUNTANT.

Quo ſemel eſt imbuta recens, ſervabit odorem.
HOR.

EDINBURGH:
Printed for A. DONALDSON, and ſold at his ſhops in LONDON and EDINBURGH.
MDCCLXVI.

7.19 General Counting-House and Man of Business - William Gordon - 1st edition - 1766

'The General Counting-House and Man of Business' is dedicated to Alexander, Duke of Gordon. This is William Gordon's second book on accounting.(1) In a note 'To the Public' he gives reasons for issuing the new text: " ... as there are many who have neither time, nor think themselves under the necessity to study those parts of a science which have no immmediate relation to the particular species of business in which they are employed, I thought models of such accounts as have been hitherto very little studied, would at once be an improvement in the art of accountantship, and an agreeable present to the public."

The book is a single volume(2) and the first 378 pages contain parts I, II and III of the second volume of Gordon's 'Universal Accountant'. The new text omits part IV of the 'Universal Accountant' (which gives 'A Brief View of the British Customs') but there are additional sections on: The West-India Counting-house (pp 379-421); The Retailer's Counting-house, or the Book-keeping proper for Shop, Warehouse, and Storekeepers (pp 422-462) and a Model of Accountantship, calculated for the Landed Gentleman, the Chamberlain, and the Farmer (pp 463-487).

It is difficult to accept, without reservations, Gordon's claim on the title page that the book also deals with 'Accounts of Business, relative to ... the Banker'. There is no consideration of a Banker's accounting records but bankers would, presumably, be interested in the contents of the book and, in that sense, could it be argued that it does contain material 'relative to ... the Banker'.(3)

The material on 'The West-India Counting-house' is based on William Weston's 'The Complete Merchant's Clerk: or British and American Counting House'(1754); this is considered in chapter 13.

The 'Model of Accountantship for the Landed Gentleman, the Chamberlain, and the Farmer' is an illustrative set of records dealing with the estate of Sir John Fullerton. There is no explanatory text for this section but the material is of interest and it is discussed in chapter 14.

The section describing an accounting system for a retailer provides for a greater use of specialised subsidiary books than in the standard version of the 'Italian Method' which is explained, and used, elsewhere in the text. The books required are: an invoice (or buying) book, a day book (or sales book), a book of charges, a journal and a ledger. There is no waste book(4) and (surprisingly) no cash book.(5) Periodically details from the specialised subsidiary books are posted to the ledger via the journal. An illustrative example for a 3-month accounting period is given.

BOOK-KEEPING MODERNIZ'D:

OR,

MERCHANT-ACCOUNTS by DOUBLE ENTRY, according to the ITALIAN form.

WHEREIN

The THEORY of the ART is clearly explained, and reduced to PRACTICE, in copious SETS OF BOOKS, exhibiting all the varieties that uſually occur in Real Buſineſs.

To which is added,

A Large APPENDIX.

CONTAINING,

I. Deſcriptions and ſpecimens of the Subſidiary Books uſed by merchants.
II. Monies and Exchanges, the nature of Bills of Exchange, Promiſſory Notes, and Bills of Parcels.
III. Precedents of Merchants Writings, peculiar to England, Scotland, and common to both
IV. The Commiſſion, Duty, and Power of Factors.
V. A ſhort Hiſtory of the Trading Companies in Great Britain, with an account of her exports and imports.
VI. The produce and commerce of the [illegible] Colonies; with a ſpecimen of the accounts kept by the factors or ſtorekeepers; and an explication of wharf and plantation accounts.
VII. The produce and commerce of the Tobacco Colonies; with a ſpecimen of the accounts uſually kept by the ſtorekeepers.
VIII. The method of keeping accounts proper for Shopkeepers or Retailers.
IX. The method of keeping the accounts of a Land-Eſtate.
X. A Dictionary, explaining abſtruſe words and terms that occur in merchandiſe.

By JOHN MAIR, A. M.

EDINBURGH:

Printed for A. KINCAID & W. CREECH and J. BELL.
Sold, in London, by W. JOHNSTON, S. CROWDER, R. BALDWIN, E. & C. DILLY, T. CADELL, and J. MURRAY.

MDCCLXXIII.

7.20 Book-keeping Moderniz'd - John Mair - 1st edition - 1773

Mair died in 1769 but, right up to his death, he had been working on a revised version of his book-keeping text and this was published in 1773 with the title 'Book-keeping Moderniz'd'. Mair considered that this revision was necessary in view of the fact that "forms and fashions in accountantship ... are in a perpetual flux".(1) The book was based on his earlier text but there was a 50% increase in the size from the 416 pages of the last edition of 'Book-keeping Moderniz'd' to 620 pages.

The organisation and numbering of chapters in the book is identical to that used in 'Book-keeping Methodiz'd' apart from the addition of a completely new 31-page section on estate accounts which is placed in the appendix as chapter X. There are, however, some changes in terminology and spelling; thus 'accompt' and 'accomptant' in 'Methodiz'd' become 'account' and 'accountant' in 'Moderniz'd'. The term 'capital' largely replaces 'stock', although 'stock' is still used occasionally. Some changes reflect the changing business environment so that, for example, the use of a bank account by a trader(2) reflects the fact that Scottish banks in the 1770's were rapidly extending their services with agencies and branches.

There were other changes in detail so that the list and description of subsidiary books is extended and the material on partnership accounts is changed. A 61-page illustrative example of partnership accounts kept in separate books is added and in this example the combined waste book/journal is used.(3) The six questions in partnership accounts had been such a popular feature of the earlier book that two other authors had reproduced them. In 'Book-keeping Methodiz'd' Mair had provided a solution for only one of these questions, he now gives solutions for five.

The 68-page example of a sole trader's accounts given in 'Book-keeping Moderniz'd' is extended by 100 pages and new features are the illustration of the Cash Book and the Trial Balance.(4)

The most interesting change is probably the fact that Mair now notes that businessmen commonly calculate profits annually: "Merchants commonly once a-year balance or close their ledger, and raise from it the materials of an Inventory to a new set of books, for the ensuing year. This they do, not purely because the spaces allotted for the accounts may, by the end of the year be supposed to be for the most part full; but chiefly with a view to discover how far they have gained or lost by last year's trade."(5) His major illustrations show this feature but he had also adopted such an accounting period in his earlier book.

'Book-keeping Moderniz'd' was very successful and nine editions were published over 35 years, the last appearing in 1807. All editions contained 620 pages indicating that there were few changes made to the original manuscript for over a quarter of a century. The only alteration that has been found (apart from changes in the dates used in the illustrative material) is a footnote in the section dealing with the tobacco trade. This notes that "matters are here represented as they were before the Independence of America was established. It is not known what changes that revolution may produce in the laws and practice of commerce with that country." Although all editions were published in Edinburgh the book was used widely as a standard text outside Scotland.

THE
MAN of BUSINESS,
AND
GENTLEMAN's ASSISTANT:

Containing a TREATISE of
PRACTICAL ARITHMETIC,
Including VULGAR and DECIMAL FRACTIONS,
IN WHICH ARE INSERTED,
Many CONCISE and VALUABLE RULES, for the READY
CASTING UP of MERCHANDIZE,
Never yet published in this Kingdom;

BOOK-KEEPING
By SINGLE and DOUBLE ENTRY,
The former upon an entire NEW PLAN,
COMPRISING
A modern and approved METHOD of keeping SMALL ACCOMPTS,
Dr. and Cr. in the WASTE-BOOK only,
Calculated for the EASE and ADVANTAGE of RETAIL-TRADERS;
TOGETHER WITH
AN ESSAY ON ENGLISH GRAMMAR.

Adapted to the Use of GENTLEMEN, MERCHANTS,
TRADERS, and SCHOOLS,

By *W. PERRY*, Master of the Academy at KELSO.

EDINBURGH,
Printed for the AUTHOR, by DAVID WILLISON:
And sold by J. MURRAY, No. 32, *Fleetstreet*, *London*;
J. BELL, *Edinburgh*; D. BAXTER, *Glasgow*; T. SLACK
and W. CHARNLEY, *Newcastle*; A. GRAHAM, *Alnwick*;
J. RICHARDSON, *Berwick*; and G. ELLIOT, *Kelso*.
M,DCC,LXXIV.

7.21 The Man of Business, and Gentleman's Assistant - William Perry - 1st edition - 1774

The year after the publication of this book, William Perry moved from Kelso to Edinburgh where he became 'Master of the Academy'.(1) The first section of the book deals with arithmetic(2) including the familiar business topics: Tare and Tret, Simple and Compound Interest, Rebate or Discompt, Equation of Payments, Fellowship, Barter and Exchange. This is followed by a section dealing with Bills of Exchange.(3)

The book-keeping material is primarily concerned with a single entry system.(4) In Perry's single entry system a waste book, journal and ledger are kept but the only accounts appearing in the ledger are: the personal accounts, of the more important customers and suppliers, and accounts for stock (ie capital), cash and balance. Records of minor debtors and creditors are kept in the waste book. The profit (or loss) for a period is obtained from the increase (or decrease) in the balance on the stock account. A comprehensive example of the system is provided with much of the information being given by way of notes placed at appropriate points in the specimen account books.

A shorter example of book-keeping by double entry is given for a general trader dealing in such commodities as rum, tobacco, muslin and wine. The accounts are balanced after a month's trading. The waste book, journal, ledger and cash book are illustrated.

The author describes the more conventional subsidiary books but notes that "Those persons ... who make use of the fewest books, are reckoned the best accomptants."

The first edition of the book finishes with a 59-page section on English Grammar and some engraved examples of Perry's 'copper plate' and 'business hand'.(5)

The 2nd and 3rd editions of the text appeared in 1777.

The 3rd edition omits the English grammar and compensates for this by (i) enlarging the arithmetic section (with a fuller treatment of annuities and an extended set of compound interest tables) and (ii) providing a better coverage of double entry book-keeping. The double entry section is extended by continuing the illustrative example for a further 3 month's trading and included in this are some examples of trading in partnership.(6)

AN

INTRODUCTION

TO

MERCHANDIZE.

CONTAINING

A compleat System of ARITHMETIC.

A System of ALGEBRA.

BOOK-KEEPING in various forms.

An Account of the TRADE of GREAT BRITAIN, and the LAWS and PRACTICES which Merchants are chiefly interested in.

In TWO VOLUMES.

VOLUME I.

EDINBURGH:

Printed for the AUTHOR;

Sold by T. CADELL, London, and

JOHN BALFOUR, Edinburgh,

M,DCC,LXXVII.

7.22 An Introduction to Merchandize - Robert Hamilton - 1st Edition - 1777/79

The title page of volume I has no mention of authorship but this is not in doubt and the dedication is signed by Robert Hamilton, Perth. Hamilton dedicates his book to the Provost, Dean-of-Guild, Bailies, Treasurer and the other members of the Council of Perth. In 1769 this council had appointed him to the post of Rector of Perth Academy, following the death of John Mair. Hamilton indicates, in the preface, that the book is intended to be suitable for use in academies and schools, and in the dedication he states that it was primarily intended for use at Perth Academy. He also hopes that the practical man of business will find the book useful. The work was first published in two volumes, volume I in 1777 and volume II in 1779, but subsequent editions were in a single volume.

Volume I (356 pages plus preliminaries) is divided into three parts. Part I is concerned with Arithmetic. Part II, which deals with Algebra, includes sections on Interest, Annuities and Reversions, the Doctrine of Chances, Annuities for Lives and Tables of Interest, probabilities of life and life annuities. Part III deals with Bills of Exchange, Promissory Notes, British and Foreign Money and Weights and Measures. Various commercial documents are illustrated and explained in this part.

Volume II also has three parts. Parts IV and V deal with Book-keeping. Part VI, on the 'State and Laws of Trade', has chapters on the State of British Trade, Custom - House Laws, Mercantile Laws (Insurance, Bills of Exchange Execution, Bankruptcy, Arbitration) and Public Funds.

The split of the book-keeping material into two chapters is interesting. Part IV is concerned with an exposition of the traditional system based on the waste book, journal and ledger, whereas part V is entitled 'Practical Book-keeping'. It is here that Hamilton breaks free from the constraints imposed by the Italian method to propose some important extensions to the basic system. Other authors, while noting that the classical system could be modified in practice, had not seen the potential for some of the developments that Hamilton proposes. There are seven chapters to part V.

Chapter I - Varieties in Italian Method: This chapter emphasises that a practical implementation of a book-keeping system may depart from the Italian method to cater for the needs of the trader, the particular circumstances of his business and the individual preferences of the accountant. Hamilton emphasises, however, that he is convinced that " a full knowledge of the regular method is absolutely necessary for understanding" some of the variations that he will introduce. In this chapter Hamilton describes the combined waste book/journal that Malcolm had introduced in 1718.

Chapter II - Method with a Cash Book and Ledger Only: This chapter describes a double entry system that may be appropriate when most of a business's transactions involve cash. The system is simpler than the Italian Method in that it requires only a cash book and ledger <u>or</u> a cash book, journal and ledger.

Chapter III - Method with Allowance of Interest: This chapter suggests the charging of imputed interest in the account books because "a merchant's gain should only be estimated by the excess of his gross profits above the interest of his stock".(1) This seems to be the first discussion of 'residual income' in an accounting text and it is considered in some detail in chapter 17 of this study.

Chapter IV - Shop-Keepers Accompts: Chapter IV considers variations to the Italian Method which are suitable for "shop-keepers, whose business consists chiefly in retail".

Chapter V - Tradesmens Accompts: This chapter is particularly important in that Hamilton develops the Italian Method into a process costing system for a textile manufacturer. This work is discussed, in some detail, in chapter 16.

Chapter VI - Land-Stewards Accompts: This chapter describes two methods for keeping the accounts of an estate. The chapter also contains an early discussion of depreciation.

Chapter VII - Farmers Accompts: Here Hamilton is concerned to provide a method of accounting that will be suitable for farmers who "have seldom leisure for much writing." The accounts are designed to assist with the management of the farm.

Part V ends by giving five problems in the design of accounting systems for the students' consideration. These problems are such an excellent illustration of Hamilton's approach to accounting that they are worthy of reproduction in full and this has been done in chapter 9 of this study.

Later editions of the Hamilton's 'Merchandize' appeared in one volume with the loss of some of the first edition material. Thus the chapter on 'Indeterminate Decimals' disappears in the 2nd edition; this is not a great loss since Hamilton admitted, in his preface to the first edition, that it could be ignored by most readers because " ... it is of little or no use in business ... " The loss of accounting material excised from chapter V of part V is, however, of considerable importance. The removal of this material from later editions has prevented Hamilton's work from receiving proper appreciation. This will be discussed in chapter 16. The accounting material in the last edition (1820) was completely rewritten by Elias Johnston and it bears no resemblance at all to Hamilton's work.(2)

7.23 The Practical Counting House - James Scruton - 1777

Although Scruton was probably not a Scot, his book has been included in this survey since he had lived permanently in Glasgow from 1749. Scruton had moved from London, at the request of the Provost of Glasgow,(1) to teach writing, arithmetic and book-keeping in that city and, at the time that he wrote this book, he was in partnership with William Gordon at the Mercantile Academy. The title of his book uses the relatively unusual term 'Accountantship'.(2)

The dedication is to John Glasford, one of the major Glasgow Tobacco 'Lords' and, according to Tobias Smollett, one of the greatest merchants in Europe.(3) An interesting feature is that Glasford's firm, and other genuine firms, appear in the illustrative material dealing with the tobacco trade.(4)

Scruton describes the method of 'Dr and Cr' in 4 short chapters.(5) Chapter I lists and describes the books "used in regular Counting Houses." Although he describes the waste book as the "most essential" book, "being the foundation of all the rest", he later states that the ledger is "the principal book of accounts. In the course of his discussion of the waste book and journal he suggests that these books may be combined and his third illustrative example shows this system in operation. Other books that he describes are: the cash book, the bank book, the debt book, the invoice book, the book of accounts current, the commission book, the bill book, the book of charges or expences; the copy book; the postage book; the sales book and the ship book.

Chapter II follows the conventional approach of analysing all transactions into Personal, Real or Fictitious categories and accounts are likewise categorised. Chapter III gives "Particular Rules for applying Dr. and Cr." and

THE PRACTICAL COUNTING HOUSE;

OR,

Calculation and Accountantship ILLUSTRATED,

In all the Cases that can occur in Trade, DOMESTIC or FOREIGN, PROPER or COMPANY;

In Buying, Selling, Drawing, Remitting, Exporting, Importing, Factorage, Brokerage, Insurance, Exchange, &c.

To which is added,

AN APPENDIX,

Containing Precedents of Writing, English and Scots, proper for every regular Counting house;

AND

A BOOK OF RATES,

Exhibiting, at one view, the DUTY and DRAWBACK upon every Commodity the British Merchant Exports or Imports, with a Summary of the Laws Respecting the same.

BY

JAMES SCRUTON,

OF THE ACADEMY IN GLASGOW,

Author of the Mercantile Penmanship.

GLASGOW:

PRINTED FOR JAMES DUNCAN, BOOKSELLER, OPPOSITE TO THE MAIN GUARD.

M.DCC.LXXVII.

chapter IV is "Of Posting and Balancing the Leger". Scruton illustrates the application of the rules that he has given by three lengthy examples.(6)

The book has a section dealing with "PRECEDENTS; or, FORMS of WRITINGS used by MERCHANTS", English, Scottish and British Precedents, computations in exchanges and insurance, a chapter entitled "A Brief View of the Business of the Custom-house" and a "Book of Rates" giving the rate of duty chargeable on various types of merchandise.

7.24 The Farmers Account-Book - David Young - c 1790

Young's Farmer's Account-Book is an analysed account book designed for recording a year's agricultural activity. No double entry system is suggested, rather the book emphasises the advantages that may be obtained from a full analysis (carried out on a daily basis) of the farmer's work.

After 4 sets of tables designed for the farmer's daily record of the weather, temperature, barometric pressure and 'Remarkable Occurences', the following analysis sheets are provided:

Tables 1 to 3, constituting a stock record system; this commences with the opening inventory and is designed to accommodate a record all acquisitions and disposals throughout the year in both physical and financial terms.

Tables 4 to 15 provide for a monthly analysis of expenditure.

Tables 16 to 27 provide for a monthly analysis of 'produce'.

Table 28 is designed to give a Summary of the Monthly Expenditure totals and the calculation of useful averages.

Table 29 is designed to provide a Summary of the Monthly 'Produce' totals and the calculation of useful averages.

Tables 30 and 31 are additional pages for the farmer to use for any other form of analysis that he considers to be useful.

Tables 32 and 33 are specimen Expenditure and Produce Summaries which have been completed to assist the reader to follow the system.

Tables 34 and 35 are blank for the farmer's own use.

Table 36 give the expense and produce of Young's own farm at Woodhead.

THE

FARMERS ACCOUNT-BOOK

OF

EXPENDITURE and PRODUCE for each Day, Month, and Year,

STATING THE

PROFIT and LOSS *per* Year upon each Article in the Farm,

CONTAINING

A REGISTER of the whole Work and Tranfactions done upon the Farm each Day.

By DAVID YOUNG.

Author of National Improvements; and, Agriculture the Primary Intereft of Great Britain.

In thefe unhappy Soils the Swains forbear,
And keep a Sabbath of alternate Year,
That the fpent Earth may gather Heat again,
And, better'd by Ceffation, bear the Grain.

VIRGIL.

Price to Non-fubfcribers Six Shillings, being a large Folio in Place of Quarto, as mentioned in the Propofals, with fundry additional Tables

EDINBURGH.

Printed for the Author, and fold by him and Mr James Ainslie Bookfeller, St Andrew's Street, New Town, from either of whom Bookfellers may be [illegible]

LIKEWISE

[illegible] Meff Aikon and Austin Seedfmen, Glafgow, Mr Adams Seedfman, Aberdeen, and Mr James Morrifon Bookfeller, Perth.—Where may be had, the [illegible] Volume intituled, *National Improvements upon Agriculture*; and the fecond Volume, *Agriculture the Primary Intereft of Great Britain.*

N. B. Commiffions may be addreffed to David Young, Perth.

Table 37 is another example but set out in a bilateral form resembling the conventional profit and loss account.

Tables 38 and 39 are for grain analyses. Grain covers: wheat, beans, pease, barley, oats, rye, meal and potatoes.

Whilst Young's method requires considerable detail to be conscientiously recorded, it is not analysed within the conventional accounting framework and from this viewpoint it is incomplete.

7.25 The Writingmaster and Accountant's Assistant - Colin Buchanan - 1798

The author of this book, Colin Buchanan, was a teacher in Greenock. Despite the title, this book is not concerned with accounting but with commercial tables and arithmetic, examples of copperplate handwriting and 'exercises for the writing scholar'. The copperplate style, which was developed at the end of the 17th century (and the beginning of the 18th), was well suited to the needs of commerce. Many of the writing masters who taught this flowing script, also taught book-keeping and both subjects were regarded as a necessary part of a commercial education. Buchanan did write on book-keeping but his works on this subject will not be considered here as they were not published until the 19th century.(1)

In general the words 'accompt' and 'accomptant' are replaced by 'account' and 'accountant' during the course of the century and Buchanan uses the more modern spelling. It is puzzling, therefore, that the Errata includes the request: "Preface, for accounts, read accompts."(2)

THE

THE WRITINGMASTER AND ACCOUNTANT'S ASSISTANT.

CONTAINING

A GREAT QUANTITY AND VARIETY

OF

PRACTICAL ARITHMETIC,

WITH

RULES AND NOTES FOR THE IMPROVEMENT OF YOUTH;

ALSO,

A VALUABLE SET OF ENGRAVINGS

OF

CURRENT-HAND WRITING AND FIGURES,

EXECUTED IN THE FIRST STYLE FROM THE AUTHOR'S MANUSCRIPT,
BY J. KIRKWOOD AND SON, EDINBURGH.

BY C. BUCHANAN,

AUTHOR OF WRITING MADE EASY.

GLASGOW;

PRINTED FOR THE AUTHOR, BY R. Chapman.

SOLD BY G. G. & J. ROBINSON, CADDEL & DAVIS, VERNOR & HOOD, AND J. JOHNSON, LONDON;

W. CREECH, AND BELL & BRADFUTE, EDINBURGH;

J. & A. DUNCAN, DUNLOP & WILSON, BRASH & REID, D. NIVEN,

A. CAMERON, AND J. MURDOCH, GLASGOW.

1798.

CHAPTER 8

THE NATURE AND OBJECTIVES OF BOOK-KEEPING

8.1 The Accounting Entity

Most 20th century accounting texts concentrate on business accounting. The same was true in the 18th century. All the Scottish authors adopted the area of Merchants Accompts as being the most appropriate for their explanation of the Italian Method because, as Malcolm says, it " ... was invented and improven, for the sake of Merchants Accompts" and "It is here we have the greatest Variety of Occurrences."(1)

For the introductory text book expositions, the accounting unit was the sole trader but, whereas it is now considered essential to distinguish between business transactions and the personal affairs of the proprietor of the business, this distinction was not observed in the 18th century.(2) The business ledger would commonly include accounts for the trader's house and his household furniture and plate and the profit and loss account would include such items as living expenses, the results of private wagers and the receipt of legacies. When the trader supplied his own capital and lived on the business premises, with his life inextricably bound up with his trade, there was logic in this practice. The practice of mixing business and private transactions seems equally appropriate when the texts are describing the accounts of the estates of the landed gentry, since here there would be just as much, and perhaps even more, difficulty and even less need to separate the estate and private affairs. When there was a need to distinguish between the interests and rights of several parties, as with the accounts of partnerships, the business unit was regarded as the accounting entity and business and private transactions were carefully differentiated.

Although 'Merchants Accompts' in the 'private sector' was invariably used by the Scottish writers as the vehicle for explaining the Italian Method, it was recognised that the system had much wider applicability. Macghie details 'public sector' areas where he considers it would be useful: "Custom-House Accompts, such as Collectors, Clerks, or Surveyors, or Comprollers of His or Her Majesty's Customs, are to keep, together with all Accompts of the like Nature, such as Accompts of the Excise, or other publick Taxes and Fonds, however the same are rais'd and apply'd, particularly it respects the following Heads, viz. Princely Accompts relating in general to His or Her Majesty's Revenues, and how His or Her Majesty's Forces by Sea and Land, are subsisted, paid, and provided for, and Salaries, Pensions, or the like are paid to Officers of State and Persons in Civil Government, to which may be added Exchequer-Accompts, Secretaries of State their Accompts, the Accompts of the Signet-Chamber, and Post-Office, &c. Political Accompts, being such as respect the Publick-good and Revenues of a City, Burgh, or Incorporation which are kept by the Treasurer or Box-master of the same."(3)

References to public sector accounting were contained in a number of the 18th century texts and also in Colinson's 'Idea Rationaria', the first Scottish accounting text. In this, Colinson indicates that he plans, at a later date, to publish a work which would include a section on " ... Princely Accompts; that is to say, one exact and compendious, clear Methode of keeping ane Accompt of his Majesties Revenues, of his Armies by Sea and Land, of his Excise, Impost, and Taxations."(4)

8.2 The Primary Objectives

Malcolm views the accounting system as providing a

model of the accounting entity: "Now, Words or Writing, are the Picture or Representation of a Thing, and ... I conceive the Merchants Books of Accompts, as a Representation, or Image of his Estate, which being a Thing subject to Alterations ... to have always the true Picture, it must suffer the same Changes with the Original, i.e. since every transaction by the Merchant, or his Doers, makes some Alteration, if not in the Value, at least in the posture of his Affairs: Therefore, a faithful record ought to be made of every Thing that any way concerns a man's Business ... ".(5)

He identifies "Men, Goods and Money" as the three types of variable in this model and he identifies a task for each of these. For transactions with Men the purpose for each person dealt with is "to know the State of Debt and Credit, i.e. what he owes me, and I owe him, with all the Circumstances". For Goods the aim is "to know the Quantity and Value purchased in any Time, and how it is disposed of ... by comparing of which, he may know what remains on Hand, and the Gain or Loss, on the Part disposed". For Money " 'tis required to know, what's received and given out in any Time, that consequently he may know the Balance in Hand".(6)

Elsewhere Malcolm recognises that a 'picture' of the whole can be obtained from the model and in his second text he notes that this is accomplished "by collecting the States of the several Parts into a complete Inventory, or Account of all one's Effects and Debts; the Difference of which is the final State of the Whole; shewing what one's free Estate is worth ... ".(7) This was accomplished in the 'Balance Accompt' which was an important feature of 18th century book-keeping practice.

In 'Book-keeping Methodiz'd' Mair describes book-keeping in more prosaic terms: "Book-keeping is an art,(8) teaching how to record and dispose the accompts of business, so as the true state <u>of every part, and of the whole</u>, may be easily and distinctly known ... The object or things of which book-keeping treats, are, the affairs, transactions, or dealings which a man of business has occassion to record and commit to writing, either for the sake of his own memory, or in order to give a satisfactory account of his conduct and management to persons concerned.

"The end aim'd at in Book-keeping is to represent distinctly the true State of one's Affairs, that is, to record a Man's Dealings and Transactions; and withall, to range and dispose the Accompts in such Order, that the books may exhibit a plain, full, and exact Account of the Condition and Circumstance of each Part of his Business; and so put the Man in case at all Times to satisfy both himself and others with respect to the State and Posture of his Affairs."(9)

Mair's emphasis is on obtaining instant information on the state of each part (as well as on the whole) of the business. This may be contrasted with modern statements of the purpose of accounting which would normally emphasise profit measurement and the use of the accounts for decision-making and control. In his elaboration of his objectives, Mair does recognise that a merchant would need to know the gain or loss on the sale of merchandise. This is, however, one item in a list, it is not emphasised as being of primary importance and Mair makes no reference to the use of accounting information for planning and decision making purposes. The aim of complete accuracy in the representation provided by the picture is emphasised later when Mair gives his view that " ... one of the Designs of Book-keeping is to put the Merchant in case at any Time to compute by the Help of his Books what he is worth <u>to a Farthing</u>".(10) These statements of the purpose of book-keeping are retained by

Mair in his second book-keeping book, 'Book-keeping Moderniz'd'.

In 'The Universal Accountant' Gordon sets out a comprehensive list of the purposes of book-keeping in a sentence which is also notable for its extraordinary length: "Book-keeping is an art, teaching how to record the dealings and transactions which a man of business hath occasion to commit to writing, and so to arrange, dispose, and adjust them, that it may be known at any period, and by any person versant in accounts, what sums are due him, by whom, and when payable; what goods he hath purchased, what of them are sold, and what remains on hand, with the gain or loss on the sales; what money, goods, or debts, he hath under the management of factors, supercargoes, or trustees, and what returns have been made him; what commissions he hath received as a factor, how they are disposed of, what returns he hath made to his employer, what reversion there is as yet in his own hands, or in the hands of debtors; what bills he hath accepted on commission, at what time, and when payable, and what funds he hath put in the hands of his correspondent to retire them; what goods or money, as a trustee, the company hath committed to his charge, what sales he hath made of the one, or application of the other; what ships he hath freighted or hired out, what insurance he hath made, and what he hath underwrote; what stock or capital he had originally, or at the preceding balance, and what improvement or diminution it hath underwent in the course of his trade; in one word, every thing that is proper to the merchant to know relative to his own affairs, or the affairs of others, with which he may be any how connected."(11)

Robert Hamilton's statement of the aims of book-keeping is more general than those given by Malcolm, Mair and Gordon. He says: "Book-keeping is the art of recording mercantile transactions in a regular and systematic manner.

A merchant's books should contain every particular which relates to the affairs of the owner. They should exhibit the state of all the branches of his business; the connection of the different parts; the amount and success of the whole. They should be so full and so well arranged, as to afford a ready information in every point for which they may be consulted."(12) Hamilton's concern with business success and 'users' needs' should be noted.

All four authors emphasise that accounting is instituted to provide the owner of the business with a means of ascertaining the state of his affairs at any time but this is but a partial explanation of its role. To complete the explanation, the views of the textbook writers must be examined to discover why they considered this information on the business's 'state of affairs' to be so useful.

8.3 Justice

In 1681 Lord Stair's codification of Scots law in 'The Institutions of the Law of Scotland' inaugurated the 'golden age of Scottish Jurisprudence'.(13) The emminent lawyer commenced his 'Institutions' by discussing 'natural justice' (an established concept which can be traced back to the great Roman jurists). He says: "Law is the Dictat of Reason ... Correspondent to these Dictats of Reason ... which are in the Understanding; There is an Inclination in the Will to observe and follow these Dicats, which is Justice ... ". He identifies the three "Principles of Positive Law" as "Society, Property and Commerce" and he explains these principles as being " ... the final causes or ends for which Laws are made, and Rights constitute and ordered, and all of them aim at the maintenance, flourishing and Peace of Society, the security of Property and the freedom of Commerce ... ".

Two years later Colinson's book similarly marked the

beginning of a period of 'Scottish Ascendancy', but this time in accounting texts (14). At the beginning of his book Colinson also emphasised the importance of justice as necessary basis for a rational society and for the promotion of commerce when he said: "As by a Rational Society, men are distinguished from other Creatures, so by Commerce, Society doth mainly subsist; and both owe their being, and Existence to Justice ... ".(15) He argues that there is a need for commercial justice to be wider than the justice which is recognised in the legal system, since " ... at all occasions the exuberant trust, allowed by one Merchant to another, in their ordinary Traffique, depending mutually on each others faith, without such nice formalities of Law, as are used in other Negotiations, doth evidently demonstrate, that Commerce to this day is maintain'd by honesty, candor, and ingenuity; upon which the Original Institution of Justice is founded."(16) He considers that the 'Regular and Ingenious form of keeping Accompts ... by Debite and Credite' is invaluable in assisting with the maintenance of justice and preventing 'disorder in the Common wealth of Traffique'.

In 1718 Malcolm also discusses the utility of accounting information by first considering the conditions necessary for the promotion of Commerce. He argues that "Societies are supported by Commerce" and, in a similar vein to Colinson, he stresses the necessity of " ... Justice a Virtue, so necessary to Society, and where that fails, Oppression takes place."(17) He points out that injustice is not necessarily wilful but that it can result from forgetfulness and the absence of an appropriate accounting system.

Stevenson makes the case even more forcefully: "For the Debitor and Creditor is pure and perfect Reason, and contains the whole material Truth and Justice of the Dealings of Men ... by following this Method, as a Man cannot be imposed upon by others, so he puts it out of his Power to impose upon them, (which ought to engage all who have a Regard to Integrity and Justice in their Dealings to follow it) ... ".(18) Here Stevenson seems to be developing the ideas of Roger North who had written: " ... for the Dr. and Cr. is pure and perfect right Reason, and contains the whole material Truth and Justice of all the Dealing, and nothing else ... ".(19)

Although Malcolm and Stevenson might seem to be developing the ideas of Colinson and North, it must be recognised that an interest in the meaning of justice, and a concern with its maintenance and extension, was widespread amongst the literati of the Scottish Enlightenment. 'Justice' was a central topic of interest to such writers as Kames, Hume and Adam Smith. It might be argued that some of the accounting writers were developing a rationale for accounting by following a distinctively Scottish concern with conditions conducive to the advance of civil society.

8.4 Efficiency and Profitability

In the 20th century accounting is commonly regarded as assisting commerce by promoting economic efficiency. It does this by providing information which encourages the channelling of resources to the areas where they can be most profitably employed. For the individual decision maker there is an emphasis on the need for the accounting system to provide 'decision relevant' information.

Although, in the early 18th century textbooks, accounting's primary role was seen as that of supporting justice in the economic system, Colinson and his successors did recognise that the Italian Method could assist in the search for efficiency and profitability. Colinson spoke of the help that book-keeping could provide in the management of the trader's resources: "If he be fortunate and acquire much, it directs him the way to Imploy it to the best advantage."(20)

Malcolm also discussed profit measurement and the use of accounting information for decision-making purposes. Moreover, there is a change in emphasis in his second book where he omits his discussion of accounting's role in maintaining justice. In this book, in the methodical statement of the aims of book-keeping, he talks of " ... Questions that may arise in the Course of Business, necessary to be Known for the Direction of our future Management ...".(21) He states that these questions can be solved by an examination of the accounts. In his discussion of estate accounts, he says: " ... is there no Pleasure for a Gentleman to know whether his Affairs prosper or go back? To know what part of his Fortune yields best, and what Part of his Expenses is greatest? That he may add and retrench as he sees most convenient: And, in a Word, so regulate his Affairs, as he may make the best he can of his Fortune and the best Use of what he receives."(22)

Stevenson too, did not neglect the uses of accounting as an aid to planning. He says: " ... when this (the calculation of the gain or loss) is once done he may very easily regulate his Management for the future, in order to pursue his real advantage ... ".(23)

Despite this recognition that a sound accounting system had utility for aiding efficiency and profitability, it does seem that this was not stressed as its primary role. In this respect the views of the theoreticians must have conflicted with the views of merchants who were undoubtedly primarily interested in accounting information which would help them to improve profitability.(24) It is possible that some of the textbook authors recognised the 'moral dimension' of accounting (25) and were uneasy with a goal of profit maximisation which might seem to conflict with their view of accounting as a tool of justice.

Adam Smith's masterpiece ('The Wealth of Nations'), which appeared in 1776, seemed to answer this dilemma by giving respectability to profit maximisation. Smith excluded " ... 'distributive justice' from the appropriate functions of government in a market society. He insisted that the only appropriate function of justice was 'commutative'; ie it should deal with the attribution of responsibility and the punishment of injury among individuals".(26) 'The Wealth of Nations' provided the trader and manufacturer with a moral justification for his pursuit of profit.(27)

This thesis provided encouragement for any accounting theorist who might wish to give more emphasise to accounting's mission of assisting efficiency. Undoubtedly Robert Hamilton would have read 'The Wealth of Nations'(28) and Smith's views may well have influenced the accounting content of his 'Introduction to Merchandize', the first volume of which was published just one year later. In this book there is a consideration of the managerial uses of accounting information and a concern over business efficiency which goes much further than that shown by his contemporaries and by those writing in the first half of the century.

It cannot be claimed that there was a major shift in emphasis in Scottish accounting from Justice to Efficiency during the course of the century, since no other writer followed Hamilton's approach, but it is right to regard 'An Introduction to Merchandize' as a major achievement. Yamey comments that, in this book "On occassions he (Hamilton) considers the rationale of particular procedures for the business man who might look to his ledger account for guidance in decision-making. In many ways it has the most modern appearance of all the early books."(29)

8.5 The Stewardship Function

Accounting's role in maintaining justice where there is the possibility of a conflict of interest, is apparent when the principal/agent relationship exists and in such cases it is termed the 'stewardship function of accounting'.

The Charge and Discharge system, used in estate accounting, was built around the stewardship function and it was an important system throughout the 18th and 19th centuries. 'Accounts Charge and Discharge' are discussed by Malcolm, Brodie and Hamilton but, rather surprisingly, they are not considered in the remaining textbooks.(30) The use of factors in trading is, however, treated as an important topic in the texts and the need for frequent reports to the employer is emphasised.

The separation between ownership and management that features so prominently in modern discussions of the stewardship role of accounting was not so much of a problem in the 18th century, although Adam Smith had noted that: "The directors of ... (joint-stock) companies ... being the managers rather of other people's money than of their own, it cannot well be expected, that they should watch over it with the same anxious vigilance with which the partners in a private copartnery frequently watch over their own."(31)

The book-keeping texts do consider co-partneries (or companies) where the management of the business is delegated to one partner and Malcolm does envisage that a copy of the balance account and profit and loss account might be provided by the Manager to another partner who requests it. "If ... the Partners have actually demanded the state of their Accompts ... you ought to give them a fair Copy of the same ... ".(32) Although the century saw the beginnings of enterprises that collected their funds from a wide range of investors, the system still had many of the features of partnerships with the copartners having, and utilising, their rights to examine the enterprise's account books or to receive fair copies of the accounts.

8.6 The Detection of Fraud and Error

Systematic accounting was recognised as a protection against fraud and error, both of which are likely to disturb justice. In the context of estate accounts, Malcolm writes: "I shall not use many Arguments to recommend regular accompting to Persons who visibly have so great use for it. If there is little to do, they have less Excuse, and if there is much, they have more need of such an Art as may enable them to know readily the distinct State and Posture of their Affairs; unless they are willing to be cheated without Controul ... ".(33) 'Controul' in this quotation seems to refer to procedures that will protect against fraud by enabling a comparison to be made between a statement provided by the servant against a master record provided by the accounting system.(34)

In addition to its value as part of a such control system, the virtues of the Italian System in identifying the presence of errors are well recognised. Malcolm makes this point: "We see now clearly the valuable Use of the mutual Connection of Accounts, and the Universal Balance of Debt and Credit; which, besides the Neatness of Stile, and the distinct Reference it makes betwixt one Account and another concerned in the same transaction, affords a curious Proof of the whole Work: So that if there is the least Defect in this Balance, we must conclude there are Errors in the Accounts; and if it holds, there is a very probable Argument, and, indeed, the best we can have, that all is right."(35)

8.7 Legal Evidence

Recourse to the law courts might be necessary to obtain justice as evidenced by the books of account. Erskine sets out the legal position as follows: "All allegations by parties to a suit must be supported by proper proof ... Books of accounts kept by merchants, tradesmen, and other dealers in business, though not subscribed, are probative against him who keeps them; and, in case of furnishings by a shop-keeper, such books, if they are are regularly kept by him, supported by the testimony of a single witness, afford a semiplena probatio in his favour, which becomes full evidence by his own oath in supplement ... ".(36)

Brodie stresses that 'accomptants' must be accurate with their records so that the " ... Accompts may be render'd Authentick, in case of any Controversy before a Judge or Magistrate".(37) Brodie was specifically referring to the importance of the journal and Mair confirms this: " ... in case of Difference betwixt a Merchant and his Dealers, the Journal is the Book commonly called for, and inspected by a Civil Judge".(38) Other writers however consider the waste-book as being more important than the journal if the records are required in evidence.(39)

Colinson provides an illustration of the role of account books in legal disputes: " ... I have seen in maters of controversie betwixt Merchants, that the one hath referr'd his difference to the others own Books, which the Magistrate forceth him to produce, and so the debate ends, As if a Foraigner had money, in my hands, some other person here pretends a debt from the said person, and so arrests in my hands; if I deny to be owing him, the other here desires the Magistrates to force me to shew my Books, and so doing I am excused at my Correspondents hands: I have seen this practised in Antwerpe, that Ancient and famous City of Trade."(40)

Mair, in the Preface to 'Book-keeping Methodiz'd' argues that many expensive law suits could be avoided if estate owners (in particular) were proficient in accounting. He also believes that judges and arbitrators must know something of accounting methods if they are to fulfill their duties effectively.(41)

8.8 Death and Business Failure; Heirs and Creditors

The advantages of a good accounting system in cases of business failure were emphasised by Colinson in the following passage: " ... if he be unfortunate it satisfies the world of his just dealing, and is the fairest and best Apologie of his Innocence and honesty to the World ... and often proves the great cause to bring him to a most favourable Composition with his Creditors ... It is a laudable custome they have in Amsterdam and Antwerpe when a Merchant comes to faile, the Magistrats appoint knowing men to search their books, and by them finding they have been direct and just in their dealings, they advise their Creditors to a favourable composition, which the most part consenting to, the rest must follow, by this means many recover again and pay their whole debt."(42)

Brodie makes the additional point that the existence of a clear set of books " ... may not only be a Satisfaction to his Creditors, but the Means of preventing Law-Suits ... "(43)

Young relates the point specifically to farming: "If a farmer was in considerable arrears for rent to the proprietor, or to other creditors, his keeping accurate books, would show to every one concerned from whence that proceded. Humanity and self interest would dictate to his creditors and friends, the duty of enabling him to rectify his errors and to support him upon the express condition, that he adopted a regular system of cropping, and kept regular books."(44)

Mair links death and business failure as both being misfortunes which would be ameliorated by the existence of good accounting records. He comments on their use "for the information of his heirs or creditors, in case he should happen to die or fail ... "(45) The emphasis is clearly on ensuring that justice is done not only to the living but also to the deceased.

John Drummond considers this last point: "...in Case of Death, his Friends or Creditors will find no Difficulty in it: So that his Family cannot suffer; and his Character of having been an exact Man, will remain after him, to the great satisfaction of Posterity".(46)

8.9 Partnership

Colinson emphasises the help that systematic book-keeping provides in facilitating the amalgamation of resources from several individuals to enable joint trading undertakings to operate. He says that: " ... Book-keeping is the only help, that encourages many to joyn their small stocks together, and by so doing, often from a small foundation Erects a most admirable Trade".(47) Later on the same page he continues: "There are two things which are supposed to be the product of this Countrey, the Manufactories and the fishing trade; which are not to be done with one mans stock, but by many: so men are oblidged to joyn in Partnership, which often blowes up with great discord, if they have not a true form to satisfie the Concerned what is become of their stocks; that let their success be what it will, one may not be wronged more then another. Both these trades have been mightily encouraged by the Kings Lawes and his money too, so it is a pitty that want of form should discourage us, which I believe is not the least cause."

At the beginning of the 18th century Edinburgh Council recognised the contribution that the 'Science of Book-holding' could make to the successful operation of partnership businesses and their wish to encourage such cooperative ventures was one of the reasons that they gave for appointing John Dickson as 'Master and Professor' of book-keeping.(48) Partnership accounts are considered in chapter 11.

8.11 Summary

All of the objectives that were considered by Malcolm, Mair, Gordon, Hamilton and their contemporaries in the 18th century continue to be valid in the 20th century but the emphasis has changed.

It seems that Colinson and Malcolm (at least in his first book) considered that, although the law might provide the framework required for the promotion of trade, commerce and the welfare of society, the regularity of the merchant's books and their completeness, when maintained under the 'Italian Method', were the instruments of ensuring justice in detail. Double entry was a 'Regular and Ingenious form' designed to assist this and to act as 'the very Scale of Commerce'.(49)

The use of accounting as a tool for improving efficiency and managerial decision making was recognised but not emphasised until Hamilton's book. Hamilton, writing after Adam Smith's revision of the concept of economic justice had legitimised the capitalist's search for profit, went further than his contemporaries by emphasising 'decision relevance' at various points in his book. It must be recognised, however, that his views were not taken up by subsequent writers. The reasons for the failure to build on Hamilton's work are unclear. It may be that within the confines of the 'Italian Method' of book-keeping, his ideas were out of place. Partly it may be that the developing profession of accountancy was establishing itself, to a considerable extent, among legal practitioners who might tend to be more sympathetic to accounting viewed as a tool of justice rather than as an instrument of efficiency.

Now, in the last quarter of the 20th century, accounting's role is regarded both as being a means of achieving justice and also as providing assistance with the efficient allocation of scarce resources. Much more attention is paid to the managerial functions of accounting but 'justice' remains firmly embedded in the system: it is present in the basic requirement that accounts should show a 'true and fair view' and in the recognition of a stewardship function for accounting. Justice has not been supplanted but some, such as Scott(50) and Williams(51) would argue that this role should receive more emphasis.

CHAPTER 9

THE BOOKS OF ACCOUNT AND THE CANONICAL SYSTEM

9.1 The Canonical System

The version of the Italian method of accounting described by the 18th century Scottish writers was standardised to such an extent that it is possible to describe a 'canonical' system. All the writers followed Pacioli by adopting his trio of principal books; the waste book, the journal and the ledger. These were augmented by a number of supplementary or 'subservient' books which were designed, in the main, to relieve the principal books of unwieldy detail.

In the 'canonical' system transactions were recorded, as they occurred in the waste book, the details of each transaction were later transcribed (or 'posted') into the journal where the necessary analysis into Debits and Credits was identified. Finally the journal entries (or 'entrances') were 'posted' to accounts (or accompts) in the ledger (or leger). Some authors proposed that the waste book and journal might be combined and there were suggestions for incomplete systems where the Italian Method was considered to be unnecessary or too sophisticated for a particular business. Apart from these variations the canonical system was adhered to for 'Merchants Accompts'.

The textbooks describe each of the principal books in some detail and their expositions of the general principles of the Italian Method are largely concerned with an explanation of the use of the books.(1) This chapter will survey the main points that they made as to the form and purpose of the principal books. Following this the various subsidiary books will be discussed.

9.2 The Waste Book (or Memorial)

The waste book(2) is described by Robert Hamilton as follows: "The WASTE-BOOK, or day-book, contains an exact register of all occurrences in business in the same order as they take place. It begins with an inventory of every thing belonging to the owner, a list of the debts due to him, and of the debts he owes to others: It is carried on with a full relation of all the money he receives, or pays; of all the goods he buys or sells; and of every other occurrence in his business. Each article should be entered as soon as the transaction takes place, and should be clearly expressed in the plainest language. It should require no supply from the accomptant's memory, but should be fully intelligible to any person, however unacquainted with the business: At the same time, it should be written with all convenient brevity; and, therefore, sometimes refers to invoices and other accompts, for particulars. The accomptant's first care should be to have nothing defective or ambiguous; his second to have nothing superfluous."(3) Additionally, in partnerships, the partnership agreement was often recorded at the beginning of the waste book.

Hamilton's comment that the merchant should not have to rely on his memory to supplement the waste book records, is in line with Malcolm's views. It was noted in chapter 8 that Malcolm believed that accounting is necessary to ensure justice and that he pointed out that injustice is not necessarily wilful but that it can arise unintentionally " ... by giving our Memory too much Trust, and neglecting to write down every Transaction of our Affairs, or setting them down in so disorderly and confused a Manner, that every Person's Right is not truly distinguished, but they are charged too much, or too little".(4) The waste book was designed to avoid this danger. Accurate and complete 'data capture' is essential in accounting and, in the 18th century canonical system, this was achieved in the waste book. All transactions were to be recorded immediately they took place in this book which thus became the organisation's database. Subsequently the details would be analysed, at leisure, in the journal and then in the ledger. Modern database accounting systems may be a return to 18th century accounting practice.

The time taken to record all transactions three times over was considerable and many would look for abbreviated procedures. The general view was, however, that if there was to be any reduction in the number of books maintained, the waste book could not be dropped, it was essential whereas the journal (to be described in the next section) was useful but not indispensible. Brodie was a heretic when he modified his orthodox statement that the waste book is " ... so material, that it cannot well be wanted ... ",(5) by noting that some traders enter " ... their Transactions at first in a Journal ... " and agreeing that such an approach is possible for the experienced practioner.(6) Admittedly an exception was made in the case of shopkeepers' accounts where Mair, Gordon and Hamilton were in agreement that there was a case for specialised subsidiary books and no need for a waste book.(7) This, however, was an exception and, in general, the waste book was sacrosanct.

The waste book has disappeared from the conventional accounting books kept in a 20th century accounting system, its place being taken by files containing the source documents from which the day books and journals are prepared. Even in the 18th century Brodie acknowledged that, some counting houses did not find a waste book essential but he considered that this short cut approach "... must render the Business of Merchants Accounts very hard to those who are unacquainted with them ... ".(8)

Although the 18th century text books give the waste

book a key position in the system, it is possible that it retained this importance in the texts after it had lost it in practice. The writers knew that a waste book was not always maintained and they frequently stated that modifications could be made for particular circumstances, nevertheless they were concerned with imparting a sound knowledge of the canonical Italian System. Their insistence on the waste book may have been an insistence that their students should adhere to proper form until they had mastered this canonical system. In the 20th century the journal, for similar pedagogical reasons, occupies a more prominent place in text books than it does in practice.

9.3 The Journal

"The JOURNAL is a fair record of all the transactions compiled from the waste-book, in the same order as they stand there; but expressed in a technical style, that it may be transferred to the ledger with more ease.

"When we are to enter any article in the journal, we must consider which accompts in the ledger it will require to be placed to, both on the Dr. and Cr. and write (the former accompt) Dr. to (the latter accompt;) then we annex an explanation of the article, and place the sum in the money column."(9)

Malcolm describes two journal formats, firstly the conventional journal and secondly the 'marginal journal'.(10) The conventional 18th century format used in the journal he describes as follows: "In the Journal, the Debtors and Creditors are both distinctly marked, tho' we find only the Word Debtor mentioned; yet the Creditors are mentioned distinctly, tho' not so directly: For we say A-Debtor to -B, &c. which constitutes B the Creditor very distinctly ... where there is one Debtor and more Creditors, and contrarily, you find in the Journal, A (for Example)

Debtor to sundry Accompts, and after the Narration, you have the Creditors mentioned, viz. to - such and such Persons and Things, or Imaginary Accompts, for the several Articles: Or sundry Accompts, Debtors to A, and after the Narration, you have the Debtors mentioned, viz. such and such Persons, &c. for the several Articles."(11) An example of this style of journal (taken from Malcolm's first extended illustration in his 1718 book) follows:

July 10th				l.	s.	d.
Voyage to Amsterdam in the Wild-Cat of Dysert, George Stirling master, Debtor to sundry Accompts, 66 l. 6s. 8d. for the following Goods, consigned to Herman Van Rymer Factor at Amsterdam to sell for my Accompt, viz.						
To Sheeps Skins for 20 Packs	L.53	6	8			
To Cash, paid Charges at Shipping	3					
To Iron, for 50 St. given to the Owners of the Ship for Freight	10					
	66	6	8	66	6	8
July 12th						
Cash, debtor to Profit and Loss, gained at Leith by a Wager upon a Horse-Race				15	-	-

It will be noted that the conventional 18th century journal does not have the two columns familiar to modern accountants.

Malcolm was rather dismissive of the journal which he describes as " ... the most useful (of the subservient books), tho' not absolutely necessary ... (since) ... we may enter Things from the Waste into the Leger immediately".(12)

Macghie writing in the same year as Malcolm, however, emphasised the legal importance of the journal: "the Journal is the Book that is only regarded, if others were to inspect the Books; as also when they are to bear Faith, when called for by any Civil Judge, for deciding of Controversies betwixt Merchant and Merchant, as is ordinary in Holland."

Because of its importance the book must be written up neatly: "All Things are to be writ in a fair Hand, avoiding all Errata's and Blots as much as can be, with the Titles of Debitor and Creditor in big Letters, or of a different Character, for Ornament."(13) Colinson had made similar points and he had urged that the journal " ... must be written with one Mans hand".(14)

There is clearly disagreement as to the relative importance of the journal and waste book. Hamilton noted that the waste book is particularly important because " ... it is the book whose authority is trusted to, and which must be exhibited to judges, or arbiters, when an accompt is disputed".(15) Perry(16) supported Hamilton's view and Hamilton probably stated the correct position when he said "As the journal is filled up from the waste-book the authority of the former is esteemed more authentic, unless there be an obvious mistake through hurry; and either of these books is depended on rather than the ledger, which, from its form, is more liable to error, and may be more easily vitiated by fraudulent design."(17)

9.4 The Combined Waste-Book/Journal

An innovation described by Malcolm is a combined waste-book/journal. He suggests this 'marginal journal' " ... because Things may be written in the Waste-Book by several Hands, and often times in haste, so that this first Copy will probably be more rude than might be wished, therefore I know some who practise this Method, viz. Out of that first

Waste-Book they compose another, differing only in this, That Things are better expressed, and the Circumstance more clear: In this Book, none but one Person writes, it is upon larger Paper, and upon the left Side of the Page there is a great Space from Top to Bottom, separate by a Line, to the Right wherof the Transaction is narrated, as aforesaid, and in that Space upon the Left, the Several Debtors and Creditors are distinctly written, without any Narration; the Names of the Debtors are first set down, and then of the Creditors, and after each the Sum for which they are Debtors and Creditors, and with each may be written the Leger-Folio, where they stand."(18)

From a 20th century standpoint, Malcolm's proposal would be regarded as the augmentation of the journal by the inclusion of appropriate narrations (the fair copy of the waste book). Initially, however, Malcolm prefers to call it a waste book and the term 'marginal journal' is introduced in his second book. In his 1718 book Malcolm provided another form of combined waste and journal book in his second illustrative set of books. He here referred to the book as a 'Waste-Book with the Journal subjoined'. A specimen entry from this illustration is reproduced below:

November 2d	l.	s.	d.
Sold for the Accompt in Company betwixt Mr David Johnston, &c. 10 Packs of Sheep Skins, at 4 l. per Pack, for ready Money	40	-	-
Debtor Cash (1), Creditor Goods in Company (9)			

In the 1731 book the marginal journal is illustrated at page 31 and in his second illustrative set of books. In this latter illustration he referred to the book as "Waste Book - In which the Debtors and Creditors are mark'd on the Margin ... ". An example of the format of this book is reproduced below:

Nov. 2					l.	s.	d.
Dr Cash	40	00	00	Sold for Account of David Johnston and Company, 10			
Cr Goods in Company				Packs of Sheep-Skins, at 4 l. per Pack, for Ready Money, is	40	00	00

It has already been noted that the waste book section of this book provides the 'Narrations' supporting the journal entries. It will be recognised that the proposal does not curtail the records but makes them more elaborate. Time and effort would only be saved in cases where the original waste book " ... is so fair and clean, as there be no need of making another Copy".(19) Malcolm considered that it was much more likely that the merchant would not be able to dispense with the separate waste book.

Malcolm's innovation was soon taken up by other writers. In 1735 William Hamilton claimed in the preface to his text (Book-keeping New Modelled) that no other writer "... has either shown such a plain and convincing Method of teaching, or yet discovered so many various Methods of framing the Journal ... ". The methods are, however, essentially those proposed by Malcolm but Hamilton assumed that no separate waste book was necessary when a combined waste-book/journal was used. His exposition illustrated, and clearly distinguished, the three waste-book/journal systems: (1) Two separate books are kept with the journal being written up from the waste book. This was the standard method. (2) Only one book is kept and the " ... Journal is upon the Margin of its Waste-book". This method is Malcolm's 1718 innovation (illustrated by him in his 1731 text). (3) Again only one book is kept but now " ... the right Debitor and Creditor (which is the Journal) is set down at the Foot of every Account of the Waste-books".(20) Malcolm had used this format in his 1718 book.

In the following year, 1736, Mair noted that 'some Moderns' had adopted the combined waste-book/journal and he illustrated the development.(21) He gave a fuller illustration in 'Book-keeping Moderniz'd'(22) and there he assumed that a separate waste book was not maintained. Scruton discussed the method in 1776 (23) and Robert Hamilton gave an illustration in his chapter on 'Varieties in Italian Method'. Hamilton noted that some merchants did combine the two books and he complained that those who omitted the narration were left with "the journal and ledger ... thereby rendered unintelligible without the waste-book".(24)

9.5 The Ledger

Colinson had called the ledger " ... the mirror of a Mans estate ... "(25) and Malcolm explains its function as follows: "The LEGER-BOOK contains all the Transactions of a Man's Affairs in such Order, that all belonging to every different Subject lie together in one Place; making distinct particular Accounts."(26)

Malcolm emphasised that the ledger is the "principal Book of Accompts".(27) His explanation of the double entry system had a concentration on the ledger and other writers adopted a similar approach although Jackson says that this was relatively unusual for the 18th century.(28) Lundin writing in the same year as Malcolm, for example, said: "The whole Art of Accompting consists in a perfect Knowledge of a Book called the LEGER, whose Name implies its Use and Design, viz. by it any that accompts this Way, may at any Time, at a View, without Trouble, be informed into any, or all the Circumstances of his Business; since in it Accompts are so clearly stated that it answers all that can be wish'd for, or expected from accompting in any Business whatsoever."(29)

The format used for the ledger in the 18th century was the conventional 'T' account format which is still used. A number of variations were suggested so that, for example, on some accounts there might be quantity columns alongside the money columns. Drummond suggested that "To avoid Multiplicity of Accompts, you can bring as many as your Paper can contain under one Title, giving them different Columns in the Leger, where every one ballances distinctly, as if they were separate Accompts."(30)

9.6 Subservient Books

Malcolm notes two reasons for keeping 'subservient' books; (a) to condense the the detail which would otherwise be recorded in a particular ledger account or another 'Grand Book' and (b) to keep like items together.

In respect of (a) he notes that: "Some of these Books are designed for abridging the Records of the Grand-Books, by keeping the Particulars of some long and tedious Accompts in Books apart, and transferring the Sums once a Week, Month, &c. as you think fit, into the Principal Books ... if the Nature of any Accompt is such, that it either gives all, or receives all, i.e. is all Debt or all Credit, then it is convenient to keep a Book express for these Articles, and bring them in, in Totals, to their Accompt in the Leger ... ".(31)

For (b) he says that the waste book " ... may either be one continued universal Record of whatever occurs in a Merchant's Business; or, because Transactions of that same Nature, will ly scattered in it as their Dates are, and even in the Leger they will be scattered upon the several Accompts to which they belong; therefore, that we may have all of one distinct Kind together, they ('some Authors') propose to keep separate Waste-Books for several Uses, for Example, in one your Inventary, and all your Accompts of buying, and other Purchases are; in another, all Accompt of Sales; in another, all Invoyces as above; 4th to contain all Payments of Debts made to or by me &c. thus they parcel out the whole Transactions of the grand Waste-Book into so many particular Books. Do in this as you think fit."(32)

It might be noted that, whereas, today, it would be usual to regard the subsidiary books as subsidiary to the ledger, the foregoing passage regards some such books as subsidiary to the waste book. A number of subservient books were suggested by the writers.

9.7 Subsidiary Books Concerned with Cash

The Cash Book "This Book is kept in a Folio-form like the Ledger, and serves to abridge the Cash Accompt there ... once a Month, this Book is posted to the Ledger; or, if you please, first to the Journal ... ".(33) Brodie dicusses the advantages that can be obtained from using a cash book. He states that it is " ... very useful to those who are in great Business, because where there is much Receiving and Disbursing of Money, the Want of a particular Book of Cash must very much swell the Ledger".(34)

With the shortage of coin that existed at various times during the century there could frequently be foreign specie among the cash received and paid. Such foreign specie would be converted to the sterling equivalent. It might be entered in a separate account for 'Foreign Coin'. Mair illustrates this approach. Alternatively there might be analysis columns in the cash book to record the detail and Malcolm says that this could be useful for bankers.(35)

The cash book was categorised as a 'subservient' book(36) but it was recognised as being extremely useful.

As the century passed its importance grew in the textbooks. Mair gives the cash book greater prominence in 'Book-keeping Moderniz'd' than he does in 'Book-keeping Methodiz'd' and Perry (in 1774) gives it a higher status than the journal. He says: "This book, to regular merchants, (being the most useful, next to the waste-book and ledger), is of great importance."(37) In 1789 Benjamin Booth, one of the English writers, considered the cash book to be "the Waste Book for all receipts and payments of money".(38)

Robert Hamilton describes a double entry method of book-keeping which is " ... in many cases, shorter than the Italian method". This method can be used where the business is mainly transacted on a cash basis. In such cases only two books are required, the cash book and the ledger. "All sums of money received, whether on personal accompts, or in payment of goods instantly sold, are entered on the Dr. of the cash-book, and posted from thence to the Cr. of the personal or real accompt in the ledger. In like manner, sums of money paid are first entered on the Cr. of cash-book, and then posted to the Dr. of the proper accompt in the ledger."(39)

Hamilton acknowledges that there will always be some transactions which it is necessary to record although no money has been paid or received. For such cases he proposes two alternative methods of proceding: 1. The 'non cash' transactions can be converted "by an easy fiction" to equivalent cash transactions. " ... if you sell goods on trust, you may suppose them to be sold for ready money, and the value, at the same time, lent to the purchaser. If you buy goods on trust you may suppose them bought for ready money, and the value borrowed from the seller."(40) 2. A journal may be kept for the non cash transactions.

Petty Cash Book Colinson describes a "Book of Petty Charges where you place small Disbursements".(41) This is a petty cash book.

Bank Book Where the merchant has a bank account in a 'public bank' the bank book is used to contain the full details of bank transactions "as the multiplicity of negotiations would swell an account in the Leger to an enormous size".(42)

Till Book Perry describes a till-book but he emphasises that this is not used as part of a double entry system. "The TILL-BOOK, so called, because the money received daily for goods sold and entered therin is put into a till; each days occurrence is added up in the evening, and at the end of every week, the sum total is carried into the waste-book. This book is only kept by Shop-keepers, who have a good deal of retail trade, and is never used in book-keeping by double entry."(43)

The Receipt Book Mair describes this book: "In this Book a Merchant takes Receipts of the Payments he makes. The Receipt should contain the Date, the Sum received expressed in Words at large, and also in Figures in the Money-columns, the Reason why, and whether in full or in part; and must be signed by the Person receiving."(44) Hamilton also makes reference to this book.(45)

9.8 Subsidiary Books Concerned with Goods and Voyages

The Invoice Book Several different types of book seem to have had the name invoice (or invoyce) book. Frequently a book with this title was used as both a sales day book and a purchases day book but it contained rather more detail than the modern day book in that all invoices were transcribed in full into it. However Scruton noted that "Many indeed reserve this book for sales alone" as the invoices from suppliers can serve as an adequate record of purchases.(46)

Malcolm's 'Invoyce Book' was of this type (ie reserved

for goods despatched) but he sees no necessity for such a book as he believes that the details should be recorded in the waste book. It has, however, been noted in 9.6 that he considers that the waste book need not be a single 'continued universal record' but that it could be useful to have separate waste books for differing types of transaction.(47) Benjamin Booth, an English writer, adopted this position when he proposed the use of separate invoice books for purchases and sales. He described the invoice-book inward as the "Waste-book for all goods imported, or purchased at home" and the invoice-book outward as the "Waste-Book for all goods sold or shipped off".(48) Perry also distinguishes two types of invoice book but his division differs from Booth's. The first of Perry's invoice books is for inland trade (it would contain copies of purchase invoices) and the second is for foreign trade (containing copies of all sales invoices of goods shipped abroad and of purchases from abroad).(49)

Book of Expences Malcolm(50) and Mair(51) describe a book of charges of merchandize which would be useful in removing some of the detail from the cash book. Scruton calls this a book of charges or expences(52) and says that it " ... contains the particular Charges on each sort of Goods and Voyages". Expense items such as: Carriage, Custom, Freight, Cranage, Wharfage, would be charged to appropriate merchandize accounts. "At the End of each Month the Money columns of this Book are added up, and the sum carried to the Cr. side of the Cash Book ... the Accompts of Goods and Voyages in the Ledger must be made Drs to Accompt Charges of Merchandize".(53) Other expenses, such as: Warehouse Rent, Shop Rent, Accomptant's Wages, Postage of Letters, "relate to Business in general, and are chargeable on no particular Accompt, these, at ballancing of the Ledger, will of course fall into the general Accompt of

Profit and Loss".(54) Drummond recommended a Book of Incident Charges which would be restricted to a record of expenses chargeable to specific batches of merchandise. "Because there are Charges which must necessarily be laid out upon Goods it is very proper you keep a Book of Incident Charges, wherein you are to state the Day when, and every particular Sum paid upon such Goods: All which being added when the whole Sale is made, comes as a Charge upon the Goods."(55)

Ship Book This is " ... a small Leger, in which no other account is raised, but one for every ship belonging to, or chartered by the merchant. The Dr. side of each of these accounts contains the expenses of victualling, fitting out, wages, &c. and the Cr. side contains all that the ship has produced for freight, passage, &c. and the sum-total of each side is carried to the Leger."(56)

Ware-House Book Drummond says: " ... it will be of great Use and Ease to you to keep a Ware-House-Book, which saves the Trouble of giving every little Sale of Goods, a Post in your Journal and Ledger. Open this Book with both Sides in View: Upon the Top for a Title, you name the Goods, and Ware-House or Cellar where they ly ... On the Left hand side keep an Accompt of such Goods you receive in ... On the Opposite Side you accompt for the Disposal of them."(57) This seems to be a composite sales day book, purchase day book and stores ledger, presumably regular totals are taken to the Goods or Merchandise Account in the ledger.

9.9 Subsidiary Books for Dealings with Factors

A Factor Book Brodie states that those who " ... seldom employ Factors and others intrusted beyond the Sea, need no other Method but to enter them with other Business in the usual Books" but where there is extensive business through factors " ... there ought to be a Separate Book, called The Factor's Book".(58) Macghie and Malcolm, however, use the name differently. For them a factor book is used to record details of goods received, as a factor, to sell for another.(59)

There is considerable room here for confusion as, it has already been noted that, Perry distinguished two types of 'Invoice Book' and that one of these was designed to contain copies of all the sales invoices made out for goods shipped abroad to factors and of purchase invoices for goods received from abroad.(60) Mair also described a book, which he called an invoice book or a factory book, which was restricted to copies of invoices of goods consigned to the merchant's overseas agents.(61)

Book of Accounts Current This book is to relieve the ledger of detail relating to accounts current. "When a factor has finished his sales of a cargo, he generally transmits an account of sales to his constituent, with a copy of his Account current".(62) Although this book is designed to contain the personal accounts of the merchant's factors, it is perhaps the precursor of the Personal ledger.

9.10 The Factor's Subsidiary Books

Commission Book The commission book is designed "To contain details of commissions, orders, and advices a merchant receives from his correspondents."(63)

Sales Book A sales book may be used by a factor (agent) to record "copies of all the accounts of sales transmitted to his employer (principal)".(64) Mair describes such a book: "It is folio'd like the Ledger, and contains upon the Right-side the Sale or Disposal of the Employer's Goods. The Left-side contains the Charges paid by the Factor, Abatements allowed to Buyers, the Factor's Commission, and neat Proceeds."(65)

Postage Book The postage book is a record of postal

expenses. "This book enables the merchant, at settling with his correspondents, to make the proper charge for postages upon this account."(66)

9.11 The Merchant's Personal Expenses

Book of Expences of Living The merchant's personal drawings and expenses were debited to the Profit and Loss Account in the 18th century and no distinction was observed between these and business expenses. In his first book Malcolm describes a 'Book of Household and Personal Expences'.(67) In his second book he calls this a 'Book of Expences of Living'. The book is to contain the detailed records of personal expenses, with the weekly or monthly totals being taken to the cash book and the debit of the profit and loss account. "By this means both the Cash-Book will be more distinct, and the Expence of Living, which otherwise would be scattered upon the Profit and Loss Account, will be here seen all at once."(68)

Macghie mentions the possible need for two books, a book of proper (ie personal) expenses and a book of household expenses.(69) Mair and Perry discuss the book of house expenses (ie the latter book).(70)

9.12 Miscellaneous Subsidiary Books

Letter Book Malcolm notes that a copy book of letters should be maintained. This is to contain copies of all letters written and received.(71) He recognises that this is not an account book and he omits any reference to it in his second book. Mair also mentions the book and he notes that letters received can be kept in "Files of Boxes".(72) Scruton describes the copy book as being designed "to contain copies of all the letters of business wrote by the merchant".(73)

Pocket Book "This is a small Book, of a portable

Size, which a Merchant carries in his Pocket when Business calls him abroad to a Tavern, a Fair, the Country, or other Places. In this he sets down the Bargains he makes, the Expenses he is at, the Debts he pays, or Sums he receives, with every other part of Business he transacts while abroad; as also any Occurence or Piece of News he thinks worth while to record. And when he comes home to his Compting-house or Shop he transfers the Things contained in this Book, each to their proper places on the Waste-book or Books subsidiary."(74)

A Memorandum Book A memorandum book might be maintained for recording important extracts from letters etc.(75)

9.13 Budgeting

The Month Book Gordon commences the second volume of 'The Universal Accountant' with a 'Dissertation on the Business of the Counting-House'. After a general discussion of the need for business planning and a good business information system. Cash and credit management are emphasised by the description of a form of cash budgeting. "In order to give the merchant a constant view of the obligations he comes under, and the means he hath of retiring them, he ought to have a book lying open in his counting-house, numbered in folios like the Leger, and divided into spaces, on the top of each which should be inserted the names of the twelve months of the year, a whole folio, more or less, being allowed, according to the extent of his dealings, for every month. On the left-hand page should be entered the payments to be made to him on each particular day of each month; and on the right hand page, in the same manner, the payments to be made by him; by comparing which, he will be at a loss upon no occasion to judge how far he may come under new obligations, or how far he may be pinched in retiring old ones, so as he may have recourse to some expedient for raising new funds to supply the emergency. ... This will likewise be a spur to the merchant to have his debts collected as they fall due ... ".(76)

The book described (and illustrated) by Gordon(77) is usually referred to as the month (or moneth) book. The objective of this book differs from that of the other books which have been described in this chapter, the other books have all been concerned with records of past transactions but this book is concerned with future plans. The book's title is not particularly descriptive but it was well established by the beginning of the 17th century. Dafforne's 'Merchant's Mirrour' had shown such a book in 1635 and the author had emphasised that he was reproducing the details from a real example. Colinson proposed such a Moneth-book "Which tells you what summes you are to pay every moneth in the year, and day when, and who is to pay you".(78) He gave an illustration of such a book. Alexander Malcolm describes a month book(79) and Scruton calls it the debt book.(80)

<u>A Bill Book</u> "The BILL BOOK is ruled in columns, which are marked in such a methodical manner, as to contain in one line the number of the bill, the drawer, the date, the person to whom payable, the usance, the time when due, whether receivable or payable, of whom and when received, or to whom and when paid, and its value. But the chief excellency of this book is, that by it a merchant can tell, at one view, all the bills he may have in hand, whose values are to be received or paid by him, and when they will become due; what bills he has drawn upon his correspondents, and what they have drawn upon him."(81) Mair, in 'Book-keeping Methodiz'd', regarded the bill book as being another name for the month book but he distinguished them in 'Book-

keeping Moderniz'd'.(82) Hamilton illustrates both a register of bills receivable and a register of bills accepted but he also says that sometimes the month book and the bill book are combined.(83)

9.14 <u>Summary</u>

A superficial view would suggest that there was no development in the area of 'systems design' throughout the 18th century, as there was little change in the books of account that the text books recommended. There were some innovations, such as the introduction of the marginal journal, a recognition that the waste book could be subdivided into specialised day books and a greater emphasis on the cash book as the century passed, but these were no more than dents in the structure and, at the end of the century, the waste book, journal and ledger remained the basis of the canonical textbook system as it was described in the main Scottish texts. It seems that Malcolm, and probably Mair and Gordon, would have agreed with North when he said: "I do not know, that any Art practised among Men, is come up to a positive ne plus ultra, but that of Accompting."(84)

Although it is true that the basic system was regarded as sacrosanct, it is suggested that this was an orthodoxy that the textbook authors promulgated, largely, for pedagogical reasons. The popularity of Mair's texts, in particular, indicates that his approach was regarded as sound by the teachers and practitioners who influenced the potential purchasers of textbooks. A comparison could be made between Mair's 'Book-keeping Methodiz'd' (first edition 1736) and an interesting text written one year earlier by an English writer, Hustcraft Stephens. Stephens' book ('Italian Book-keeping Reduced into an Art') breaks with the traditional method of exposition so that it contrives, for example, to describe the structure of the Italian System without any reference to the waste book and it only discusses that book when page 119 is reached. Stephens' book is undoubtedly of considerable merit as an original and scholarly exposition of the Italian Method, but it went only to a second edition(85) whereas Mair's book was a best seller which continued to be used long after his death.

The view of the Scottish writers, that it was essential to cover the canonical system before moving on to variations that might apply in practice, can most clearly be seen in Hamilton's 'Introduction to Merchandize' where a distinction is made between 'Italian Book-keeping' (dealt with in part IV) and 'Practical Book-keeping' (in part V). At the conclusion of part V, a remarkable set of problems is given on the design of accounting systems. These are so challenging that they would not be out of place in a modern advanced text and they are worth reproducing here.

"We shall conclude this PART by proposing a few cases for a trial of the learner's skill in inventing suitable forms of book-keeping.

"I. A society of merchants raise a stock of £40,000, for carrying on the business of banking. The stock is divided into 100 shares of £400 each, and any partner may hold one or more, not exceeding five, and may transfer them under certain restrictions. They circulate their own notes by lending money on cash-accompts, or by discounting bills. In this last, they observe a rule, that they will not discount beyond a certain sum on bills, where the same person is bound either as drawer or accepter. The business is conducted by directors chosen annually at a general meeting of the partners, and by proper officers under them. They balance their books and divide their profits once a-year. Require a proper form for their accompts?

"II. Require the best form for conducting the books of

societies for the benefit of widows or the aged, or for insurance of lives? ... (The student is here referred to a section of the text which describes these societies).

"III. Require a proper form for an insurance-broker's books? ... (The student is here referred to a section of the text which describes the work of insurance brokers).

"IV. A bleacher takes in linen at his field, and employs agents at several towns in the neighbourhood for the same purpose. Required a form of conducting his accompts, which, besides containing the value of the work done at the field, and the expence, will exhibit the quantities received from, and returned to each agent, and the quatities from each, still on hand; and also a comparison of the expence on the coarser and finer kinds, to assist the proprietor in judging whether the prices affixed to the different kinds be in due proportion to the charge?

"V. A brewer purchases barley, and converts it into malt; he also occasionally purchases and sells malt; he carries on the different branches of strong ale, small beer, and porter-brewing; and desires a form of book-keeping that shall exhibit his expence and sales, his debts and credits, the quantity of malt obtained from barley, the quantities bought, sold or consumed, the quantities of beer of different kinds obtained from malt, and compared with the price of the barley, and a comparison of the profit on the different branches of his business.

"VI. Required a scheme of book-keeping for the linen manufactory ... " (The accounting system for the linen manufactory referred to by Hamilton will be discussed in some detail in chapter 16).

This series of questions (which adopts the modern case study approach) is a clear indication that Hamilton, at least, did not regard the basic book-keeping system, that he introduced in part IV, as being anything other than a framework which must be adapted to make it suitable for the requirements of a particular application. Other authors were not so clear on this point but the fact that they introduced a wide range of subsidiary books shows that they did appreciate that the basic system could, with advantage, be modified to make it more suitable for particular circumstances.

CHAPTER 10

BALANCING THE BOOKS

10.1 General Comparison with Current Practice

Current commercial accounting practice requires a profit and loss account and balance sheet to be prepared at regular (usually annual) intervals. The profit and loss account is part of the double entry system but the balance sheet is not a ledger account but a listing of account balances, and it is, therefore, not itself an integral part of the double entry system. Often carefully prepared versions of the balance sheet and profit and loss account are drawn up and distributed to a range of interested parties. These documents are subject to voluminous regulations in an attempt to ensure that they present a true and fair view.

Things were different at the start of the 18th century. Although it is true that Colinson (in 1683) closed his specimen accounts at 6-monthly intervals, a major difference between practice then and today, is that it was unlikely that a 17th century merchant would balance his books at regular intervals. Often the books would only be closed when they became too full and a new set was to be started.(1) This practice would not cause major problems if the merchant was an owner/manager with free access to the business's accounting records and in close touch with its daily operations. It was later developments, such as the separation of operational management from a large diffused body of share owners and the growth of tax legislation, which made regular financial reporting essential.

Despite the last comment, regular balancing became more usual during the first half of the 18th century and, as early as 1718, both Malcolm and Macghie were noting that merchants <u>commonly</u> balanced their books at regular intervals.(2) Later Mair, Gordon and Hamilton made similar comments and adopted annual balancing in their illustrative examples.

When the 18th century merchant closed his books a profit and loss and balance account were prepared but the balance account (unlike the balance sheet) was a ledger account and thus part of the double entry system. Documents described as profit and loss sheets and balance sheets did feature in some of the 18th century texts but it must not be assumed that these are equivalent to the modern balance sheet and income statement. Some copies of the profit and loss account and the balance account might be made and distributed to a few individuals (eg partners) but there is little reference to this in the texts and, in general, partners had access to the books.(3) When Hamilton, for example, says that there would be difficulty in laying before the partners "a state of their affairs" if a trader's private affairs were recorded in the same books as the partnership business, he is assuming that these books would be laid open for the inspection of the partners.(4)

10.2 <u>The Objectives of 'Balancing the Ledger'</u>

Winjum has discussed the closing (balancing) of a trader's books in the 250 years up to 1750; his view is that: "Evidence contained in early textbooks supports the conclusion that early writers regarded the bookkeeping objectives accomplished in the closing process as more important than the determination of total enterprise income".(5)

This opinion is endorsed by Yamey, who says: "The early counterparts of the modern profit-and-loss account and balance sheet were largely by-products of the double-entry bookkeeping process".(6) He provides some evidence for this view from account books that have survived from the 17th century and he quotes some of the 18th century accounting authors as additional support. Mair's description of the process of 'balancing the ledger' as one of separating "the articles of stock that lay ... diffused through the whole Ledger" from the "refuse and dregs",(7) he would regard as part of this support.

It will be argued here that Mair's description should not be taken as implying that 18th century profit and loss and balance accounts were prepared primarily for technical book-keeping reasons. There was less emphasis on a <u>regular</u> determination of the merchant's position and on <u>regular</u> calculations of his profit, than there is today but these were growing in importance as objectives from early in the century.

Two decades before Mair, Malcolm (1718) had given the objectives of balancing as being: " ... in Order both to making up a State of the whole Affairs, and for the changing of the Books, or the Transportation of the Accompts from old to new Books, which begin with the compendious State of the Accompts abstracted from the former".(8)

Macghie (also in 1718) clearly stated that the balance of the profit and loss account would " ... shew how much is gain'd on the whole Year's or half Year's &c. trading".(9)

10.3 <u>Profits for Branches of Trade</u>

Before regular annual summaries of income and expenditure became 'common' accounting procedures reflected an alternative (and not necessarily inferior) view of profit. The merchant's attention (and the consequent accounting emphasis) would be concentrated on the progress and ultimate profitability of each of his individual ventures or consignments and he would would wish to have their profitability measured as they were completed rather than on an annual basis. Using the popular tree metaphor, the emphasis was on an assessment of the fruit from each 'branch of trade', as and when it came to fruition. The emphasis did not change instantaneously when annual balancing was introduced and there was some conflict between the two views of profit. Techniques for dealing with incomplete 'ventures' within a framework of regular balancing, were not developed for some time.

An accountant in the 20th century opens the profit and loss account at the end of the accounting period but in the 18th century the profit and loss account would stand open continuously ready to receive profits and losses as they were calculated. Malcolm, whilst explaining this point, emphasises that it is not necessary, or convenient, to take a gain or loss to the profit and loss account on the occasion of each sale. It is the cumulative gain or loss from each 'profit centre' (to use a more modern term) which is transferred, on the completion of the venture, to the profit and loss account. He says: "For Example, an Accompt of Wine is opened in the Leger, wherein is entered on the Debtor side the Quantity purchased with the first Cost and Charges; if these Wines are disposed of at Several Times; and this recorded on the Creditor side, there is no Necessity, nor would it be at all convenient to calculate the Gain or Loss at every Sale, but when the whole is disposed, or when we prepare to know how the total State of Gain or Loss stands, then may it be done, and the Gain or Loss set upon the least side, and carried to the opposite Side of the Accompt of Profit and Loss."(10)

This emphasis on the branches of trade leads to another difference between 20th and 18th century accounting in that the modern accountant would, normally, expect a firm's ledgers (excluding the personal ledgers) to contain rather more expense accounts than asset accounts, but, in the illustrative ledgers of Malcolm, Mair, Gordon and Hamilton, there are few accounts for individual types of expense. The sparing use of such accounts arises for two reasons: (i) because, wherever possible, expenses are debited (and income credited) to relevant asset accounts to enable a profit (or loss) to be calculated for each branch of trade, and (ii) because income and expenditure accounts are often combined to create a branch of trade. It is the results of the individual 'branches of trade' or 'profit centres' that are collected in the profit and loss account.(11)

Macghie considers that: " ... often-times the Accompt of Profit and Loss, ought to be subdivided into its several Branches, such as Interest-Accompt, Insurance-Accompt, Provision-Accompt,(12) Charges Accompt, &c. besides a general Accompt of Profit and Loss, into which all these at length terminate, together with other Things which cannot be otherwise denominated, than by the general Title of Profit and Loss".(13) Earlier (p 9) he had also listed Bottomery Accompt, Wagers Accompt, Promises Accompt and Hazard Accompt and later (p 50) he added: Rentals Accompt, Accompt of Ships Voyages, Proper Expences,(14) Household Expences and Exchange Accompt. Macghie's listing of expense and income accounts will seem more familiar to 20th century accountants but it must be remembered that the emphasis on 'branches of trade' means that many of the expense and income figures will be the result of offsetting debit and credit items.(15)

For a shopkeeper's accounts Gordon did advocate that expenses (other than the prime cost of the merchandise) should be debited to the profit and loss account rather than to the merchandise account. He says: " ... debit profit and loss for every charge that is not the price of goods; such as chest, wrapper, and package of any kind, cartage, carriage, &c. although it is stated by the seller."(16) Gordon's reason for this departure from normal 18th century practice is not based on any distinction between product costs and period costs but on practicalities. His method is to " ... render the prime cost of every particular in a bill of sales more easy to be discovered".(17)

10.4 Joint Costs and the Allocation Problem

The wish to show the outcome of the individual branches of trade could easily lead to problems of joint cost allocation. Edwards has noted that: "The bookkeeping literature of the 18th and 19th centuries abounds with examples of consignment accounts, voyage accounts and accounts showing the profit on the sale of different types of commodities by the same business."(18)

Robert Hamilton gives examples of this type and these demonstrate that he is well aware of the 'joint cost problem'. In this respect Yamey has pointed out that Hamilton is in advance of his contemporary, Adam Smith, whose 'Wealth of Nations' contains nothing helpful on the subject.(19) Hamilton outlines the relevant considerations in the course of a commentary on one of his extended illustrations. In chapter I of part IV during the explanation of an example, he says: "When we import a cargo of different kinds of goods which could not well be separated, such as iron and deals; of which the one is necessary for ballast, and the other to complete the lading, it is proper to join them in one accompt, and compute the profit or loss on the whole together. Here we open an accompt of goods from Gottenburgh, and distinguish the iron and deals in inner columns, which is better than to open one accompt for iron and another for deals. Perhaps there might be gain on the one and loss on the other; but as we were obliged to import both togeher, it is the success of the whole that we should inquire into."(20)

In another section a similar point is made: "When the

American trade was open, a considerable number of ships were built in the northern provinces, and sent home to Britain for sale. The ships were generally loaded with lumber to the West-Indies, and there took in sugar on freight for London. Sometimes they made several voyages before they came home. As the purchase of the ship and success of the voyages are properly but one adventure, they are joined in the same accompt, and the gain estimated on the whole."(21)

The second example is particularly interesting, as the lumber dealing and the ship purchase and sale are dealt with as a single venture, whereas the results of the sugar transactions are calculated separately and a freight charge is imputed to enable this to be done. This is a sophisticated method of dealing with the joint cost problem but Hamilton was not the only writer to suggest its use.

Malcolm had earlier used the approach in 'A Treatise of Book-keeping' when he was considering the problem of measuring the separate profitability of two connected branches of trade. He says: "If you employ your Ship in Trade; then to keep a clear and separate Account of the Gain and Loss by your Ship, and by your Merchandize, charge your Goods (or the Voyage Account, ...) with the Freight, as you would pay it to a Stranger; and place all the Charges of Reparations and Navigations to the Debt of the Ships Account, and the Freight to the Credit".(22)

In summary, Hamilton considered that discretion should be exercised in the identification of branches of trade (or profit centres) because taking the subdivision too far would lead to spurious apportionments of joint costs which would not help in the assessment of branch profitability. In some cases however joint activities could be meaningfully disaggregated and Hamilton and Malcolm demonstrate how this could be achieved by the use of appropriate imputed costs, based on external market prices. The joint cost problem remains a topic of debate and controversy today(23) and the advice given by Hamilton and Mair would not seem out of place, or at all dated, if it were to be introduced into the modern debate.

It will be recognised that, unless all branches of trade are to be consolidated into one, there will inevitably be expenses which it is difficult, or impossible, to allocate meaningfully to specific branches. Such expenses would be taken to the profit and loss account. Malcolm notes this when he says: "Things will of Necessity come to the Profit and Loss Account, which in Effect are neither Gain nor Loss; as Interest paid or received for the Loan of Money; for though there is no other Account to carry this to, yet there may be more gained by the Use of the Money borrowed, than the Interest; which Gain will fall upon the Account to which the Money was applied, and from this carried at last to the Profit and Loss Account ... ".(24)

10.5 Sophistication in Profit Measurement

It is too readily assumed that 18th century profit measurement methods were crude whereas they often showed considerable sophistication. In addition to Hamilton's recognition that joint cost apportionment should be avoided and the use of imputed costs by both Hamilton and Malcolm, other examples can be provided. Malcolm, for example, recognises that the difference between (a) discounts received (or allowed) because of defects in the goods supplied and (b) discounts received (or allowed) for payment before the due date, can be important if 'branch of trade' profits are being calculated. He considers that the former type of discount is properly regarded as affecting the profit on the goods whereas the latter is a financing gain (or cost).(25) Some of Robert Hamilton's contributions in this field will be considered in later chapters.(26)

Not all 18th century accounting writers were as sophisticated as Malcolm and Hamilton, but when accounting methods are alleged to be crude, it is necessary to consider whether 20th century criteria are being inappropriately applied. The failure to make periodic charges for depreciation in the profit and loss account might be considered in this light. Depreciation does not feature in the text book discussions of merchants' accounts but depreciation accounting is closely connected with regular periodic profit calculations and when Hamilton deals with estate accounting, where regular annual accounting periods were used, he does discuss depreciation.(27) When 'branch of trade' profit rather than annual profit is the focus of attention the need for periodic depreciation charges is at least debatable.

10.6 Accrual Accounting

Similar points should be borne in mind when the 18th century cavalier approach to accruals and prepayments is considered. It is clear that the 18th century text book writers did not regard merchants' accounts as a form of cash flow accounting, nevertheless there is difficulty in claiming that they advocated full accruals accounting. In general, they seemed to pay no attention to the identification of accruals and prepayments at the time when the books were balanced. This may have been because the use of regular accounting periods had not completely supplanted the earlier emphasis on 'branch of trade' profit. For the latter, the identification of accruals and prepayments was less necessary as it was assumed that the books would remain open until the branch had come to fruition. This explanation receives added force from the discussions of estate accounting and farm accounting where the use of annual accounts and the attempt to relate income and expenditure to a year's activities was well established. Here Hamilton, for example, gives detailed instructions for ensuring that the profit and loss account gives the profit for the year's crop.(28)

In 'Merchants Accompts' it seems to have been thought unnecessary to be overworried about accruals and prepayments even when the income (or expense) was clearly related to the passage of time. An example is interest receivable.(29) Malcolm is completely indifferent between three approaches for accounting for such interest; (i) entering all the interest when the loan is made, (ii) charging interest "from Term to Term as it falls due" or (iii) entering the interest when it is paid.(30) The accounts were being prepared for the merchant, he would be aware of the convention that was being used and would not be misled.

Even the apparent exceptions, must be looked at with care. Malcolm, for example, discusses the use of an 'Accompt for household &c Expences out-standing' in his 1718 book(31) and he adopts a more general approach using an account with the title of 'General Account of Out-standing Charges' in his 1731 book.(32) In neither case, however, does he relate the need for this account to the closing of the books, rather the objective seems to be to get a debit for the expense into the appropriate asset account or the profit and loss account, as soon as possible.

William Hamilton however does seem to acknowledge the problem and to suggest an answer. He also uses the example of outstanding Household Expenses. He says: "If you were owing any Part of these Expences, then would Profit and Loss be Debitor to them for what was due, and Cash would be Creditor only for what was paid out of it. But there is a shorter Way than this of bringing the Accounts of so many Men into your principal Books for such Trifles, and this is by making your general Account of personal and Household

Expences Debitor to personal and Household Expences outstanding, which comprehends all these small Creditors under this Account ... ".(33) He gives an example of such an accrual in his third set of books.

10.7 The Balance Account

Earlier sections of this chapter have dealt with the profit and loss account but the balance account also played an important part in the process of closing the books and the functions of this account and its construction will now be considered.

In 'Book-keeping Methodiz'd' Mair develops the conventional arboreal description of the nature of 'stock' into a more general agricultural metaphor to explain the purpose of the balance account. He describes the merchant's stock as: " ... the Fund for Traffick, and it is worthwhile to observe how it spreads, and diffuses itself in a Course of Trade, branching out into a Multitude of various Accompts, which all depend and hang on it, as the Branches on the Root. It is to a Merchant someway like Seed to the Husbandman, which is sown in the Spring, adorns and beautifies the Fields in Summer, and appears with quite another Face than what it had before, is cut down in Harvest, and gathered into the Barn, where being separated from Chaff and Straw, it again resumes its former Shape, with Increase or Diminution, according to the Nature of the Soil and Season, and becomes Seed for the ensuing Year. Thus when a Merchant begins to trade, his Stock dissipates and scatters, spreads, sprouts, and shoots out into a Variety of Accompts, and these again into others, proceeding in a constant Succession, and continual Flux, till by this Propagation a whole Ledger, consisting perhaps of 200 or 300 Folios, be replete, and ripened as it were into a Harvest. Upon this the Books are shut up, and the Articles of Stock that lay lately diffused through the whole Ledger, and seemed to possess so large a Field, being now separated from Refuse and Dregs, shrink again within the narrow limits of the Balance-Accompt, being enlarged or lessen'd, or only varied, according to Success and the Chance of Trade. From this it passes into the Inventory of the new Books, where it takes the same Turn as before, and again is brought to the Ballance Accompt, and from it to the next Inventory; and thus goes on in a circulatory manner, while the merchant continues to trade."(34)

It is noteworthy that Mair has no explicit statement that the balance accompt shows the state of affairs at the balancing date, but implicitly this is the case, if the new opening inventory is based on the closing balance Accompt and other authors do make such a claim for the account. Malcolm makes the claim and, in doing so uses the more conventional metaphor of the tree; he writes: "There may be a change of the State of the Stock, as to its constituent Parts, which is the effect of the various tossing this Stock about in Trade, and the frequent Changes that are made of one Thing for another in that Course ... The Question now is, How the Alterations that befall the Members of the Stock shall appear? None of these will be on the Accompt of Stock, because, according to the fundamental Rules, as Things change and come in place of one another, they are charged and discharged in their particular Accompts: It is plain therefore, that the present State of the Stock can only be known, by examining the State of every particular Accompt, by which we may find what Effects of every Kind we have, and what Debts are due both to and by us; These being all collected into an Accompt called Ballance, will shew us the present and true State of our Stock ... as the Stock-Accompt with its Members, and these variously changed by the future Negotiations, give us an Idea of the opening and spreading of a regular Accompt, so will the Beauty of this Art appear us agreeably, when we see how orderly these manifold Accompts are closed and shut up again, and finally terminate in this one Accompt of Ballance, which presents us with the true State of Affairs, after all the Alterations that have happened, since the making up of our last Inventory: For as this Accompt of Stock is the Root or Capital, and its Branches the Subjects of the future transactions, so the Ballance - Accompt is the Metamorphosis of it, shewing, how, by the Course of Trade, the several Members are changed, some being encreased, some decreased, others expunged or lopt off, and new ones grown up."(35)

It might be noted that in the discussion of the balance account (and more generally in the explanation of the double entry system) the 18th century writers had no terms to describe what are now called 'assets' and 'liabilities'. Gordon talks of an " ... inventory of the money, effects and debts belonging to him (the trader) and the debts due to others".(36) Malcolm, Mair and Hamilton sometimes talk of 'effects and debts'. The former term seems to have been used in a vague sense and any reference to 'debts' had to be qualified by an explanation of whether the debts were owing by or to the trader.

If the balance account is intended to " ... shew us the present and true State of our Stock" then Yamey rightly stresses that: "A distinction must be drawn between a balance account drawn up on the basis of the account balances appearing in the ledger, and a balance account incorporating the facts as revealed by an actual inventory where the possessions of the firm are examined and valued."(37)

It is surprising that none of the 18th century writers discusses this point. One possible explanation is that any required adjustments were made to the opening Inventory rather than to the closing balance Accompt, where the latter was not regarded as showing a just view. There is possibly an example of this in the specimen accounts provided by Colinson. Colinson's illustrative accounts are for a year's transactions (1 January - 31 December, 1682) divided into two six-monthly periods. In opening the accounts for the second period Colinson introduces a journal entry which involves a small adjustment to the profit and loss account. From the viewpoint of 20th century practice, this would have seemed more appropriate if it had been made before closing the books.(38)

A better example is provided by Brodie, also in an illustrative example for two consecutive accounting periods (this time of unequal length). Again an adjustment to the opening inventory of the second period is made. In this example there is no hint of the existence of any accrued expenses when the books are closed at the end of the first period and the profit and loss and balance accounts are prepared. When the new books are opened, however, Brodie introduces accrued rent and accrued expenses. This means that the opening balance on the stock (capital) account in the new books is lower than the closing balance in the old books. The journal entries Brodie gives are as follows:

				l.	s.	d.
Dr Stock				56	-	-
Cr Profit and Loss for a Year's Rent,						
and Taxes of my House and Warehouse	L30	15	-			
Petty Charges, Pocket Expenses,						
and little Incidents,	25	5	-	56	-	-
Dr Profit and Loss				56	-	-
Cr Cash paid the above Charges				56	-	-

(39)

No other examples have been identified but all the authors were consistent in stressing the importance of accuracy in the opening inventory.

It must also be remembered that modern accounting systems (based on historic cost principles) do not fully achieve what Yamey is advocating and yet they contrive to produce accounting statements which are claimed to give a 'true and fair' view.

10.8 The Treatment of Non-Business Items

It was noted in chapter 8 that the strict distinction between business and non-business, assets, liabilities and transactions, which is now regarded as so fundamental, was not observed by the writers that we are reviewing.(40) Colinson(41) comments on the reluctance of some merchants to include all their personal wealth in the business books but he does not relate this to any theoretical objection that the trader has but rather to his "fear that others see his Books". Although he does not consider this a valid reason (since the trader can always 'seal up the accompt' of stock) he acknowledges that " ... a man may have a private stock ... and a stock in trade also; but then he must bring none of his private stock into his trading stocks Books, lest he confuse himself. Wherein can this private stock consist? it must be in Lands, Houses, Rents, Jewels, and House-furnishing, &c. for which private stock let him keep a Book, which he may easily do apart."(42)

Colinson clearly considers this system less satisfactory than recording everything in the trade books; his recommendation is: "Let a man place all in his Books as his Condition is" and he does include private stock in his illustrative example. Mair does not even discuss the possibility of omitting non business assets, he says: "It is usual for merchants to erect a general accompt, by the title of Plate, and jewels, which is debited for all the plate, jugs, spoons, rings, watches, &c. they had at first setting up, or which they have occasion afterwards to purchase."(43)

Where the stock (ie the capital) account includes the merchant's personal stock it would still be possible to exclude changes in the value of the non business stock from the profit and loss account and thus restrict the latter account to business profits and losses. Mair refers to the possibility of crediting the receipt of a legacy or the gain on a wager etc directly to Stock in his first book,(44) but in 'Book-keeping Moderniz'd' he states, unequivocally, that such items should be credited to profit and loss account(45) and this latter practice was more generally approved. Malcolm, for example, makes it clear that he considers that the profit and loss account should not be reserved solely for business gains and losses. He advocates debiting it with the trader's household costs and crediting it with non-business gains, such as legacies received. In one example that he gives, the expense of a wager is debited to profit and loss, and elsewhere there is an example of a wager won by the merchant "there being no Peace concluded between Britain and Spain ... ". The winnings are credited to profit and loss.(46)

Malcolm justifies this approach as follows: " ... I would keep the Stock-Accompt clean of every Thing but what belonged to the last Inventory, for it is the proper Office of the Accompt of Profit and Loss to receive all the Encrease and Decrease of the Stock, until we make a new Inventory, and consequently a new Accompt of Stock".(47)

The balance on the profit and loss account is thus the cumulative increase, or decrease, in the merchant's stock that has arisen since the books were opened; this balance is only transferred to the stock account when the books are ultimately closed.

10.9 Asset Valuation - Merchandise

The section on 'The Retailers Counting-house' in Gordon's 'General Counting House' describes the process of valuing unsold merchandise when the books are being closed: "Merchandise-account, contains on the debtor-side, the prime cost of all the goods which have any how come into the retailer's hands since the books were opened, with all those he had on hand at opening the books; and, on the creditor-side, all the sales that have been made since the books were opened, and the prime cost of all the goods that have been sold. Wherefore, if the goods have been all disposed off, the inner column on the creditor-side, and the money-column on the debtor's side, will be equal, and the account will in that case be closed with profit and loss for the difference of the outer columns: If the inner column on the creditor is less than the debtor money column, it will be equal to the prime cost of the goods already disposed of, and the difference will just balance the goods on hand. In this case, credit the account with balance for this difference, and extend it to the outer column, and debit the account with profit and loss for the difference of the outer columns."(48)

Gordon's system (which was also that suggested by most of his contemporaries) would today be described as a perpetual inventory system. Malcolm considers the question of a shortage on the Accompt of Goods. He states that the 'Value' (presumably the cost) of the goods lost could be charged to profit and loss Accompt but he seems to prefer not to make such a transfer as the loss will automatically reduce the profit obtainable from the merchandize.(49)

Colinson, Malcolm, Macghie, Brodie, Stevenson, Gordon, Perry, and Scruton all value unsold goods at cost(50) but the most popular author, Mair, is vague on the subject and Yamey considers that: "The valuation of assets did not trouble the great majority of authors of books on bookkeeping and accounts up to the middle of the nineteenth century. In those cases where an author stated the basis for the valuation at which an asset is to be transferred to the closing balance account, usually no reason was given for the choice of basis."(51)

Malcolm was one of the few who did provide a reason for using cost as the basis; he values goods as 'they cost you' in preference to the 'current rates' because otherwise "you bring in Gain and Loss into your Accounts which has not yet actually happened, and may perhaps not happen".(52) Malcolm also recognises that the valuation basis may depend on the purpose of the exercise and that this might lead to the use of replacement cost: "But if your Accounts are balanced, in order that your Effects may be disposed of to your Creditors for Payment of your Debts, it seems just that they be valued at the current Rates; or with such Allowances as Merchants have from one another."(53)

Drummond mentions the use of realisable value as the basis of valuation in the opening inventory. He says: "Some in their Inventary value Goods as they desire to sell them, but I know of no Reason for this, but to make a Man appear rich by his Inventary, and, at ballancing, his Gain appear little."(54) The implication of the last remark seems to be that either there will be less inventory on hand when the books are balanced, or else that the closing inventory is valued at cost.

10.10 <u>Value to the Owner</u>

Although the majority of 18th century writers proposed the cost basis for inventory valuation, it was not universally accepted. Hamilton is one of the dissidents. He says: "It is proper, before balancing, ... to take an exact inventory of the goods on hand, as far as can be done;

and affix a moderate value to each article, according to the current prices at the time; such a value as the owner would be willing at present to buy for. It is much more proper to value the goods on hand in conformity to the current prices, than at prime cost: For the design of affixing any value is to point out the gain or loss; and the gain is in reality obtained so soon as the prices rise, or the loss suffered so soon as they fall."(55)

Although inflation was at a very modest rate for the period from 1750 to 1800,(56) Hamilton clearly considers that it is important to recognise price fluctuations in the profit measurement system and his valuation method is, in essence, that favoured in the Sandiland's Report(57) on 'Inflation Accounting'. The Sandiland's Committee uses the term 'value to the owner' which was used by Professor Bonbright in 1937 (58) to describe this value concept. Another authority, Professor Baxter, uses the term 'deprival value'.(59) Bonbright was the first to discuss in detail 'value to the owner' and he gives the following definition: "The value of a property to its owner is identical in amount with the adverse value of the entire loss, direct and indirect, that the owner might expect to suffer if he were to be deprived of the property."(60) This definition is fuller than Hamilton's but Hamilton's definition captures the essential points and, although it might be argued that he had not worked out all the implications of the method, he is undeniably adopting the same approach as Bonbright and his definition is rather simpler.

Hamilton and Gordon positively advocated a physical stock count(61) and Malcolm considered the question of inventory shortages, which seems to imply that a count was undertaken. Malcolm's suggestion that no action should be undertaken where there is an inventory shortage, because the loss will automatically find its way into the profit and loss account, is not an adequate answer to Professor Yamey's objection to items appearing in the balance account that are not based on 'an actual inventory'. With Professor Yamey's criticism in mind, it is appropriate to look at the valuation bases suggested for other assets.

10.11 Asset Valuation - Debtors

Malcolm gives the following example of the valuation of 'debtors' and the treatment of 'bad debts': "Of Desperate Debts When a Debt becomes lost by the Circumstances of the Debtor, I would not any longer encumber my Leger with that Person's Account; but discharge it by Profit and Loss. Or if I do not actually discharge the Debtor; and look on the Debt only as desperate for the Time, but which may afterwards possibly be recovered; I would not discharge the Account absolutely, but only transfer it from the Debtor's Particular Account to a General Account of Desperate Debts; and there let it stand, till it's either recovered, or till I look upon it as irrecoverable; and then it's discharged out of this Account."(62)

This treatment can make sense if a comprehensive record rather than profit measurement is the primary objective. Hamilton agrees with Malcolm's suggested treatment, but he is more cautious about writing off desperate debts and he recommends that, even where a debt is written off to profit and loss account, a record of it should be maintained in a separate book in case it should, at some future time, become recoverable.(63)

10.12 Asset Valuation - Fixed Assets

Eighteenth century writers did not use the term 'fixed asset'(64) but their approach to the valuation of such assets as Houses and Ships can be examined. Malcolm had a very liberal attitude to such matters. He says: "For

Accounts of Houses and Ships: You may value them at the first Cost; and when that is stated on the Creditor-side, the Difference of the Debt and Credit is Gain or Loss, arising from the Difference of the Reparations, &c. and the Rents or Freights. Or you may take the Difference of the two sides, and state as the Balance due to you; by which means the Value of the Thing will appear less and less at every balancing, till it's nothing. And then in a new Inventory you enter it again, at what Value you think proper; and sometimes also you may appear to be a Loser, which must go to Profit and Loss; but the first Method I think the best: And though these Subjects do not really keep up their Value, yet I would continue them at the first Value till they were disposed of, or lost; or you may chuse to state them at another Value from Time to Time, as you think they are then really worth."(65)

In interpreting this quotation it must be remembered that it assumes that any expenses relating to the asset will have been debited to the asset account and any income derived from the asset will have been credited. At the balancing date a decision has to be made as to how much to transfer to the profit and loss account as the gain (or loss) derived from owning the asset, the balance will be taken to the balance account as the asset's 'book' value.

Malcolm is suggesting three possible valuation methods: (i) 'first' cost, (ii) opening balance less net income, (iii) valuation at the balancing date.

Under (i) The transfer to profit and loss will be the net income from the asset ignoring any charge for depreciation.

Under (ii) There will be no transfer to profit and loss account, all income derived from the asset is regarded as reducing the investment in the asset.

Under (iii) The asset's value is appraised at the date

when the books are balanced. This may result in a depreciation charge or an appreciation credit to profit and loss account.

Yamey confirms that all three bases were used in practice.(66) Method (i) is Malcolm's preferred approach but, in the last sentence of the quotation, he mentions the possibility of combining methods (i) and (iii).

Drummond considers the valuation of an estate by reference to the income that it yields. Discussing the value that is to appear in the opening inventory, he says: "You are to give the Name of, and Place where your Land-Estate lies valuing it at the Number of Years purchase it is worth."(67)

10.13 The Annual Calculation of Profit

Yamey considers that it was the advent of general limited liability which decisively changed accounting practices by requiring the preparation of regular (annual) accounts,(68) although Pollard notes an earlier tendency in this direction when he says: "Again and again, where long series of accounts survive, it will be seen that where they have not been regularly periodic before they become so at some time during the eighteenth century."(69)

Some of the textbook authors at the start of the century had commented on a 'common' practice of balancing the books once a year. Malcolm and MacGhie were the earliest. Malcolm noted that: "It (the balancing of the books) is done as oft as a Merchant pleases, when he would know the State of his Stock, and this is commonly once a Year ... ".(70)

In his second book he makes the point that balancing the books does not force the merchant to open a new set of books: "If you propose to make an Inventory for the Satisfaction of knowing the State of your Affairs, without designing a new Leger; then make up your Balance, and Profit and Loss, upon a Loose Sheet ... without writing any Thing in the Leger ... ".(71)

In the first edition of 'Book-keeping Methodiz'd', Mair noted the common practice of annual balancing but he did not then relate this to the need for an annual profit figure. His example of the accounts of a merchant deals with a year's transactions. In the 3rd edition (1749) he states annual balancing is generally adopted by overseas storekeepers in the tobacco trade.(72) Similarly, in chapter VIII of the appendix to the 5th edition (1757), annual balancing and the annual preparation of a profit and loss account are assumed in the new material concerned with " ... the method of keeping accompts proper for shopkeepers or retailers".(73)

In 1765 Gordon wrote: "Merchants generally, at some fixed period, once in the year, balance or close the Leger, not only because the spaces allotted for the accounts may be for the most part full but likewise to show the merchant a true state of his affairs, and what increase or diminution his capital hath suffered by last year's transactions."(74)

In the first edition of 'Book-keeping Moderniz'd' (1773) Mair made the same point in words which are very similar to those used by Gordon.(75)

Hamilton's 'Introduction to Merchandize' followed closely on the heels of Mair's 'Book-keeping Moderniz'd' and, while also emphasising the need for an annual profit calculation, it takes the matter further by considering criteria for determining an appropriate financial year-end date. Hamilton says: "Merchants generally balance their books once a-year. The design of this operation is, to collect the various branches of their business diffused through the books, into a concise abstract; to ascertain their gain or loss since the last balance; and exhibit the present state of their funds. If the business be of such a kind, that most of the branches naturally come to an issue at a certain time of year, that time is the proper for making the balance. Otherwise the end of the year, or the least busy time, may be chosen."(76)

10.14 Work Sheets and Accounting Statements

During the century, the text books had moved to the acceptance (and advocacy) of an annual calculation of profit with the preparation of an annual profit and loss account and an annual balance account within the merchant's ledger. During the second half of the century the preparation of a separate profit and loss sheet and a balance sheet (outside the ledger) was described by some of the authors but there was some variation in the use of these terms.

In 1762 Stevenson used the term balance sheet and he illustrates such a document having the following columns: Accompts upon which there is Gain, Accompts upon which there is Loss, Effects on Hand, Debts due to me, Debts due by me.(77) This 'balance sheet' has many similarities to an 'extended trial balance' which is a commonly used work sheet in the preparation of finacial statements. It might also be regarded as a combined income statement and balance sheet.

Hamilton gives an example of a profit and loss sheet and balance sheet which are more like the 20th century financial statements which bear those names but they are also (in part at least) work sheets.

Professor Watanabe has discussed the work sheets described in the early textbooks.(78) He identifies Simon Stevins' "Staet of Capitael" and "Winst en Verlies" as the first examples of working sheets.(79) The next examples that he gives are the descriptions provided by Macghie, Malcolm, Mair and Hamilton.(80) Although he considers that Malcolm and Hamilton did provide an advance, in that their working

Specimen Profit and Loss Sheet and Balance Sheet from Hamilton's Merchandize

PROFIT AND LOSS SHEET.

	L	s	d		L	s	d
Salt	—	11	4	Meal	9	18	—
Charges Merchandize	13	14	2	Port-wine	6	15	—
Proper Expences	32	15	10	Paper	4	18	6
				Yarn	2	3	2
	L47	1	4	Calicoes	1	13	4
* In Leger	4	4	10	Diaper	—	15	10
				Iron	2	7	11
	L51	6	2	Clover-ſeed	5	—	1
				Lint-ſeed	—	18	—
				Share of ſhip Hazard	23	—	—
				Train-oil	8	—	—
					L65	9	10
Nett gain	16	13	8	* In Leger	2	10	—
	L67	19	10		L67	19	10

*Summary figures for expenses and income.

BALANCE-SHEET.

	L	s	d		L	s	d
Caſh	8	3	10	Meal, outcome 3 b. *			
Meal, 124 b. at 13s 4d	83	14	—	Royal Bank	201	3	2
Yarn, 474 ſp. at 2s	47	8	—	William Bruce	20	—	—
Amiſſing ½ *				Thomas Sharp	8	—	—
Houſe in Edinburgh	300	—	—		L229	3	2
James Boſwell	37	11	—				
Henry Hardie	31	2	6				
David Miller	18	—	—				
J. Cuthbert	5	6	3				
Iron, 40 ſtone, at 3s 4d	6	13	4				
J. Henderſon	7	4	—				
W. Hunter	18	13	6				
James Dalton	35	15	—				
Clover-ſeed, 300 lb. at 6d	7	10	—				
Inlake 10 lb. *							
J. Scott	4	7	6				
Share of ſhip Hazard	140	—	—				
George Gordon	6	3	4	STOCK	528	9	1
	L757	12	3		L757	12	3

*Notes of inventory shortage and surplus.

sheets are also used to survey the trader's financial position and details of the profit calculation, nevertheless he does not believe that they can be categorised as true financial statements.

In the 18th century the extensive use of agents and factors in overseas trade necessitated regular financial reports by the factor to his principal(81) but the need for regular financial reporting by business managers to a widely dispersed ownership did not exist. Although there were many examples of absentee ownership in the 18th century and Scottish partnerships with over 100 partners,(82) the development of financial reporting procedures largely occurred in the following century with the growth of limited liability companies.

Yamey has rightly emphasised the importance of the effect that 19th century company legislation had on financial reporting.(83) The profit and loss account and the balance sheet were largely created to meet the needs of the new type of business organisation but there were precursors and Hamilton's profit and loss sheet and balance sheet may be considered as such. His statements are partly (perhaps even primarily) working papers but he may be hinting at an enlarged function for them when he notes the need to set out the balance sheet items in a suitable manner. He says: "Thus is the state of a person's affairs brought together, in a short compass, under his view; and the articles of the balance sheet supply materials for a new inventory. It is convenient, however, to alter the order, and arrange the real accompts together, and the personal ones together."(84) Whether this is sufficient to give Hamilton's balance sheet the status of a 'financial statement' is a matter of judgement.

CHAPTER 11

ACCOUNTING FOR PARTNERSHIPS

11.1 Definitions - Legal and Accounting

Partnerships were important in the development of the economy of 18th century Scotland(1) and sound book-keeping practices were essential to foster the mutual trust that was required among the partners. The text book authors recognise this factor and the first Scottish writer Colinson, gives it particular emphasis, at the beginning of his book, where he claims that book-keeping is the only technique that makes partnership arrangements feasible for many traders. He argues that it is " ... obvious to all Considering persons that this honourable and profitable Science of Book-keeping is the only help, that encourages many to joyn their small stocks together ... ".(2) Most of the authors dealt with the topic of accounting for partnerships but they generally considered it to be an advanced topic. Colinson, for example, describes it as " ... the difficultest part to learn of all the Book-keeping ... ".(3)

The Partnership Act (1890) has now provided a concise definition of partnership as "the relationship which subsists between persons carrying on a business in common with a view of profit"(4) but, in the 18th century, terminology and definitions were varied. In the major codification of Scottish law undertaken by James Viscount of Stair in 1681, partnership is discussed under the heading 'Society, where, of Copartnery', and the following definition is given: " ... society may be described 'a contract, for communicating the profit or loss of that which is brought into the society, proportionably according to the share and interest of each partner'."(5)

Forty years on, Forbes, another Scottish legal writer, provides a definition of 'partnership' that is more in line with that of the 1890 Act: "Partnership is a Contract, by which two or more Persons join in common Money or Goods, and Labour or Service, for carrying on some lawful Commerce, Work, or other Business, that they may share among them all the Gain or Loss thence arising."(6)

'Society', 'partnership' and 'association' are all used in the 18th century but the most commonly used terms in the Scottish accounting texts are: 'company' and 'copartnery' and the application of accounting to partnerships is usually called 'Company Accompts'. Malcolm, Mair, Gordon and Hamilton all included material on 'company' accounts in their texts and Mair and Hamilton provided formal definitions of 'partnership'. Hamilton's definition is similar to that given by Forbes: "Partnership is a contract among two or more persons, to carry on a certain business, at their joint expence, and share the gain or loss which arises from it."(7)

In contrast, Mair's definition has an unusual emphasis. He says: "Partnership is that Branch of Trade which is managed and carried on by a Trustee, in the Name, and for the Account of the Partners, that is, when a joint Stock,(8) made up by two or more Merchants, is deposited in the Hands of one Person, to be employed by him in a Way of Commerce, according to Instructions."(9)

Mair states that normally the partners choose one of their own number to be the 'partner-trustee'(10) and Macghie also mentions this feature when he states: " ... the whole Management of the Affair being usually committed to one of the Partners, who in that respect serves the Company in Quality of a Factor, for which he is to have his Provision ... ".(11)

Mair is following the terminology adopted by Macghie

and Malcolm when he uses the term 'partner trustee' but Malcolm also refers to this individual as the 'accountant and chief manager' and there is the assumption that he will maintain the partnership's acccounting records. Macghie notes that alternatively " ... the Company may employ a neutral Person to do all this, who in this Respect is properly their Factor".(12)

Only in his second book does Mair recognise that there may be partnerships in which the partners share in the management of operations but he considers that these are likely to be small ephemeral arrangements. "There is a kind of company-accounts, wherein the partners promiscuously take a share in the management, and co-operate with one another; and these are commonly small adventures, and short of continuance."(13)

11.2 Types of Partnership

Scottish law gave the partnership legal recognition as a separate entity which English law did not. "A partnership ... may perhaps be defined a contract by which two or more form themselves into a society, capable, under a particular name or firm, of dealing as a separate person, and contracting with others all the relations of debtor and creditor ... "(14)

The Scottish book-keping authors describe several different types of partnership. Malcolm makes a distinction between standing or 'fixt' (or fix'd) companies and 'unfixt' (unfix'd) companies(15). He relates the adjective 'fixt' to the company's stock (or capital). A 'Fixt Company' is one with a " ... fixt Stock which every Partner furnishes his Share of, and this to be the subject Matter of all the subsequent Transactions of Trade".(16) An 'Unfixt Company' has "no standing and fixt Stock; but, for Example, buy from Time to Time Parcels of this or the other Kind of Goods, to be disposed of in domestick or foreign Trade, and withdraw their (ie the partners') Shares of the Value sold, when they please; by which Means their Stocks or Effects in Company, perpetually vary according to the Value of these different Transactions, and such Partnership may be entred into for one single Parcel of Goods or Voyage, or they may continue for some Course of Trade".(17) Mair uses the term 'fixed company' to describe companies "whose Trade is considerable, or who have the Prospect of dealing long that way"(18) but he does recognise that the partners in such fixed companies would commonly leave the balances on their stock accounts as a fund for continuing 'adventures'.(19)

Hamilton discussed the various types of partnership from two viewpoints, accounting and legal. In part IV, which concerns Italian Book-keeping, he distinguished 'occasional' partnerships from 'fixed' partnerships.(20) In part VI, in the chapter dealing with 'Mercantile Laws', he gave a more detailed analysis. Here he described four types of partnership:

"(I) "Occasional joint trade, where two or more merchants agree to employ a certain sum in trade, and divide the gain or loss so soon as the adventure is brought to an issue. ...

"(II) Standing companies, which are generally established by written contract between the parties, where the stock, the firm (21), duration, the division of the gain or loss, and other circumstances, are inserted. ...

"(III) Companies, where the business is conducted by officers. There are many companies of this kind in Britain, chiefly established for purposes which require a larger capital than private merchants can command. ... The capital is condescended on (22), and divided into a certain number of shares, whereof each partner may hold one or more, but is generally restricted to a certain number. Any partner may transfer his share; and the company must admit his assignee as a partner. The death of the partners has no effect on the company. No partner can act personally in the affairs of the company; but the execution of their business is intrusted to officers, for whom they are responsible; and, when the partners are numerous, the superintendency of the officers is committed to directors chosen annually, or at other appointed times, by the partners.

"(IV) Companies incorporated by authority. A royal charter is necessary to enable a company to hold lands, to have a common seal, and enjoy the other privileges of a corporation. A charter is sometimes procured, in order to limit the risk of the partners; for, in every private company, the partners are liable for the debts, without limitation; in incorporated societies, they are only liable for their shares in the stock of the society. The incorporation of societies is sometimes authorised by act of parliament; but this high authority is not necessary, unless for conferring exclusive privileges."(23)

Hamilton does not specifically state that companies of types II and III are 'fixt' companies but this is the implication. Malcolm only considered the 'private partnership'(24); presumably he would have regard Hamilton's type IV corporation as a 'public partnership' although neither author uses this term.

It has been noted that the 18th century Scottish writers used the terms 'copartnery' and 'company' as synonyms. In England, however, a distinction was being drawn between copartnerships and companies, with the latter term being restricted to bodies created by Act of Parliament or Royal Charter.(25)

In the following century, Lorimer, writing on Scots law, made the following distinction between joint stock companies and partnerships: "The leading distinction, independent of statute, between a joint stock company and a proper partnership, consists in the shares of the former being transferable to purchasers, heirs, or creditors, without the consent of the remaining share-holders; whereas, in partnership, the adoption of new partners is either forbidden, or allowed only with the consent of the whole members of the existing firm."(26)

With this distinction Hamilton's type III partnership might seem to be a joint stock company but there is a difficulty with such an interpretation. Although Lorimer states that his distinction applies 'independent of statute', he was writing after the 1719 Bubble Act had been repealed. This act had imposed a prohibition on partnerships with freely transferable shares and Hamilton was writing while the act was still on the statute books. The topic will be considered further in 11.8.

11.3 Limited Liability

The type III partnership may have been a 'joint stock company' but Hamilton was clear that the liability of partners in such an unincorporated company could be not limited, by appropriate clauses in the co-partnery agreement, to the capital that they had agreed to contribute. Earlier in the century, the Scottish courts seem, in one case,(27) to have decided that partners could use unincorporated joint stock companies as a vehicle for obtaining the benefits of limited liability.

DuBois gives some of the details of this case: "In 1756, the creditors of a small unincorporated joint stock company engaged in the fishing trade, the Arran Company,(28) by a suit in the Court of Session, Edinburgh, sought to submit the individual property of the members of the company to the payment of the debt. The defendants' counsel argued that this type of organization was modeled on the societe en commandite of Holland and France, and that the liability of the members was limited to the sum subscribed."(29)

The copartnery agreement provided that "nothing herein contained shall be understood to import a Power to the Directors to compel any partner or Subscriber to pay or contribute any more Money to the Stock than the Sum by him subscribed". The decision was in favour of the defendants and the case was considered to confirm the view that, in Scottish partnerships, partners could restrict their liability to the amount of capital that they had agreed to contribute.(30)

Seventy years later, Bell justified this decision by arguing that companies operating under a descriptive name that did not identify the partners, where the partners (or shareholders) held "small transferable shares vendible in the market", implied " ... a credit entirely different in nature and object from that which belongs to private partnership; a reliance on the stock of the company; a comparative disregard of the personal credit of the shareholders; an attention confined to the reality of the fund, and the good discretion of the management".(31)

This was certainly not the position that obtained in England. In 1745 the attempt to form a British Linen Co-Partnery with both Scottish and English partners almost foundered on this point. The Scottish partners had signed the agreement but there was a problem with some of the prospective London partners because they feared that, if the partnership failed, they would be individually liable for all of its debts. Ebenezer McCulloch, one of the managers of the co-partnery, wrote as follows to a prospective London partner: " ... if the opinion of the ablest Judges and Lawyers of this country that that clause will save every particular person from being affected with the Company's Debts to a greater extent than his share or shares paid in, should not prove altogether satisfying to answer these doubts stirred up, Pray, would not a Royal Charter effectually do it".(32) A Royal Charter was obtained because of the English fears.(33)

The distinctive Scottish position on limited liability did not last long. In 1772 the Ayr Bank (Douglas, Heron and Company) failed. This unincorporated partnership had 226 partners and, in the case of Douglas Heron and Company v Hair, the Court of Session applied, without qualification, the viewpoint that the members of such an unincorporated joint stock company were individually liable for the company's debts.(34)

Since the Treaty of Union, Scots law had been moving closer to English law. The Ayr Bank case illustrates this infiltration in the field of business (company) law. It was no longer regarded as appropriate for Scottish lawyers to make analogies with the Continent. The English system was in control.(35) Five years after the failure of Douglas Heron and Company, Hamilton wrote his 'Introduction to Merchandize', and his section on the legal liability of partners clearly recognised the law as it was set out in that case.

11.4 Profit Sharing

Seventeenth and eighteenth century partnership agreements were frequently complicated, with capital provided unequally by the partners and consequential arrangements for allowing interest on capital contributed. Sometimes distributions of profit were limited to interest on capital as was the case in the New Milns Manufactory agreement of 1680: "That at the third yeir we shall onlie begin to receave our bygone annual rents if ther be so much free profites, and so therefter yeirlie for the first seven yeirs at least to receive onlie the rent of our monie if the profite affoord it, the excrescent advantage runneing up to a greater stock for the wholl Society untill the Society shall think fitt to divide proportionally, the gain that is by and attour the interest and rent."(36)

There might also be an agreement to pay salaries and commission to those partners who actively participated in the running of the business.

In the absence of express agreement among the partners the law would provide the profit sharing rule but the rule given in the 18th century legal and accounting texts differs from that given in the Partnership Act 1890. This act provides that, in the absence of any agreement to the contrary, partners share profits, and losses, equally.(37) Forbes said: "Money or Goods only, or Labour and Service only may be contributed by all the Partners; or Money and Goods by some, Labour and Service by others: Whereof the Contribution may be equal, or unequal. Where nothing is expressly agreed as to the Communication of Gain or Loss, all are to share therein, proportionably to their Contribution of Money, or Goods, or Pains. If the Shares of Profit and Loss, that every one is to expect, be expressed, that must be observed; whether it be agreed, that those shall be equal, where the Contribution is unequal; or unequal, where the Contribution is equal."(38)

The computational aspects of the division of company profits is discussed in some of the accounting texts and in many 18th century arithmetic texts under the heading of the 'Rule of Fellowship'.(39) Where the textbooks contained both business arithmetic and accounting, this discussion did not form part of the book-keeping section of the text.

11.5 Accounting for an Investment in a Partnership

The accounting texts consider the records that are necessary in the case of partnerships where "the Accounts and chief Management are under the direction of another Partner".(40) Malcolm makes a distinction between the form of the records that are suitable if the partnership is 'unfixt' and those which are appropriate when it is 'fixt'.

In the case of an investment in an 'unfixt' company " ... the Manager is obliged at all Times to exhibite fair and distinct Accompts of the State of Affairs to his Partners; I have no more to do but to keep plain Accompts of what I give, or owe to the Company, and what I receive".(41) Where, for example, the partner-trustee is AB, this is achieved by opening two accounts for 'my' dealings with AB.

The first account is to record my investment in,(42) and contributions to the running of, the partnership (as debits) and drawings and other amounts received from the partnership (as credits). Malcolm suggests that an appropriate name for this account is 'AB my Accompt with him in Company' but Mair and Hamilton give alternative names that may be more appropriate in some circumstances such as: 'Goods in Company with AB' or 'Voyage in Company with AB'. The writers suggest that the title of the account should indicate the extent of 'my' interest in the partnership profit and expense. 'AB my Accompt with him in Company' " ... contains the value of your share on the Dr. and the returns obtained on the Cr; and the balance shows the present extent of your property in the funds of the company; and, when all your share is withdrawn, it shows your gain or loss".(43)

The second account is to record any other dealings that occur with the partner-trustee, AB. Suggested titles for the second account are: 'AB <u>his</u> proper Accompt' (Malcolm) or 'AB <u>my</u> proper Accompt' (Mair and Hamilton) or 'AB my Accompt Current' (Mair - although he does not approve of this title). As an example of the use of this account consider the case of amounts due to me from the partnership; these would be credited to 'AB my Accompt with him in Company' and debited to 'AB his proper Accompt'.

For recording investments in 'fixt' companies, Malcolm gives a different set of instructions. As for 'unfixt' companies there will be an account for dealings with the partner/trustee, ie if the partner/trustee is AB there will be 'AB his proper Accompt', but now all transactions with the partnership will be channelled through this account apart from the initial investment which is debited to 'AB my Accompt with him in Company'. "When I am concerned in a standing Company, I make my Accompt in Company with A.B. &c., ... Debtor for my Share, stocked in or owing, and this Accompt I never touch more till the Company-Accompts are examined and ballanced with the Managers; and then if I withdraw my Stock, this Accompt is Creditor for it; what Gain or Loss falls to my Share, I state to the Accompt of Profit and Loss."(44)

The 'Accompt in Company' is treated as an investment account which is to be recorded and maintained at cost. Mair's treatment is not in such precise detail as Malcolm's but it seems to give a similar result: "If after the goods are disposed of, you take up your Share of neat Gain, continuing your Share of Stock, as a Fund for a new Adventure, charge Cash Dr. to Profit and Loss, for the Sum received, and let the Accompt in Company stand as it is. N.B. This is the ordinary Case in fixed Companies."(45)

Malcolm explained the importance of maintaining both accounts since 'AB my Accompt with him in Company' is a 'Trust' account and "must be distinguished from the real and absolute Debts betwixt us, upon other particular Dealings". The question of the partner's liability for the debts of the partnership is not discussed by Malcolm but it may be a consideration behind his wish to distinguish between 'trust account' balances and 'real' debts. Hamilton is concerned with an individual partner's responsibility for the partnership debts and, in particular, for cases where: " ... the funds of the company are incumbered with considerable debts". In such cases he argues that " ... it will be proper to notice them in the inventory of our private affairs".(46) He suggests that the share of partnership debts should not be entered in the 'investment account' but that it should be shown in a separate account called, for example, 'Manufactory Debts'.

11.6 Partnership Accounts

It was assumed by the 18th century writers that one of the partners would assume the role of 'Accountant and chief Manager'(47) with the responsibility of maintaining the partnership accounting records. It is possible that, in describing this partner as 'Accountant', the word is being used in two senses, 1. as meaning the person who is to maintain the books of account and 2. as the person who is required to provide an account because he is a trustee.(48)

For 'unfixt' or occasional partnerships (joint ventures in modern terminology) the partnership accounts might be kept in the accountant's own books. As partnership goods are acquired they would be debited to an 'Accompt of Goods in Company with AB'. In addition the accountant keeps accounts for each partner's dealings with the partnership. For a typical partner (say AB) there will be an account to record his initial and subsequent inputs of capital; this would be headed up 'AB his Account in Company with --- '. Any amounts withdrawn from his stock by the partner would be debited to this account. Additionally each partner may have an account for any other transactions he is involved in with the 'Accountant and Chief Manager', other than as a partner. For AB, this would be termed 'AB his Proper (or Particular) Account'.(49)

Hamilton comments that this "accurate method" is "seldom used, on account of its prolixity, but deserves the attention of the learner, because it unfolds the general principles of book-keeping, and may be altered or abridged, as the particular circumstances of the business require".(50) Hamilton identifies three defects of the method as follows:

(a) It often requires two records for a transaction, the first record to deal with the transaction itself, the second to apportion the cost or revenue derived from the transaction over the partners.

(b) It does not exhibit the articles that are paid into or drawn out from the partnership in any one account.

(c) "Another inconvenience is, that you cannot lay before the company a state of their affairs, without either the trouble of transcribing, or the disagreeable necessity of submitting your private business, which is recorded in the same books, and intermixed with their transactions, to their inspection."(51)

Because of these defects, Hamilton argues that it is preferable to keep separate books for any partnership even if it is occasional.(52)

11.7 Separate Partnership Books

If separate books are maintained for the partnership, there should be a company ledger, waste-book and journal (but the waste-book can double as a journal in Malcolm's system). In his first book Malcolm says that the accounts of a 'fixt' company are better kept in separate books;(53) in his second book he is even more insistent that: "The Affairs of this Kind of Society, especially those of a more publick Nature, must be recorded in distinct and separate Books"(54) and Hamilton agrees.(55)

The ledger will contain two accounts for each partner,

one an 'Accompt in Company' and the other an 'Accompt Proper' (or a particular Accompt).(56) The contents of the accounts are not the same for 'fixt' and 'unfixt' companies. For a 'fixt' company AB's Account in Company is credited with his share of the stock "... and it stands so, for there goes no other Thing to that Accompt, except the Company increase or diminish their Stock, or at a ballancing of their Accompts".(57) Malcolm is more insistent on this point than the other writers but it is apparent in the other texts. AB's 'Particular Account' is to be debited with amounts paid to the partner from the company and credited with amounts lent or otherwise paid by him to the company (except for any introduction of new capital). The balances of the 'Particular Accounts' "are understood to be owing to, or by the whole Company".(58)

Mair suggests that, in addition to the foregoing accounts there could be a 'Stock in Company Accompt' which is "only a Collection of the Sums that stand upon the Credit-sides of the Partners Accompts in Company, exhibiting at once the total Sum of the Inputs, (this) is not absolutely necessary ... except in the Books of large and fixed Companies, for in such the smallest Piece of Form is not to be neglected".(59) Malcolm also considers this approach: " ... if you would have an Accompt, in which all the Shares of the Stock should be seen at all Times, and no other Thing, then make Cash, &c. in Company, (viz. the Things stocked in) Debtors to Stock in Company for the Shares; but immediately Balance this Accompt of Stock, and make it Debtor to our Accompts in Company".(60) An account of this type would be useful where the number of partners (or shareholders) was large (consider the 226 shareholders of the Ayr Bank). Malcolm also points out that it would be appropriate if some partners do not contribute the full amount of their agreed share capital immediately. The account bears some resemblance to an Issued Share Capital Account in modern company accounting.

Malcolm emphasises that the manager's own transactions with the company must be recorded both in his own books and in the company's books. He explains that " ... I consider my self in a double Capacity. 1. As Book-keeper to the Company, I do every Thing as if I were not a Partner. But, 2. As I am, I must give my self Accompt (1731 book has the plural 'Accounts') in their Leger, as I do to the rest of the Company; and if at any Time the Company require to balance their Books, I am accountable for all the Balance of Money or Goods found to be in my Hands by these Accompts, and for what I am Debtor on my particular Accompt, or any other Partner or Person whatever, 'tis all understood to be Effects belonging to the whole Company; and what I or any Partner (or any other Person) is Creditor for on our particular Accompt, or our Accompt in Company is a Debt due by the whole Company to be cleared out of the foresaid Effects; and thus I have a distinct state of their Affairs, and can make up my Accompts with Ease."(61)

11.8 <u>The Transfer of Shares in a Partnership</u>

The South Sea Bubble burst early in the 18th century (1720). Trading in the stock of the South Sea Company(62) reached a feverish pitch in that year and a sudden collapse followed that led to the ruin of many. The government reacted to the emergency by pushing a bill through Parliament which became 'An Act to Restrain the Extravagant and Unwarrantable Practice of Raising Money by Voluntary Subscriptions for Carrying on Projects Dangerous to the Trade and Subjects of this Kingdom'. This statute became known as 'The Bubble Act'.

The Bubble Act provided, inter alia, that: "the acting or presuming to act as a corporate Body or Bodies, the raising or pretending to raise transferable Stock or Shares, the transferring or pretending to transfer or assign any Share or Shares in such Stock or Stocks without Legal Authority, either by Act of Parliament or by any Charter from the Crown to warrant such acting as a Body Corporate ... shall for ever be deemed to be illegal and void and shall not be practiced or in any wise put in execution".

There is some doubt about the act's applicability to Scotland(63) and Section 25 did provide: "that nothing in this Act shall extend or be construed to extend to prohibit or restrain the carrying on of any home or foreign Trade in Partnership in such Manner as hath been hitherto usual."

If the act had been generally interpreted as having important repercussions in Scotland one might have expected some reference to these in the accounting texts. There was, however, no such discussion. Although the Bubble Act had ostensibly banned partnerships with freely transferable shares, Hamilton's description of the different types of partnership (quoted above pp 227-8) makes it clear that he considered that it was possible to create an unincorporated joint stock company in which the members had a right to transfer shares freely.

Malcolm deals with the accounting records required for such 'share' transfers and it is useful to compare the treatment of this topic in his 1718 book (which was published before the Bubble Act) with the change in emphasis in his second book-keeping book (which appeared 11 years after the Bubble Act).

In 1718 Malcolm said: "If the Company being (for Example) five in Number, take in a sixth, quitting him 1/6 of their Stocks. I would make their Accompt in Company Debtors to their particular Accompts for the 1/6 Part, and when they receive it, their particular Accompts are Debtors, or receiving it immediately, their Accompts in Company Debtors to what they receive; and for the Partner now taken in, I make his Accompt in Company Creditor by his particular Accompt, or by what he pays in for his Share. If he pays or is owing any Thing of Allowance to the Company for his Privilege, Profit and Loss in Company is Creditor for it, by his particular Accompt, for what he pays ... ".(64) The last sentence of this quotation seems to be referring to a share premium.

The 1718 explanation had assumed that there was agreement among the existing partners on the admittance of the new partner. In Malcolm's 1731 book the emphasis has changed. The text now deals with an individual partner selling his shares to an outsider, the agreement of his fellow partners is not mentioned. "If any Partner sell his share, or any part thereof, the Person to whom he sells, must have an Account in the Company's Books; and his Account in Company, be Creditor by the Seller's Account in Company, for the Value. Or, if there is a Stock Account, make the Partner (who transfers) His Account in Company, Debtor to Stock; and this, Debtor to the new Partner's Account in Company. Also observe, That if he who transfers, owes that, or any Part of it, to the Company; then, the company having consented to this transfer, make the new Partner's Account Debtor to the others Particular Account for what is owing to the Company; and if the Company take in one or more Partners afterwards, making hereby an Addition to the Capital, enter these Partners shares as the former were; and if these pay or owe any Thing to the Company, more than their Stock, for being taken in; it goes to the Profit and Loss Account."(65)

11.9 Summary

Partnerships played an important part in the

development of industry and commerce in 18th century Scotland. The industrial developments required large amounts of capital and the status of the Scottish partnership as a separate legal entity made it easier for businesses with a large number of owners to operate as partnerships, without experiencing the legal difficulties which might arise in England.(66) The contemporary accounting texts assumed that unincorporated companies with transferable shares could be formed in Scotland, and they did not even consider the possible application of the Bubble Act to prevent this.(67) The accounting texts described a form of organisation, 'the fixt company', which had similarities to the modern limited liability company and (although this was not discussed in the accounting texts) it was widely assumed, for much of the century, that it was possible for a Scottish co-partnery agreement to confer this benefit on its members.

Methods of accounting for transferable shares in such companies, were developed and even the question of shares issued at a premium was discussed although the suggested treatment of such premiums (crediting them to Profit and Loss Account) is no longer acceptable.

Partners would commonly have access to the partnership books but it was recognised that some partners might, alternatively, request a 'State of their Accompts'. Malcolm says that if such a request is received from a shareholder, it should be complied with, since he is entitled to "a fair copy of the same".(68)

As the role of partnerships in the Scottish economy became more important, the textbook writers began to adapt the Italian system to deal with joint stock organisations where the share capital was contributed by a large number of dispersed partners, each of whom had the power to sell his shares without the prior approval of his partners. In their descriptions of 'Merchants' Accounts' the 18th century accounting writers were reluctant to deviate from the canonical Italian method. The developments that they describe in partnership/company accounting, however, demonstrate that, when necessary, they were willing to adapt the system and further it shows that the Italian method was flexible enough to deal with changing patterns of business organisation.

CHAPTER 12

ACCOUNTING FOR THE TOBACCO TRADE

12.1 Background

The 3rd edition of Mair's 'Book-keeping Methodiz'd' appeared in 1749 with a new chapter (chapter VI) devoted to "The Produce and Commerce of the Tobacco Colonies, viz. Virginia and Maryland; with a Specimen of the Accompts usually kept by the Merchants or Storekeepers there".(1) The need for such a chapter would have been obvious to someone living so near Glasgow in the middle of the 18th century. The Union of Scotland and England, in 1707, had legitimised Scottish participation in the profitable tobacco trade and the Scottish tobacco trade was based entirely on Glasgow. The route north of Ireland to North America was the quickest route (by two or three weeks)(2) from Britain; Glasgow was ideally situated and its share in the trade increased dramatically. In 1738 the Scottish trade was 10% of the British total, in 1744 it was 20%, in 1758, 30%, in 1765, 40% and in the years 1768-70 it reached 50% of the British total.(3)

The Glasgow tobacco trade was essentially an entrepot trade with the unprocessed tobacco leaf being exported from the Clyde to the Continent in exactly the same condition as it had arrived from America. Both the Northern and the Southern routes to the Continent were used. Mair's new section illustrated the accounting records and procedures used in the tobacco trade, but it also went beyond this and described the industry in some detail. The importance of the trade to the Virginian and Maryland economies was clearly set forth in statistics on the volume and value of the trade and much of the information is of considerable historical interest. For example, Mair names the American tobacco warehouses as they existed in the mid 18th century: "Those on the south side of Potomack river are, Wicomico, Coan, Yeocomico, Nomony, Mattox, Boyd's-hole, Caves, Acquia, Quantico, Occoquan, Huntin-creek, and Falls. Those on the north side of Rapahannock, are Indian Creek, Deep Creek, Glascocks, Totuskey, Nailers, Bray's Church, Gibson's, Falmouth. On the south side of the river are, Urbanna, Hob's-hole, Port-Royal, Fredericksburgh, &c."(4)

Another book which illustrates some features of the tobacco trade is Scruton's 'The Practical Counting House' (1777). The author, writing in Glasgow, dedicates his book to John Glasford (or Glassford), one of the great Glasgow 'tobacco lords' and Glassford's firm appears in the main illustrative example.(5) Scruton clearly intends this to be a realistic 'case study' as a number of other firms and individuals who were active in the tobacco trade, also appear in it. These include: Alexander Speirs, John McCall and Co and Houston's and Co.

12.2 Organisation of the Trade

Devine distinguishes two systems for carrying on the tobacco trade in the 18th century, these were the 'consignment system' and the 'store system'.(6)

The consignment system was typically used by London merchants. Under this system three parties were involved: the London firm of merchants, the merchants' factor in North America and the planter. The planter retained the legal ownership of the tobacco but consigned it to the factor whose London principals disposed of it in Britain and on the Continental markets. The London merchant acted as agent for the planter and charged a commission and handling charges for this service. The planter bore the cost of insurance and freight; he also bore the risk.

The second method was the store system and this was

typical of Glagow trade from about 1740.(7) Under this system the Glagow merchant established a store (or stores) in the tobacco colonies. This store, managed by the merchant's factor, sold goods to planters on (generous) credit terms on condition that they would sell their tobacco to the factor. Adam Smith commented on the store system as follows: "Even the stores and warehouses from which goods are retailed in some provinces, particularly in Virginia and Maryland, belong, many of them, to merchants who reside in the mother country, and afford one of the few instances of the retail trade of a society being carried on by the capitals of those who are not resident members of it."(8)

Scruton's main illustrative example deals with the accounts of a merchant who has two such stores in America, in Blandford, Virginia and in Baltimore, Maryland. The second store is managed by Robert Lawson. Here again Scruton is using a real person.(9) James Lawson, a Glasgow tobacco trader, did have a son named Robert. Devine notes that "Almost every figure of note in the (tobacco) trade had spent some time in Virginia or Maryland as an apprentice, as a storekeeper or as a factor. James Lawson's son, Robert, followed the conventional route. In 1763 he was almost sixteen and had spent four years at grammar school, two at college and 'about one year at Counting, Book-keeping and French'. He was now sent to Maryland under the supervision of his father's partner there."(10)

Scruton gives details of the type of goods that were sent to these stores: "To the continent of America, we export wearing apparel, household furniture, silk, woollen, and linen manufactures, iron, cordage and sails, great guns, small arms, ammunition, lead, brass, iron and steel, with every thing else which may serve for the luxuries as well as conveniencies of life, excepting provisions, with which, in general, they are plentifully supplied within themselves."(11)

John Gibson, a contemporary Glasgow accountant/ merchant, was critical of the 'stores system'; he described the evolution of the method (and some of its dangers) as follows: "So sensible were the people of Glasgow of the advantages which they had procured by the Union, that no sooner was the treaty signed, than they began immediately to prosecute the trade to Virginia and Maryland; they chartered vessels from Whitehaven; they sent out cargoes of goods, and brought back tobacco in return. The method in which they proceeded in this trade was certainly a very prudent one, a super-cargo went out with every vessel, who bartered his goods for tobacco, until such time as he had either sold all his goods or procured as much tobacco as was sufficient to load his vessel, he then returned immediately; and, if any of his goods remained unsold, he brought them home with him ... soon after the year 1740 a new mode was adopted ... factors were established in the country, who received the goods, and remitted the tobacco; these goods they gave credit of to the planters, on condition that they should receive their crops of tobacco, when ready for the market: for several years this method succeeded extremely well ... but the trade, after the period of 1750, being exceedingly increased ... ambition for who should be possessed of the largest share of the trade took possession of them; they lent to the planters large sums of money, in order to secure them for customers, they gave them unlimited credits; and thus ... rendered the commerce with the people of America, rather a speculative, than a solid branch of business" .(12)

Mair recognised the two methods of trading and he estimated that three quarters of the tobacco brought to Britain was purchased in exchange for European and 'Indian' goods (the store system) and the remaining quarter was "consigned, and sent over to Britain, mostly to London, by the Planters themselves; which is paid for generally in Bills ... ".(13) In his illustrative example he uses the stores system.

Although the store system was clearly successful and, presumably, appropriate for Glasgow, it might seem strange that Glasgow merchants, who would have had much more difficulty in obtaining the necessary funds than their London counterparts, should opt for a method of trading which would seem to require more capital and to be accompanied by greater risks. Pares attempts to answer this query: "It is a paradox that Glasgow, where capital was scanty and difficult to mobilize, went in for a type of trade which, to all appearance, required a large capital, whereas the London factors pretended to act as mere agents, leaving most of the burden of finding the capital to the planters. Yet these appearances were very deceptive. The Glasgow merchants, who bought their tobacco in Virginia, could limit the size of their operations very much better than the London factors who merely handled cargoes for a commission; for there was no limit at all to the advances into which the latter might be led. Thus it was the London factor, outwardly a mere agent, who became the planter's banker, much more so than the Glasgow merchant." (14)

12.3 The Tobacco Warehouses

Mair describes the legal and quality control procedures installed in Virginia and Maryland to facilitate the trade: "The purchasing of Tobacco in the Colonies, is now, by an Inspection-law, made easy and safe both to the Planter and the Merchant. This Law took place in Virginia in the year 1730, but in Maryland not till the year 1748. The Planter, by virtue of this, may go to any Place, and sell his Tobacco, without carrying a Sample of it along with him; and the Merchant may buy it, though lying 100 miles ... from his store, and yet be morally sure with respect to Quality and Quantity.

"For this purpose, upon all the rivers and bays of Virginia and Maryland, at the Distance of about twelve or fourteen Miles from one another, are erected warehouses ... To these warehouses all the Tobacco in the Country must be brought, and there lodged, before the Planters can offer it for sale."(15)

"The Tobacco being thus lodged in the Warehouse, the Planter goes to the Merchant, sells his Tobacco, and delivers him the Notes ... the Notes ... circulate, and pass from hand to hand, without Indorsation; the Title or Property in the Tobacco lying entirely in the Possession of the Notes." (16)

12.4 Currency in the Tobacco Colonies

Adam Smith comments on the scarcity of gold and silver coinage in the tobacco colonies: "Gold and silver ... very seldom appear in the commerce between Great Britain and the tobacco colonies. Maryland and Virginia have little occassion for these metals in their foreign as in their domestic commerce. They are said, accordingly, to have less gold and silver money than any other colonies in America. They are acclaimed, however, as thriving and consequently as rich as any of their neighbours."(17)

When money passed hands in trading transactions it was likely to include a significant number of foreign coins. When, for example, John Robertson, the 'superintending factor' for William Cunningham and Co., purchased bills from the Cabin Point factor in 1770, he remitted in payment: 227 pistoles of different kinds, 20 carolines, 3 3/4 moyderes, 7 ducats, 10 guineas and 75 half guineas.(18) Neither Mair nor Scruton specifically mention any problems of this nature but the offset of the amount due to a planter (for tobacco purchased) against the amount due from him (for his purchases from the store) minimised the necessity for cash transactions. Barter was very prevalent.(19)

Because of the shortage of coin the tobacco notes, referred to by Mair, served as a form of money in Maryland and Virginia. In Virginia all the public debts such as "the Parson's Stipend, the Clerk or Precentor's Salary, the King's Attorneys and Sheriffs Fees, the Maintenance and Cloathing of the Poor, the Expence of Ferries, the building and repairing of Churches, Prisons, &c." and "most of the private Debts" were settled "not in Cash, but in Tobacco".(20) If Alexander Malcolm (chapter 3) had been successful in his application for the position of rector at St Mary's, Dorchester County in 1753, his salary would have been paid in 40,000 lbs of tobacco per year.(21)

In this connection, Mair notes that the merchants often acted as tax collectors in that " ... when a Planter sells a Hogshead of Tobacco, he desires the Merchant to charge him with so much to the Sheriff, and give the Sheriff Credit for the same. When the Sheriff has got a great many of these small Credits in the Merchant's Books, the Merchant pays him the total at once, and thereby saves him a good deal of Trouble."(22)

12.5 The Store Accounts

Mair distinguishes the ideal system that should be installed (using an invoice-book, a waste book, a journal, a warehouse-book, a sales-book and the ledger) from the incomplete system that is more likely to be in use. He states that, in practice, the local agent keeps only a ledger for the goods sold from the store, and a warehouse or tobacco book for the tobacco purchased. Neither a journal nor a waste book is normally maintained. The ledger contains only cash, personal and ship accounts. " ... to save writing, no accompt of goods is kept"(23) and there is no profit and loss account: "The Ship-accompts contain, upon the Dr Side, the Goods taken from the Store for the Ship's Use, with Charges paid for Repairs, Flat-hire, to Jobbers, &c. These Accompts are commonly left open, as they have nothing on the Cr Side, and could only be closed by Profit and Loss; which Accompt is never kept. A Copy of the Ship-accompts is usually sent home by the Ship for the Information and Satisfaction of the Owners.

"The Warehouse or Tobacco Book contains a list of all the Tobacco that passes through the Storeskeeper's Hands; and is ruled with Columns, for the Date of the Notes, the Time when received, the Persons of whom received, the Folio of the Ledger where posted ... ".(24)

Mair states that the "Storekeepers generally balance their Books once a-year: On which occasion they make out two fair Copies of the whole Books; one of which they send home to Britain for the Use of their Employers, and the other they retain in the Store."(25)

12.6 The Merchant's Accounts

The merchant who uses the 'store system' opens a ledger account for the store. This is debited with the cost of goods sent to the storekeeper (or supercargo). When the 'abstract of the balance'(26) is received the details will be used to calculate the profit on the store and the amount due by (or to) the storekeeper. The profit is taken to the profit and loss account and the amount due from (or to) the storekeeper is transferred to his account current. Scruton's example of the transactions with Robert Lawson, the storekeeper in Baltimore, are reproduced here. The details are not a direct transcription of the ledger accounts from the text because such a transcription would hide much of the detail.

ROBERT LAWSON MY STORE IN BALTIMORE

	£	s	d		£	s	d
1775				1775			
Jan. 1 Balance of Goods	3020	-	-				
Feb. 16 Sundries, per the Fanny, Linnen, shoes, pumps tape, laces, curtains matrasses, pillows, desk, book case, chairs, card table, backgammon tables, boxes, men and dice, cutlery, scissors, spurs, pistols, candlesticks etc.	1016	1	3	Dec 31 Robert Lawson my Account Current	4906	9	-
Calendering, porterage, lighterage, tonnage &c. to Greenock	13	7	10	Robert Lawson outstanding Debts	876	1	-
Shipping charges	5	12	1				
Insurance at Campbells office at 2 per cent	25	17	6				
Feb 24 Goods shipped per the Diana, Manchester checks, corderoy.	80	-	-				
Packing and shipping charges	2	10	-				
Insurance at 2 per cent	2	1	3	Balance of Goods	1227	-	-
Dec 31 Profit and Loss	2844	9	11				
	7010	-	-		7010	-	-

ROBERT LAWSON MY ACCOUNT CURRENT

1775		£	s	d	1775		£	s	d
Mar	25 Bills Payable for his draught at 60 days sight	200	-	-	Mar	18 Tobacco per the Margaret	635	-	-
						28 Advance made by R. Lawson to the captain	20	-	-
					April	23 flax-seed per the Susan of Baltimore	90	-	-
					June	5 Foreign Currency Joes and dollars	1087	12	11
Dec	31 Robert Lawson My Store in Baltimore	4906	9	-	Dec	31 Balance	3273	16	-
		5106	9	-			5106	9	-

CHAPTER 13

ACCOUNTING FOR THE SUGAR TRADE

13.1 The Sugar Colonies

The 5th (Edinburgh) edition of Mair's 'Book-keeping Methodiz'd' appeared in 1757 with an additional 127 pages, 97 of which were devoted to accounting for the sugar trade.(1) Gordon also dealt with accounting for this trade in 'The General Counting-House and Man of Business',(2) in a section on 'The West Indian Counting House'.

The description of sugar trade accounting by Mair and Gordon is a good example of the plagiarism that existed at the time. Mair's text in chapter VI is based entirely on a book published in 1754, 3 years earlier than the Edinburgh fifth edition of 'Methodiz'd'. The source book for this material is William Weston's 'The Complete Merchant's Clerk: or British and American Counting House'.(3) Gordon's material is also a direct copy from the same source and there is evidence that Gordon possessed a copy of this book, since the copy in the antiquarian library of the Institute of Chartered Accountants of Scotland bears the hand written inscription "E Libris Gulielmi Gordon 1756".

It is interesting to determine the time lag that occurs between an economic change taking place (such as the emergence of the sugar industry as an important economic institution in Great Britain) and its recognition in the accounting texts. The sugar industry in the British controlled Island of Barbados began early. The first sugar factory on the island, and in the English New World colonies, was built in 1641 by Colonel Holdip.(4) According to Beer: " ... a few years later it (sugar) was the 'soul of trade of this island'. Customs duties paid in London on Barbados imports in 1655 was £12,930 of which £11,422 was on sugar."(5)

In Jamaica the transition to sugar monoculture was slower. In 1672 there were 70 sugar works, 60 indigo works and 60 cacao works on the island. By 1757, however, when Mair introduced the topic into 'Book-keeping Methodiz'd', sugar was supreme there too. Mair puts the point succinctly: " ... sugar cane is the glory of the West Indies, and the sugar and rum thence arising may be called the staple commodities of these islands."(6)

Mair refers to Jamaica, Barbados and the Leeward Islands as the sugar colonies. Despite the dominance of sugar in the economies of these colonies in the 17th century, the trade did not become of major significance to Britain until the mid 18th century. Woodruff discusses its growth and the importance of this to Britain: " ... so rapid was the development of the cane sugar industry in the West Indies in the 18th century and so important did the sugar trade become, that at the time of the treaty of Paris in 1763 some Englishmen considered it more important to maintain the sugar growing island of Guadeloupe than the whole of Canada. Growing supplies of raw sugar and improved methods of refining, developed in the 18th-19th centuries, placed sugar within the reach of an increasing number of Europeans. Between 1700 and 1760 United Kingdom consumption alone increased sixfold."(7)

In the light of the subsequent history of the West Indies, Mair's description of sugar as 'the glory' of those islands could be disputed, but the economic importance of the trade in the 18th century cannot be questioned.

13.2 Sugar Manufacture and the Plantation Accounts

At the beginning of the 18th century a typical West Indian sugar plantation would have had a workforce of about 100 and it would have utilised 80 acres of land. To put this into context it must be noted that, at the same period, farms of more than 30 acres were uncommon in Britain. Sugar production was, however, more than farming, it combined agriculture and industry. On top of the agricultural processes of planting, weeding and cutting, there were the manufacturing processes of grinding, boiling and refining the sugar, and, perhaps, the distilling of rum. "A sugar plantation was a factory set in a field."(8)

It might be thought that this environment would have led to the development of cost accounting systems with an emphasis on efficiency. It does not seem, however, that there was any attempt to devise such costing systems. The standard form of accounting used seems to have been very basic and Mair devotes only one page to the accounting records maintained by planters for the expenses of growing the cane and converting it to sugar, mollases and rum.

This discussion is in a section on 'Wharf and Plantation accompts briefly explained'. In this section Mair states that the plantation accounts are *not* normally kept on a double entry basis. He describes three books which are generally kept, these are:

"1. The *Boiling-house book*, which contains an account of all the sugar that is potted.(9) This is subscribed by the white man on duty, and examined weekly by the overseer.

"2. The *Still-house book*, which contains an account of all the rum produced. This too is subscribed by the person on duty, examined by the overseer, and shown to the proprietor's attorney, or transmitted to the proprietor himself in Britain.

"3. The *Plantation-book*, which contains an account of all the sugar, rum, and other produce, rolled off the plantation, and to whom sold; with an account of all the provisions and other things bought, and from whom; as also, an account of the number of servants and negroes belonging to the plantation ... ".(10)

This brief treatment recognises that the plantation owners would often be absentee proprietors with a local attorney but it is disappointing that no consideration is given to the accountability problems of such a situation. Weston, in contrast, was very critical of the planters' systems. Mair does not take up this line nor does he adopt Weston's sarcastic comments on the poor calibre of plantation clerks. Weston had complained that: "Planters think any thing fit for a Plantation Clerk, that can write and cast Accompts, and in fact, as times at present are in the West-Indies, they make any thing a Clerk; for if a man is recommended to a Factor, who in Point of Honour is obliged to patronize him, and he finds his Abilities but indifferent, he provides for the young Man both in Pleasure and Experience, by recommending him to the Freedom of a Planation Imprisonment, where he may remain many years, and know no more of Trade and keeping Books than at his first Arrival: For the Overseers who estimate the Force of their Understanding, by that of their Power, will persist in having the Books continued in the OLD Way, against all Remonstrances to the contrary."(11)

Weston notes that under the 'OLD Way' the plantation books "are generally kept without any regard to double Entry, containing only an Account of the Produce sent to Market, and Provisions expended ... ".(12) He argues for an improvement in accounting practice by the adoption of "Books to be conducted with the Proprietory of Double-Entry".(13) He believes that a proper double entry system would improve efficiency and help to check on the honesty of the planter's agents.

Because the standard of accounting in plantations was so poor, planters often had to guess details of the plantation's profitability and value. "There are in print many calculations of the profits of a plantation; since the authors were usually arguing for a remission of taxes or some other favour from the government, they often contrived to show that these profits were a minus quantity. But, when they were talking among themselves sugar planters seem to have expected their estates to yield them at any rate 10 per cent, some said 15 per cent, interest on their capital."(14)

If Weston is to be believed, the poor quality of the plantation book-keepers was a major cause of the generally poor standard of accounting on the sugar plantations. Certainly the conditions were too unattractive for educated Scots to have considered such a post, other than as a last resort.(15)

13.3 The Sugar Trade

Mair gives a useful description of important features of the sugar trade between the West Indies and Britain and the financing of this: "Goods sent from Britain to the sugar-colonies for sale there are generally consigned to factors there; or sometimes factors are sent over and settled in the colonies by British merchants who employ them. Two, three, or four of these factors are commonly joined in a company or partnership, that, in case of the death of any of them, the business may nevertheless be carried on by the surviving partners, and so the employers in Britain suffer no loss, at least not have their affairs thrown into confusion, or any stop put to their trade, by such an accident. This precaution is the more necessary, as the West Indies are reckoned a sickly climate."(16)

This section is very similar to the first paragraph of Gordon's chapter on 'The West Indian Counting House'(17) and both are clearly based on a paragraph in Weston's book.(18) Weston goes on to describe the accounting procedures commonly followed on the death of a partner(19) and Mair deals with this later.(20)

Mair describes a typical arrangement as follows: "A partnership of factors being thus established, they provide themselves in a shop or house ... A single factory of this kind is capable of transacting business for several merchants, or for several companies of merchants in Britain."(21)

The factors were commission agents acting for both the West Indian sugar producers and British merchant houses. They sold sugar on commission for West Indian principals to British merchants and they sold other goods for these same British merchants (again on commission) to the sugar producers. The system had been established for some time. Richard Pares has described how Azariah Pinney set up as a factor in Nevis in the 1680's.(22) Azariah had been deported, with £15 in his pocket, to the West Indies for his part in the Monmouth Rebellion of 1685. In the years 1686-90 one of his brothers, Nathaniel, consigned to him goods worth £618. Over the same period Azariah sent to Nathaniel 153,297 lb of sugar in various hogsheads, butts, tierces, and barrels besides small quantities of cotton and Spanish money. In these transactions Azariah was Nathaniel's agent, receiving a commission on the business done, but the business grew from these small beginnings and Azariah was soon acting as a factor outside the family circle. There is little detail available of his trading but we find him dealing in dry goods from Europe (sugar-bags, scissors, etc) and American produce (corn and boards).(23)

It seems probable that he did not long confine himself to acting as agent for others but that he soon set up as a merchant buying and selling on his own account and from this he developed to become a planter and landed proprietor.(24)

Although Weston's book is concerned with book-keeping, his business experience enables him to adopt a very practical approach and he gives guidance on such matters as the storage of various types of goods: "Let your Beef, Pork, &c be stowed in Tiers, fore and aft the Store, with their Bungs upermost, to prevent losing the Liquer which presently decays them; stopping the front Barrel of each Tier, to prevent their rolling forward, which may not only endanger the Goods, but yourself. I would not stow whole Barrels above three, nor half Barrels above four, Tier in height; for the Weight of the upper, may destroy some of the lower Tier, whose Barrels are defective." (25).

13.4 The Factor's Commission

Mair gives details of the various types of factor's commission and the rates that were commonly used: "The commission allowed to factors in the sugar-colonies was formerly very high. At present it is 5 per cent. on sales, 3 per cent. for insuring the debts, and 5 per cent. on returns. By insuring the debts, I mean, that the factor is accountable for them; so that if any person to whom he sells his employer's goods on trust, should turn insolvent, the loss is the factor's not the employer's. And this is constantly the case in the sugar-colonies, unless the employer, to avoid paying the 3 per cent. signify to the factor that he chuses to run the risk of the debts himself. When the factor is accountable for the debts, the sales are considered as ready money, and the neat proceeds ought to be remitted in six months at furthest after the goods are sold. Factors too have an allowance of 3 per cent. on sales, in name of storage; but this does not extend to the sale of negroes, because negroes are commonly lodged in the ship until disposed of."(26)

These rates tally with those that Azariah Pinney considered proper in 1708: "5 per cent for sales and 3 per cent storage, and 5 per cent returns, 3 per cent storage, 2 per cent horse hire, and on disbursements for freight of wines 5 per cent has been and is usually charged ... others might perhaps agree otherwise."(27)

13.5 The Factor's Books

Mair(28) and Gordon(29) list and describe the account books commonly maintained by factors in the sugar colonies. These are:

- Invoice Book
- Waste Book (and its subsidiary books)
- Journal
- Ledger
- Sales Book.

The invoice book contains copies of all invoices for goods received from the factor's employers, for resale on their behalf. As the goods remain the property of the consignors they are not recorded as purchases by the factor and the invoice book record of their receipt is thus a 'memorandum' record that does not constitute an entry into the double entry system itself.

The waste book is similar to the waste book used in 'proper trade'.(30) The subsidiaries of the waste book are the memorandum book and the cash book. The former "is commonly of a long narrow form"(31) and it is kept in the store to record the details of all sales transactions as they take place. Gordon says: "This book lies open in the store throughout the day, into which the storekeeper inserts, with all possible despatch, the transactions of the day with regard to sales, whether for ready money, or on time: and when store-business is over, the clerk retires into the counting-room, and, from the Memorandum, copies the transactions of the day fair into the Waste-book."(32)

The cash book is regarded by both Mair and Gordon as a subsidiary of the waste book not as a ledger account. Mair states that it " ... serves to abbreviate the Cash account in the Ledger, into which it is posted monthly".(33) Both writers emphasise that it is desirable for individual partners to initial the cash book entry when they receive cash.

Mair illustrates the normal form of journal which is prepared from the waste book but he also describes, and illustrates, the alternative system in which the waste book and Journal are combined in a single book which he terms a day book. Gordon uses a variation of this second method. In Gordon's combined journal/waste-book the journal entries are shown on the left hand side of each page and the waste book entries on the right hand side. The waste book description of each record then constitutes a narration for its journal entry.

"The Ledger is of the usual form; but sometimes has a column next to that which contains the day of the month, in which is inserted the page of the Journal, or Day-book, the several entries are posted from."(34) Mair goes on to say that " ... the Ledger is begun, carried on, and at last finished, without any Stock-accompt (i.e. Capital Account), which is not necessary, and which factors never use... "(35) but there is an Accompt-current for each partner. Capital accounts and fixed asset accounts are considered to be unnecessary because the books are only concerned with a fairly restricted number of 'projects' or 'ventures'.

The sales book records the sales achieved by the factor for each consignment received and the expenses and commission which are to be deducted from the proceeds. The book forms the basis for the 'Account Sales' which is sent to each employer when the transactions involving his consignment(s) have been completed.

13.6 <u>The Slave Trade</u>

Slavery was an essential part of the West Indian

plantation system and the voyage from Africa to the West Indies was the centre of this infamous triangular trade. British merchants sent cloth, beads, weapons and tools to Africa in exchange for slaves, the slaves were then transported to the Caribbean and exchanged for sugar which was sent home to Britain. Mair notes that: "The great advantage of the African trade is, that it carries no money out, supplies our plantations with negroes, and brings in a great deal of bullion for negroes sold to the Spanish West Indies."(36)

The West Indian factors also managed the sale of African slaves. Mair says that: "With consigned negroes the factor receives no formal invoice, as he does with other goods; the captain of the vessel only upon his arrival delivers to the factor a note or memorandum specifying what number of negro men, women, boys and girls, he has on board for sale, exclusive of the priviledged slaves belonging to himself, to the doctor, or any other person".(37) Mair provides the following example of the memorandum:

Kingston, Jamaica, April 1. 1765.

Received of Captain Bell, of the Rose of Liverpool, just arrived from Africa, the following list of negroes, on account of Martin Steel and Company, merchants in Liverpool, for sale and returns, viz.

57 negro men.
45 boys.
44 negro women.
17 girls.

Signed per ditto Bell. (38)

The sale of the slaves was recorded in the factors'

sales book in the same way as the other merchandise.

Sales on account and risk of Martin Steel and Company, per the Rose, Capt. Bell.

1765	To whom sold.	Negroes 57 men	45 boys	44 women	17 girls	Price	l.	s.	d.
Apr.									
4	Bonds	4	6	5	3	at £48 at £30			
						at £45 at £30	687	0	0
15	John Cole	2				at £50	100	0	0
25	George Gordon		2			at £30	60	0	0
28	Heavy Money	6	4	6	4	at £50 at £30			
						at £50 at £30	840	0	0
May									
5	Bonds	20	12	24		at £48 at £32			
						at £47	2472	0	0
18	John Brown	8		6	4	at £50 at £48			
						at £30	808	0	0
June									
3	Cash	1					48	0	0
8	Ditto	10	12			at £47 at £28	806	0	0
14	Peter Tom	1					48	0	0
17	Cash			1			46	0	0
24	Ditto		2		1	at £28	86	0	0
28	Ditto	2	3		1	at £46 at £25	191	0	0
July									
6	Ditto	1	3	2	2	sickly	90	0	0
	Dead	2	1		2				
		57	45	44	17		6282	0	0

C H A R G E S

July 6						
To Cash, paid						
import-duty on 163 negroes,	81	10	0			
Capt. Bell, coast-commission	241	12	3 1/2			
Dr Ward's fee,	7	18	0			
House-hire for 13 sick negroes	6	10	0			
Dr Ward, for extraordinary medicines to the sick	7	10	0			
For provisions towards maintenance of the cargo	96	13	4 1/2			
To Profit and Loss, for commission at 5 per cent.	314	02	0	755	15	8
To Martin Steel and Company's accompt-current, for neat proceeds, when received,				5526	4	4

Errors excepted,

Kingston, Jamaica, July 6. 1765.

Per the Rose, Capt. Bell.

Sands, Gordon, and Watts.

Mair notes that the factor " ... sells off the negroes as he would do any other sort of merchandise; with the difference only, that negroes are generally sold either for ready money, or on bond, or mortgage. As negroes by long keeping turn out an expensive cargo, daily maintenance adding considerably to the prime cost, factors think it their duty to dispose of them as speedily as possible; and always endeavour to manage so as to be able to remit, if not the whole, at least a large share of the neat proceeds by the return of the ship."(39)

There was a high death rate of slaves because of the cramped, unhygenic accommodation to which they were confined during the voyage to the West Indies. Mair's example notes five deaths in the sales book. Pares suggests that one reason why planters were so unsure as to the profits that they were making was that the investment in slaves "was subject to a terrible depreciation allowance"(40) which the planters neglected to charge as an expense in computing their profits.

13.7 Mair's Illustrative Example

The material reproduced in the last section is from an extended example which Mair provides to illustrate the accounts of factors in the Sugar Colonies; Gordon also gives a worked example. Both illustrations are based on Weston's book but Mair's example is fuller than that used by Gordon.

Mair's illustration deals with a Jamaican partnership of factors, Simon Sands, George Gordon and William Watts with premises in Kingston. From the beginning of January to mid July 1765 these factors receive "for sale and returns":

From George Buchan, London a consignment of pumps, boots and shoes, china, candles and linen.

From Robert Green and Company, Bristol a consignment of saddles, stockings, nails, three inch cordage, pease, bottled ale and a copper boiler, together with wine and malmsey picked up when the ship called at Madeira.

From John Scot and Company, Glasgow flowered lawns and 234 barrels of herrings together with butter, mess beef, mess pork and tongues picked up when the ship called at Cork.

From Martin Steel and Company, Liverpool 163 slaves from Africa.

In return Messrs. Sands, Gordon and Watts sent:

To George Buchan 5 hogsheads (8,408 lbs) of Muscovado sugar and 320 ozs of silver.

To Robert Green and Company 28 puncheons of rum, 61,560 lbs of ginger, logwood and lignum vitae

To John Scot and Company pymento, bags of cotton, coffee, fustic, ebony, 936 ozs of silver and 13 rials.

To Martin Steel and Company 16,471 lbs of sugar, mahogany planks, 1,000 ozs of silver and 200 double doubloons.

Gordon's similar (but shorter) illustration omits any reference to the slave trade. The realism of the details in these illustrations of trade with the sugar colonies is confirmed by Scruton who says: "To the sugar colonies we export provisions, linen and woollen cloths, hard-ware, shoes, stockings, &c. and, in return, we receive sugar, rum, mollasses, mahogany, cotton, coffee, hardwood, cedar, indigo, pimento, ginger, cocoa, preserves, citron water, and great variety of preserves."(41)

Mair's example runs from the beginning of January 1765 to July 10th. At this latter date the books are balanced. " ... factors never think of balancing their books, nor look upon them as ready for a balance, till the outstanding debts are paid in, and returns shipped, or remittances made to their employers; for the chief design of balancing the Ledger is to discover the amount of neat gain since the books were begun, and to make a dividend of it equally among the partners. Now this cannot be done till payment of the debts is received, and the neat proceeds be remitted; because till then the commission, and other profits on returns, are not stated, and no dividend can be made of money not received."(42)

The profit is thus calculated for a set of 'projects' on the completion of these and not at annual intervals. The major part of the factors' profit is derived from the commission (5%) and storage charges (3%) on goods sold for the employers and the commission (5%) on the sugar, rum and other goods sent to the employer. There are however other gains such as that arising from an accepted practice of charging for wharfage and negro hire at a rate above the cost actually incurred.

The expenses and gains are transferred in the normal manner to a profit and loss account and the balance on this is taken to the factors' accompts-current. Because the books are only closed when all transactions are fully complete, "The only accompts that now remain open, are Cash and the Partners accompts-current. Now, the difference of the sides of these several accompts-current, are the shares of gain still due to the partners; whose sum, if the books and balancing work be right, will be equal to the difference of the sides of the Cash-accompt, which is the sum that remains to be divided among them: and accordingly these accompts are all closed, and the balance of the books finished, by making the following entry in the Journal, and posting it to the Ledger; namely, Sundries Drs to Cash. viz. Each Partner's accompt-current, for the respective sums due to them."(43) This final entry records the payment of the cash balance to the partners.

CHAPTER 14

ESTATE ACCOUNTS

14.1 The Objectives of Estate Accounting

The 18th century estate owner's income was frequently derived from a variety of sources such as rents, farming and even manufacture. In such cases it would be preferable if the estate accounts could be organised so as to exhibit the financial outcome of each 'accomptable branch'(1) of activity. The objectives might be very similar to those of a merchant's accounting system although some estate owners could be less interested in maximising monetary returns.

In a small estate the management function might be handled by the estate owner himself and he might even keep his own accounts(2) but in large estates managerial problems were often tackled by devolving responsibility to a steward or chamberlain. This was a solution to one difficulty but it gave rise to another, the problem of accountability. The estate owner would now expect the accounting system to ensure that the chamberlain accounted fully for all the resources received on his (the principal's) behalf.

Pollard has pointed out that the form of accounting that had developed for the administration of large estates differed, in important respects, from that adopted for merchants accounts.(3) The former had become the 'Account Charge and Discharge' system where the main emphasis was on the prevention of embezzlement by the estate factor. The latter used the Italian Method. Despite the widespread use of the 'Account Charge and Discharge' method, few of the 18th century accounting authors discuss it; those who did discuss estate accounting seem to have been anxious to demonstrate the universal applicability(4) and superiority of the Italian Method. They believed that this method could answer both the estate owner's need for a method which showed the outcome of the various 'accomptable branches' and his need for a system that would ensure justice in the principal/agent relationship.

14.2 Textbook Coverage of Estate Accounting

Several of the 18th century Scottish authors, including Malcolm, Mair, Gordon and Hamilton, discussed estate accounting in their books.

Alexander Malcolm described an Estate Accounting system, including 'Accompts of Charge and Discharge', in the appendices to both 'A New Treatise of Arithmetick and Book-keeping' (1718) and 'A Treatise of Book-keeping' (1731). In the second book there are few changes from the material contained in the first but the changes that are made, are significant.(5)

Gordon in his second book-keeping text includes a 'Model of Accountantship, calculated for the Landed Gentleman, the Chamberlain, and the Farmer'.(6) At the beginning of the book he optimistically claims for this section that " ... the Leger ... may be so short, and withall so distinct, that it will prove an amusement than a trouble to a Gentleman of fortune to keep his own accounts".(7) Gordon's 'model' is in the form of a worked 'case study'. There is no accompanying text, apart from two brief footnotes, but some interesting details can, nevertheless, be obtained from the illustration.

Mair says nothing of estate accounting in 'Bookkeeping Methodiz'd' but he does consider the topic in chapter IX of the appendix to 'Bookkeeping Moderniz'd'.(8) This chapter bears some resemblance to the material given by Gordon but it is better constructed and easier to follow. Mair claims that, although the example that he provides is concerned with the accounts of a landed estate, "from the specimen here exhibited, it will be easy to frame books proper for the purpose of the farmer."(9)

Robert Hamilton describes and illustrates 'Accompts of Charge and Discharge' in Volume I of his 'Introduction to Merchandize' (1777). Volume II (1779) has a chapter on 'Land-Stewards Accompts'.(10)

The current chapter will be largely based on the works of these four writers but others will be referred to as appropriate. In particular the English writer Roger North will be quoted at times because Malcolm had clearly read his book and there is some similarity in the treatment of certain topics although Malcolm's writing is in no sense a copy of North's.(11) Reference will also be made to an important 'Memorial on Estate Accounting' which was written by an 18th century Edinburgh accountant, Francis Farquharson, for the assistance of the Duke of Gordon.(12) This memorial is evidence that practising accountants were recommending the use of the Italian Method for estate accounting.

It will be necessary to consider the accounts of both the estate owner and those of his chamberlain. Although some of an estate's income and expense would often be connected with its farming activities (and this will be discussed), farming accounts will be looked at, in more detail, in the next chapter.

14.3 The Accounting Period

In one important respect estate accounting at the beginning of the 18th century was more modern than merchants accounts at the same date. This was because it was common in estate accounting to have accounts prepared at regular (annual) intervals. The 'crop year' system was often used. Under this system the period from (say) Whitsun 1720 to Whitsun 1721 was referred to as 'Crop (or Cropt) 1720'.(13)

Malcolm considers the question of the appropriate date for commencing the accounting year: " ... consider what is the best time for beginning the Accompts; if the Rent is all Money. the Beginning of the Year or of January(14) will do well, and the Accompt of Arrears will be what's due preceeding Martinmas last(15); but when there is Oats, Barley, &c. which is commonly payable betwixt Christmas and Candlemass, it will be best to begin the Accompts 1st of March, that there may be as little Arrears as possible; beside what is resting(16) of Corns, &c. can now be charged in Money, because the Term of Delivery is past, and before this Time, there is commonly a published Rate set upon Farm Corns &c. at which Rate the Tenants are obliged to pay to their Masters what they failed to deliver. In each Tenants Accompt, let there be as many Columns as there are Species of Rents payable by that Tenant, with the Money Columns last ... "(17)

The adoption of a regular pattern of annual accounts resulted in much closer attention being paid to accruals and prepayments at the financial year end than there was when merchants accounts were being explained. There was also an interesting development in accounting for depreciation, a topic which is completely ignored in the textbook treatment of merchants accounts. These aspects will be considered later in the chapter but first the recommended books of account will be described.

14.4 The Estate Owner's Books

In the appendix to 'A New Treatise of Arithmetick and Book-keeping', Malcolm discusses Estate Accounting.(18) He sets the scene for his discussion by making certain assumptions: " ... I take for Example, a Gentleman of a plentiful Fortune, whom I shall suppose willing to bestow Time and Pains in keeping regular Accompts of his Concerns, upon prospect both of Pleasure and Profit from his Labour. The subject Matter of the Accompts to be kept is, in general, the Product of his Estate, and the disposal thereof. But there are many accomptable Branches here, so that a mere Cash-Accompt of Receipts and Expence will not serve: For I shall suppose a Gentleman is concerned with Rents, which he either gathers himself, or by Factors or Bayliffs,(19) who are accomptable to him; with the Management of Lands in Hand: with Interest Money received or paid, or both; with House-keeping, which he ought to take accompt of; with the ordinary and extraordinary Expences of his Retinue and Pleasures, &c. ... And the chief Encouragement to this Work is, That by a regular Accompt, where every Thing is carefully Recorded, a Man can discover what is the Occasion of his Loss, what Branch has failed, and consequently he will foresee the Way to help such Misfortune for the Time to come, if the Fault was his own, and if not, it is at least a Pleasure to be conscious of this".(20) Malcolm suggests that the following books are required:

A Waste Book " ... containing a plain Narration of all Things as they occur ... ".(21) As with a merchant's waste book, this book would commence with a " ... full and exact Inventory ... of all your Personal Estate viz ready Money, Jewels and Plate, and all Manner of Household Furniture, Books and Pictures, &c Stock of Corns, and Cattle upon the Grounds in Hand, Corn, Meal, &c in the Grannaries, and other Kind of moveable Effects, the seed in the Ground, also the Stores of Provision of all Sorts which are at present in the House, Money lying out upon Interest and Arrears of Rents due by Tenants, &c. &c."

Roger North also recommended the maintenance of a waste-book but Francis Farquharson's memorandum to the Duke of Gordon does not list it as being necessary.

A Cash Book "This is a very necessary Book, because much of a Gentleman's Concerns runs thro' his Cash; and this Book ought to be filled up daily".(22) This is very similar to the wording used by North(23) and both North and Malcolm state that the cash book would be written up from the waste book.(24) It is interesting that the cash book receives more emphasis in estate accounting than in discussions of merchants accounts. Malcolm advocates balancing, and carrying forward a balance, at the end of each page of the Cash Book rather than carrying forward the totals of both sides. Farquharson describes a cash book in his Memorandum on Estate Accounts and he makes the practical point that all the Duke's petty expenses could be entered as a single "Slump article at the end of the month". This 'slump article' is a balancing figure which is calculated as follows:

"1766 May 26 Cash received to be Debites ...		£3,000 - -
Cash paid Creditor	£1500.	
Cash in hand	1400...	2,900 - -
Deficiency		£ 100 - -

Therefore at the ballancing, Cash is to be credited thus
1766 May 26 By Cash laid out in pocket expenses since the last ballancing ..... £100 - -"

Farquharson also suggests that the vouchers should be filed.(25)

Malcolm considers that, if the estate is not too large, a Waste Book and a Cash Book might be the only books necessary. Although this would not constitute a double entry system it could be perfectly satisfactory and answer all the estate owner's needs. In such cases Malcolm suggests that a monthly Digest or Abstract could be prepared with the payments summarised under appropriate headings such as Household Expenses, Apparel, Wages, Interest, Books etc. and similarly the receipts analysed into such categories as Rent, Interest, Cattle Sales, Corn Sales etc. " ... and if all these accomptable Titles be written down successively under one another, and the Page divided into 12 Columns, bearing upon the Top the 12 Months, then this will serve for the whole Year's Abstract, and must therefore be set in some separate Place of the Book ... ".(26)

A Book of Accompts with Tenants This would be a book " ... where in distinct Places every ones Charge and Discharge may be plainly and fairly written, without any great Formality of Stile; tho' you may give it the Show of a Debtor and Creditor Side ... it will be so much more the distinct ... ".(27) Each account would open with any arrears of rent and then the debit for the current year's rent would be entered. Malcolm stresses that this is not part of the double entry system, stating that "The current Years Rent is not to be taken into the Inventory; but according as it is paid, so it will be entred in the Books".(28)

Malcolm points out the advantages of closing off the accounts in this book as the balances are agreed. The book may be extended to include accounts with other persons with whom the gentleman has dealings. North also recommends the use of a 'Book of Accompts stated with Tenants'.(29)

A Book of Petty Accompts This book is considered useful for recording dealings with Servants and Workmen.(30) North also suggests the use of this book.(31)

A Book of Real Accompts This book would contain an " ... Accompt of Cattle, Corn, and other Stock or Furniture; to know at all Times, what you have, and how it is disposed of".(32) This book may be combined with the Book of Petty Accompts.

A Ledger The above books are deemed to be essential but for a full accounting system, Malcolm (and North) consider that a Ledger, and possibly a Journal, should be kept. Malcolm introduces and discusses the following ledger accounts: 'Accompts of Household Furniture, Books, etc'; 'Accompt of House-keeping' (to include the expenses of 'apparel', the cost of educating children and the expense and income from orchards and gardens); 'Accompt of Equipages' (the cost of horses, coaches etc. and expenses of the 'retinue, parade or sport'); 'Accompt of Cash in the House Keepers Hands' (written up each month from statements provided by the housekeeper); 'Accompt of Husbandry' (debited with seed, utensils, wages, 'cattle of the plough' etc and credited with the proceeds from the sale of corn, corn taken for housekeeping and corn taken to the granary); 'Accompt of Grazing' (debited with opening stock of cattle, dairy utensils, wages and expenses, credited with revenue from sale of cattle, wool, dairy produce and with goods taken by the housekeeper); 'Granary Accompt' (debited with opening stock and corn received from Husbandry and from tenants); 'Land Rents Accompt'; Personal Accounts; 'Accompt for the Steward'; 'Profit and Loss Accompt'; 'Balance Accompt' and the Estate (Stock) Account.

In Gordon's illustration of a 'Model of Accountantship, calculated for the Landed Gentleman, the Chamberlain, and the Farmer'(33), the opening inventory includes the following: Cash, Cash with a Banker, Rent in Arrears, Bills Receivable, Corn in Stack (Corn seems to be a generic term covering wheat, barley, oats, peas and beans), Corn in Granaries, Corn Manufactured (oatmeal), Provender (hay) and Cattle. The details from the inventory, are journalised and posted to the 'leger' with the corresponding credit being to Moveable Estate Account (Stock Account). Various liabilities are also listed and debited to the same Moveable Estate Account.

Where the estate is managed by a chamberlain there will

be an account for him. Malcolm discusses the contents of this account which will be opened with a debit balance which represents arrears of rent etc outstanding at the beginning of the accounting year. During the year any cash received from the chamberlain will be credited to the account but most of the detail will be taken from the Account of Charge and Discharge that he submits at the year end.

Malcolm advocates a separate ledger for dealings with tenants. He acknowledges that a criticism of his system of estate accounting might be that it employs too many books. He believes, however, that a single ledger would not be so useful since many of the accounts relate to dealings with "a simple Kind of People, who will require very particular and distinct Accompts, and every thing said in the plainest Manner". For this reason he believes that it is better to keep a separate book for dealings with tenants; additionally this, and other subsidiary books, will relieve the ledger of detail.

Farquharson's memorial for the Duke of Gordon also proposes separate books (ledgers) for certain types of transaction. Specifically he suggests: 'A Book for recording the Chamberlains Accompts', 'A Book for the Dukes Household and family Expense' and 'A Book for the Dukes farm'. He illustrates some of the accounts which should appear in the ledger and states that the aim should be to "show at a view the state of all the Dukes affairs".

14.5 Accruals in Estate Accounting

Malcolm shows a concern with accruals in his discussion of estate accounting which is completely absent from his section on merchants accounts. This can clearly be seen in his treatment of interest. He says: "Erect an Accompt of Interest Debtor for all you pay, and Creditor for what you receive; but the best way is, to place this Accompt the

Interest at the Term when they are incurred or become due, and place the same also to the Persons Accompt to, or by whom due; and when paid, charge or discharge them. But at making up the general balance, it will be fit to calculate and state what's incurred to that Time, (whether it is a Term of Payment or not) that the balance may give a compleat View of the present State of affairs. After this close the Accompt with Profit and Loss."(34)

Malcolm's discussion of the Accompt of Housekeeping and the Accompt of Equipages is interesting. In both of these accounts the debit side is a mixture of assets and expenses. The material dealing with the Accompt of Housekeeping is reproduced here: "ACCOMPT of Housekeeping, Make it Debtor for all the Utensils of Kitchen, Dairy, Brew-House, &c. and for the Store of Provision at present in the House, as per Inventory, and for what's afterwards purchased, also, for all the Expences of House-Keeping, as Money expended, Corn and Cattle, &c. brought in for the use of the House, Wages paid to Servants belonging properly to the House-Keeping. It is Creditor for what is due to the servant of Wages at making up the Inventory, and afterwards for all the Waste which happen to be sold of that which was formerly brought in, and charged to that Accompt."(35)

The above quotation makes it clear that any accrued wages at the beginning of the year are to be credited to the account. Malcolm also provides instructions on balancing the account at the end of the year but, in 'A New Treatise of Arithmetick and Book-keeping', he neglects to make any reference to accruals at the year end.

Later Malcolm realised that this section was unclear (or incomplete) and in the corresponding section in his second book the discussion is amplified. The passage in 'A New Treatise' reads as follows: "This accompt is closed with Balance for the Utensils and Provisions remaining, and after this with Profit and Loss for Difference, which is the neat Expenses of House-Keeping within the Time of the Duration of this Accompt."(36) This is corrected in 'A Treatise of Book-keeping' to read: "This Accompt is closed, Creditor, By Ballance, for the Value of the Utensils and Provisions remaining, and Debtor, To Ballance, for what is unpaid of the Servants Wages, for which it was at the Beginning made Debtor; after this it is closed with Profit and Loss, for the Difference, which is the neat expenses of House-keeping, within the Time of the Duration of this Accompt."(37)

14.6 The Estate Capital Account

The authors distinguish between the Heritable (or Real) Estate and the Moveable Estate. Mair describes the position as follows: "The landed gentlemen (sic) ... has, properly speaking, two estates, ... , the one moveable, the other heritable. The moveable part, or the moveables, are his ready money, the victual he has on hand, his cattle, furniture, equipage, and utensils, with the debts due to him; the heritable part is the mansionhouse and farms, the rents arising from which, when received, become moveables."(38)

Mair did not open separate 'stock' accounts for each type of 'estate' but Gordon did. It was not, however, considered essential for the recorded figure of estate capital to contain an estimate of the capital value of the heritable property, even when separate Real and Personal Estate accounts were used, in such cases the Real Estate Account might be used solely to record the rental income derived from the heritable estate. In addition to separate accounts for the Heritable Estate and the Moveable Estate, Gordon also provided a Current Account for the estate owner. The balances of this Current Account and the Heritable Estate Account were transferred to the Moveable Estate

Account at the end of the year.

If it was wished to show the capital value of the heritable estate in the estate books, Malcolm explained how this could be estimated by capitalising the rents. In the 18th century it was common for part of the rent to be paid in kind rather than in cash, this 'victual' rent had first to be converted into money, then " ... reckoning at 20 (or as many as you please) Years Purchase, the Sum is your real Estate, in Distinction from what is called the personal Estate, consisting of moveable Effects, as Money, Cattle, House-Furniture, Arrears of Rents, &c.".(39) The figure of 20 years assumes an interest rate of 5% which was the legal maximum at the time that Malcolm was writing.(40) Malcolm, however, considers that this calculation and refinement 'is needless'.

14.7 The Home Farm

Gordon's example provides an account for the home farm of an estate (the Mainse of Fullhall) which is cultivated by or for the proprietor. This account calculates the profit or loss from operating the farm. Although farm accounting will be considered in the next chapter, it is appropriate to briefly examine Gordon's material in the context of estate accounting since the procedures that he suggests are relatively sophisticated.

The debits to the Mainse of Fullhall Accompt include the costs of wages, hay, manure, draining, reaping, land tax, repairs and inclosing but there are also certain notional charges. There are charges made for the rent of the farm (credited to the Heritable Estate Account) and for the consumption of wheat, oats, barley, peas and beans (credited to Corn in Granaries Account). On the Credit side the income from the sale of dairy produce is measured by the cash received but other produce is credited at current market prices. There is a notional income receivable from the grazing of family cattle. The profit from the farm is taken, at the year end, to Sir John Fullerton's Account Current. It is clear that it is considered useful to attempt to measure the profitability of the individual parts of the estate's activities.

14.8 The Chamberlain's Accounts

Where the estate owner employs a chamberlain or steward to collect the estate rents and manage the estate, the chamberlain will keep accounts of his transactions and the textbooks discuss the form of these accounts. The books kept by the steward will be very similar to those that the landowner would keep and Robert Hamilton's treatment of estate accounting is strictly a discussion of the books that would be kept by the 'land-steward'. Hamilton advocates that the books should be kept "on the principles of double entry" but he suggests that "the form need not be rigidly observed". He names only two books, the journal and the ledger. Malcolm gives a longer list: a 'Waste-Book', a 'Cash Book', a 'Book of Real Accompts' (for dealing with other "real Effects, besides money, they have taken the charge of") and a 'Book of Accompts with Tenants', but the last three books could be considered as part of the ledger.

14.9 A Rental Book

Rents constituted an important part of the income of an estate and, since the collection of rents would often be delegated to a chamberlain, the rent records are discussed at this point.(41) Malcolm suggests that a Rent Roll of the Estate should be kept.(42) This should be updated frequently "because Rents rise and fall sometimes" and he recommends that the records should be kept in a Rental-Book.

Money was scarce in Scotland, particularly at the

Rental of the Estate of Sunnybanks, for crop 1768.

Farms.	Tenants.	Infield acres.	Outfield acres.	Wheat, 18 s.	Barley, 14 s.	Meal, 12 s.	Ducks. 1 s.	Hens. 1 s.	Convertion. L. s.	Money. L.	Amount. L. s.
No 1. Woodhead,	John Kier,	200	180	80	80	80	12	36	178 8	65	243 8
2. Hazelfield,	James Brown,	190	160	85	90		24	24	141 18	100	241 18
3. Cowlairs,	George Gray,	210	200	75	75	70	36	24	165 —	150	315 —
4. Carmore,	Joseph Hill,	230	210		90	90	30	30	120 —	110	230 —
5. Glenside,	Andrew Bell,	240	120	50	50	50	48	36	114 4	150	264 4
6. Craigends,	David Young,	260	190	60	70	80	42	42	155 4	160	315 4
7. Moortown,	Allan Key,	250	140	70		60	18	48	102 6	90	192 6
8. Rosemount,	Sir James ——	210	190							200	200 —
Total,		1800	1390	420	455	430	210	240	977 —	1025	2002 —

Total amount of real rent,	— —	L. 2002
Duty to the crown,	— — —	2
Free rent,	— — —	2000

Land tax, ministers stipends, schoolmasters salaries, and other public burdens, paid by the tenants.

MAIR'S SPECIMEN 'RENTAL'

beginning of the century, and it was common for part at least of the rent to be paid in kind.(43) The details would be recorded in the Rental Book in analysis columns.

Each page of this book would be: " ... divided in Columns for the following Uses, let the Names of the Grounds and Farms be first upon the left Hand, in the next set the Name of the Tenants; then in so many distinct Columns every Kind of Rent which is paid, as Oats, Barley, Capons, Weathers, &c. and Money in the last Place; the Columns being inscribed with these Names, set under the Quantities payable ... "(44)

Farquharson in his memorandum prepared for the Duke of Gordon, gives a description of the Rental Book which is similar to that provided by Malcolm, but he also recommends the preparation of a "List of all the Publick and private Burdens payable out of each (estate), whether payable by the Heritor or tennent, such as Ministers stipends, Schoolmasters Salarys, Land Tax, a note of the valued rents; feu and teind duties, annual allowances to Chamberlains, Clerks, Forresters, officers etc ... ".

Hamilton seems to assume that the detailed rent records would be kept in the ledger but neither he nor Malcolm give any examples of rent records in their books. Gordon and Mair, however, do provide illustrations of a Rent Roll which they term a 'Rental of an Estate'.(45) Mair's example (of the "Rental of the Estate of Sunnybanks, for crop 1768") is reproduced here.

Stevenson gives details of the dates at which the rent is typically payable: " ... Money Rent is payle. at Candlemas and Whitsunday 1761, each of these Terms 1/2. The Victual payle. between Christmas 1760 and Candlemas 1761. The Kain payle. from Candlemas 1761 to Easter."(46)

Although the component parts of the rent are due at a various times throughout the year, the whole amount is usually charged to the tenant in the Rental Book at the beginning of the year (1 November). Hamilton, however, says that this should be done "at the terms when the rents fall due".

In Mair's example about half of the rent is shown as being payable in various forms of farm produce, wheat, barley, meal, ducks and hens. Here, in 1768, the victual rent is converted into cash for accounting purposes, but the payment is partly in kind. In the case of the poultry rent the ducks and hens are paid over but the tenants have agreed to settle the meal-rent by paying the calculated cash amount (by accepting bills for payment at a later date). Each tenant has an account with appropriate analysis columns for recording the rent charge and the subsequent payment (discharge) of this.

Other authors do not convert the victual rent into cash. In such cases the Estate (Capital) Account or the Rental Account will have multiple analysis columns to record the various types of rent. Hamilton describes both methods. Malcolm's discussion of the problem is as follows: "In such Estates where there is Oats, Barley, &c. paid in the Rent, the total yearly Rent is not known by the Rental-Book in Money Value, because the Price of these Changes; but the true Design of a Rental-Book is no more than to know the yearly Rent, of every Species ... "(47)

Stevenson's illustrative Waste-book records the sale of the Barley Rent of an Estate: "I have this Day agreed with Peter Brewer that he is to take all the Barley Rent of my Estate of Greenside, being 24 Chalders, which the several Tenants are obliged to deliver to him betwixt and Candlemas next, under the Penalty of 20 d. per Boll, in case of failure, agreeable to a Contract betwixt us of this Date, he being obliged to pay me at the Rate of 11 s. per Boll, 1/2 at Candlemas, and the other Half 6 Months after, and I have given him my Precepts upon the ... tenants ... ".(48)

In Mair's example, not only does the estate owner sell the right to the wheat and barley rent, but also he is able to do this for a higher price than that used earlier when converting the rent to money. A profit is recorded and this is taken to the Profit and Loss Account in contrast to the rental income which is taken directly to the Estate (Capital) Account.

Malcolm notes that sub totals can be calculated for each 'Mannor' or 'Baronry'. "And at last make an Abstract of the Whole for the Totals of each Mannor; the Sum of this Abstract is the Total Year's Rent".(49) He goes on to say that "If you please to make another Money Column, in it you may set the yearly Rent according to the Valuation by which publick Taxes are paid, and this you may call the Parish Value."(50) He also discusses the question of 'teinds'.(51) Frequently the teind duty payable by the landowner was transferred, by him, to the tenant, Malcolm advises that:

"If the Teind payable out of the Lands is included in the Rent-roll, it must be deducted from the Sum, the Remainder is the neat Rent belonging to the Master; but if you put that in the Rental, it is best set down in a separate Article; and in summing up the Columns, keep the Rents and Teinds distinct."(52)

Other potentially useful information can be recorded in the Rental. In Mair's illustration, for example, the land is divided into 'infield' and 'outfield' and the acreage of each is given. The infield is the plot of land nearest to the farmhouse - this land had more attention paid to it than the larger outfield which was poorer and often badly tended.(53) Gordon uses the term 'arable acres' for 'infield' and 'improveable acres' for 'outfield'.

14.10 Accompts Charge and Discharge

The account charge and discharge system is a system of accounting, and associated audit procedures, which emphasises the stewardship function. "The steward was charged with the sums for which he was responsible (opening balance, plus receipts), and discharged of his legitimate payments; the end balance showed what he must hand over to his lord or keep in his charge for the next period."(54) Chatfield says that the system was developed in 15th century Scotland for controlling King James I's revenue(55) but Jones has pointed out that the English Exchequer Pipe Rolls system is very similar and much older.(56) North, writing in 1714, equated the two methods by referring to 'charge and discharge' as the 'Chequer Way'.(57)

Accepting that in origin the system was not Scottish,it was popular in Scotland where it has been used almost down to the present. In 1903 Lisle could write: "In Scotland the accounts of many institutions and societies are published in the form of Accounts Charge and Discharge, ..."(58)

Malcolm and Hamilton discuss the Accompt Charge and Discharge system and Hamilton describes its form as follows: "An accompt of charge and discharge ... contains, on one side, the articles entrusted to the care of a factor, for which he is accountable; on the other side; the manner in which he has rendered accompt for the same; and concludes with the balance which remains in his hands, or which is due to him by his employer."(59)

Brodie illustrates this by the heading of the example of an Account of Charge and Discharge that he provides:

ACCOMPT of CHARGE and DISCHARGE by THOS. TRUSTY, Steward to J. OPULENT, Esq; of BELMOUNT.

The said Thomas Trusty his charge,

1777.		Wheat Qu.	L.	s.	d.
Jan. 1.	To balance of former accompt,	—	100	—	—
	To arrears due by tenants, per accompt,	500	460	—	—
	To wheat in granary,	700			
May 15.	To rent of the estate of Belmount for one year, per rental,	600	1200	—	—
Dec. 31.	To value of wheat 300 qrs. sold, per accompt,	—	450	—	—
		1800	2210	—	—

The said Thomas Trusty, his discharge.

		Wheat Qu.	L.	s.	d.
Dec. 31.	By cash paid J. Opulent's order, per accompt,	—	1500	—	—
	By wheat sold to sundries, per accompt,	300			
	By wheat delivered to J. Badger, per order,	1200			
	By arrears due by tenants, per accompt,	180	460	—	—
	By debts outstanding for wheat sold,	—	120	—	—
	By wheat remaining in granary,	120			
	By a year's salary,	—	50	—	—
	By balance in the steward's hands,	—	80	—	—
		1800	2210	—	—

HAMILTON'S ILLUSTRATIVE

ACCOMPT CHARGE AND DISCHARGE

King Edward's-Castle, Twentieth October, MDCCXXI.

John Faithful, Steward.

This Day, James Royal, Esq. hath given me in Charge, all his Estates in the Country, and all Debts due to him by Bond, or otherwise, appointing me his Steward, or Chamberlain, to collect all his Rents, Sums of Money, and Interest upon Bonds, &c. and to dispose of the Grain, and Poultry, &c. after the Family has no further Demand on the Tennants, all which I Accompt for, as follows, viz."(60)

Brodie then provides 'A Yearly Abstract, or General Distribution' in bilateral form, with the left hand side headed 'Charge' and the right headed 'Discharge'. This is supported by the following schedules and accounts:

A Rent Roll,

An account for each tenant,	)The accounts are in bilateral
	)form, with each debit side
An account for each debtor,	)headed 'Charge' and each
	)credit side headed 'Discharge'

A list of tradesmen's bills paid by the steward,

A list of wages on 'Improvements',

A list of wages paid to household staff.

Hamilton's illustrative specimen of an 'Accompt of Charge and Discharge' is reproduced. His comments on this are as follows: "Stewards on landed estates, and collectors of the revenue, generally make up their accompts in this form. The student will observe, that instead of charging the several articles at the time they are received, the whole sum which the factor is employed to collect is charged at once; but any part which he is not able to recover before the accompt be settled, is admitted as an article of discharge, unless the factor be bound as cautioner(62) for the payments. If there be any goods intrusted to his care they are charged and discharged in separate columns. And, as the design of the accompt is to exhibit the state of the affairs under his management in a concise point of view, the amount of the articles alone is inserted, and the particulars of each are drawn out in separate accompts, to which the general accompt of charge and discharge refers."(63)

The account is essentially a statement of resources received and dispersed by the steward not a statement of the estate's income and expenditure. It could thus be a defective vehicle for assessing the estate's position. Against this, the merit of the system was its simplicity. North comments: "For when you talk to plain Men, of the Relation and Mutual Dependence of Accompts, and the Perpetual Balance, they are amazed, and straight Demand to know plainly, what is theirs, and what not? Therefore the Chequer, and most ordinary Ways of Render, are to run the whole Accompt, however large, and diffused, into Two Articles only collatable as Mine and Thine; or Charge and Discharge: For that answers the plainest Demand, what all this is for, and all that is against you."(64)

In view of the systems widespread, and continued, use in Scotland down to the present(65), one would have assumed that it would have warranted a prominent place in most of the Scottish texts. It is, therefore, peculiar that only three of the 18th century Scottish writers on accounting (Malcolm, Brodie and Hamilton) describe the operation of the system.

The reason may be that 'accompts charge and discharge' was not considered as part of the Italian System. Furthermore it is not a complete system but rather the term describes a statement that could be readily prepared from the books if the chamberlain used the Italian Method. Malcolm integrated the method into the double entry system but Hamilton's discussion of the subject is not in part IV of his book (which deals with Italian Book-keeping) but in part III on 'Bills, Invoices, Accompts, Monies, Weights, and Measures'. Brodie also distinguishes his method of estate accounting from the method of 'Debitor and Creditor.'

Textbook-writers may have considered the subject as outside the scope of a book-keeping text but additionally (or alternatively) they may have assumed for themselves the evangelical role of promoting the merits of the Italian System against inferior systems. They would certainly be aware of the charge/discharge system and the terms charge and discharge were, not infrequently, used in explaining the Italian Method. Hamilton recognises that: "An ACCOMPT of CHARGE and DISCHARGE is of the same nature as an accompt current."(66) The tenants' accounts in the estate books could also be viewed in this way and Malcolm proposes that the tenants' accompts should be designed so that " ... every ones Charge and Discharge may be plainly and fairly written ... "(67)

14.11 Accounting for Depreciation and the Audit of Investment Decisions

In his discussion of 'land-stewards accounts' Hamilton suggests a 'going concern' historical cost approach for the valuation of a fixed asset. He says: "If a sum of money, suppose L.500, be expended to improve the farm, which the proprietor does not expect to draw back in less than 10 years, the whole sum, at the end of the first year, is considered as part of the stock on the farm; but, at the end of the second, when one-tenth part, or L.50, was expected to be drawn back, the remainder only, or L.450, should be considered as part of the stock; and this allowance is gradually diminished L.50 each year, till it be exhausted. If no returns be expected for several years, the allowance is not diminished till the time when benefit was expected.

This, however, should be regulated by the hopes entertained when the money was expended, and not by the success of the improvements; and then the balance of the farm-accompt, in the successive years, will show how far the improvements have exceeded or fallen short of expectation".(68)

The foregoing is interesting as an early, if rudimentary, discussion of depreciation.(69) The quotation also shows a recognition of the problem involved in relating ex post reports of an investment decision's outcome to the ex ante appraisal which led to the decision. This problem is still unsolved but Hamilton's view that depreciation charges "should be regulated by the hopes entertained when the money was expended, and not by the success of the improvements" is relevant to the continuing discussion.

14.12 Estate Accounting and the Development of the Accountancy Profession

Eighteenth century Scottish estate owners needed frequent access to accounting, financial and legal expertise and owners of large estates relied heavily on their 'doers'. Although overstated, there is a substantial core of truth in Lockhart's observations on this topic: "The country gentlemen of Scotland, from whatever causes, are generally very much in debt. Their writers, or, as they call them, their agents or doers, are of necessity acquainted with the many secrets which men in debt must have; they are themselves the bankers and creditors of their clients. In short, when a gentleman changes his man of business, his whole affairs must undergo a complete revolution and convulsion; and in Scotland, it is a much easier thing to get rid of one's wife, than of one's doer."(70)

The demand for such services gave impetus to the young accountancy profession which was developing from those Edinburgh lawyers who began to specialise in accounting in the second half of the 18th century. These accountants were able to provide four separate (but linked) services for those connected with large estates. Firstly, the large landowners were active in the agricultural improvement movement, this required funds and the accountants were able to give advice. Secondly, when estate owners found themselves in financial difficulties, accountants were often appointed as trustees or judicial factors. Thirdly, following the '45 Rebellion, many estates were forfeited and the need to keep accounts for these gave work to a new profession of accountancy.(71) Fourthly, accountants were needed to undertake the audit of estate accounts which were particularly necessary when estates were in the hands of trustees during the minority of a landowner. The agricultural improvement movement was strong in Aberdeenshire. Speaking of that region Grant notes that " ... between 1667 and 1771 a large proportion of the county passed into the effective control of the wealthy landlords and landed aristocracy. From holding under 30 per cent of the county in 1667 they had advanced to hold about 50 per cent by 1771."(72) This advance was made despite the damage to fortunes of many major families caused by such set backs as their involvement in the '15 and the '45 rebellions.

This chapter has included several references to an interesting specification of a 'model' estate accounting system, prepared, in 1766 by Francis Farquharson, for the Fourth Duke of Gordon, when the Duke assumed management of his estate from 'his Tutors and Curators'. Farquharson was to continue as the Duke's accountant until his (Farquharson's) death. This appointment called for more than just technical expertise, considerable tact was required since Francis was not only a professional advisor but also the confidant of both the Duke and his wife (Jane Maxwell). This was a difficult position as the Duke was anxious about his wife's spendthrift tendencies and the duchess was continually complaining of the inadequacy of her annual allowance of £4,000.(73)

14.13 Summary

Estate accounting in the 17th century had been based on the account charge/discharge system but those 18th century accounting writers who discussed estate accounting, advocated the Italian Method (or some single entry variation of this). The emphasis in estate accounting was on control and accountability and the charge/discharge system had developed specifically to meet this need. It was not designed to assist with the measurement of profitability and efficiency but it could give some limited help in these areas. Pollard has pointed out that the system: " ... provided a general view of the estate, and since incomes, such as rents, sales of timber, etc., were usually grouped together in some commonsense way, e.g. by manors, unchanged over the years, it also provided a kind of check on the efficiency of the estate, as it was possible to compare from year to year the movement of rents between village and village, or the proportions of rents in arrears, or, on the expenditure side, the salaries or other expenses on the upkeep of the farms."(74)

The 18th century writers were convinced however that the double entry method was far superior and few of them even mentioned accounts charge and discharge. They believed that the Italian Method could not only achieve the desired element of control but that it could also show the profitability of the various accountable branches much more directly and it could assist in decision-making. Gordon's use of an imputed rent charge to the Home Farm is clearly intended to give the estate owner information which would help in decision making. Malcolm similarly compares the profit obtained by farming with the rent that could be obtained by letting. In the estate ledger there will be an 'Accompt of the Husbandry' and an 'Accompt of the Grazing'. Malcolm states that these two accounts can show the " ... Advantage of keeping Land in Hand, and whether you make the Rent of it; for these ought also to be in the Rent-Roll at what Value you think fit ... ".(75) In some respects estate accounts seem to have been more closely geared to answering questions of profitability and efficiency than were merchants accounts.

CHAPTER 15

FARM ACCOUNTS

15.1 Agricultural Progress

Scottish agriculture at the beginning of the 18th century was in a poor state. A basic form of crop rotation (barley one year, oats the next) was normally used. The quality of the grain was extremely poor so that commonly only three seeds of oats were harvested from one sown. The farm worker would cut this meagre harvest with a sickle, not a scythe, and would thresh it with a flail. Agricultural implements were crude and unwieldy and efficiency was further hampered by the absence of enclosures. The land was frequently farmed on a run-rig basis.(1) The difficulty of communication and transportation was another hindrance to progress.

In the latter part of the 17th century three Acts had been passed which were designed to improve the efficiency of agricultural operations in Scotland. First a 1669 Act provided for the fencing of land.(2) Then two 1695 Acts authorised the division of common land among local land owners(3) and the consolidation of land held on run-rig tenancy.(4)

As the 18th century passed improvements took place; these developments were led by the nobility and gentry. The Honourable Society of Improvers was founded in 1723. New vegetables were introduced, potatoes (1739), turnips and cabbage and the average weight of animals doubled over the century. From 1750 onwards considerable improvements took place. Marshes were drained, scientific crop rotation was introduced, the scythe replaced the sickle, iron ploughs replaced wooden ploughs and threshing machines (invented by James Meikle) came into use. This period is often referred to as the Agricultural Revolution. The Lothians, and later the Aberdeen area, were to the fore in the agricultural improvement movement. In the north and west sheep farming prospered leading to unemployment and consequential emigration.

15.2 Farm Accounting - Single Entry Systems

Although, in general, the textbook authors were convinced that the Italian Method of Book-keeping had universal applicability, some contemporary writers were not convinced of the usefulness of converting a mercantile accounting system to serve the uses of farmers. In 1771 the prolific English agricultural writer, Arthur Young (1741-1820) wrote: "It is not long ago since a specimen of accounts was laid before the public, consisting of several books, in imitation of merchant accounts; but I humbly think that too complicated methods should not be recommended, lest the farmer, instead of being enlightened, should be disgusted. The grand object is to keep a ledger, or an account for every article in the farm; in which an account should be opened for every field in the farm, or at least for every arable field, and one for all the grass. The farmer should in this book directly, without the intervention of a waste-book or a journal, enter all his expences; but, for doing this, he must take the trouble of dividing his rent to every field, so that the account may be complete, and not have an article for rent alone, unless it be a mere memorandum; and, before he balances his books at the end of the year, it is necessary for him first to cast up the sundry accounts, such as tythe - poor levey - various expences - and divide them in the same manner as rent."(5)

Arthur Young's viewpoint seems to be shared by Robert Hamilton (who includes a chapter on 'Farmers Accompts' in his 'Introduction to Merchandize') and also by David

Young,(6) a Perthshire Land-surveyor, who published his 'The Farmers Account-Book' about the year 1789. Neither of these advocates a full double entry system for farmers and they both suggest that an account should be kept for each field.

Hamilton suggests the use of a single book for the accounting records of farmers "as men of this profession have seldom leisure for much writing ... ".(7) He claims that this method is "very concise, yet generally sufficient". The method involves using a modified form of cash book. The receipts side has two columns, one for cash receipts and the other for the farmer's debtors as they arise. When (for example) a credit sale is made an entry is made in the debtors column, when the debtor pays a cross is placed against this entry and the cash received is entered in the cash column. On the credit side cash payments and credit purchases are dealt with in a similar manner. Once a month (or once a quarter) Lists of Debtors and Creditors are prepared from the uncrossed items in the debtors' and creditors' columns.

15.3 The Farmer's Profit and Loss Account

Hamilton assumes that the farmer will require an annual calculation of his farm's profitability and his method enables him to achieve this on an accruals basis rather than on a cash basis.

"Once a year we make out a state of the gain or loss as follows: To the sum of the cash-column on the Dr. side, or money drawn from the sale of the crop, we add the amount of debts due to us, and the estimated value of any part of the last crop that remains on hand. If any of the money received this year be in payment of the former crop, the sum of these articles must be subtracted. Thus we obtain the value of the crop. Then, to the sum of the cash-column, on the Cr. side, or amount of expence, we add the debts due by us, and subtract from the amount any sums that were paid for debts contracted before the present year. Thus we obtain the expense of raising the crop; and this, compared with its value, shows the gain or loss. But, if the value of the stock (i.e. the Capital) be increased or diminished, or money sunk for improvement, allowance must be made for it, as directed paragraph 31."(8)

David Young's book is a specialised book on farm accounting but not a text book as such. It is designed as an analysed account book for recording a year's activity (in considerable detail) but explanatory text and illustrative examples are added.(9) Included are tables designed for the annual calculation of profit.(10) Specimen figures are provided as an example(11) but no clear instructions are given as to how adjustments are to be made for changes in stock holdings, debtors, creditors etc.

It should be noted that the selection of an appropriate financial year is implicit in Hamilton's reference to the gain (or loss) on the crop. Elsewhere Hamilton had stressed the importance of establishing an appropriate year end date.(12)

15.4 Management Accounting for the Farmer

Hamilton suggests that the 'intelligent husbandman' will keep additional records to "record the progress of his operations, and ... the success of his management". One such book is the FIELD-BOOK. This book is to contain an account for each field and it is clear that Hamilton considers that the book would have a useful role in providing information for decision making purposes.

The expense and produce (income) of each field is entered into its register and "The register of the same field, in successive years, is continued from page to page, that the success of the different manures, rotations, and methods of treatment, may be easily compared, and a judgement formed of the whole, when continued for a sufficient length of time."(13)

Hamilton provides an example which illustrates the success of a rotation of wheat, barley and hay following a fallow period and a plentiful application of manure and lime. This example is reproduced below:

No. 1. Westfield, Soil light loam.			Expence	Produce
1772 10 Acres. rent 30s. L.15			L. s. d.	L. s. d.
	FALLOW			
Jan. 20 to 24	12 yokings ploughing			
May 18 to 21	10 ditto ditto			
30	2 ditto harrowing			
June 15 to 18	10 ditto ploughing across			
20	3 ditto harrowing			
	37 yokings at 2s.	L3 14 0		
	100 loads at 3s.	15 - -		
	200 bushels lime at 2s.	20 - -	38 14 -	
	WHEAT			
Aug. 15 to 19	10 yokings ploughing			
20 to 21	2 yokings harrowing			
	12 yokings at 2s.	L1 4 -		
20	21 Sown 4 quarters at 42s.	8 8 -		
Oct. 1	draining	4 -		
1773.				
Mar. 12	weeding	6 8		
Aug. 1 to 15	reaping at 5s.per acre	2 10 -	12 12 8	
	120 threaves wheat			
Nov. 20	40 quarters at 42s.			84 - -
	4 qrs. per acre			
	10 returns per feed			
	Carried Forward		51 6 8	84 - -

	Brought Forward		51 6 8	84 - -
	BARLEY			
Oct. 1 to 14	11 yokings ploughing			
Mar 15	10 ditto ditto			
April 1	2 ditto harrowing			
15 to 18	9 ditto ploughing			
19	2 ditto harrowing			
	34 yokings at 2s.	L3 8 -		
19	sown 5 qrs. barley at 25s.	6 5 -		
20	breaking clods	15 -		
1774				
Aug. 8	reaping at 5s. per acre	2 10 -	12 18 -	
	150 threaves barley			
Dec. 1	28 qrs. barley at 24s.			33 12 -
	2.8 qrs. per acre			
	5.6 returns per feed			
	HAY			
	1 qr. 4 bush. ryegrass sown with the barley, at 4s. per bushel	L2 8 -		
1775	200 lb. clover seed at 6d.	5 - -		
June 1	mowing at 2s. per acre	1 - -		
20	winning and stacking	2 10 -	10 18 -	
Sept.30	32 loads hay atL1:5s.	L40 - -		
	3.2 loads per acre			
	12 oxen pastured on the foggage 6 weeks at 2s. per week	7 4 -		47 4 -
	four years rent		60 - -	
			135 2 8	164 16 -

Hamilton explains some of the technical terms and the method used to calculate the cost of a yoking: "A yoking is the work performed by one man and two horses or cattle.(14) If four horses be yoked in the plough together and two men employed, this must be reckoned two yokings; and a like proportion for a greater or less number. There are generally two yokings a-day in summer and one in winter. To ascertain the expence of a yoking, add the charge of maintaining and upholding the cattle, the purchase, and repairs of plows, harrows, harness, &c. and divide the sum by the number of yokings in a year; to the quotient add the daily wages of the servant, and the sum is the expence per yoking. If the servant be paid by the year, his wages and maintenance may be divided by 300, allowing 65 days for Sundays, holidays, and accidents. The expence of reaping an acre is computed by dividing the whole expence of the harvest by the number of acres."(15)

Young is primarily interested in providing the farmer with a decision support system. In the introduction to 'The Farmers Account-Book', he stresses the importance of accounting as an aid in improving the profitability of the farm: "It is an object of great importance to every farmer, especially to young farmers, that they keep distinct accounts of expenditure and produce for every article by itself. The want thereof has ruined many. When a person is losing every year by his farm, and defective in keeping proper accounts, he cannot give a satisfactory account from whence such loss arises, either to himself or others; nor can he apply a proper remedy ... When regular accounts are kept, and where different schemes of improvement are tried, the produce will show which is the best."

Young also sees advantages to be obtained from comparisons made among farmers. "It would be the greatest advantage if every member of Farmers clubs were to keep such accounts, and compare them with one another."

He illustrates a record for individual fields with details which are similar to those provided by Hamilton.

Table XXXVII

Sketch of Expenditure relative to a Farm of 120 Acres, divided into six Fields of 20 Acres each, Carse Ground, or good Clay Soil, at 40s. per Acre of Rent.

	Total			Average		
Field No 1. and 2.						
for Wheat after Fallow	L.	s.	d.	L.	s.	d.
Five plowings of 20 acres, the first plowing in November	50	0	0	2	10	0
Forty bolls lime per acre at 2s. per boll, or 6d. per bushel	80	0	0	4	0	0
Ten tuns dung per acre, at 3s. per tun	30	0	0	1	10	0
Seed two bushels per acre, at 5s. per bushel	10	0	0		10	0
Cutting and carriage 15s. per acre, threshing 12 bolls per acre at 10d.	25	0	0	1	5	0
Two years rent, and incidents for articles that may be omitted	86	0	0	4	6	0
Total expence of a field for wheat	281	0	0	14	1	0

	Total			Average		
Produce Field No 1. and 2. of Wheat	L.	s.	d.	L.	s.	d.
Twelve bolls per acre, at 20s. per boll	240	0	0	12	0	0
Straw and chaff, at 4s. per boll	48	0	0	2	8	0
Total Produce of field of wheat	288	0	0	14	8	0

	Total			Average		
Field for Beans, No 3.	L.	s.	d.	L.	s.	d.
Three plowings of 20 acres, the first in November preceding	30	0	0	1	10	0
Twenty tuns dung per acre, at 3s. per tun, laid on in autumn	60	0	0	3	0	0
Seed beans six bushels per acre, at 3s. 6d. sown in February per bushel	21	0	0	1	1	0
Cutting, carriage and threshing 12 bolls per acre	21	0	0	1	1	0
Rent and incidents for articles that may be omitted	46	0	0	2	6	0
Total expence of a field for beans	178	0	0	8	18	0
Produce Field No 3. of Beans						
Twelve bolls per acre at 14s. per boll	168	0	0	8	8	0
Straw and chaff, at 3s. per boll	36	0	0	1	16	0
Total Produce field of beans	204	0	0	10	4	0

Field No 4. for Barley	L.	s.	d.	L.	s.	d.
Three plowings of 20 acres, the first in November or December	30	0	0	1	10	0
Seed barley, clover and hay seeds	23	0	0	1	3	0
Cutting, carriage and threshing 12 bolls per acre	21	0	0	1	1	0
Rent and incidents for articles that may be omitted	46	0	0	2	6	0
Total expence of field of barley	120	0	0	6	0	0
Produce Field No 4. of Barley						
Twelve bolls per acre, at 14s. per boll	168	0	0	8	8	0
Straw and chaff, at 2s 6d per boll	30	0	0	1	10	0
Total Produce field of barley	190	0	0	9	18	0

(addition error)

	Total			Average		
Field No 5. for Clover	L.	s.	d.	L.	s.	d.
Red Clover two cuttings of 20 acres, at 2s. 6d. each cutting	5	0	0	0	5	0
Winning and carriage, &c. part of which eat green in straw yard and stables	15	0	0	0	15	0
Rent and incidents for articles that may be omitted	46	0	0	2	6	0
Total expence of a field of clover	66	0	0	3	6	0
Produce of Field No 5. of Clover						
One cutting of 300 stone, or three tuns per acre, at 4d. per stone	100	0	0	5	0	0
Second cutting ditto 150 stone, at 3d. per stone	37	1	0	1	17	6
Total produce of field of clover	137	10	0	6	17	6

Field No 6. for Oats	L.	s.	d.	L.	s.	d.
Plowing and harrowing 20 acres, 15s. per acre	15	0	0	0	15	0
Seed three bushels per acre, at 3s. per bushel	9	0	0	0	3	0
Cutting, carriage and threshing 12 bolls per acre	22	0	0	1	1	0
Rent and incidents for articles that may be omitted	46	0	0	2	6	0
Total expence of a field for oats	92	0	0	4	5	0
Produce of Field No 6. of Oats						
Twelve bolls per acre, at 12s. per boll	144	0	0	7	4	0
Straw and chaff, at 3s. per boll	36	0	0	1	16	0
Total Produce of field of barley	180	0	0	9	0	0

	Total			Average		
Total produce for one year	999	0	0	8	6	6
Total expenses for one year	737	0	0	6	2	10
Balance Profit	262	0	0	2	3	8

Although these figures are for one year, Young is interested in making comparisons over several years and he presents an eight-year summary of the results of his farm at Woodhead.

15.5 Woodhead Farm Results

Young's Table 36 contains "an account of the real expenditure and produce for the first eight years upon the farm of Woodhead belonging to the Right Honourable the Earl of Kinnoul, and possessed by David Young". The totals for this are as follows(16):

Year	Annual Produce £	Annual Expenditure £	Deficiency £
1763	97	650	553
1764	494 (should be 394)	801	407
1765	191	852	661
1766	426	818	392
1767	446	827	381
1768	334	916	582
1769	783	810	27
1770	429	581	152
	3,100	6,255	3,155

Young points out that the expenditure figures should be adjusted by the stock on hand at the year end but he does not provide these figures so that it is not possible to calculate the annual loss. It could be that much of the expenditure was of a capital nature. Nevertheless the picture is not very healthy and Young frankly admits this:

"The reader will no doubt be a little surprised at the balance against this farm in the space of eight years ... I must acknowledge I laid by far too much out upon it, which I was enabled to do as I cleared from my business in Perth about £200 yearly ... This table is not produced here as a pattern, but rather as a beacon, or warning for other farmers to take care how they engage, or attempt to improve a muirland farm, upon so short a lease as this was, being only for twenty one years ... The short tack, and the low rent, was a great motive with me to improve it rapidly, but the great sums at first laid out increased the interest so much that this of itself was more than a rent, and the muirs not giving a proper return at first increased the balance every year."

Whether a farmer would be attracted by David Young's system, which required so much detailed record keeping and yet seemed to have been so unsuccessful in warning its originator of the financial mess that he was getting into, is rather doubtful. Young, however, has no doubts about its usefulness and it is clear that he regarded it as a management accounting system.

15.6 Summary

Eighteenth century Farm and Estate Accounting emphasised the preparation of regular (annual) accounting summaries. The identification of expenditure and income with regular accounting periods, led naturally to the interperiod comparison of results and the use of such comparisons for managerial purposes. Hamilton and Young describe the benefits of such information.

Towards the end of the century Sinclair's semi-official Board of Agriculture (17) was very active in publishing reports on the state of agriculture in counties throughout England and Scotland. Many of these reports included accounting information and this was frequently supplied in the bilateral form suggesting that the potential readers would be familiar with this. David Young's namesake, Arthur Young, the Board's secretary, was prolific in his agricultural writings and these too made frequent references to accounting and stressed its importance.(18) For example, he says " If a farmer knows not the degree and amount of profit or loss on every article, and by every field, it is impossible he should possess a due experience of the past, or ever be able to make it a guide to the future ... ".(19)

CHAPTER 16

ROBERT HAMILTON AND THE ORIGINS OF COST ACCOUNTING

16.1 Cost Accounting Writers of the Eighteenth Century

The British industrial revolution, which began in the 18th century, gave an impetus to the development of improved management information systems(1) but there was little supporting writing on industrial cost accounting, not only in that century, but also for most of the next.(2) Although it seems that cost accounting practice was in advance of the textbook expositions, the position must not be overstated. Some manufacturers had developed accounting systems which included some form of cost accounting but " ... the development of accounting as a tool of industrial management in this period, was patchy and uneven"(3) and industrialists often experienced difficulty in calculating the costs and profitability of different branches of trade.

The 18th century textbook expositions did display an increasing emphasis on the managerial uses of accounting for merchants, farmers and estate owners but only three British accounting authors discussed industrial costing. Two of the writers were English, James Dodson(4) and Wardhaugh Thompson(5). The third was the Scot, Robert Hamilton. After the writings of this trio nothing further of importance appeared (in English) until the end of the next century. Hamilton's 'Introduction to Merchandize' is undoubtedly the most important from this group. It not only introduces some important practical costing techniques but also combines these with a sound development and exposition of the theory in a structure which emphasises the role of opportunity cost and the managerial uses of costing as an aid to improving efficiency.

Hamilton fully recognised that the management of more complex production systems required more detailed cost information than could be obtained from the transaction based system used in 'merchants accounts'. His suggestions for an improved system are contained in chapter V of part V of his 'Merchandize' which deals with 'Tradesmens Accompts' (the accounts of 'artificers and manufacturers'). In this chapter he is critical of manufacturers who maintain only a day book and a ledger (perhaps supplemented by a cash book and invoice book), and he describes the books that he would recommend.(6) He suggests that a model system would contain: a Book of Material (ie a stores ledger), a Book of Wages (for recording and charging out wages), a Book of Work (a cost ledger which also records goods sent to and received from outworkers), the Journal (for recording purchases, sales, etc and a monthly summary of the quantity and value of work manufactured) and the Ledger " ... which, besides personal accompts, should contain, Accompts of Stock, Profit and Loss, and Cash. Accompts for the different branches under which the expence of the business may be distributed, as, materials, wages, upholding of machinery, rents, excise, incident charges, &c. A general accompt of the trade or manufacture ... " (this is a Work-in-Progress Account) and " ... one or more accompts for manufactured goods ... " (these are Finished Goods Accounts).(7)

Hamilton's suggestion that expenses should be recorded in appropriate expense accounts, is in line with current practice but, in the 18th century it was much more common for expenses to be debited directly to 'venture' or other 'profit centre' accounts. Another development occurs when Hamilton suggests that the expense account balances should be transferred at annual intervals to the 'work-in-progress' account, so that the annual profit on manufacture can be calculated. Accounting texts were beginning to advocate the regular annual calculation of profit in the second half of the 18th century, before then the balancing of the books had often been carried out at irregular intervals. It should be noted that Hamilton assumes that profit is to be recognised when manufacturing is complete, not deferred until sale. Unsold goods are valued at selling price but he describes one system which allows for the books for a given year to be kept open until all the production for that year is completed.(8)

Hamilton illustrates his chapter on 'Tradesmens Accompts' with examples based on a shoemaker's business and a linen manufactory. Dodson also illustrates the accounts of a shoemaker's business and Thompson uses the example of linen manufacture.

Both Wardhaugh Thompson and Robert Hamilton introduce a form of process costing for a linen manufacturer but Hamilton's system is much more advanced and, whereas Thompson specifically states that his details are not taken from practice,(9) the detailed observations made by Hamilton seem to suggest that his system may have been in operation.(10) A comparison of the two expositions will be made at appropriate points in this chapter and it might be noted that there could be some discussion on whether Thompson's book (1777) did precede Hamilton's. Hamilton's second volume (containing the costing material) is dated 1779 but it might well have been written two year's earlier when volume one was published.(11) James Scruton, writing in Glasgow (also in 1777) provides an explanation of the 'Laws and regulations, relative to the imports and exports of linen' in his book 'The Practical Counting House' but he does not discuss accounting for the linen trade or manufacture.

In his discussion of process costing, Hamilton proposes

a system that incorporates both transfer pricing and profit centres. Despite this important contribution to the development of cost accounting in this barren period, the value of his work was unrecognised by his contemporaries (including Johnston who revised the book) and immediate successors and, right up to the present, it has failed to obtain the recognition that it deserves.

The difficulty of obtaining access to the first edition of Hamilton's book is, at least, part of the reason for this neglect. Hamilton's most complete discussion of his cost accounting system is only given in volume II of the first edition of 'An Introduction to Merchandize' which was published in 1779. Subsequent editions appeared in a single volume and the material in chapter V was seriously compressed (mainly by the omission of an important example) and it disappeared entirely from Johnston's 'new-modelled' edition of 1820. This space saving exercise was unfortunate. It seems clear that earlier commentators have not had access to the first edition of Hamilton's text and this has meant a less than complete appreciation of the worth of his work. In this chapter, in the absence of an indication to the contrary, all references will be to the first edition.

16.2 The Scottish Linen Industry

Hamilton's linen manufacture example is by far the more important and the more detailed of the costing illustrations that he provides. It was natural for Hamilton, a Scot, to base his exposition on textile manufacture. His father had started as a cloth merchant before moving into papermaking and publishing and, by 1777 when Robert was writing his 'Introduction to Merchandize' in Perth, textile manufacture had become very important in that town.(12) It can be assumed that Hamilton would know of the local manufactories and their business methods and his discussion is, thus, likely to have been based on fact.

In other respects, the linen industry was an obvious practical setting for introducing costing since it was the first major industrial success in Scotland and a case can be made for believing that the origins of industrial cost accounting were in this industry.

The manufacture of linen was one of Scotland's oldest trades and at the time of the Treaty of Union (1707), textiles and black cattle were the only Scottish exports to England. The importance of the textile trade was emphasised by Scottish supporters of the Union and the progress of the linen industry was aided by assistance given by the Board of Trustees for Fisheries and Manufactures in Scotland which was founded in 1727 to administer the funds provided by the Treaty of Union.(13)

At the beginning of the century it was recognised that the bleaching process was a major weakness of Scottish linen manufacture; at that time, to be well bleached the cloth had to be sent to Holland or England. In the 18th century there was considerable experimentation in this area and much improvement was achieved but the capital investment required was significant. In 1728 the Board of Trustees assisted James Adair of Belfast with the establishment of a bleaching field in Galloway(14) but it was on the east coast that some of the main developments took place. Progress was not rapid nor was it one of uniform advance but "Output rose three-fold in volume and four-fold in value between years 1736-40 and 1768-72 - nearly thirteen million yards were woven yearly at the latter date".(15) By the end of the century Scottish linen manufacture had become a major British industry.

The story is well told by Durie in his book 'The Scottish Linen Industry in the Eighteenth Century'.(16) Durie lists five main steps that were involved from flax to finished cloth: (i) growing and harvesting the flax; (ii) rippling (removing the seed), retting (separating the fibres), scutching (removing the bark) and heckling (combing out the fibres); (iii) spinning; (iv) weaving; (v) bleaching.

The need to assess the profitability and efficiency of operations in each of these processes required a development of the accounting system.

16.3 Textile Manufacture and the Proto-Factory

One of Hamilton's contemporaries in Perth was William Sandeman who founded a substantial bleachfield. The site is now of interest to industrial archeologists: "Five miles upriver from Perth is the bleachfield and village of Luncarty, which was established by William Sandeman in the period 1732-69; at first 50 acres in extent, by the 1880's Luncarty, with its great lade system, occupied 130 acres."(17)

Sandeman's interest in book-keeping is shown by the fact that he was a subscriber to Stevenson's 'Book-keeping by Double Entry' in 1762. A year before this he had submitted a petition to the Trustees for Improving Fisheries and Manufactures in Scotland asking for support for his Luncarty Bleachfield on which he had spent £3,500 sterling over ten years.(18) He had then prepared the following statement of capital invested:

MR SANDEMAN'S BLEACHFIELD TOTAL EXPENSE TO THE 4 AUGUST 1761

Accompt of Money expended, upon Luncarty Bleachfield from the beginning of the Year 1752, when it began to be fitted up, as yearly laid out

1752 October Amount of an Accompt sent the Honbl Trustees for the manufactures, for Levelling and Laying out Twelve Acres Bleaching Ground, and Building a Boiling House, with a House for a Water Milne, for Washing and Rubing Cloth after the Irish Method		£755 6 4 1/2
1753 Further Laid out before the above works were compleated	£470 6 0 1/4	
A Press, for Lapping after the Dutch method	73 3 3	543 9 3 1/4
1754 A House for Holding a Beetling machine, and a Room for Lapping Cloth	£175 7 7 1/2	
A Beetling Machine	102 15 11 1/4	
Fencing about the Waters	28 8 1	306 11 7 3/4
1755 A Drying House	£133 2 4	
Fencing about the Waters	23 6 7 1/2	156 8 11 1/2
1756 Sundrie New Uttencils, Large Kieves &c		26 15 8
1757 A machine, for pounding Ashes, with Improvements on Rubbing Boards		47 13 8 1/2
1758 A Dwelling House	£200 0 0	
Sundrie Improvements on the Machinery & Laying out more Bleachfield ground	78 13 5 1/4	278 13 5 1/4
1759 A Large House to Contain 18 Tubs, for 36 women to Wash and Rub Cloth after the Dutch Method, and Laying out 3 Acres Bleachfield		193 19 6 1/2
1760 A large House for Servants, also a House for Rinsing & Blewing the Cloth & laying out One & a half Acres more Bleachfield Ground		177 15 11 3/4
		£2486 14 7

MR SANDEMAN'S BLEACHFIELD TOTAL EXPENSE TO THE 4 AUGUST 1761 - CONTINUED

1761					
	These two Houses are built and presently finishing	A House 36 feet long by 20 feet wide, for Holding Milk Casks & Kieves for souring the Cloth	£30	0	0
		A House 32 feet long by 24 feet wide, the ground floor for Holding Ashes & other Materials, & having two Timber floors for holding & Lapping Linen	150	0	0
	Part of the Machinery already made and materials preparing & Sundrie Tradesmen at Work	A House for Containing a New Washing Miln, Rubing Boards and a Beetling, Estimated at	120	0	0
		A House for Bucking the Cloth with Boilers, Kieves & other Uttencils	160	0	0
		A Compleat Sett of Machinery viz a Washing Miln, Rubing Boards, & Beetling machine, with Cannal, for the water & Miln Wheel Estimated at	200	0	0
		A Drying House to be Large	200	0	0
		A Dwelling House, to an Overseer with Room for holding Cloth	150	0	0
		Laying out & Inclosing 40 Acres at Work Ground for Dry Bleaching of Coarse Linen	20	0	0
			£1030	0	0

Luncarty Bleachfield 4th Augt 1761 (19)

Mr Sandeman's submission to the Trustees for Improving Fisheries and Manufactures in Scotland serves to emphasise the complexity of just one part of textile manufacturing and the capital investment required. The complete process was the most capital intensive of all industrial processes in the second half of the 18th century. Although it was not until 1787 that the first mechanised flax-spinning mills appeared in Scotland, well before then there had been developments in the system of manufacture which required considerable investment. These changes have led some commentators to talk of the 'proto-factory'.(20) The requirement for a significant investment of capital in buildings and equipment was one feature of the proto-factory, another two features were the use of a supervised labour force working at the employer's premises and the development of production methods that were designed for 'flow production'.(21) Hamilton's genius is demonstrated by the fact that he considered the accounting implications of each of these developments and incorporated appropriate techniques into his system of accounting.

Hamilton's treatment of two of these developments will be considered in this chapter. The effect of the third (the requirement for a significant investment of funds in the business) will be discussed in chapter 17.

16.5 Wage Earners and Accounting for Wages

Textile manufacture was very important in providing employment in 18th century Scotland and changes which were introduced in the pattern of employment had important repercussions in the economy. In the second half of the century a pronounced increase in the demand for textiles led manufacturers to move from the 'domestic' or 'putting-out' production system, where the processing was carried out in the workers' own homes, to a centralised administrative system which could give them greater control over the productivity of the work staff. Pollard discusses this change.(22) In the new system those employees working on the employer's premises as wage earners might receive a day wage rather than the piece-rate system of remuneration which was often used for outworkers. Johnson (23) considers that these changes encouraged the development of cost accounting.

Whereas Thompson's description of textile cost accounting assumes the domestic system, Hamilton's is not restricted in this way but his illustrative 'Book of Wages' is for a shoemaker's business. He suggests that this would contain " ... the names of the journeymen and other servants employed, the work they are employed at, the number of days and, rate per day, if they be paid by days-wages, or the quantities of work done, and rate, when paid by the piece. It may be filled up once a week, or oftener, if necessary". "In some trades, it may be convenient to keep the book of wages in the form of a ledger, and allot an accompt for each journeyman, where the quantity and value of the work he performs is entered".(24)

Although the decision orientated features of Hamilton's system are very marked, the foregoing quotation does not expressly advocate the recording of a dayrate worker's output nor the calculation of unit costs. The absence, at this point in the text, of any specific comment on employee productivity has led Sutcliffe and Burrows(25) to express the view that: "Conceivably the wage book would lend itself to ... determining the productivity of employees, but its application for such purposes was not considered. The detailed employee records were developed not to generate information on employee performance, but to provide an additional safeguard against fraud: to ensure that employees were paid only once for work completed".

Although the first sentence is factually correct, it is

considered that other material in the chapter can only lead to a rejection of the view given in the second sentence. The misunderstanding must have arisen because Sutcliffe and Burrows did not have access to the first edition of 'An Introduction to Merchandize' which is more detailed on this and other related topics. Hamilton clearly did intend his system to provide the manufacturer with the 'information he needed to judge alternative opportunities' (26) and, to this end, he did have an interest in the evaluation of worker productivity. In his linen manufacture example he points out that, although the wages payable to weavers employed in the manufacturer's own workshop may well be less than the remuneration of outworkers for the same output, this benefit has to be balanced against the workshop expenses. He outlines a procedure for making such an evaluation: "In order to judge which is most beneficial, he may open an accompt of weaving, and enter the wages paid to his own weavers, and the expenses attending the work-shop, on the Dr. and the wages which would have been paid to other weavers, on the Cr. The balance shows the gain or loss by weaving it at home; and the expence of weaving, when delivered out, is transferred to the Dr. of the brown linen accompt".(27)

This describes a sophisticated form of analysis. Unfortunately the paragraph (along with other important material) disappears from the second and later editions of the text.

16.6 Flow Production and Process Costing

With an absence of mechanisation, for most of the century, conventional definitions of 'factory production' do not fit the production methods that were in use. A major feature of the textile proto-factory at this time was, however, the inauguration of flow production, which might or might not utilise machinery for its execution.(28) Such a 'flow of production' features prominently in Hamilton's discussion of a process costing.

Hamilton introduces his illustration of a linen manufacturer's process costing system as follows: "Suppose a linen manufacturer who purchases or imports rough flax, dresses it by his own servants, and sells such kinds as do not suit his purpose; delivers the rest to be spun, and receives the yarn from the spinners; weaves part in his own ware house by journeymen, and delivers the rest to other weavers; gives out the linen to be bleached, and receives and sells it when white." (29)

The costing system makes use of a number of specialised 'subsidiary' books for recording the inputs of resources and the quantities and values of material flowing through the processes. The system that Hamilton describes is an integrated one so that the ledger includes appropriate process accounts which contain summarised information on the purchase of the rough flax and the details of the above-listed processes in:

an accompt of rough flax,
an accompt of dressed flax,
an accompt of yarn,
an accompt of brown linen and
an accompt of white linen.

In addition there might also be:

an accompt of weaving (when some of this is performed within the manufacturer's own work-house) and
an accompt of boiling (when the manufacturer has his own boiling house).

The system can be described schematically as follows:

SUBSIDIARY BOOKS	LEDGER ACCOUNTS	
	ACCOMPT OF ROUGH FLAX S.156	
	Balance	Sales →
ROUGH FLAX BOOK (prime cost of flax, expenses of dressing and quantities processed)	Purchases	Transfers to Dressing Shop
	Profit/Loss on sale of Rough Flax	Balance
	ACCOMPT OF DRESSED FLAX S.156	
	Balance	Sales →
DRESSED FLAX BOOK (quantities of flax received from Heckling Shop; delivered to and received from spinners; cost of spinning)	Transfers into Dressing Shop	
	Heckling Expenses	Transfers to Spinners
	Profit/Loss of dressing flax	Balance
	ACCOMPT OF YARN S.156	
	Balance	Sales →
YARN BOOK (quantities and value of yarn received from spinners; expense of spinning, yarn delivered to weavers and linen returned; sales of yarn)	Spinning Cost	Transfer to Weavers
	Dressed Flax	- Internal
		- Outworkers
	Profit/Loss by Spinning	Balance

SUBSIDIARY BOOKS | LEDGER ACCOUNTS

ACCOMPT OF BOILING S.158

Costs of Boiling 'Materials, rent, wages and other expences'	Revenue from Boiling - External - Internal
Profit/Loss from Boiling	

ACCOMPT OF WEAVING WITHIN THE WORKHOUSE S.157

Transfer from Yarn Accompt	Value of Work completed - evaluated by reference to wages which would have been paid to out-workers - transferred to Accompt of Brown Linen
Work House Rent	
Expense of Looms	
Wages Paid	
Profit on Weaving within Work House	

BLEACHING BOOK (quantities delivered to and received from bleach fields, expenses of bleaching)

ACCOMPT OF BROWN LINEN S.156

Balance	Sales
Cost of Boiling	
Received from Weavers	Transfers to Bleachfields
Purchases	
Weaving Cost	
Profit/Loss by Weaving	Balance

SUBSIDIARY BOOKS	LEDGER ACCOUNTS	
	ACCOMPT OF WHITE LINEN	S.156
LINEN BOOK (quantity and quality of linen produced; total cost of production; sales proceeds)	Balance	
→	Brown Linen	Sales →
	Bleaching Cost	
	Profit/Loss by Bleaching	Balance

16.7 Non-Industrial Cost Accounting

Wells(30) has pointed out that the emphasis on identifying the outcome of each of the various 'branches of trade', which was a feature of the 17th and 18th century expositions of mercantile and estate accounting, led naturally to 'departmental accounts' which were precursors of industrial cost accounting systems, such as Hamilton's. Wells reproduces a 'Meal Accompt' from Hamilton and an earlier example from estate accounting from Monteage(31) which illustrate this point.

Concurrently with the developments in industrial cost accounting there was a parallel development in farm accounting. Arthur Young (32) proposed a farm accounting system in which there was a 'departmental' ledger account for each field. His view was that the farmer's ' ... accounts may be said to be the foundation of good husbandry'(33) and he continually emphasised the benefits of appropriate analysis and regular (annual) summaries of farm and estate activities. In his extensive analyses of the financial implications of alternative agricultural plans he often used the T account format as a convenient way of marshalling the anticipated costs and benefits and this suggests that he believed that his readers would be familiar with this framework. Hamilton's farm accounting system (described in chapter 15) had provided for a 'Field Book' with separate accounts for individual fields(34) which was similar to that suggested by Arthur Young.

Established 18th century mercantile and estate accounting systems thus used departmental or 'branch of trade' accounts which could be adapted to provide improved financial record keeping methods for farming (where the Agricultural Revolution was underway) and manufacturing (to meet the needs of the Industrial Revolution). Wells considers that these accounts " ... provide a unique example of a technique originating in one set of circumstances and being adapted as circumstances changed".(35) Hamilton's process costing system and his field book can be interpreted in this way.

16.8 Transfer Pricing

An important feature of Hamilton's system is that he proposes that transfers from one process to the next should be made at market price. Again there is a parallel with farm and estate accounting where transfers from one 'branch' of business to another might be recorded at such prices.(36) In contrast, Thompson records inter process transfers at cost, not market value.

An implication of Hamilton's approach is that the processes are 'profit centres' and the balances on:

> the 'accompt of dressed flax',
> the 'accompt of yarn',
> the 'accompt of brown linen' and
> the 'accompt of white linen'

show respectively:

> 'the gain or loss by dressing flax,'
> 'the gain or loss by spinning,'
> 'the gain or loss by weaving' and
> 'a comparison of the profit obtained by selling the linen, white or brown'.

Where accounts are kept for weaving and boiling these show:

> "the gain or loss by weaving ... at home"
> (rather than using outworkers)(37) and
> "the gain or loss by boiling".(38)

The comparison of the weaving costs of wage earners and outworkers has been discussed earlier in this article. The process of determining the profit from boiling is only advocated when the manufacturer undertakes not only the boiling of his own yarn but also does such work for others. Where the manufacturer does not do such outside work, an accompt of boiling is deemed unnecessary since " ... the expence of boiling, along with that of weaving, may be entered on the Dr. of the brown linen accompt". The reasoning behind this approach is discussed below, in section 16.9.

A comparison can be made between the analysis of a textile manufacturer's profit using Hamilton's system and the analysis given in the 1748 Profit and Loss Account of the British Linen Company.(39) This company (40) seems to have used out-workers and subcontractors, but it did have its own bleachfield.(41) The Profit and Loss Account shows the company's profit from each of the following sources: Fine Linen, Coarse Goods, Hemp, Yarn, Dressed Flax and

Undressed Flax.

The firm of Marshalls of Leeds was using a comparable system in the early 19th century: "It is reasonable to suppose ... that machine records were started soon after 1804 ... clerks in the mill's office ... condensed the records of the four main departments - hackling, spinning, weaving and bleaching - on a half yearly basis showing the inputs and outputs by quantity and value for each grade of raw material processed, constructing in effect a set of process accounts".(42)

Hamilton makes no provision for the elimination of unrealized profit in the year-end inventory valuation, but, apart from this, his system identifies many of the features of a modern integrated costing system, although it was written when the Industrial Revolution was scarcely underway.

Hamilton's transfer pricing method was retained in the second edition of 'Merchandise' but the detailed examples of the application of the method to different processes were removed and the text is not so clear. He states that the monthly transfers from the 'general accompt of the trade or manufacture' (ie the Work-in-Progress Account) to the Finished Goods Account should be made at "the value of goods manufactured". By this last phrase he must mean a standard selling price since he assumes that the Work-in-Progress Account will show a profit (or loss) and that a further profit (or loss) will arise in the Finished Goods Account if the actual selling prices differ from the standard selling prices. Littleton (43) is critical of this part of Hamilton's work but the criticism is based on a misunderstanding arising from the use of one of the later editions in which the explanation of the system was curtailed.

Over 100 years later Norton's 'Textile Manufacturers'

Book-keeping'(1889), agrees entirely with Hamilton's method of judging profitability: " ... the only method of testing the economy of manufacturing departments that the author has found to be altogether satisfactory and reliable is ... Credit each department with standard prices for its work done, and Debit it with its proportion of the expenditure".(44) Littleton is enthusiastic about Norton's book, which he considered to be one of three influential books on cost accounting to appear in England at the end of the 19th century;(45) it is ironic, therefore, that, because of a misunderstanding, he should have been so disparaging about Hamilton's approach 110 years earlier.

16.9 <u>Joint Costs and Decision-Making</u>

Pollard states that 18th century manufacturers were unable to deal with costing for joint products, he says " ... not even the principles could be worked out".(46) There were also problems in farming where the use of field accounts seemed to require an apportionment of rent, tythes, poor levy etc.(47) Yamey(48) has pointed out that Hamilton demonstrated an enlightened approach to the joint cost problem and this has been considered in chapter 10.(49)

Hamilton's chapter V on 'Tradesmens Accompts', contains further evidence that he <u>had</u> worked out the 'principles'. His emphasis in this chapter on the managerial purposes of accounting, leads to a decision orientated consideration of the circumstances which should apply before a 'profit centre' is established. Hamilton says: "If all these branches of business were necessarily connected, and the manufacturer had no other choice than to purchase the rough flax, and carry on the successive operations, it would be sufficient to keep his books in a form that should exhibit the gain or loss on the whole; but, if he has an opportunity of beginning or desisting at any stage of the manufacture, his books should exhibit the gain or loss on each operation separately. He may purchase dressed flax or yarn; he may sell the linen before it be bleached; and, since he chuses to unite the several trades of flax-dresser, spinner, weaver, and bleacher, it is proper he should have a separate view of the success of each. This is the leading principle by which his books should be regulated."(50)

Hamilton avoids any pointless consideration of alternative apportionment bases, instead he considers the fundamental question of the circumstances in which it is appropriate to analyse profit to individual activities. He propounds the 'leading principle' that the calculation of the profit for any given 'stage of the manufacture' is only appropriate when there is "an opportunity of beginning or desisting" at that stage. If there is such "an opportunity of beginning or desisting" there is an opportunity cost involved in a decision either to begin or to desist.

Hamilton does not use the term 'opportunity cost' but it is clear that he understands the use of this important concept. The following extract from the first edition of 'Merchandise' illustrates his use of the opportunity cost approach. "Several other articles may require attention. For instance, if he boils the yarn, to prepare it for weaving, the expence of boiling, along with that of weaving, may be entered on the Dr. of the brown linen accompt. But, if he keeps a boiling house, and performs that operation upon yarn belonging to others, as well as his own, it will be proper to open an accompt of boiling, and enter the value of materials, rent, wages, and other expenses, on the Dr and the sums received for boiling yarn belonging to others, or chargeable on his own, at the same rate, on the Cr. The balance of this accompt will show the gain or loss by boiling."(51)

The technique described in the above quotation is not

unique to Hamilton. Other 18th century writers were also aware that it might sometimes be necessary, or useful, to impute a cost for the services of an asset (or profit centre). In particular this was advocated when a merchant owned a ship in which he transported both his own goods and the goods of others. In such cases, if the merchant wished to determine the separate profitability of the ship and the goods which were transported in it, there could be difficulties involved in attempting to apportion the transportation cost but these could be avoided by charging the merchant's own consignment at the normal commercial rates. Malcolm, Hamilton and Scruton all have examples where they suggest this opportunity cost approach.(52)

Hamilton's 'leading principle' and his opportunity cost imputations would seem to provide a useful framework for tackling the joint cost apportionment problem. Two hundred years after his views were first published, accountants are now taking the problem seriously;(53) in so doing they could, with advantage, consider Hamilton's valuable contribution to the debate.

16.10 Summary

Hamilton's chapter on 'Tradesmens Accompts' is important because it contains an early description of a completely integrated process costing system, but this is only part of its value. The chapter is also noteworthy because of its modern approach to cost accounting, Hamilton's system is a modern system. Throughout he emphasises managerial considerations, he discusses the joint cost problem and the case for profit centres. The techniques that he suggests include transfer pricing and the use of opportunity costs.

This chapter has pointed out that the value of Hamilton's work has been insufficiently recognised. Some serious misunderstandings of its worth have arisen because the versions of 'Merchandize' which most researchers have consulted, have not included Hamilton's full text. The complete description of his costing system only appears in the first edition which has not been published in facsimile form and which is held by relatively few libraries.

Despite the fact that most commentators have not seen the complete version of Hamilton's writings on cost accounting, they are generally complimentary about the truncated version that appeared in later editions. Chatfield sees it as an important description of the integration of cost and financial accounting,(54) and Crossman considers it to be an interesting early example of a cost control system.(55) Garner is impressed by the material, but he takes its omission from the 1820 edition to be a recognition by Hamilton of its lack of contemporary relevance.(56) The truth is that none of Hamilton's accounting writings survived the zeal of Johnston's misguided revision.

For whatever reason Hamilton's work had no influence on his contemporaries and nothing of any note was published (in English) on the subject of costing for over 100 years. There were developments on the continent (France) during the first three quarters of the 19th century(57) but there was no consideration of cost accounting, in any English language text, until Garcke and Fells produced their book on 'Factory Accounts' in 1887 and George Pepler Norton's 'Textile Manufacturers' Book-keeping' appeared in 1889.(58)

Because of the importance of Hamilton's contribution to costing, the fact that this appears, in its complete form, only in the first edition of his 'Merchandize' and the relative difficulty of obtaining access to this edition, the relevant chapter is reproduced here as an appendix.

CHAPTER 16

ROBERT HAMILTON AND THE ORIGINS OF COST ACCOUNTING

APPENDIX

AN INTRODUCTION TO MERCHANDIZE - ROBERT HAMILTON
1st Edition - Vol 2 - 1779 - PART V - CHAP V

TRADESMENS ACCOMPTS

152. Artificers and manufacturers sometimes keep only a day-book and ledger; the former, for entering goods sold, or work done on credit; the latter for personal accompts: And perhaps a cash and invoice-book.

A more compleat method is necessary for exhibiting the materials used, the work done, and the profit acquired. The subsidiary books most useful for these purposes are,

I A BOOK of MATERIALS, where the quantities purchased and consumed are entered in separate parts, or on opposite pages.

II A BOOK of WORK, where the quatities of materials delivered to journeymen, the quantities of wrought goods received in return, the dates of the delivery and return, the value of the materials and wages; and the value of the wrought goods are entered in separate columns.

If the business consists in any operation performed on goods belonging to others, this book must contain columns for the quantities received from our employers, the work done, and the delivery of the goods when improved or converted, the charge, and, perhaps, for the payment. By this means, it will be a check upon the ledger, and may sometimes supply the place of one.

Several books of this kind will sometimes be needed. The exact form must be regulated by the nature of the articles. We shall have occasion to give some specimens afterwards.

III A BOOK of WAGES, which contains the names of the journeymen and other servants employed, the work they are employed at, the number of days, and rate per day, if they be paid by days-wages, or the quantities of work done, and rate, when paid by the piece. It may be filled up once a week, or oftener, if necessary. The following is a specimen of a shoemaker's book:

Jan. 2. to 7.	A.Hart,	foreman,cutting and attending customers per week		L - 12 -
	Tho. Hill,	4 pair mens shoes at 1s 8d	L - 6 8	
		3 pair boys, 1s	- 3 -	- 9 8
	Ja. Campbell	4 pair womens shoes, at 1s 2d	L - 4 8	
		6 pair girls do. 10d	- 5 -	- 9 8
	Ja. Hill	3 pair boots, at 3s	- - -	- 9 -
		Paid 7th January		L 2 - 4

In some trades, it may be convenient to keep the book of wages in the form of a ledger, and allot an account for each journeyman, where the quantity and the value of the work he performs is entered. If they then be regularly paid, the payments may be marked below; if otherwise, they may be marked on the opposite page of the folio.

153. The principal books are,

I. The JOURNAL, which contains the Purchases, Sales, Cash-transactions, and the like; and a Monthly Abstract of the quantity and value of work manufactured.

II. The LEDGER, which, besides personal accompts, should contain,

Accompts of Stock, Profit and Loss, and Cash.

Accompts for the different branches under which the expence of the business may be distributed, as, materials, wages, upholding of machinery, rents, excise, incident charges, &c.

A general accompt of the trade or manufacture. To the Dr of this accompt, the balances of the accompts of materials, and other expences, are transferred at the end of the year; on the Cr. the value of goods manufactured each month is entered. The balance shows the gain or loss, allowance being made for the value of goods not yet compleatly manufactured, and therefore not entered in the Cr.

One or more accompts for manufactured goods, where the quantity made is entered monthly on the Dr. and the monthly sales on the Cr. These accompts will balance by the value on hand, if the prices be constant; but, if the prices vary, the balance, compared with the value on hand, per inventory, will show the gain or loss by the alteration.

The ledger is posted, by double entry, from the journal.

These general directions will be useful in most kinds of trades and manufactures; they will answer every purpose of regularity and information, and do not require much writing that can well be spared. Their particular application, and the number and form of the subsidiary books, will be different, according to the nature and extent of the business. We shall select one instance, and point out the method more particularly.

154. Suppose a linen manufacturer who purchases or imports rough flax, dresses it by his own servants, and sells such kinds as do not suit his purpose; delivers the rest to be spun, and receives the yarn from the spinners; weaves part in his own ware house by journeymen, and delivers the rest to other weavers; gives out the linen to be bleached, and receives and sells it when white.

If all these branches of business were necessarily connected, and the manufacturer had no other choice than to purchase the rough flax, and carry on the successive operations, it would be sufficient to keep his books in a form that should exhibit the gain or loss on the whole; but, if he has an opportunity of beginning or desisting at any stage of the manufacture, his books should exhibit the gain or loss on each operation separately. He may purchase dressed flax or yarn; he may sell the linen before it be bleached; and, since he chuses to unite the several trades of flax-dresser, spinner, weaver, and bleacher, it is proper he should have a separate view of the success of each. This is the leading principle by which his books should be regulated.

155. The following subsidiary books may be used:

I A flax-book in which is entered the prime-cost of each matt or parcel, the expense of dressing, the quantities and values of the several kinds of dressed flax it produces. It may be kept in the following form:

No.25.

f21.	L2	10		28lb. at	3½d	L -	8	2	Profit
charges	-	5	-	19	6½d		-10	3½	
	L2	15	-	54	10d	2	5	-	
				101		L3	3	5½	L- 8 5½

No.26.

f35.	L3	10	-	10lb. at	4d	L -	3	4	
charges	-	6	-	14	8d		- 9	4	
	L3	16	-	17	10d		-14	2	
				63	1s	3	3		
				104		L4	9	3	- 13 3

II Another flax-book, in which is entered the quantities and kinds of dressed flax received from the heckling shop. In another part of this book there is entered the quantities delivered to the spinners, and columns are reserved for marking the yarn returned, and expense of spinning. The following is a specimen:

DATE	SPINNERS	FLAX DELIVERED		VALUE		WHEN RECEIVED	YARN		CHARGES		SPINNING		TOTAL		COST PER SPINDLE		
		lb.	d.	s.	d.		fp	h	s.	d.	s.	d.	s.	d.	s	d	q
Jan 3	Ann Stewart	3 at	10	2	6	Jan 13	3	3	1	4	5	-	7	6	2	-	-
5	Cath Scott	2	12	2	-	20	3	-	1	6	4	6	6	6	2	2	-
6	Jane Saddler	4	8	2	8	Feb 1	4	-	1	-	4	-	6	8	1	8	-
8	Christ. Ritchie	6	7	3	6	2	4	-	1	-	4	-	7	6	1	10	2
12	Janet Arthur	5	-	2	9												

III A yarn book, in which the quantities and values of the yarn received from the spinners, and expense of spinning, are entered, when the yarn is returned. From this the reserved columns in the flax book are filled up. In a separate part of this book, the yarn delivered to the weavers is entered, and columns reserved for marking the linen returned. The form is nearly the same as that of the flax book. If part of the flax or yarn be sold, it may be entered in a separate part of the respective book.

IV A bleaching book, in which the quantities delivered to the bleachfields are entered, and columns reserved for marking the linen returned, and expence of bleaching.

V A linen book, ruled with a variety of columns, for entering the number, measure, and fineness of each piece, the quantity and quality of yarn used, the expence of yarn, weaving, and bleaching, the total expence, and the sale. These particulars are collected from the books already described.

(SEE FACING ILLUSTRATION)

Other columns might be ruled for the flax, the charge of spinning, the rates, and the profit.

Besides these an invoice book, cash book, and day book, or sales book, should be kept in common form.

156. The principal books are, 1. The Journal, in which the sales are entered from the day book; the money received and paid, from the cash book; and monthly abstracts of the dressing, spinning, weaving, and bleaching, from the respective subsidiary books. The Ledger, which, besides personal accompts, and those of stock, cash, profit, and loss, and its subsidiaries, contains the following:

Accompt of rough flax, which contains the quantities bought on the Dr. and the quantities sold or delivered to the dressing-shop on the Cr.

Accompt of dressed flax, which contains the quantities

No	Yarn Quality Sp	H	Value L.	s.	d.	Weaving L.	s.	d.	Bleaching L.	s.	d.	Total Expence L.	s.	d.	Length Yds	Breadth in	Hundreds	Rate per Yard s.	d.	Value L.	s.	d.	Sold for L.	s.	d.
1	10	4	1	1	8	-	8	4	-	6	3	1	16	3	25	36	14	1	8	2	1	8	2	1	8
2	15	3	1	7	6	-	10	-	-	8	-	2	5	-	48	36	10	1	2	2	16	-	2	16	-
3	10	4	1	1	8	-	10	-	-	6	-	1	17	8	24	40	12	1	10	2	4	-	2	4	-
4	16	6	2	8	-	-	18	-	-	12	-	3	18	-	36	30	18	2	6	4	10	-			
5	17	3	1	11	2	1	1	-	-	12	-	3	4	2	32	36	8	2	-	3	12	-	3	12	-

received from the dressing-shop, the value of the rough flax, and expense of dressing, on the Dr. and the quantities sold or delivered to the spinners, with the value, on the Cr. This accompt exhibits the gain or loss by dressed flax.

Accompt of yarn, which contains the quantities bought or received from the spinners, the value of the dressed flax, and expence of spinning, on the Dr. and the quantities sold, or delivered to the weavers, with the value on the Cr. This accompt exhibits the gain or loss by spinning.

Accompt of brown linen, which contains the quantities bought or received from the weavers, the value of the yarn, and expence of weaving, on the Dr. and the quantities sold or delivered to the bleachfields, on the Cr. The accompt exhibits the gain or loss by weaving.

Accompt of white linen, which contains the quantities received from the bleachfields, the value when brown, and expence of bleaching, on the Dr. and the sales of the white linen on the Cr. This accompt exhibits a comparison of the profit obtained by selling the linen, white or brown.

The articles in all these accompts are posted monthly from the abstracts entered in the journal, referring to the subsidiary books for particulars. It will be convenient to rule inner columns for arranging the matter which each accompt contains. Thus, the accompt yarn may be ruled with several inner columns on both sides, for entering the quantities of each kind received and delivered, also, a money column, on the Dr. for entering the value of the flax spun monthly, and another for the expense of spinning. The sum of these columns is extended to the outer column.

157 The linen woven in his own workshop will be done at a cheaper rate than that which is executed by other weavers; but, in return for this, he has the rent of the work-house, and expence of providing and upholding the looms, to

discharge. In order to judge which is most beneficial, he may open an accompt of weaving, and enter the wages paid to his own weavers, and the expenses attending the work-shop, on the Dr. and the wages which would have been paid to otjer weavers, on the Cr. The balance shows the gain or loss by weaving it at home; and the expence of weaving, when delivered out, is transferred to the Dr. of the brown linen accompt.

158. Several other articles may require attention. For instance, if he boils the yarn, to prepare it for weaving, the expence of boiling, along with that of weaving, may be entered on the Dr. of the brown linen accompt. But, if he keeps a boiling house, and performs that operation upon yarn belonging to others, as well as his own, it will be proper to open an accompt of boiling, and enter the value of materials, rent, wages, and other expences, on the Dr and the sums received for boiling yarn belonging to others, or chargeable on his own, at the same rate, on the Cr. The balance of this accompt will show the gain or loss by boiling.

159. By following this method, the goods on hand, at every stage of the manufacture, will be exhibited in the accompts of rough and dressed flax, yarn, white and brown linen. As there will always be flax in the hands of the spinners, yarn in the looms, and linen at the bleachfields, it would be more agreeable to strict form (Part IV Section 71) (1) if other accompts were opened, under proper titles, for entering the goods that were delivered out for these different operations. Without this, there is a chasm betwixt the connecting entries; the value of flax delivered is entered on the Cr. of the flax-accompt when delivered, but is not brought to the Dr. of the yarn-accompt till the

yarn be returned. This irregularity, however, is attended with no onconvenience, if the subsidiary books above described be kept; and, as it cannot be avoided, without a good deal of additional trouble, the accompts already enumerated will be sufficient. The values, however, of the flax, yarn, and linen, delivered out, must be computed, and entered in the respective accompts, when the books are balanced.(2)

160. The owner of the books, perhaps, may chuse to distinguish the gain or loss on the manufacture of materials purchased each year, although the operations be not compleated till the following year. For this purpose, the books of 1777 must be kept open till all the flax purchased that year be spun, woven, and bleached. In the subsidiary books, where the spinning, and other operations, are entered, the quantities obtained from the materials of the present and former years must be distinguished, and the same distinction preserved in the journal-abstracts. When the new ledger is opened, the balance of the cash, white linen, and personal accompts, only, are transfered to it. The new accompt of rough flax is only opened when new purchases are made, and the accompt of dressed flax, yarn, and brown linen, when the materials of the present year's purchase are advanced to that stge of manufacture. The articles relating to the former materials are entered monthly in the old ledger. The flax delivered to the spinners, on the Cr. of dressed flax, and, together with the expence of spinning, on the Dr of yarn; the yarn delivered to the weavers on the Cr. of yarn, and together with the expence of weaving, on the Dr. of brown linen; the dressing and bleaching in the same manner. When all the linen is bleached and returned, the old books are balanced, and the value of linen produced from last year's materials, but manufactured this present year,

is transferred to the Dr. of the linen accompt in the new ledger, where all the sales from the beginning of the year are entered.

By this method, the expence of spinning, weaving, and bleaching the old materials, are entered on the Dr. of the respective accompts, in the old ledger, but the corresponding entries will be found in the cash-accompt (perhaps some of them among the personal accompts) of the new one. This destroys the equal balance of the opposite sides in both. The Dr. side of the old ledger will be heavier, and the Cr. side of the new one. To remedy this, the new books must be charged Dr. to the old ones, before balancing for the amount of the expenses laid out this present year, in compleating the manufacture of materials purchased last year. The equilibrium of both ledgers is then restored, and the old one is ready to balance.

CHAPTER 17

ROBERT HAMILTON AND RESIDUAL INCOME

17.1 Rate of Return Calculations

The investigation of profitability via an analysis of the relationship between profit and capital employed is now an established feature of accounting control systems, but this has not always been the case. Pollard says: "The merchants and money lenders of fourteenth-, fifteenth-, and sixteenth-century Italy, among whom modern accounting practices first arose, were indeed interested in profits ... but there was in their case no sense in which they could relate profits to any fixed investment or 'capital' of a firm as a whole: their calculations showed the costs and returns from individual journeys, or individual commodities, and were designed to allow an appropriate division of profits among the shifting groups of associates for each separate venture."(1)

Although the features described by Pollard were being modified in the 18th century they are still apparent in the 18th century book-keeping texts (particularly in the first half of the century). It has been emphasised that the procedures that these books described proposed the opening of an account for each individual venture or voyage or 'branch of trade'; assets and expenses attributable to a particular venture were to be debited to the venture account and revenue was to be credited.(2) No distinction was made between capital and revenue expenditure as it was intended that the account should remain open to cover the venture's complete history. At the venture's termination the results were calculated and transferred to the profit and loss account.

If the books were closed at regular intervals(3) there

might be a need to balance a venture account before it had run its term. The procedures suggested for such cases were diverse. It will be appreciated that at the balancing date, a decision was required on how much of the balance on the venture account should be taken to the profit and loss account and how much should be transferred to the balance account (to be carried forward to the next period). There is no indication that the textbook writers regarded this as an important decision and this suggests that the interruption in the record of the venture's progress was frequently regarded as an unfortunate nuisance rather than an opportunity to assess its interim profitability.

The combination of features described above, would complicate any attempt to calculate a rate of return on capital employed by a trader or manufacturer, although this could be more readily undertaken for the capital contributed by partners in a 'fixt' partnership(4) and for prospective rates of return on proposed investments. An example of the use of such prospective rates is the 17th century 'prospectus' issued in 1681 by Sir James Stanfield for the New Mills Cloth Manufactory.(5) This gave the forecast expense and revenue in considerable detail and emphasised that it was anticipated that the profit would be in excess of the legal rate of interest (5%).

Although the regular closing of the merchant's books became an established feature of the accounting texts in the first half of the 18th century, the texts placed little emphasis on the regular (annual) calculation of profit until the second half of the century.

By the end of that century, the calculation of a rate of return was commonly being suggested, and made use of, by agricultural commentators.(6) The process was easier in farm and estate accounting where the annual calculation of profit was a long established practice. Occasionally estimated rates of return were being made for other forms of business enterprise where there was continuity and the requirement for a substantial investment. We can, for example, point to rate of return calculations which were made for West Indian sugar plantations(7) and mines,(8) both being cases that required a substantial investment for an extended time period.

Bryan Edwards, writing of an 'average' sugar plantation, estimated that " ... it requires a capital of no less than thirty thousand pounds sterling to embark on this employment with a fair prospect of advantage".(9) On page 255 of his History he analyses this as follows:

Lands		14,100	(£ Jamaica currency)
Buildings		7,000	
Stock: 250 negroes	17,500		
80 steers	1,200		
60 mules	1,680	20,380	
		41,480	
£42,000 Jamaica currency is		£30,000	(Sterling)

The Gross Revenue he estimates at:

200 hogsheads of sugar	£3,000	(Sterling)
130 puncheons of rum	1,300	
	£4,300	
and expenses are	£2,150	

" ... leaving £2,150 sterling ... clear profit to the planter, being seven per cent on his capital, and £50 over, without charging, however, a shilling for making good the decrease of the negroes, or for the wear and tear of the buildings, or making any allowance for dead capital ... ".(10)

It has been argued that this is an understatement of the rate of return that was frequently obtained by sugar plantations(11) but the point being made here is that this was an accepted method of assessing profitability and that rate of return calculations were attempted.

17.2 Residual Income

The Industrial Revolution produced conditions where it was particularly important to be able to compare profit with capital employed, but Hamilton was the only 18th century writer of an English language accounting text to discuss this topic, despite the fact that the preparation of annual accounts for merchants and manufacturers had become an established feature of the system described by the accounting authors at the end of the century. Hamilton considers this topic in chapter III of part V of his 'Merchandize' under the title 'Method with Allowance of Interest'. In this chapter he proposes an alternative to the rate of return calculation by suggesting that a period's profit should be charged for the use of funds employed in earning it.(12)

This measure of business performance has resurfaced in recent years and it has been extensively discussed in the management accounting literature under the name 'Residual Income'.(13) This name seems to have been introduced by the General Electric Company(14) who were using the method in the 1960's although they 'apparently' do so no longer.(15).

Despite its absence from all but Hamilton's text, the method, but not the name, was used in 18th century Britain.(16) Example of its use will be given later in this chapter. At the beginning of the century the method would seem to have had at least two practical advantages over the Rate of Return Method, irrespective of any theoretical advantages that it it may also possess. Firstly the method was practical and it could be used whereas Pollard is correct in saying that the calculation of rates of return was (at that time) largely impracticable. Secondly, in copartnerships, the problems arising from unequal capital contributions could be dealt with by allowing interest on the partners' capitals.(17) The method may well have had its origin in its use by partnerships.

Hamilton was well aware of the method's advantages. He advocated its use as <u>the</u> measure of business success and seems to have placed rather more importance on it than on his process costing material, as the residual income chapter was exempted from the second edition cuts whereas some important costing material was excised.

17.3 The Interest Rate

The medieval objections to usury had been moderated by the 18th century. Adam Smith notes that: "In some countries the interest of money has been prohibited by law. But as as something can every-where be made by the use of money, something ought every-where to be paid for the use of it."(18)

He notes however that: "In countries where interest is permitted, the law, in order to prevent the extortion of usury, generally fixes the highest rate which can be taken without incurring a penalty."(19)

Gordon, writing in 1763, says that the rate of interest paid on a loan: " ... may be under the rate established by law, if it is so stipulated betwixt the parties, but never can be above it, without incurring a severe penalty on the part of the lender ... the interest of money was reduced to 5 per cent from the 29th of September 1714, and this statute continues in force to this day."(20)

It seems, however, that this maximum rate was not always observed since Malcolm says that "If any Thing besides the legal Interest is paid for the Loan of Money, it has nothing to do with the Person's Account."(21) This seems to mean that any interest paid in excess of the legal maximum should be recorded as miscellaneous expenses and should not be identified with the lender's account. Since Malcolm (who was later to enter the Church) generally takes a moral standpoint, his comments suggest that it was not considered immoral to exceed the maximum rate of interest.

Although the interest rate on a loan would vary with the risk involved and the reputation of the borrower, it was possible, from the founding of the Bank of England at the end of the 17th century, to speak of a 'general rate of interest'(22) and Hamilton refers to this in his description of his 'Method with Allowance of Interest'. He says: "In all commercial countries there is a fixed rate of interest, and the merchant's gain should only be estimated by the excess of his gross profits above the interest of his stock. The latter may be obtained with little risk or trouble; the former alone is the reward of his industry and the compensation for his hazard. And, if the profit of his trade be less than his stock would have yielded at common interest, he may properly account it a losing one."(23) It was this 'fixed rate' of 5% which was commonly considered to be the appropriate rate in the 18th century calculations of residual income.

Hamilton wrote this during his time at Perth. Ten years previously another Perth citizen, the linen manufacturer William Sandeman, was very conscious of the points made by Hamilton in the above paragraph. Sandeman wrote in a letter: "I have dealt my self to the extent of £10,000 p.a. for these two years past in the linen trade, and have not made common interest of the money employed ... ".(24)

17.4 Interest as Opportunity Cost

In making the comparison between the return from his

investment in the linen trade and the return that he could have obtained at common interest, Sandeman is adopting an opportunity cost viewpoint. He implies that he regards the cost of his 'money employed' in the linen trade as being the lost opportunity of investing it elsewhere at 'common interest'.

One hundred and fifty years earlier Robert Loder's farm accounts (for the period 1610-20) show that he also recognised the opportunity cost of the investment in his farm. Each year he explicitly charged against his farm profits the cost of his investment.(25) Parker describes the development of the opportunity cost concept and its use in business decision making,(26) he discusses Loder's use of opportunity cost but otherwise concentrates on the 19th and 20th centuries. Robert Hamilton and Arthur Young were, however, discussing the concept in the 18th century.

In his agricultural writings Young gives many examples of estimated 'yearly accounts' (ie profit and loss accounts) for given investments and specified farming plans.(27) In these he regularly makes a charge for interest. He provides an explanation for this in a discussion of a particular scenario where an individual has the choice of either working as a farm labourer or investing his savings of £100 in a small farm:

"Now as he maintained himself by his labour before, and saved something besides; and, as he does no more than maintain himself after he is a farmer, without security from the misfortunes of bad crops; it is extremely evident, that he loses the interest of his money by turning farmer.

"But as all contingencies are hazardous, the loss attending this farm is best stated thus:

	l.	s.	d.
Deficiency,	2	19	0
Interest of stock,	5	7	0
Total loss,	£8	6	0" (28)

Hamilton expresses his view as follows: "If we buy goods at long credit, and sell them for ready money, or on short credit, we may happen to have the money in our hands for some time; and, as we may lend it out at interest, or employ it in other branches of our business, during the interval, the advantage arising from it ... should be added to the profits, or deducted from the loss of the accompt which yields it." (29)

This advocacy of use of opportunity cost as a managerial tool, should be contrasted with the views of the economists of the period. In the 'Wealth of Nations' Adam Smith recognises 'opportunity cost' in the course of a discussion of the payment of bounties and, in particular, the bounty paid on the exportation of corn. He says: "Unless the price of the corn when sold in the foreign markets replaces, not only the bounty, but this capital (i.e. the capital required to grow the crop), together with ordinary profits of stock, the society is a loser by the difference."(30)

This discussion is in a macro economic context but elsewhere Smith discusses the nature of profit and interest from an individual's viewpoint: "Whoever derives his revenue from a fund which is his own, must draw it either from his labour, from his stock, or from his land. The revenue derived from labour is called wages. That derived from stock, by the person who manages or employs it, is called profit. That derived from it by the person who does not employ it himself, but lends it to another is called the interest or the use of money. It is the compensation which the borrower pays to the lender, for the profit which he has an opportunity of making by the use of the money."(31) Although Smith uses the word 'opportunity' in the foregoing quotation he fails to consider the alternative opportunities open to the entrepreneur for the employment of his own capital and this means that he does not recognise that merchant's profit is partly (foregone) interest. In contrast Hamilton (and Young) see this clearly and advocate the charging of the foregone interest as an opportunity cost when the trader (or farmer) uses his own capital. The influence of Adam Smith is apparent in Hamilton's approach in chapter III (and elsewhere) but here Hamilton goes further than Smith and succeeds in converting Smith's analysis to a management decision-making end. This is a significant step forward.(32)

17.5 Accounting for Residual Income

Hamilton is aware of the problems that arise when an attempt is made to calculate the residual income of the individual branches of a business; he says: "It is easy to form a general estimation of his profits in this sense, by deducting the interest of his nett stock from the gain which the balance of his books exhibits. But it is a matter of some difficulty to determine the gain or loss on each branch of his business, with allowance of interest for the money employed in it."(33)

Because of these problems, Hamilton advocates the incorporation of interest charges into the double entry system. He recognises that accrual accounting is unsuitable for this purpose and he sets forth, in sections 9 to 13, an alternative system of cash accounting.

Although Hamilton provides a brief example of the operation of his system, a more detailed illustration is provided here to facilitate the explanation.

Hamilton's method requires two ledgers. Ledger 1 deals only with transactions that involve (i) the receipt or payment of cash and (ii) credit transactions where interest is chargeable or receivable. It " ... contains the stock, profit and loss, and subsidiary accompts in the common form ... " but the only personal accounts included are those that bear interest. Accounts dealing with 'goods and voyages' are kept in 'a peculiar form'. "On the Dr. of the accompts of goods, there is entered the sums of money paid out for purchase or charges; and on the Cr. the sums received, for what is sold." Credit purchases and sales are not entered in this ledger until the cash is paid or received. The accounts in this ledger are provided with interest columns to calculate interest payable and receivable from the date that the transaction takes place. In the example an interest rate of 10% has been used and it has been assumed that all transactions take place half way through the accounting period.

Ledger 2 records the credit transactions and the cash settlements necessary to ascertain amounts owing and the inventory balances; it " ... contains accompts of goods and voyages, in the common form, and all personal accompts, except those on which interest is computed".

A trial balance extracted from ledger 1 should balance, ledger 2 will not balance. For the example the opening balances are:

	Ledger 1		Credit Transactions		Ledger 2	
	£	£	£	£	£	£
Venture 1	1600 100*		150		1750	
Venture 2	1200 200*		350		1550	
Debtors					300	
Cash	1000					
Loan		100				
Creditors				500		500
Capital		4000				
	4100	4100	500	500	3600	500

The balances in the centre columns arise from credit transactions (sales on credit) which will not be entered in ledger 1 until cash passes. The starred items represent the cost of the goods sold in these credit transactions. During the year the following transactions take place:

Cash Purchases	Venture 1	£1500
	Venture 2	1500
Credit Purchases	Venture 1	2050
	Venture 2	1650
Cash Sales	Venture 1	2000
	Venture 2	1000
Credit Sales	Venture 1	2500
	Venture 2	2700
Receipts from Debtors		4500
Payments to Creditors		3200

It is assumed that the interest rate for the loan is 10% and that all cash balances earn interest at this rate. The balances of goods on hand at the period end are £1000 for Venture 1 and £1300 for venture 2. Elsewhere Hamilton advocates the use of deprival value to value unsold goods but here it will be assumed that they are to be valued at cost. The ledger accounts would be written up as follows:

L E D G E R 1

VENTURE 1

	INT			INT	
Opening Stock			Cash Sales	100	2000
- in hand	60	1600	Receipts from		
- sold on credit	10	100	Debtors	110	2200
Cash Purchases	75	1500			
Payments to			Closing Stock		
Creditors	00	2000	- in hand		800
Interest		135	- sold on credit		400
Profit and Loss		65			
		5400			5400

LEDGER 1

	INT		VENTURE 2	INT	
Opening Stock			Cash Sales	50	1000
- in hand	20	1200	Receipts from		
- sold on credit	20	200	Debtors	115	2300
Cash Purchases	75	1500			
Payments to	60	1200	Closing Stock		
Creditors	60	1200	- in hand		500
Interest		110	- sold on		
			credit		600
Profit and Loss		190			
		4400			4400

	INT		CASH	INT	
Opening Balance	100	1000	Cash Purchases		
Cash Sales			- Venture 1	75	1500
- Venture 1	100	2000	- Venture 2	75	1500
- Venture 2	50	1000			
Receipts from			Payments to		
Debtors	225	4500	Creditors	160	3200
Interest		165	Closing Balance		2465
		8665			8665

LOAN (bearing interest)	
Balance	100
Interest	10
	110

L E D G E R   1

INTEREST

Loan Interest	10	Venture 1 (imputed interest)	135
		Venture 2 (imputed interest)	110
Capital	400	Interest Received	165
	410		410

PROFIT AND LOSS

		Venture 1	65
Capital	255	Venture 2	190
	255		255

CAPITAL

		Opening Balance	4000
		Interest	400
		Profit	255
			4655

L E D G E R   2

VENTURE 1

Opening Stock	1750	Cash Sales	2000
Cash Purchases	1500	Credit Sales	2500
Credit Purchases	2050		
Profit and Loss	200	Closing Stock	1000
	5500		5500

LEDGER 2

VENTURE 2

Opening Stock	1550	Cash Sales	1000
Cash Purchases	1500	Credit Sales	2700
Credit Purchases	1650		
Profit and Loss	300	Closing Stock	1300
	4600		4600

CREDITORS CONTROL

Cash	3200	Opening Balance	500
Closing Balance	1000	Credit Purchases	3700
	4200		4200

DEBTORS CONTROL

Opening Balance	300	Receipts from Debtors	4500
Credit Sales	5200	Closing Balance	1000
	5500		5500

Hamilton assumes that the cash in hand will not be able to earn interest and he recognises that this will create a difference between interest on the capital invested and interest charged out to profit centres. He argues that this difference should not be large: "The balance of the interest-accompt will be nearly equal to the interest of the nett stock. It would be exactly equal, if no money were at any time kept on hand; and, as merchants are careful to regulate their affairs so as never to have much unemployed, the difference will not be considerable."(34) If the difference were to be excessive this would indicated that the cash balance was not being controlled efficiently.

The method proposed achieves the objective of identifying the interest element of profit centre profits and Hamilton is enthusiastic about its merits. He does, however, recognise that it is considerably more complex than the conventional procedures: "This form of book-keeping is the most perfect of any; but the additional trouble is considerable. It is therefore improper where the articles are small and numerous; but when the articles are generally extensive, and the credit long, it may be used to advantage. If it be thought too tedious to follow it through every branch of the business, we may confine it to accompts of greater extent and importance, and keep the others in the common manner."(35)

Anthony has recently proposed a system of accounting for interest with some similarity in its aims to that described by Hamilton. Before dismissing Hamilton's suggestions of accounting for interest as impracticable and unnecessary, Anthony's views might be noted, he says: "Although there is general acceptance of the fact that interest is an element of cost, the tendency is to dismiss rather quickly the idea that this cost should be recorded in the accounts, on the grounds that it is not feasible to do so and that even if it were feasible, the effort would not be worthwhile."(36) Anthony argues that " ... the idea is both feasible and beneficial".

17.6 Residual Income in Practice - Ex Post Calculations

Although there is no evidence that Hamilton's 'most perfect' accounting system was ever used, there is evidence that a charge for the cost of capital was not unusual in 18th century accounts. Pollard says: "... there is much evidence to show that "profits" in common parlance, were often understood to be the surplus <u>after</u> interest was paid."(37) As recently as 1887 James Molleson, an Edinburgh accountant, noted that "Some people think that five per cent. interest should be calculated on capital before profit is reached", although he did not personally approve of this, except for partnerships.(38)

A 1748 Profit and Loss Account for the British Linen Company provides an illustration of the interest charge:

Profit and Loss section of 'Abstract of the Balances and of the Profit and Loss of the British Linen Company at 12 January 1748'

<u>Abstract of Profit and Loss from 24th Sept 1746</u>
<u>To 12th January 1748</u>

Dr			Cr
To Int. on the Capital at ? 1747 for the Int due ye Proprietors on four Calls to that time	£754 14 -	By Gain on the following (39) Heads Viz Accompt of Fine Linen Old Acct	£237 9 8 4/16
Deduct due fr them	339 8 10	Accompt of Coarse Goods do	124 5 - 3/16
	£415 5 2	Hemp	43 8 2
To Charges of Management	273 11 4	Accompt of Yarn	262 7 10 6/16
To Interest Accompt, paid	278 13 -		
		Accompt of Dress'd Flax	15 17 8 6/16
		Accompt of undress'd Flax	319 15 2 3/16
	£967 9 6		1003 3 7 6/16

Brought Forward	967 9 6	Brought Forward	1003 3 7 6/16
		Loans on Bills for Interest	1 13 1
		By Discompts allowed for Sundries to the Com £16 4 8 5/16 Deduct Allowed by the Com 8 3 8 11/16	8 - 11 10/16
To Balance free of all Charges excepting the Premium due to Directors & Managers	142 6 9	By Insurance Accompt Gain'd by not insuring (40)	96 18 7
	£1109 16 3		£1109 16 3

(41)

A factor which would seem to have encouraged the use of an interest charge in the above example was that interest on the capital contributions of partners was part of the profit sharing scheme.

The textile trade continued to use residual income in the 19th century. Stone notes its use by the Charleton Cotton Mills in Manchester from 1810 to 1889 (42) and Norton, at the end of the century, is definite in his advice that it should be used by textile manufacturers. He says: "An important charge, which should never be omitted in calculating the profit of a business is interest upon the Capital employed therein."(43)

The reason he gives is that there is an opportunity cost and this must be recognised. "If the Capital were borrowed the business would have to pay interest thereon and the proprietor of the concern could obtain interest on his capital if it were employed elsewhere; consequently the concern should be charged with interest as an expense of the business."(44)

In farming in the 18th century, where the preparation of regular annual accounts was normal, Young, the English agricultural writer, illustrates the use of residual income by an English farmer (a Mr Ruggles) in the 1780's.(45) In analysing his operations for a period from Michaelmas 1784 to 31 December 1787 he charges interest at 5% on 'capital employed' (note that he uses this term). The capital employed is calculated as follows:

	£.	s.	d.
"The live and dead stock of the farm, taken by appraisement, March 27th, 1784; also manuring, feed, and tillage, paid the outgoing tenant to Lady-Day, 1784, valued by Mr. John Harrison, for Mr. Brice and Mr. Ruggles.	289	4	0
Labour, rent, rates, taxes, &c. &c. the second half year, to Michaelmas, 1784.	357	14	7
Total first stock of the farm, or capital employed	646	18	7"

17.7 Ex Ante Residual Income

The foregoing examples illustrate the use of 'ex post' Residual Income as an measure of past performance but Residual Income can be estimated in advance of entering a venture in an attempt to assess its attractiveness as a worthwhile investment. This Annual Value would be an alternative to the calculation of the venture's Present Value.(46) Hamilton does not suggest the use of residual income in this way but material in his arithmetic text shows that he was aware of the possibility of using 'rate of return' calculations for this end.(47)

The Edinburgh Linen Copartnery's appraisal (in 1757) of the costs and benefits of installing 100 looms, provides an example. In this appraisal the calculations, which are designed to identify the annual benefit and the annual cost, include an interest charge at 5% on the investment in the looms. There is also a charge for "use of the Looms" which may be assumed to be a year's depreciation. There is no indication as to how this is calculated.(48) The appraisal is as follows:

Estimate for 100 Looms 5 May 1757

Calculation of the Charge and discharge of 100 Looms to be employed in the Weaving of Sheetings & Edinburgs

80 Looms employed in Weaving Edinburgs would produce in the year		1120 Webs	
20 Ditto in Weaving Sheetings from 6 to 10 hundred would produce		320	
		1440 @ 3/6	£252

	sh	d				
Reeds to each Loom	2	10	for Edinburgs			
Coams	1	10				
Leathers & Cords		6				
Use of the Looms	1	10				
Temples & Shuttles		6				
80 Looms @ 7/6 per year				£30	-	-
	sh	d				
Reeds for Sheeting	4	6				
Coams	2	7				
Leathers & Cords		6				
Use of the Loom	1	10				
Temples & Shuttles		7				
20 Looms @ 10 -				10	-	-
House Rents @ 6/8 per Loom				33	6	8
Dressing and Tallow @ 9d per piece				54	-	-
Brushes 150 pair @ 1/4				10	-	-
Expense in engaging Weavers				12	10	-
Warehouse Rent				8	-	-
Coal & Candle				7	13	3
1d per Web to Inspectors				6	-	-
Foremans Wages				25	-	-
Clerk for Writing up the principall Books				10	-	-
Drink Money to Carters				3	3	-
				£209	12	11

Total Brought Forward			£209 12 11
Interest on the Value of			
Utensils per other side(49)			10 1 1
			£219 14 -

		Charge	Discharge(50)
Bro' Over		219 14 -	252 - -
To Warping			
12384 Pcs yarn @ 1/2d	25 16 -		
By Cash paid to the Warpers	19 17 8		
Gained on Warping			5 18 4
Total Gain on the factory for one year		38 4 4	
		£257 18 4	£257 18 4

17.7 Summary

The increasing rate of economic development in 18th century Scotland and the increasing amounts of capital that this required led traders to compare their business profit (or prospective profit) with the capital that they had invested (or might invest). One way of relating capital to business operations is to charge these operations with the cost of the capital employed. This method was used quite frequently towards the end of the century and its introduction was made easier as the practice of preparing regular annual accounts was also becoming more common. The method was particularly appropriate for use in companies or copartnerships where the partners had contributed unequal amounts of capital. The partnership agreement might then provide for the use of an interest charge as a method of allocating profit. The distinction between appropriations of profit and charges against profit was not recognised at this time.

Hamilton would have been aware of the use of this 'Method with Allowance of Interest' and he realised its importance. Adam Smith had discussed 'lost profit' as an opportunity cost in 'The Wealth of Nations' but he did not relate this concept to the individual business man and he did not think of it as a decision making tool. Hamilton, however, appreciated that making a charge for the foregone interest on the trader's capital could provide him with useful information because: " ... if the profit of his trade be less than his stock would have yielded at common interest, he may properly account it a losing one".

Hamilton seems to have been the first to have discussed residual income in an accounting treatise although there were earlier examples in agricultural texts. Hamilton is also unique in having set out a method by which it could be incorporated into the accounting system. In addition to his other contributions to the development of accounting, he deserves to be remembered as the first advocate of this important, if controversial, measure of operating performance. The mystery remains as to why no other accounting writer considered the matter until Norton discussed it in his book which was published over 100 years after the first edition of Hamilton's 'Merchandize'.

Because of the importance and contemporary relevance of Hamilton's discussion of this topic, his 'Method with Allowance of Interest' is reproduced in the following pages as an appendix.

CHAPTER 17

APPENDIX

AN INTRODUCTION TO MERCHANDIZE - ROBERT HAMILTON 1st Edition - Vol 2 - 1779 - PART V - CHAP III

METHOD WITH ALLOWANCE OF INTEREST

8. In all commercial countries there is a fixed rate of interest, and the merchant's gain should only be estimated by the excess of his gross profits above the interest of his stock. The latter may be obtained with little risk or trouble; the former alone is the reward of his industry and the compensation for his hazard. And, if the profit of his trade be less than his stock would have yielded at common interest, he may properly account it a losing one.

It is easy to form a general estimation of his profits in this sense, by deducting the interest of his nett stock from the gain which the balance of his books exhibits: But it is a matter of some difficylty to determine the gain or loss on each branch of his business, with allowance of interest for the money employed in it.

The accomptant will readily perceive, that, for this purpose, interest must be computed in the several accompts of goods and voyages on which money has been advanced; and, if this interest be deducted from the gross gain, or added to the loss, the real success of each branch will be exhibited.

The common order of an accompt of goods in the ledger is by no means proper for instituting a computation of interest. The goods are entered on the Dr. when bought, and on the Cr. when sold; and, if interest were computed thereon, it would extend from the time of purchase to the time of sale; whereas it ought to extend from the time of advancing the money till the time of recovering payment. For this purpose, accompts of goods must be kept in an order that exhibits the extent and continuance of the advance; where nothing is entered on the Dr. till the money be laid out, and nothing in the Cr. till the money be recovered. Progressive computions of interest on these accompts, drawn out as directed PART I. #118. will shew what the money employed in each branch of trade would have yielded at common interest, and consequently determine the real gain or loss.

If we buy goods at long credit, and sell them for ready money, we may happen to have the money in our hands for some time; and, as we may lend it out at interest, or employ it in other branches of our business, during the interval, the advantage arising from it, computed as above, should be added to the profits, or deducted from the loss on the accompt which yields it.

The accomptant will understand how this may be done, if he apprehend this leading idea, that the property of goods in some sense, is not acquired till paid for; and, in some sense, not conveyed till payment be received.

The books required are, a Waste-book, Journal, and two Ledgers.

9. I. The Waste-Book. In the inventory, the debts due to us are not placed after the goods in the common form, but are arranged under the title of the goods from which the debts arose. Thus, wine on hand, and debts for wine formerly sold, are arranged and extended together; and, though some kinds of goods be entirely sold, if part of the debts arising from their sale be still owing, the tilte must be continued in the inventory, and these debts arranged under it. Thus, the inventory will contain, first, the

ready money on hand; then the goods on hand, and debts arising from each; and lastly, the debts owing us, for money lent or otherwise, not connected with any accompt of goods. In like manner, the list of debts due by us is arranged under the titles of the goods purchased.

Purchases and sales are entered in the common manner: But when payments are received or made on personal accompts, the kind or kinds of goods for which the debt was contracted, are mentioned.

10. II The Journal. In order to understand the journal, the accomptant must observe that it is to prepare for the first ledger, which contains no personal accompts, except those on which interest is charged. The articles proper to be entered in the Journal are selected from the waste-book, and different marks are prefixed to the articles entered and to those omitted.

The journal-entries are as follows: for the inventory, Sundries Drs. to Stock; Cash, for ready money; Goods, for value on hand, and outstanding debts; and Personal Debtors, for other debts.

When goods are bought for ready money, Goods Dr. to Cash; when sold for ready money, Cash, Dr. to Goods.

When goods are bought or sold on credit, there is no Journal-entry, unless interest is to be computed from the time of sale; in which case, the entry is the same as in the common form.

When payments are received, Cash, Dr. to Goods, for which the debt was owing. When payments are made, Goods Dr. to Cash.

When goods are sent abroad, Voyage Dr. to Goods, if formerly our own, or, To Cash, if bought for ready money, and for charges. But, if the goods be bought on credit, there is no journal-entry when purchased, and the entry, when paid, is Voyage Dr. to Cash. The journal-entries, in other cases, will be obvious, if the nature and design of the ledger be understood.

11. III. The FIRST LEDGER, Which contains the stock, profit and loss, and subsidiary accompts in the common form, accompts of goods and voyages in a peculiar form, and such personal accompts only as interest is regularly charged on.

On the Dr. of the accompts of goods, there is entered the sums of money paid out for purchase or charges; and, on the Cr. the sums received, for what is sold. The balances shows how much money we have employed in every article of our trade, when the Dr. is greater; or how much money we have in hand, by dealing in certain articles, if the Cr. in any accompts be greater.

This ledger is posted from the journal described above, in the common manner.

12. IV. The SECOND LEDGER contains accompts of goods and voyages, in the common form, and all personal accompts, except those on which interest is computed. It may be posted immediately from the waste-book; or, if the accomptant pleases, he may keep a second journal, to prepare for it.

13. When the goods are to be balanced, we must compute and charge interest on every real and personal accompt in the first ledger; then we collect the debts which are owing to us, under the titles of the accompts from which they proceeded. As the accompts of goods in the second ledger contains the quantities bought and sold, we shall find, from the balance of their inner columns, whether the whole be disposed of, or how much is on hand: And, as the sales are entered in the Cr. in the second ledger, when they happen

but in the former, not till payment be recovered, we shall find how much is still owing, by comparing the Cr. of the corresponding accompts in the different ledgers. We may affix a mark to such articles in the second as are also in the first; and the remaining ones must be selected and arranged under the value of the goods on hand; or, if partial payments be made, the balance must be taken.

Now, if we have paid for all the goods, the Dr. of the accompt in the first ledger exhibits the price for which we bought them, the charges paid out, and the allowance of interest for advance: The Cr. contains the money we have received for them; and the balance, collected as above shows the value still on hand, together with the extent of outstanding debts. If these be added and compared with the sum of the Dr. the gain or loss will be ascertained.

But if the whole, or part of the goods, be still owing by us, we must make allowance for the same, before we can ascertain the gain or loss.

The accompts of goods, when the gain or loss is charged, will balance by the amount of the value on hand and outstanding debts, or, by the difference between that amount and the debts which we owe on these goods. The same observations and rules apply to voyages, ships, or property of any kind. When the balances of all the accompts in the first ledger are collected, the stock and balance accompts will correspond, as in the common form.

If a debt has become desperate, it should be omitted in the list, under the title of the goods; by which means, losses by bad debts will be referred to the particular accompts on which the debts were contracted; and, as some branches of trade are more exposed to this kind of hazard than others, the merchant will have the advantage of knowing the actual success of each when every loss arising from it is included.

The Balance of the interest-accompt will be nearly equal to the interest of the nett stock. It would be exactly equal, if no money were at any time kept on hand; and, as merchants are careful to regulate their affairs so as never to have much unemployed, the difference will not be considerable.

This form of book-keeping is the most perfect of any; but the additional trouble is considerable. It is therefore improper where the articles are small and numerous; but when the articles are generally extensive, and the credit long, it may be used to advantage. If it be thought too tedious to follow it through every branch of the business, we may confine it to accompts of greater extent and importance, and keep the others in the common manner.

CHAPTER 18

SUMMARY

18.1 The Scottish Accounting Texts

Double entry book-keeping developed in Italy in the 13th and 14th centuries.(1) There is considerable variety in the early accounting records that have survived from this period but, by the time that Luca Pacioli first described the technique in print, in 1494, the procedures were fairly well standardised. Pacioli's book was a major influence on subsequent book-keeping texts and many relied heavily on it. Knowledge of the Italian Method spread quite rapidly during the 16th century. Book-keeping texts were published in those countries where trade was most active and during the 16th and 17th centuries Dutch and Flemish writers were pre-eminent. In the 17th and early part of the 18th centuries Scottish (and English) merchants often acquired their knowledge of book-keeping in Holland and the first Scottish author (Colinson, 1683) was influenced considerably by his knowledge of Dutch practice.

In the 18th century a number of Scottish treatises on book-keeping appeared and the high calibre of some of these soon gained them the status of standard texts. Malcolm and Macghie wrote important books in 1718 and Malcolm's second book appeared in 1731. These were followed by Mair's popular and influential book-keeping series (which was published regularly from 1736 to 1807), books by Gordon (1763/65 and 1766) and Hamilton (1777/79). Yamey has described the 18th century as period of 'Scottish Ascendancy' in accounting texts.(2)

The books produced by these writers were important (a) in spreading a knowledge of the Italian Method of book-keeping, not only in Scotland but also in England, Ireland

and America, and (b) in providing support for the developing Scottish economy. The writers specifically incorporated material which they considered would be relevant for the Scottish merchant.

18.2 The Demand for Accounting Texts

At the start of the century there was no accountancy profession and those few who did possess a knowledge of the craft of book-keeping would usually have obtained it by working as apprentices in a merchant's counting house, usually in Holland, or by attending a Dutch commercial school. Early in the century the town councils of Glasgow and Edinburgh realised the advantages of a wider knowledge of the subject and appointed official teachers.

As the century passed, the formal teaching of book-keeping in Scottish schools expanded and Mair's role in the development of commercial education in Scotland was particularly important in that he pioneered the developments at Ayr Grammar School when, in 1746, its programme was broadened to include mathematics, science and book-keeping. Later he moved to Perth to head the new Academy there which was specifically created to provide a new style of curriculum with an emphasis on science, English, civil history, mathematics and book-keeping.(3) Robert Hamilton took over the rectorship at Perth on Mair's death. The achievements of Perth Academy under the leadership of Mair and Hamilton soon led to the foundation of similar academies in other parts of Scotland.

The new academies typically included mercantile studies as an important part of the syllabus. Alongside this development there was a rapid growth in the number of private educational establishments run by writing masters and book-keeping teachers. Alexander Malcolm wrote his book-keeping books whilst he was a private teacher of mathematics and book-keeping in Edinburgh and Aberdeen in the first half of the century and William Gordon operated his mercantile academy in Glasgow (and later in Edinburgh) in the second half of the century.

Although not a major trading power, economic progress was being made in Scotland during the 18th century and this and the emerging capitalist spirit created a need for a growing number of book-keepers and a more general knowledge of the double entry system. The demand for textbooks on book-keeping and business mathematics for the young merchant, the pedagogue and his pupils was strong. Moreover the market was not confined to Scotland; after the Union of 1707, Scotland was part of a leading trading nation and the market for the texts was a British demand.

18.3 Meeting the Demand

Accounting texts are economic goods and their publication depends both on demand and supply. It has been argued above that the Scottish demand for good book-keeping textbooks was part of a larger British demand. Given this there seems no obvious reason why the texts should not have been supplied from England. To suggest that Scotland might produce such books might, in fact, seem to be to suggest an unlikely discontinuity in the existing pattern since, up to this time, only the leading commercial nations had produced important accounting texts.

In fact, Scotland was very well placed to meet the need and it took the opportunity presented to it. 18th century Edinburgh was a printing and publishing centre with cost advantages over London and there were university educated teachers such as Malcolm, Mair, Gordon and Hamilton who were qualified to write texts on book-keeping, mathematics and many other topics. Their efforts received positive encouragement from the Scottish Enlightenment which had created an atmosphere which was conducive to academic publishing. Another contemporary accounting writer recognises this when he says: "Learning in general, and particularly that of the Arts and Sciences, is now come to great heighth, and it seems to meet with encouragement everywhere, especially that which tends to the advancement of Trade and Manufactures."(4)

18.4 The Coverage of the Texts

Although the Scottish texts were well written, their approach was a traditional one in that they concentrated on 'merchants accompts'. Malcolm, after a general theoretical introduction, states that he is using 'merchants accompts' as the vehicle for explaining the 'Method of Accompting by Debtor and Creditor' because this is the application which is most fully developed and which is the most convenient for exhibiting a wide variety of transactions to the reader. Mair, Gordon and Hamilton adopt similar schemes.

There was an additional advantage to this approach in that it gave the Scottish texts a wider appeal and access to a larger market than was open to those writers who chose to use the narrower application of estate accounts as the basis of their texts. Two of the most noteable English books of the time(5) did concentrate on accounting for estate owners. These were well written and interesting texts but they did not prove so popular as Mair. Estate accounting is also discussed by the Scottish writers and they emphasise that the technique that they are explaining is comprehensive in that it can readily deal with the accounts of "kingdoms, farms, manufactures, or families".(6)

Malcolm, Mair, Gordon and Hamilton all covered certain basic material which they regarded as being essential for a proper understanding of the system and likely to be of use to most merchants. In addition some of the writers allocated specialised chapters to deal with accounting for areas of activity that were particularly important in Scotland. Glasgow's flourishing trade with North America was recognised by Mair when he introduced a chapter on the tobacco trade into the 3rd edition of 'Book-keeping Methodiz'd' (1749). He also included a chapter on the sugar trade from the 5th edition of 1757. Although the tobacco trade collapsed with the American War of Independence, the West Indian sugar trade continued to expand and partially filled the gap. The linen industry, which became Scotland's main manufacturing industry during the century, was used by Hamilton to introduce his costing system.

The books also accommodated material on the changing form of business organisation. Larger business units were being formed in the course of the century. All the textbooks included material on company (or copartnership) accounts. The authors were aware of the importance of this topic and they specifically identified copartnerships where the capital was fixed, shares were transferable and the management was delegated to a partner trustee. This type of partnership seems to have had many of the features of a joint stock company. The question of the legality of such companies, in the light of the provisions of the Bubble Act, seems not to have caused concern.

18.5 The Canonical System - The Books of Account

Not only did the Scottish authors have the ability to write good textbooks but also they had an infectious enthusiasm for the Italian Method which made them very effective propagandists as well as textbook authors. They were, indeed, so eloquent in their praise for Pacioli's system that they might be criticised for their apparent unwillingness to consider any improvements.(7) It is likely that, in some respects, accounting practice was in advance of accounting theory as set out in these texts but this is not necessarily a valid criticism. Whilst it is true that the authors did attempt to instil a feeling of reverence for the standard system, it can be argued that they adopted this approach because they regarded it as pedagogically correct. Once the student had mastered the standard system they were quite willing to discuss variations designed to make the method more suitable for particular applications.

Using this normative approach the 18th century writers took their task to be the explanation of the canonical Italian system. As far as the books of account were concerned, this system was based on the use of Pacioli's three books: the Waste Book, the Journal and the Ledger.

All the authors did, however, explain alternatives to the canonical system once they had explained that system in full. Hamilton provides a good example of this. He divides the accounting material of his 'Introduction to Merchandize' into two parts: 'Italian Book-keeping' (part IV) and 'Practical Book-keeping' (part V). This division recognises the need to modify the standard system to suit the circumstances of particular requirements. Part V contains many valuable suggestions for improvements to the standard system but Hamilton still regarded it as essential for the student to have covered the basic framework in part IV.

Early in the 19th century James Morrison of the Mercantile Academy at Glasgow, contrasted those writers, such as Malcolm, Mair, Gordon and Hamilton, who "have tenaciously adhered to the Italian Method, with three Books only" with those who had developed a system based on a number of specialised 'Subsidiary Books'.(8) This distinction can rightly be made but it should not be overemphasised. By the end of the century more and more specialised books were being described by the Scottish writers. Several authors acknowledged that the Waste Book was not always maintained but throughout the century it hung on to its place as a key book although increasingly the Marginal Journal, which Malcolm had introduced as early as 1718, appeared in the illustrative material.

As time passed the cash book also began to achieve more prominence. This book had received more attention in texts dealing with an estate owner's accounts and the English writer North, who wrote such a treatise, explains the reason for this when he distinguishes between " ... a Gentleman, who receives and spends ... " who has " ... most of his Business run through his Cash" and a merchant who " ... deals by Barter, Exchequer, and Assignment, whereof a small Portion comes into his Cash".(9) The increasing use of cash by merchants as the century passed, necessitated a more prominent role for the cash book (although there was probably some delay before this was recognised in the texts).

In the 19th century the canonical framework used by the textbooks did change but the transition was not an instantaneous switch to the use of specialised day books. The 18th century saw the texts moving gradually towards the new system, whilst retaining the formal framework of the Italian System. In the 19th century the new paradigm was adopted. The Scottish writers did not make this step but their books had prepared the way for the new system.

18.6 Profit Measurement for 'Accomptable Branches'

In 1718 both Malcolm and Macghie noted that it was common for merchants to balanced their books at regular intervals (usually annually or six monthly) but the writers may have been adopting a normative approach to their subject as studies of extant account books do not seem to confirm their claim.(10) The balancing procedures involved the preparation of a profit and loss account but Malcolm and

Macghie (in 1718), and later Mair (in 1736), had no particular emphasis on the need for regular calculations of profit. The merchant was assumed to be more interested in the profits earned by each of his individual ventures, consignments, voyages or 'accomptable branches' than annual profit.

Except for a few general expenses which were debited directly to profit and loss account, all expenditure was charged to an appropriate branch of trade (or venture) account. The intention was that each of these venture accounts would remain open until the venture was complete. It follows that there was no necessity to distinguish between capital and revenue expenditure and depreciation was not a problem if the account remained open until the expiration (or disposal) of any depreciating assets.

When the accounts were balanced, which not infrequently was only when the books had become full, there was a need to place a value on any branches which had not come to fruition. The textbooks describe the necessary procedures but they do not worry overmuch about the choice between alternative valuation bases presumably because the accounts were being prepared for the merchant himself and he would recognise the significance of whatever convention was adopted.

Accruals and prepayments were given scant attention in merchants accounts until some time after the use of regular accounting periods became the practice.

18.7 Imputed Transactions

The situation in merchants accounts should be contrasted with that applying in farm and estate accounting, where the system of annual accounts was firmly established. In estate and farm accounting, procedures for making adjustments for accruals were described by Malcolm.(11)

Depreciation was also a relevant consideration in such cases where the annual crop was regarded as a branch of trade and Hamilton includes an interesting discussion of this topic in his chapter on 'Land-Stewards Accompts'.(12)

When criticism is voiced of the Scottish writers' neglect of accruals, alternative valuation bases, depreciation and the distinction between capital and revenue in their discussion of accounting for trading activities, it should be remembered that the criticism presupposes a concern with regular accounting periods and the distribution of regular financial reports which was largely absent for most of the century. If the accomptable branches of the 18th century merchant are to be regarded as profit centres, it must remembered that they are profit centres without an emphasis on the time dimension. The methods advocated by the textbook writers should not be criticised for failing to answer a purpose which they did not accept.

In fact, both Malcolm(13) and Hamilton(14) advocate quite sophisticated techniques for obtaining the profit of each accomptable branch of trade. Where internal transactions occur between two branches they suggest that it can be useful to impute appropriate charges. This kind of adjustment was proposed when a trader owned a ship which was used for transporting both his own and customers' goods. To determine separately the profitability of the ship and the goods, both Malcolm and Hamilton suggest that a freight charge should be debited to the goods and credited to the ship account.(15) In estate accounting the goods and services absorbed by the home farm were similarly to be transferred at the going rate.(16)

Hamilton went further than his contemporaries by recognising the existence of the 'joint cost problem' and specifying a criterion which would enable a distinction to be made between those cases where it was appropriate to calculate the separate cost (and separate profitability) of connected activities and those situations where this was a meaningless exercise.(17) Hamilton's views on this problem are still valid.

18.8 Profit Measurement for Regular Accounting Periods

The regular calculation of business profits became more important as the century passed. In 1763 Gordon noted that it was an ojective of the annual balancing of the books. He says: "Merchants generally, at some fixed period, once in the year, balance or close the Leger, not only because the spaces allotted for the accounts may be for the most part full, but likewise to show the merchant a true state of his affairs, and what increase or diminution his capital hath suffered by last year's transactions."(18)

In his second book Mair agreed with Gordon by making a similar statement, but there was still no improvement in the discussion (or lack of discussion) of accruals and prepayments. The difficulty was that of reconciling the older orientation, with its emphasis on each voyage as a 'branch of trade', with the new emphasis on a regular annual assessment of the total activities. The textbook recognition of the problem was tardy and Littleton claims that, of some 50 texts published between 1788 and 1899, only about 10% deal with accruals.(19)

In other respects the emphasis on 'branch of trade' accounts may have been instrumental in encouraging useful developments in farm and estate accounting and in Hamilton's process costing system.

In 1779 Hamilton acknowledges that regular annual balancing is the common practice and he gives a specimen Profit and Loss Sheet and Balance Sheet in his book. Although these were precursors of the modern financial statements which bear similar names, Hamilton's 'sheets' were primarily worksheets used as part of the annual balancing procedures.

The Profit and Loss Sheet and Balance Sheet did provide a summary of the period's transactions and period end position but there was no suggestion that such statements should be routinely prepared for distribution although Malcolm recognised that partners might legitimately request a 'State of their Accompts'.(20) For the majority of businesses, however, there was no separation between ownership and management so that regular reports of stewardship would have been superfluous. The merchant's account books were primarily maintained for his own use; he would have free access to them and would be in close touch with the daily operations of the business.

18.9 The Objectives of Accounting - Efficiency and Justice

A 20th century apologist for accounting would stress the contribution that it makes at the level of the individual (in providing information which is 'decision relevant') and at the national level (in promoting the efficiency of markets). The 18th century writers also considered that book-keeping assisted in promoting trade and commerce but they envisaged the mechanism for achieving this rather differently. They viewed the major benefit of the Italian Method as arising from the order that it imposed on chaos and its assistance in preserving justice by acting as the 'scale of commerce'(21). Order and justice were necessary for commerce to flourish.

Within the individual organisation there is again a difference between the modern perception of accounting's role and that considered as applying in the 18th century. Littleton and Zimmerman have said that: "A great deal, perhaps most, of accounting's service capacity for society is derived from the aid it renders to business management ...

Better managerial decisions became possible when the continuity of enterprise operations and a periodic review of status and results were recognized ... Further steps in this same direction were taken when exchange-priced transactions affecting several operational periods were carefully apportioned between fiscal periods and, in industrial accounting, between manufacturing process and/or product units."(22)

The emphasis given in the 18th century textbooks was different. Malcolm, Mair and Gordon did recognise the managerial uses of accounting but their stress was not on assisting the entrepreneur to maximise his profits but rather on the 'justice' of the record provided by the Italian Method.

This might be thought puzzling as the developing economy at the beginning of the 18th century was a capitalistic economy and Marshall has described how some of the Scottish entrepreneurs at that time were using accounting information to control and expand their businesses.(23)

Gordon (whose bill discounting activities seemed to exhibit some of the features of a capitalistic approach to affairs) emphasises, however, that it is not in a trader's own best interests for him to concentrate exclusively on profit maximisation: "It is the trader's interest to conduct his affairs with judgement and oeconomy; but his duty and interest are equally concerned, that all his negotiations be founded on integrity and honour."(24)

It has been claimed that Calvinism and Adam Smith legitimized the spirit of capitalism and the use of the merchant's accounting system in his search for profits. When the Italian Method was so used, the textbook emphasis provided an added bonus by emphasising that its use provided assurance that business was conducted with 'integrity and honour'. It is too simple to oppose justice and efficiency. Both have always featured as aims of accounting. The emphasis on 'objectivity', the requirement that accounts shall show a 'true and fair view' and the recognition of an important stewardship function for accounting are all accepted by the professional accountant of today as they were by accountants at the beginning of the 18th century. Similarly it has always been recognised that the merchant could obtain useful advice on the management of his business from his account books. Despite this it must be recognised that the textbook emphasis has changed and the stress seems now to be on accounting's role in assisting with the efficient allocation of scarce resources whereas most of the 18th century writers did not feature this so strongly.

18.10 The Genesis of Management Accounting

Hamilton was not mentioned in the previous section because he placed a much greater emphasis on providing information relevant for management's needs than did the other writers. 'An Introduction to Merchandize' is important because it contains an early decription of a completely integrated process costing system. Hamilton's treatment of this is particularly noteworthy because of its modern approach. Throughout he treats cost accounting as management accounting so that he discusses the case for profit centres, the problem of joint cost apportionment, transfer pricing and the use of opportunity costs.

The increasing rate of economic development in 18th century Scotland and the increasing amounts of capital that this required led traders to compare their business profit (or prospective profit) with the capital that they had invested (or might invest). One way of relating capital to business operations is to charge these operations with the cost of the capital employed. This method was used quite frequently towards the end of the century and its introduction was facilitated as the practice of preparing regular annual accounts was also becoming more common. The method was particularly appropriate for use in companies or copartnerships where the partners had contributed unequal amounts of capital. The partnership agreement might then provide for the use of an interest charge as a method of allocating profit. The distinction between appropriations of profit and charges against profit was not recognised at this time.

Adam Smith's discussion of 'lost profit' as an opportunity cost(25) was adopted, adapted and refined by Hamilton to provide this useful measure of operating success. Some agricultural writers (noteably Arthur Young) had advocated the charging of interest in computing a farmer's profit before Hamilton wrote on the subject but Hamilton's description seems to be the first in an accounting text and he also provides a method of systematically incorporating the interest imputations into the accounting records.

Hamilton's work on cost accounting and residual income has been insufficiently recognised. Some serious misunderstandings of the worth of his costing chapter have undoubtedly occurred because most researchers have not had access to Hamilton's full text, which only appears in the first edition. This edition is quite difficult to locate and it has not been reproduced in facsimile form.

Partly for this reason Hamilton's important innovations on cost accounting and residual income had no influence on his contemporaries and he has received insufficient attention in works on the development of accounting. After Hamilton's book nothing of any note was published (in English) on these subjects for over 100 years until the appearance (in the 1880's) of three books on cost accounting.(26)

18.11 The End of the Scottish Ascendancy

Although Mair's book continued to appear in new editions up to 1807, the Scottish Ascendancy in book-keeping texts effectively ended with Hamilton's text. The achievement of this group of Scottish writers is that, through the medium of a series of important texts, they successfully presented and promoted the technique of Italian Book-keeping, which was relatively unknown at the beginning of the century, into a position where it was universally accepted as indispensible in any business organisation. Further developments might have been anticipated from the Hamilton's 'Merchandize' in that it was an innovative book with several features which might have seemed particularly relevant for business conditions towards the end of the century. These develoments did not occur and, ironically, the loss of this leadership occurred simultaneously with the development of book-keeping into the new discipline of accountancy and the birth of the Scottish accountancy profession.

At the start of the 18th century a few teachers and writers of book-keeping texts were undertaking book-keeping work for merchants but by 1800 the new discipline of accountancy had become firmly established as an area of expertise which sustained a sizeable group of practitioners. In Edinburgh this body of practitioners included many lawyers who had developed a specialism in accountancy and this came to be regarded as a branch of the legal profession. Well into the 19th century this viewpoint continued.(27) The book-keeping texts of Malcolm, Mair, Gordon and Hamilton were probably inappropriate for the new race of accountants who would often have obtained their training as apprentices in legal offices. The worth of Hamilton's book was not appreciated by those who emphasised the legal aspects of accountancy.

18.12 Accounting as Part of the Enlightenment

This book has concentrated on the works of an important group of 18th century Scottish accounting writers. In chapter 1 the question was posed as to whether the Scottish Ascendancy in accounting texts (which they achieved) can be considered as part of the Scottish Enlightenment.

If the Scottish Enlightenment had a focus it was probably a focus on the improvement of society through a study of the "science of man"(28) and the laws underlying human behaviour. Supporting this concern there was an emphasis on the need to communicate new ideas, advances in knowledge and improvements in the practical arts. The Enlightenment's achievements in encouraging educational texts was significant and, in chapter 1, we claimed that the stream of influential accounting text books can be recognised as being an important part of this flood of improving literature.

Subsequent chapters have shown that the subject matter of these texts was also intimately concerned with the Enlightenment's focus on the improvement of society. Early in the century Malcolm argued that "Societies are supported by Commerce" and he claimed that a sound system of book-keeping is a prerequisite for ensuring the justice which is required for the promotion of commerce and hence the advancement of society.(29) Colinson, the first Scottish accounting author, held similar views. The texts convey their authors' excitement and enthusiasm for the outstanding virtues of the technique that they are explaining. They did not view the Italian Method as a useful but optional technique, rather they thought of it as a major advance which would lead to profound improvements in trade and commerce (and society). Gordon, for example, considered that "Regular books frequently examined, will contribute more to prosperity in trade, than great address and abilities without them."(30) In addition to its contribution in this respect, the authors were clearly captivated by the elegance of the Italian System. They would have agreed wholeheartedly with Sombart's view that "double-entry bookkeeping can be contemplated not without awe and admiration as one of the most artistically arranged structures produced by the admirably rich formative capacity of the European human spirit."(31) In support of such a view Malcolm quotes with approval North's belief that " ... besides the real Value of it (book-keeping) in Life, every ingenious Gentleman may have Reason to know this Art, as a Sort of human Learning".(32)

In the 20th century accounting is seldom described in such terms but Hatfield has attempted to reinstate some of its lost glory by an appeal to its history. In a well known essay, he sought to " ... remove the stigma attached to accounting by showing that in its origin it is respectable, nay, even academic: that ... it has from time to time attracted the attention of men of unquestioned intellectual attainment; that it justifies itself in that it has arisen to meet a social need".(33) This study of Scottish Accounting in the 18th century has produced support for Hatfield's claims.

The case for considering the 'ascendancy' in accounting texts as part of the achievements of the Enlightenment can also be argued from a consideration of the 'unquestioned intellectual attainments' of the main writers. Alexander Malcolm, John Mair, William Gordon and Robert Hamilton were polymaths of considerable intellectual attainment. Robert Hamilton (Professor of Natural Philosophy, and later

Mathematics, at Marischal College, Aberdeen) could, without question, be included in any list of Enlightenment luminaries for his major work on the national debt and his social writings as well as his contribution to the development of accounting.(34) The other three accounting authors also display the versatility of the period; so that, for example, Malcolm wrote a major work on music, Mair was a pioneer of science education in the school curriculum and Gordon campaigned for the inclusion of accounting in university studies.

The books, therefore, had an origin which was both 'respectable' and 'academic'. The fact that they were extensively reprinted and that they were read widely throughout Britain and America, is proof enough of their quality and the fact that they met a 'social need'. It has been shown that some of the texts were more than sound utilitarian manuals; they were also well written and innovative. Although they were practical, technical works they were also part of the general intellectual ferment of the Scottish Enlightenment and should be seen as part of this movement which produced the more renowned works in economics, philosophy, law and science. If the accounting writings lack the glamour of some of the other publications of the period, and some of the other works of their authors, they had an influence which is arguably just as profound. Some of the writings demonstrate significant advances in accounting thought and the development of some ideas and techniques which remain relevant and important more than 200 years later.

GLOSSARY

" ... as every Artist has a Set of Words and Ways of Speaking, which they have a Liberty and Right to use, as being peculiar to the Art they profess; so Merchants have theirs ... In all Merchants Writings, ... when written by a Person of Skill and Experience, there is a concise, emphatick Diction, a certain peculiar use of Words and Phrases, which is a kind of Elegancy that runs through and adorns the whole, and at the same Time shows the Ability of the Accomptant".(Mair, J, 'Book-keeping Methodiz'd', 1736, pp 6/7).

Abatement " ... by Abating a Debtor of a Sum resting, you take as you and he can agree, without respect to the Sum lent, or Term of Payment when it comes due by Rebatement ... " (Brodie, 'A New and Easy Method of Book-keeping', 1722, p 4 of Second Waste-Book). Mair distinguishes 'abatement' from "discount or rebate" which latter two terms refer to a "regular Deduction from any Sum, according to the Rate of Interest on account of Payment per Advance" (Mair, 'Book-keeping Methodiz'd', 1736, p 29).

Accompt, account Often used in the plural to refer to the 'Italian Method of Book-keeping' but also used for many different types of business statement so that the third chapter of part III of Hamilton's 'An Introduction to Merchandize' (entitled 'Merchants Accompts') deals with Bills of Parcels, Invoices, Accompts Sales, Accompts Current and Accompts of Charge and Discharge'. The word could also refer to various types of calculation as in the title of Newall's book 'The Merchant's Companion: being a more Exact. Quick and Easy Way, for making up of Accompts'.(Newall, W,

Glasgow, 1715) Gradually as the 18th century passed the modern spelling 'account' replaced 'accompt'. Accompt is used by: Colinson (1683), Drummond (1718), Lundin (1718), Malcolm (1718), Macghie (1718), Mair (1736), Stevenson (1762); both forms of spelling are used by: Brodie (1722), Malcolm (1731), R Hamilton (1777); Account is used by: W Hamilton (1735), Gordon (1763 and 1766), Mair (1773), Scruton (1777), Young (c 1790). Even at the end of the century 'accompt' hung on; in 1798 Buchanan uses 'accounts' (and 'accountant') in his book ('The Writing Master and Accountant's Assistant') but his list of errata notes that this should be 'accompts'.

Accomptant, accountant The term accomptant was originally used for someone who was required to account to another. "Thus in mediaeval times the person giving up the account always refers to himself as the "computans" or accountant." (Murray, D, 'Chapters in the History of Bookkeeping, Accountancy and Commercial Arithmetic', Glasgow, 1930, p 15) Dodson uses the word in a analogous sense when he says: "The Person ... whose Transactions are registered, is called the ACCOUNTANT",('The Accountant, or, the Method of Book-keeping deduced from clear principles', 1750, p i) and Colinson is also adopting this definition when he says that book-keeping " ... is a Science absolutely necessare for all Accomptants".(Idea Rationaria', 1683, p 1) In the 18th century 'accomptant' is sometimes used to mean someone who is (or should be) adept at calculating; in this sense it features in some book titles such as George Brown's book of tables which he called 'Arithmetica Infinita, or the Accurate Accomptant's Best Companion'.(Edinburgh, 1718) Murray gives more examples of this use.(op cit, pp 11-13)

Glossary

The more modern meaning is 'one who keeps accounts'. This is the usage adopted by Gordon in the title of his book 'The Universal Accountant and Complete Merchant'.(1763) In the name of Gordon's book there is the implicit assumption that the merchant will be his own accountant but in the second half of the century 'accomptant' or 'accountant' was the job description of those whose living was obtained from maintaining accounting records.

Accountant and Chief Manager The term used by Malcolm to describe the person (normally a partner) who manages the affairs of a partnership and maintains the accounting records (Malcolm, A, 'A Treatise of Book-keeping', 1731, p 65). See 'partner-trustee'.

Accountantship Used by Scruton in the title of his book 'The Practical Counting House; or, Calculation and Accountantship Illustrated', (Glasgow, 1777). Gordon (Scruton's partner) also uses the term ('The Universal Accountant and Complete Accountant', 1763, vol II, p 13).

Agio "An Italick word importing a conveniency, and is used to signify the difference of the value of current money and bank notes, in Venice and Holland, which is commonly 3 or 4 per cent. in favour of the notes. Also the reward given for changing one coin or species of money for another" (Mair, 'Book-keeping Methodiz'd', 1736, appendix, p 56).

Alligation A branch of commercial arithmetic which is concerned with questions relating to the mixture of several ingredients. Usually the object is to determine the cost (or price or some other quality) of the resulting mixture but it also covers the calculation of the proportions of the various ingredients which should be used when the desired average cost (or price or quality) is given.

Alphabet An alphabetical index. "...an Alphabet or Index-Book, into which are entered the Names of every Title of Accompt, with the Folio of the Leger where they stand ... " (Malcolm, 'A New Treatise of Arithmetick and Book-keeping', 1718, p 117).

Annual Rent Interest. Colinson's Question 29 is as follows: "Q. If you borrow money on Interest, What is Debitor? A. Cash Debitor to him that lends the money for the principal summe, and Interest Accompt Debitor to him for the annual rent, so long as you agree" (Colinson, 'Idea Rationaria', 1683, p 8).

Asset This word is not used in 18th century accounting books. It is difficult now to imagine how an accounting text could be written without using the term (or a synonym) but Gordon illustrates how they managed. He talks of an "inventory of the money, effects, and debts belonging to him (the trader), and the debts due to others" ('The General Counting-House and Man of Business', 1766, p 422).

Assignation An order made by the Assigner on one of his debtors (called the Assigned) requiring him to pay an amount to one of the Assigner's creditors (called the Assignee), (Mair, 'Book-keeping Methodiz'd', 1736, p 32). Colinson's Question 85 is as follows: "Q. Suppose you did give him ane Assignation or precept upon another for that summe? A. Then he is Debitor to the person, upon whom I have drawn the precept" ('Idea Rationaria', 1683, p 14).

Auditor "In a legal Sense, Auditors are Persons appointed by the Judges, in an Action of Accompt, to adjust the Differences between the Parties, in order to joyn Issues upon Facts not agreed. In a Revenue Sense, they are Officers in the Exchequer, to whom all stating Accompts belong. And in a Common Sense, every Person who professes the formal stating and adjusting of Accompts extrajudicially, is called an Auditor, and his Work, when perfected, an Audit. An Auditor differs from an Accomptant, as an Accompt rendered differs from an Accompt kept" (North, 'The Gentleman Accomptant', 1714, Vocabulary). North is notable among the 18th century writers in emphasising auditing.

Balance, Ballance " ... by the word Balance merchants understand the difference betwixt the sums on the Dr and Cr sides of any accompt. Which difference being entered on the defective side, the accompt is said to be balanced; that is, to have the sums of the Dr and Cr sides evened, or made equal" (Mair, 'Book-keeping Methodized', 1765, p 79). "Ballance, this proceeds from the Analogy of Accompts with Weights. When the Sums opposed are equal, the Accompt ballanceth; and the difference of unequal Sums is called the Ballance because that added to the lesser, makes them equal, and that closes the Accompt" (North, 'The Gentleman Accomptant', 1714, Vocabulary).

Balance Accompt The account to which all asset, liability and stock (capital) balances are transferred when the books are closed. Also forms the basis for the new inventory prepared when the new books are opened.

Balance Sheet This term has a variety of meanings in the 18th century and the early part of the 19th. Stevenson uses it for an extended trial balance, ('Book-keeping by Double Entry', 1762). Hamilton illustrates a balance sheet which is more in keeping with the modern definition as a statement of assets and liabilities. "The Dr. of the balance-sheet contains every kind of property belonging to you, and every debt owing to you; and the Cr. contains every debt owing by you: Therefore the difference of the sides exhibits your nett estate" ('An Introduction to Merchandize', 4th edition, 1799, p 292, para 50). Hamilton's Balance Sheet is, however, primarily one of the Working Papers prepared in closing the books. Even as late as 1844 there is no unanimity in the use of the term so that one of the forms issued by the Registrar of Joint Stock Companies, in connection with the 1844 'Act for the Registration, Incorporation, and Regulation of Joint Stock Companies', shows a 'Balance Sheet' which includes Receipts and Expenditure for the accounting period (Wordsworth, C, 'The Law of Railway, Banking, Mining, and other Joint Stock Companies', London: William Benning and Co, 5th edition, 1845, pp 251/252).

Bank Dollar Dutch currency. "Sums of Money at Amsterdam are distinguished into bank and current. The current money is the real coin which circulates in the country. The bank money is imaginary, being the property which a person possesses in the treasure lodged in the bank. Money paid into the bank of Amsterdam cannot be redrawn; but those who pay it have credit in the bank-books, which they can transfer at pleasure; so that it circulates in payments, and answers the purposes of trade, with equal or greater ease than real money" (Hamilton, 'An Introduction to Merchandize', 1788, p 227).

Barter " ... is the trucking or exchanging one commodity for another".(Mair, 'Book-keeping Methodiz'd', 1736, appendix, p 57) The early writers discuss barter, eg Colinson includes a barter transaction in his illustrative example on 7th January 1682 (Colinson, 'Idea Rationaria', 1683).

Bill of Exchange "A Bill of Exchange may be defined a written Mandate of the Drawer to his Correspondent, ordering him to pay to the Creditor in the Bill, the Sum therein contained, at a certain Time, and sometimes in a particular Place, for some Cause mentioned in the Bill itself" (Mair, 'Book-keeping Methodiz'd', 1736, appendix, p 14). This definition is retained throughout all the editions of 'Book-keeping Methodiz'd' but it it is replaced in 'Book-keeping Moderniz'd' by the following simpler definition: "A short written order for money, to be received in one place or country, for value paid in another" ('Book-keeping Moderniz'd', 1773, p 351).

Bodomrie, Bottomry, Bummery (North) "Bottomry, is the borrowing of money on the bottom of a ship, for which a high rate of interest, sometimes 30, 40, nay 50 per cent. is to be paid upon the safe arrival of the ship: but if the ship be lost, neither principal nor interest can be demanded" (Mair, 'Book-keeping Methodiz'd', 1736, appendix, p 58). "Bodomry is the Money lent to the Masters of Ships when, after a long Voyage, they fall short of Money to buy Provisions, or for their other necessary Expence; or when they are drove by Stress of Weather into a strange Port, and require Money for their Sustenance, or Repairing their Ships. It ... is allowed by the Laws and Statutes of all Countries; even 30 or 40 per Cent Interest in regard that the Lender, who always gives his Credit on the Faith of the Ship, and not the Master, can make no Demand of his Money, if the said Ship happens not to make a safe Voyage home ... " (Brodie, 'A New and Easy Method of Book-keeping', 1722, p 8). See Malcolm (1718) p 123. "Bummeries, or as the Etymon is, Bottom Marine, signifies certain Bargains for vast Interest upon Loans of Money, to stand or fall intirely upon the Return or Loss of Ships. Which Contingency sanctifies the Bargain, and makes it not Usurious within that Statute, whatever it may be by the Law of Conscience" (North, 'The Gentleman Accomptant', 1714, Vocabulary). See 'Usury'.

Book-Holding Book-keeping. "The Council of Edinburgh considering how necessary the Science of Book-holding is for the Advantage of Trade and Commerce ... Do therefore Nominat and Authorize ... John Dickson to be Master and Professor thereof within the City" (Edinburgh Evening Courant, 15 October 1705). "It is interesting to note that a more literal translation from the Dutch, 'book-holding', was in use in Scotland. The Scottish National Dictionary cites the following from the Scots Courant of 16 March, 1716: "John Morison, A M is to begin his lessons of ... the Italian Method of Book-holding".(Parker, R H, 'Reckoning, Merchants' Accounts, Book-keeping, Accounting or Accountancy? The Evidence of the Long Titles of Books on Accounting in English 1543-1914', printed in 'External Financial Reporting', edited by Carsberg, B and S Dev,

Prentice - Hall International, 1984, p 116) The Dutch word is 'boekhouden'. The French is 'tenue des livres'.

Bounties " ... are certain premiums allowed for the exportation of certain British manufactures".(Gordon, W, 'The Universal Accountant', vol I, 1763, p 182) "Bounty Money, is that which Merchant Exporters of Corn, when the Price is low, Receive as a Premio for the Exportation. This was at first Temp. Car. 2. laid on, on purpose only to lessen his Treasure, and has been a publick Nuisance ever since." (North, 'The Gentleman Accomptant', 1714, Vocabulary)

Box-Master Macghie uses this as a synonym for 'treasurer' (Macghie, 'The Principles of Book-keeping Explain'd', 1718, p 11) See 'Cash'.

Branch (of trade) The word branch is not used to mean an organizationally distinct department. Any distinguishable part of a merchant's trade (eg a particular consignment or a particular voyage) may be regarded as a branch of trade. Colinson refers to Cash as a branch of stock.('Idea Rationaria', 1683, p 6) Compare with the modern French usage of 'branche'.

Brokers "are a kind of Factors: They are commonly persons who have been bred merchants, and have had misfortunes in the world: they must be men of skill and experience, their business being to find out customers to merchants, and to assist merchants in making bargains".(Mair, J, 'Book-keeping Methodiz'd, 1736, appendix, p 58)

Glossary

<u>Butt</u> " ... of sack, 2 hogsheads; of currants, from 15 to 22C" (Mair, 'Book-keeping Methodiz'd', 1736, appendix, p 59). "Sold to Peter Couper, 5 Butts of Cherry Seck ... " (Colinson, 'Idea Rationaria', 1683, Wastebook, 3 January 1682).

<u>Cancel</u> "CANCEL, is a Word well known to mean the making a Writing void by dashing Lines over it. But true Cancelling is, when it is done so Diagonally, as to produce Squares Arras-wise (as Workmen say.) For the Lattice of the Seat, or Office, in which the ancient Secretary of State sat, was framed in that manner, which being called Cancellae, he that sat infra Cancellas, was called the Chancellor; so between the Choir and Nave of Churches. The like now in Italy is used in Windows, and called Jalousia. Taking the Seal off a Deed is called Cancelling, but improperly; but it being the Delivery back of the Deed to be cancelled, it makes it void" (North, 'The Gentleman Accomptant', 1714, Vocabulary).

<u>Candlemas</u> The feast of the purification of the Virgin Mary, February 2, one of the Scottish quarter days. "Custom has fixed on two terms in the year as the periods from which the rents of that year are to be accounted in bonis of the life-renter; the one half at Whitsunday, when the corns are presumed to be fully sown, and the other half at Martinmas, when they are reaped."(Erskine, J, 'Institutes of the Law of Scotland', 1773, II, ix, para 64). The other Quarter Days are: Whitsunday (15 May), Lammas (1 August) and Martinmas (11 November).

<u>Capital</u> The term was used in its modern accounting sense (eg Stevenson, 'A General Discourse', 1732, p 8; Gordon,

Glossary

'The Universal Accountant', 1765, vol II, p 16; Mair, 'Book-keeping Moderniz'd', 1773, p 16) but 'stock' was more commonly used by the 18th century accounting authors. Malcolm uses 'Capital Stock'.('A Treatise of Book-keeping', 1731, p 38). Both 'capital' and 'stock' are used in Smith's 'Wealth of Nations'(1777).

Carolus, Carolusus (Colinson) An English gold coin of the time of Charles II, the coin features in Colinson's illustrative Cash Book valued at 23 shillings sterling (Colinson, 'Idea Rationaria', 1683).

Cash "This word Cash is used now generally for money Accompts, it comes from the Italian word Cassa, which is a money Chest ... " (Colinson, 'Idea Rationaria', 1683, p 6). Thirty five years after Colinson's note, Macghie still thought it necessary to explain the word: "Cash (a Title for Money)" ('The Principles of Book-keeping Explain'd', 1718, p 2). Other writers also note the derivation. Brodie, ('A New and Easy Method of Book-keeping', 1722), commences an illustrative Waste-Book as follows: "Inverness, 24th August, 1721 ... I have Ready Money in Chest L1037 - 11 - 8" and he calls the Cash Book 'The Money or Chest-Book' (p 14). See 'Mr. Chest and Mr. Box'. (Littleton, A C and B S Yamey (editors), 'Studies in the History of Accounting', Sweet and Maxwell, 1956, pp 266-271).

Cautioner Scots Law term, one who becomes security for another. " ... unless the factor be bound as cautioner for the payments" (Hamilton, 'An Introduction to Merchandize', vol I, 1777, p 351).

Glossary

Chamberlain "the factor of an estate etc." (Robinson, M (editor), 'The Concise Scots Dictionary', Aberdeen University Press, 1985). "There is a kind of Stewards, who are not Domestick Servants (and in Scotland, we call them rather Chamberlains or Factors) to whose care is committed the collecting of Rents."(Malcolm, 'A New Treatise of Book-keeping', 1731, appendix, p 30).

Charge and Discharge (an Accompt of) "An accompt of charge and discharge ... contains, on one side, the articles entrusted to the care of a factor, for which he is accountable; on the other side; the manner in which he has rendered accompt for the same; and concludes with the balance which remains in his hands, or which is due to him by his employer" (Hamilton, 'An Introduction to Merchandize', vol I, 1777, p 350).

Check Note " ... whenever he wants to pay a tradesman, as, suppose £50 he writes a bill, as follows, in a check note given him for that purpose:

No 182 6th January 1774

Pay Mr Edward Needful, or bearer,

Fifty pounds

To Cashiers of the Bank W.P.

(Perry, 'The Man of Business', 1774, Note on p 2 of Waste Book). This is the only reference to cheques located in the 18th century Scottish accounting texts.

Glossary

Closs " ... is an allowance to the buyer of 2lb for every 3cwt. for the turn of the scale, in selling by retail" (Perry, 'The Man of Business', 1774, p 149).

Company Partnership; "When a Joint-Stock is employ'd in common among several Persons in the way of Trade, their Accompts are nam'd Company Accompts, wherein each Person shares of the Gain, or suffers Loss in proportion to his Share in the Stock. The Management of these Accompts is usually committed to one of the Partners, who, in that respect, acts a Factor to the rest, for which he has usually a Provision as other Factors, and his respective Share in the same stock" (Brodie, 'A New and Easy Method of Book-keeping', 1722, p 12).

Company Accompts (or Accounts) Partnership Accounts. " ... when the same (ie the trade) is managed both for my self and others (the Accompts ... are always termed Company-Accompts)" (Macghie, 'The Principles of Book-keeping Explain'd', 1718, p 6).

Current Dollars, Currant Dollers (Colinson) Dutch currency, see Bank Dollars. Colison's illustrative Cash Book values 'Legg or currant Dollers' at 56 pence, whereas 'Rix or Bank-dollers' are valued at 58 pence ('Idea Rationaria', 1683).

Customs "Customs are certain duties or tolls, imposed by the sovereign, or legislative power of the nation, on certain imports and exports, for the maintenance and support of government, receivable at the customhouse, and regulated by tariffs, or books of rates; the principal whereof may be reckoned tonnage, poundage, old subsidy, new subsidy, 1/2,

2/3 subsidy, &c" (Gordon, 'The Universal Accountant', vol I, 1763, p 182).

Day Book A generic name for the Waste Book or Journal. " ... the Waste-Book is plainly a Journal, i.e. a Day-Book: But to distinguish two Books, which agree in this Respect, that they are both properly Day-Books; the one is called the Waste-Book, and the other the Journal ... " (Malcolm, A, 'A Treatise of Book-keeping', 1731, p 28). Hamilton uses the term day book to refer to a combined waste book and journal (Hamilton, 'An Introduction to Merchandise', vol II, 1779, p 242).

Dead Stock Used by Stevenson to refer to 'Rings, Jewels and Plate' included as assets in his example of estate accounting (Stevenson, 'Book-keeping by Double Entry', 1762). Gordon uses the term to refer to merchandise for which there is no demand ('The Universal Accountant, 1765, vol II, p 2).

Debenture "At the Custom House: a certificate given to an exporter of imported goods on which a draw-back is allowed, or of home produce on which a bounty was granted, certifying that the holder is entitled to the amount therein stated" (Oxford English Dictionary). "The Allowance given by Law for every Barrel of White Herrings 2s. 8d. and for every Barrel of Salmon 4s. 6d. is a Profit that doth arise upon the Fish a Month after Exportation, when you get out a Debenture from the Custom-House, certified upon either the Commissioners of Customs, or Excise ... " (Brodie, 'A New and Easy Method of Book-keeping', 1722, p 4 of Second Waste-Book). Drummond discusses the effect of debentures on the cost of curing fish in his essay on 'The Method of catching and curing Cod-

Fish ... ' which is appended to 'The Accountant's Pocket Companion'.(1718, pp 34-37) Scruton gives examples of the various types of debenture.('The Practical Counting House', 1777, pp 362-394) North's definition differs from the foregoing: "Debentures are properly the Paper-Tickets given out to Seamen or Soldiers, instead of Money due to them to a time for their Pay; and supposed to be made good out of Money to come in. But these are commonly sold at low Rates for present Coin, especially to great Officers and their Clerks, who smelling the Money in the Wind, by their Jackalls buy up the Debentures, and so forestal the poor Men of their Dues."(North, 'The Gentleman Accomptant', 1714, Vocabulary)

Debt Book "In this book is specified the date of every payment, to be paid or received."(Scruton, J, 'The Practical Counting House', 1777, p 5) The book is a cash budget. Malcolm and Gordon call this book a 'Month Book'; Mair calls it a 'Month Book' or a 'Bill Book' in 'Book-keeping Methodiz'd',(1736, appendix, pp 9-11) but he distinguishes between these in 'Book-keeping Moderniz'd'. (1773, pp 336/337)

Delivery Accompt A Delivery Accompt in buying is debited when goods are bought for delivery in the future (the supplier being credited). A Delivery Accompt in selling is credited when goods are sold for delivery in the future (the customer being debited). When the goods are received or delivered a transfer is made to the relevant goods account. Colinson introduces these accounts as part of the procedures to follow in accounting for fore-hand bargains. (Colinson, 'Idea Rationaria', 1683, p 9, also Ledger A, F10)

Glossary

Desperate Debts Bad and Doubtful Debts (Malcolm, 1731, pp 52/3). "If you have to deal with several bad Debtors, of whom you do not expect Payment soon, or perhaps scarcely ever; ... I would erect a general Accompt, under the Title of Desperate Debts, and make it stand Dr. for all such Debts, till I receive Payment, or found them irrecoverable" (Mair, 'Book-keeping Methodiz'd', 1736, p 30).

Dinmont "A wether between the first and second shearing, i.e. between one and a half and two and a half years old" (Scottish National Dictionary). "Sold to Robert Forrester 3 Scores and 4 Dinmonts, for 3 Scores payle. at 12s. 6d. Luck-penny deduced £37 5 0" (Stevenson, 'Book-keeping by Double Entry, 1762, example of farm accounting).

Discount " ... a regular Deduction from any Sum according to the Rate of Interest on account of Payment per Advance" (Mair, 'Book-keeping Methodiz'd', 1736, p 29). See 'rebate'. "Bankers in discounting bills, find the interest of the sum drawn for, from the time the bill is discounted until it be due; which interest is more than the discount" (Perry, 'The Man of Business', 1774, p 159). "Discount, in the artificial Sense signifies a sort of Trade in buying Bills of Exchequer, Tallies, and the like, before the time of Payment; and so much as is given less then the Import, is called the Discount, being the Premio for laying down the Money beforehand. This often covers great Frauds; for many Men declining, will contrive Bills to be drawn on purpose to be discounted, which is paying intolerable Usury; and so they hold up, by robbing Peter to pay Paul, till they break, to the Disappointment of the last Discounters" (North, 'The Gentleman Accomptant', 1714, Vocabulary).

Glossary

Doer An agent, the term is used by Malcolm, " ... the merchant, or his Doers ... " ('A New Treatise of Arithmetick and Book-keeping', 1718, p 124), and by Mair, " ... Manager or Doer for the Company ... " ('Book-keeping Moderniz'd', 1736, p 46).

Dollar "a piece of foreign coin, about 4s. 6d" (Mair, 'Book-keeping Methodiz'd', 1736). The word is a corruption of the German 'Thaler'. Although by the 18th century the word was used to describe a variety of foreign coins, it had earlier been used for certain Scottish coins.

Double Entry Used in title of Stevenson's book (1762), earlier used by Webster (1721) and Weston (1754). Adopted by Mair in the 5th edition of 'Book-keeping Methodiz'd' (1757) in his Sugar Trade chapter (based on Weston) and used on the title page of Mair's 'Book-keeping Moderniz'd (1773).

Double Usance See Usance. Written as 2 Usance. "Q. what if you pay the Bill that run on 2. Usance presently rebating at 1. per Cent?" (Colinson, 'Idea Rationaria', 1683, p 13).

Draw-Back " ... is a sort of Discount, but is used in Custom-house Business only, and is when an importer upon Exportation is to have the Custom paid back again, in Money or Discount" (North, 'The Gentleman Accomptant, 1714, Vocabulary).

Eln, Ell The Scottish eln (or ell) was 37.059 inches (compared with 45 inches in England). "I have 1000 Elns fine linen at 2sh 6d Ster per Eln" (Macghie, 'The Principles of Book-keeping Explain'd', 1718, In illustrative Waste-book).

Glossary

Entry, Entrance "Entry, in Accompts is only the writing the Parcels into the Books in due Order and Form" (North, 'The Gentleman Accomptant', 1714, Vocabulary).

Exchange " ... taken in its restricted sense, is a commerce in money, or the exchanging one species of money for another" (Stevenson, 'A Full and Practical Treatise upon Bills of Exchange', 1764, p 2).

Factor (1) "Factors are merchants agents, residing abroad, constituted by letters of attorney to act for their constituents" (Gordon, 'The Universal Accountant', vol I, 1763, p 231). (2) See Chamberlain.

Factory Accompts (or Accounts) Accounts maintained for trade undertaken as a factor (Macghie, 'The Principles of Book-keeping Explain'd', 1718, p 6).

Feu Duty An annual sum payable to the superior or feuar of land in return for the right of exclusive possession or use of the land in perpetuity.

Feuar One who holds land in feu.

Fictitious Accompts "Fictitious or Nominal Accompts, are such as are contriv'd on Purpose to supply the Defect of a Debitor or Creditor ... And therefore, e.g. when I receive any Thing, without giving out or delivering (or being in the least obliged to give out or deliver) any Thing in Compensation thereof, as in the Case of a Gift, or any Kind of neat Gain; then I say, I must contrive a Creditor, to which the Thing received must be made Debitor, which in general must be Accompt of Profit and Loss, or a particular Branch thereof, viz. Interest-Accompt, Proper Charges-Accompt, Accompt of Household-Expenses, Insurance Accompt, Bottomry-Accompt, Accompt of Wagers, Promises, Hazard, &c. ... The same might be said as to the Converse, when we give out or deliver any Thing, without receiving or expecting to receive any Thing in Compensation therof ... " (Macghie, 'The Principles of Book-keeping Explain'd', 1718, pp 9/10).

Firm 'Firm' is not used in the modern sense of meaning a partnership but rather the 'style' or name of a partnership under which it trades. "Two or more merchants in company assume some denomination, which is called their firm, under which their business is conducted; and all the partners use it in subscribing papers which relate to the business of the company" (Hamilton, 'An Introduction to Merchandize', 4th edition, 1799, p 216). "All debts contracted under the firm of the company are binding on the whole partners ... " (op cit, p 525). The Oxford English Dictionary acknowledges this meaning.

Fixed (or Fixt) Company A fixed company is a company (partnership) with " ... a fixt Capital Stock, of which every Partner furnishes his Share; and this to be the subject Matter of all the subsequent Transactions of Trade" (Malcolm, 'A New Treatise of Arithmetick and Book-keeping', 1718). The adjective 'fixt' refers to the stock (ie the capital) but companies (or partnerships) with a fixed capital are likely to be fairly substantial. Mair refers to " ... fixed companies, whose trade is considerable, or who have the prospect of dealing long that way" (Mair, 'Book-keeping Methodiz'd', p 50)

Folio "The two pages of the Book (i.e. the Ledger) lying open before you, on your Right and Left Hand, are numbred alike; ... and therefore both together are called but one Folio".(Macghie, 'The Principles of Book-keeping Explain'd', 1718, p 3) The word is derived from the Latin 'folium' a leaf; this is another example of the use of the tree metaphor in accounting.

Fore-hand Bargain This is a bargain where some (or all) of the consideration is pre-paid. Malcolm provides a definition " ... where Goods are bought or sold to be delivered at a certain Time afterwards, either with a Penalty, or not; and Money, or other Effects, given per Advance of the Price; as is common in such Cases".('A Treatise of Book-keeping', 1731, p 47) He gives the following example in a specimen Waste-Book: "Sold on Fore-hand Bargain to William Smith, 8 Bales of French Paper, at £4 per Bale, to be delivered 5 August next. Given me per Advance an Assignation on Daniel Trader, payable on Demand for £18. The rest payable at Delivery £14" ('A New Treatise of Arithmetick and Book-keeping', 1718). The journal entry for this is Dr: William Smith £32; Cr: Delivery Accompt of Sales £32; Dr: Daniel Trader £18; Cr: William Smith £18. An earlier example appears in the records of the New Mills Cloth Manufactury "Edinburgh, the 12th May, 1703. ... ane bargaine of oakin timber that David Vertie made a foirhand bargaine with him for ... ".(Scott, W R, 'The Records of a Scottish Cloth Manufactory at New Mills, Haddingtonshire 1681-1703', Edinburgh: Scottish Historical Society, 1905, p 347) Colinson (1683) discusses accounting for fore-hand bargains on p 9.

Gabel " ... an old word for tribute or custom paid to the Prince or Lord. Also an excise in France on salt" (Mair, 'Book-keeping Methodiz'd', 1736, appendix).

Gain and Loss Accompt Drummond uses this title for the Profit and Loss Account ('The Accomptant's Pocket-Companion', 1718, p 8). Gordon refers to an 'Account of Loss and Gain', ('The Universal Accountant, 1765, vol II, p 16) but more generally he uses 'Profit and Loss Account'.

Grand Book of Accounts The Ledger, used by William Hamilton ('Book-keeping New Modelled', 1735, p 2).

Guinea, Guinie (Colinson), Guinee (Colinson) An English gold coin so called because it was originally made from metal imported from Guinea. Included in Colinson's illustrative Cash Book with a value of 21s 6d sterling, ('Idea Rationaria', 1683). "By a proclamation issued Dec 22nd 1717, the guinea was made current at 21s" (Bithell, R, 'A Counting-House Dictionary', London, 2nd edition, c 1880).

Hanse " ... a society of merchants incorporated for promoting the interest of trade, and the safe conveyance of merchandise from one kingdom to another" (Mair, 'Book-keeping Methodiz'd, 1736, appendix, p 63).

Hanse-towns " ... certain free towns in Germany, in number twenty-seven, as Hamburg, Lubeck, Magdenberg, &c. joined in a league offensive and defensive against all enemies"

(Mair, 'Book-keeping Methodiz'd', 1736, appendix, p 63).

Hansel, Handsel " ... i.e. Hand-sale, money received upon the first sale of any part or parcel of goods, or the money received first in the morning. Also a new-year's gift" (Mair, 'Book-keeping Methodiz'd', 1736, appendix, p 63). The first instalment of a payment.

Hazard Accompt " ... when you borrow Money on Bottomry, charge Cash Dr to Hazard-accompt for the sum received" (Mair, 'Book-keeping Methodiz'd', 1736, p 29). If the ship arrives safely the credit balance on the Hazard Accompt (plus interest) is cleared by repayment of the loan. If the ship is lost the credit balance is transferred to Profit and Loss Accompt.

Heavy Money "bullion, or uncoined money" (Mair, 'Book-keeping Methodiz'd', 1736, appendix).

Heckle An instrument for combing flax.

Hog "Young sheep are called hogs from Martinmas after they are lambed till they are fleeced next year" (Scottish National Dictionary). Used by Stevenson in his illustration of farm accounting ('Book-keeping by Double-Entry', 1762).

Hogshead "a vessel containing 63 gallons" (Mair, 'Book-keeping Methodiz'd', 1736, appendix).

Imaginary Accompt An alternative term for an account that North and Malcolm would call a 'Mediate Accompt' but also used as a synonym for 'Fictitious Accompt' (Yamey, B S,

Glossary

'Pious Inscriptions Confused Accounts; Classification of Accounts: Three Historical Notes', printed in Edey, H and B S Yamey (editors), 'Debits, Credits, Finance and Profits', Sweet and Maxwell, 1974, p 157)

Imaginary Species "In the commerce of exchange from Britain, they use three sorts of species; two of which are imaginary, and one real. The imaginary species are pounds and pence, there being no such species of coin current in the country." (Stevenson, 'A Full and Practical Treatise upon Bills of Exchange', 1764) In Scotland, in the early years of the 18th century, the Scottish merk was an example of imaginary species.

Index " ... in the beginning of this Book (the leger) is the Index with the 24. A, B, C. Letters, to place down every Accompt, where or what leaf it stands on in the Leger".(Colinson, 'Idea Rationaria', 1683, p 4) Colinson omits the letters J and U from his index. Hamilton also talks of 24 letters.('An Introduction to Merchandize', vol II, 1779, p 280)

Insurance-Reckoning An account that shows the profit or loss on insurance, explained by Colinson in questions 56-59. ('Idea Rationaria', 1683, p 11) The Insurance-Reckoning account only records the result of 'insuring other mens goods'. Insurance premiums paid are not entered in this account but are debited to the relevant voyage or venture account.

Inventar, Inventare, Inventary, Inventory An inventory of a merchant's possessions and debts, the first item to appear in the Waste-Book when the books are opened. Colinson uses 'inventar' ('Idea Rationaria', 1683, p 6) and 'inventare' (p 7). Malcolm uses 'inventar'. "For other Things, as Furniture, entrusted with a House-Keeper, there ought to be an Inventar ... " ('A New Treatise of Arithmetick and Book-keeping', 1718, appendix, p 30). Elsewhere (facing page 194) he uses 'Inventary': "The Inventary (taken this Day) of the whole Estate, and Debts owing to me A. M. Merchant in Edinburgh" ('A New Treatise of Arithmetick and Book-keeping', 1718, facing p 194). In his second book Malcolm uses inventary and inventory. Mair uses 'inventary' in the first edition of 'Book-keeping Methodiz'd'(1736) but in subsequent editions this is changed to 'inventory'.

Invoice-tare See tare.

Jacobus An English gold coin of James I (James VI of Scotland); appears in Colinson's illustrative Cash Book with a value of 25s sterling ('Idea Rationaria', 1683).

Journal "The Journal is the Book wherein the Transactions recorded in the Waste-Book are prepared to be carried to the Ledger, by having their proper Debitors and Creditors ascertained and pointed out" (Mair, 'Book-keeping Methodiz'd', 1736, p 8).

Journal Entrance, Journal Entry, Journal Post "every Case or Example ... of the Waste-Book when entered in the Journal is called a Journal Post or entrance" (Mair, 'Book-keeping Methodiz'd', 1736, p 11). In later editions (eg 1765 edition, p 11) 'entrance' becomes 'entry'. 'Journal entrance' is used by Macghie ('The Principles of Book-keeping Explain'd', 1718, p 2).

Journalize To record in the journal. William Hamilton uses the word: "I shall shew in a very convincing Manner, how to journalize every Subject of the Waste-book" ('Book-keeping New Modelled', 1735, p 5). Also used by Gordon ('The Universal Accountant', vol II, 1765, p 33). Macghie uses 'journalizing' ('The Principles of Book-keeping Explain'd', 1718, p 47).

Kain, Kane A payment in kind, especially of poultry, made by a tenant of land as part of his rent. "The Kain payable from Candlemas 1761 to Easter" (Stevenson, 'Book-keeping by Double Entry', 1762, entry in illustrative estate memorial, 1 November 1760).

Lammas The feast of the first fruits (the wheat harvest), August 1, one of the Scottish quarter days. The other quarter days are: Martinmas (11 November), Candlemas (2 February) and Whitsunday (15 May). Lammas and Candlemas are normally the dates when rents fall due.

Last A measure for fish, grain, flax, leather etc, Mair gives details in his 'merchants dictionary' ('Book-keeping Methodiz'd', 1736, appendix). "9 January 1705 Bought of Peter Winchester the following Goods, payable in 3 Months, viz 20 Lasts of Salmond, at L.30 per Barrel" (Macghie, 'The Principles of Book-keeping Explain'd', 1718, illustrative set of books).

Glossary

Ledger, Leger "The Name, Leger, comes, very probably, from the Latin Word Legere, to gather; because in it are gathered into distinct Accounts, the Transactions relating to every Subject, which are scattered in the Waste-Book, according to their Dates. Some Authors write it Ledger, and derive it from an Italic Word, which signifies Sleight, or Art; because that appears most in this Book." (Malcolm, 'A Treatise of Book-keeping', 1731, p 6) North adopts the second view: "Ledger ... comes from the Italians Leggiero, because the Entries are short and sleight".('The Gentleman Accomptant', 1714, Vocabulary)

Ledger Entrance, Ledger Entry An entry in the ledger. " ... in the Ledger-Entrance, express the Name and Quantity of those Wares bought or Sold". (Mair, 'Book-keeping Methodiz'd', 1736, p 25) In later editions 'ledger-entrance' becomes 'ledger entry'.

Liability This term was not used in the 17th and 18th century texts. Colinson talks of "Debts which I am owing to several Persons" and distinguishes these from "Debts owing by several Persons" ('Idea Rationaria', 1683, Waste-Book A, p 1)

Luck-penny "A sum of money given for luck, e.g. that returned traditionally by the seller to the purchaser of goods, esp. live stock or grain, by way of discount." ('Scottish National Dictionary') "Sold to Robert Forrester 3 Scores and 4 Dinmonts, for 3 Scores payle. at 12 s. 6 d. Luck-penny deduced £37 5 0." (Stevenson, 'Book-keeping by Double Entry, 1762, example of farm accounting)

Glossary

Martinmas The feast of St Martin, 11th November (or in some parts of Scotland 28th November); one of the Scottish quarter days. The other quarter days are: Candlemas (2 February), Whitsunday (15 May) and Lammas (1 August). Martinmas and Whitsunday are term days when a tenant enters or departs from leased property.

Mediate Accompt Another term for Imaginary Accompt. The word mediate arises because the account is " ... put betwixt one Accompt and another" (Malcolm, 'A New Treatise of Arithmetick and Book-keeping', 1718, pp 122/3). until the nature of the transaction is confirmed. Malcolm gives the example of a conditional debt ie the debt is conditional on a future event occurring, until the debt is confirmed (or rejected) the debt can be recorded in a Mediate Accompt. Malcolm adopted this term from North who uses it in 'The Gentleman Accomptant' (1714, p 15).

Memorial Talking of the Waste-Book Malcolm says " ... we might more reasonably call it The Memorial Book (as some Authors do) because in its principal Use and Design, 'tis no more" (Malcolm, 'A Treatise of Book-keeping', 1731, p 4).

Merk Originally a certain weight of gold and silver and used as a money of account from early times with the value of two thirds of the pound Scots or 13 shillings and 4 pence Scots. By the 18th century this was equivalent to 13 1/3 d sterling. A silver coin of this denomination was coined at intervals from the reign of James VI in 1578 to that of Charles II. As a money of account the name persisted into the 18th century ('Scottish National Dictionary'). Colinson's illustrative Cash Book includes merks, valued at

14d sterling, ('Idea Rationaria', 1683) and Macghie also introduces them into his explanatory set of books ('The Principles of Book-keeping Explain'd', 1718).

Milree, milreis, millrines (Colinson) A Portuguese gold coin and money of account. The milree features in: Colinson, ('Idea Rationaria', 1683, illustrative cash book); Macghie, ('The Principles of Book-keeping Explain'd', 1718, illustrative set of books) and Gordon ('The Universal Accountant', vol II, 1765, pp 290-323, specimen III).

Moneth Book, Month Book Colinson describes a Moneth Book " ... which tells you what summes you are to pay every moneth in the year, and day when, and who is to pay you" ('Idea Rationaria', 1683, p 2). Mair, Gordon and Hamilton call this book the Month Book. Scruton calls it the Debt Book. In 'Book-keeping Methodiz'd', Mair regards the Bill Book and the Month Book as being the same, but in 'Book-keeping Moderniz'd' he distinguishes between them.

Mortgage " ... a pawn of land, houses, or goods, laid for money borrowed, to be the creditor's for ever if the money be not paid at the day agreed on" (Mair, 'Book-keeping Methodiz'd', 1736, appendix, p 66).

Neat, Nett or Net "NEAT or NETT, Italian for clean, and means the Debt or Sum reduced to a clean State, after all Deductions, Repairs and Allowances set off" (North, 'The Gentleman Accomptant', 1714, Vocabulary). "Paying of neat yearly rent (after deduction of feu duty, Minister's stipend, and School master's salary ... about £1040 sterling" (Caledonian Mercury, 21 April 1764, p 195).

Glossary

Neat Stock Capital. Gross Stock would be the value of the assets; gross stock less liabilities is Neat Stock. The term is used by Mair ('Book-keeping Methodiz'd', 1736, p 5).

On time To sell on time is to sell on credit terms. To buy on time is to buy on credit terms. Colinson gives the following question and answer: "Q. If you sell half (of a parcel of goods) for ready money, and half upon time? A. The Buying Man Debitor to the goods for all, and then Cash Debitor to him for what money is received" ('Idea Rationaria', 1683, p 8).

Par "Par, is one of the burning Words of this Age, and relates to the Currant Values of Funds, Stocks, Credits, Tallies, &c. which are sometimes over, and rarely Par; which Word speaks the general Sense of it, in Equality, and so is used in Accompts" (North, 'The Gentleman Accomptant', 1714, Vocabulary).

Par of Exchange " ... is when he to whom a bill is payable, receives of the acceptor just so much money in value as was paid to the drawer by the remitter" (Mair, 'Book-keeping Methodiz'd', 1736, appendix, p 68).

Parcell, Parcel A batch of transactions. "This Debitor and Creditor must be formed out of the Waste-Book parcells" (Colinson, 'Idea Rationaria', 1683, p 4). "Containing Directions for Posting Parcels or Transactions of Trade in the Waste-Book ... " (Macghie, 'The Principles of Book-keeping Explain'd', 1718, heading of chapter II, p 12). North's use of the term differs slighlty from the foregoing: "Parcel, Italian Partita, means all that is wrote in

Accompt, and posted into the Ledger in one Sum ... " ('The Gentleman Accomptant', 1714, Vocabulary). These uses of the term 'parcel' are extensions of the more obvious use of the word to describe a batch of merchandise " ... such Partnership may be entered into for one single Parcel of Goods ... " (Malcolm, 'A New Treatise of Arithmetick and Book-keeping', 1718, p 163).

Partnership " ... is that Branch of Trade which is managed and carried on by a Trustee, in the Name, and for the Account of the Partners, that is, when a joint Stock, made up by two or more Merchants, is deposited in the Hands of one Person, to be employed by him in a Way of Commerce, according to Instructions" (Mair, 'Book-keeping Methodiz'd', 1736, p 46). Robert Hamilton's definition is more modern: "Partnership is a contract among two or more persons, to carry on certain business, at their joint expence, and share the gain or loss which arises from it" ('An Introduction to Merchandize', vol II, 1779, p 524).

Partner-trustee "Merchants upon entring into Partnership generally chuse one of their own Number, to whom they commit the Management of their Company-concerns, who, on account of his being Partner, as well as Manager or Doer for the Company, is called Partner-Trustee, and shares of Gains and Losses that happen, according to his Share of the Stock ... " (Mair, 'Book-keeping Methodiz'd', 1736, p 46). Malcolm also uses the term.

Personal Accompts " ... are such, as have only the bare Names of Persons for their Titles, and arise from my dealing with such Persons as are neutral, or Strangers in a common

Way of trading, viz. in buying and selling upon Time, or bartering, borrowing, lending, promising, wagering, etc. or when they respect me as my Correspondents, (i.e. my Imployer or Factor) or Partners in Factorage or Company Accompts, where such Accompts are only meant of such Persons their particular Accompts" (Macghie, 'The Principles of Book-keeping Explain'd', 1718, p 9).

Post An entry into one of the accounting books. The word's meaning is not restricted to transcriptions into the Ledger from a Book of Prime Entry. " ... Every Case or Example of the Waste-Book when entred in the Journal is called a Journal Post or Entrance" (Mair, 'Book-keeping Methodiz'd', 1736, p 11). "Containing Directions for Posting Parcels or Transactions of Trade in the Waste-Book ... " (Macghie, 'The Principles of Book-keeping Explain'd', 1718, Heading of chapter II, p 12). "Posting, Italian Appostare, from Positio, placing to Accompts" (North, 'The Gentleman Accomptant', 1714, Vocabulary).

Post-Book Malcolm uses this term to refer to an accounting book containing personal accounts but not maintained on a double entry basis. He suggests that small traders might have " ... a common Post-Book for the Persons with whom they Deal upon Trust, in which they give every Debtor or Creditor an Accompt, with Debt and Credit both on one Side, either with a double Money Column, or constant Deductions, as the Debts and Credits succeed one another ... " (Malcolm, 'A New Treatise of Arithmetick and Book-keeping', 1718, appendix, p 30). North distinguishes the 'Merchant's Ledger' from a 'Tradesman's Post-Book' "which apes the Ledger" but is defective in any "Connexion of Accompt" which is the

Glossary

"Cement that joins all finally in one Ballance" ('The Gentleman Accomptant', 1714, p 42). The Oxford English Dictionary gives it a wider meaning "A book in which accounts are posted; a ledger."

<u>Precepts</u> Scottish legal term. A document instructing or conferring authority to take certain action. "This Day sold for ready Money 10 Chalders of Pease, at 8s. per Boll, and have given off my Precepts for the same to William Hardie upon the following tenants, to be delivered upon Sight of the Precepts, ... " (Stevenson, 'Book-keeping by Double Entry', 1762, illustrative estate memorial 25 January 1761). 'Precept' is used by Macghie to mean a bill of exchange: " ... for the Price thereof he has given me an accepted Precept or Bill, on George Sharp, payable in 1/mo" ('The Principles of Book-keeping Explain'd', 1718, illustrative set of books, January 9, 1705).

<u>Premium, premio, proemio</u> "Premium, money given for insuring ships, goods, houses &c." (Mair, 'Book-keeping Methodiz'd', 1736, appendix, p 69). Colinson (1683, p 11) uses 'premio'. Drummond (1718, p 14) and Macghie (1718) use 'proemio'.

<u>Pricking</u> "PRICKING is a Method used in examining a Set of Books, to find out Errors. Each Parcel is seen in the Journal, and compared with the Ledger-Entries, both Dr. and Cr. and when that is found right, a Point of the Pen (for Neatness) is put to each Line to enter; and then in future Examinations, those are flipt, and they go on to others; for the Point shews the Examination hath gone so far" (North, 'The Gentleman Accomptant', 1714, Vocabulary).

Glossary

Promise - Reckoning An account debited when the trader promises to pay a given sum if certain conditions are fulfilled (the credit being to the potential creditor) OR an account credited when the trader is promised a certain sum if he complies with certain conditions (with the promisor being debited). Colinson ('Idea Rationaria', 1683, pp 9/10) discusses this and he gives examples in the illustrative books (Waste-Book, 12 January 1682 and Ledger A, F 11).

Proper Used to mean 'personal'. Gordon has an example of an account headed 'Ship Jenny proper', indicating that the ship is owned solely by the trader ('The Universal Accountant', vol II, 1765, pp 304/305). In contrast another account is headed 'The Ann galley in company with Dale of Leghorn 2/3 and self 1/3' (op cit, pp 300/1). 'Proper' is from the Latin 'proprius' = 'ones own'.

Proper Accompts (or Accounts) The accounts of a sole trader or, more precisely, that part of a trader's accounts which deals with his trading as principal on his own account, not through an agent. "If no Man is concerned with you in any Branch of Trade, you keep only Proper Accompts" (Drummond, 'The Accomptant's Pocket-Companion', 1718, p 5).

Proper Expences (or Charges) Drawings by owner of business. "That you may know your Expence, you make an Accompt of Proper Charges, in which you class ... Pocket Money, Diet, Lodging, Washing, Apparel, &c." (Drummond, 'The Accomptant's Pocket-Companion', 1718, p 12). 'Proper expenses were commonly charged to the merchant's profit and loss account. "The amount ... is not properly loss, but, as it has the same effect in diminishing the stock, it is placed in the same manner to the Dr. of profit and loss" (Hamilton, 'An Introduction to Merchandize', p 269).

Proper Trade Is trade "which a Merchant carries on for himself ... Proper Trade is either Domestick or Foreign. Proper domestick Trade is that which a Merchant carries on by himself, without the Help of a Factor. Proper foreign Trade, is the Business that occurs to a Merchant by employing a Factor" (Mair, 'Book-keeping Methodiz'd', 1736, p 20).

Provision "A factor's wages called also his commission or provision" (Mair, 'Book-keeping Methodiz'd', 1765, p 226). Colinson records commission received in a Provision Accompt ('Idea Rationaria', 1683, Ledger A, F 22).

Real Accompts "Real Accompts are such, whereby we denominate Things of all Sorts; whether Money, Wares, Moveables, Houses and Possessions of all Kinds, whether the Wares be in our Hands, or in the Hands of our Factor or Partner" (Macghie, 'The Principles of Book-keeping Explain'd', 1718, p 9).

Rebate " ... a regular Deduction from any Sum according to the Rate of Interest on account of Payment per Advance" (Mair, 'Book-keeping Methodiz'd', 1736, p 29). See 'discount'.

Reparation Robinson, M ('The Concise Scots Dictionary', Aberdeen University Press, 1985) gives the definition: "Furniture, furnishings" but the word seems to be used to mean 'repairs', eg " ... the Expence of Reparations,

Taxations, and Improvements" (Malcolm, 'A Treatise of Book-keeping', 1731, p 47).

Rix Doller Colinson's illustrative Cash Book records such coins with a sterling value of 58d ('Idea Rationaria', 1683). These coins seem to be Dutch but coins with this name were issued in several countries.

Sequestrate Remove and place in the hands of a trustee or sequestrator.

Share The textbooks show the word 'share' beginning to take a specialised meaning as a 'share of the capital'. " ... if you would have an Accompt, in which all the Shares of the Stock should be seen at all Times ... then make Cash, &c. in Company ... Debtors to Stock in Company for the Shares; but immediately Balance this Accompt of Stock, and make it Debtor to our Accompts in Company" (Malcolm, 'A New Treatise of Arithmetick and Book-keeping', 1718, p 174).

Specie(s) Money in the form of minted pieces of metal.

Specie Book Colinson uses this as an alternative name for the Cash Book ('Idea Rationaria', 1683, p 3).

Staple "a city or town appointed by the government, a public mart for merchants to bring goods to for sale" (Mair, 'Book-keeping Methodiz'd', 1736, appendix, p 72). To promote its trade with Scotland the Netherlands established the Scottish Staple in the 14th century; from 1543 this was situated at Veere. Privileges were granted to Scottish merchants providing that the Scottish trade was concentrated at this port. In 1683 Colinson dedicated his book ('Idea Rationaria') to Mr James Kennedy, Lord Conservator of the Priviledges of the Scots Nation in the ... Netherlands for his efforts in " ... restoring to its former luster and prosperity, that Ancient Policy of our Nation ... The Staple at Campheer:" The system had broken down by the 18th century and the Staple was finally closed in 1799 although the office of Conservator continued until 1847.

Stock Capital. Sometimes linked with the word capital as 'capital stock'. Malcolm uses 'Capital Stock' on p 38 of 'A Treatise of Book-keeping' (1731) and North had previously used it on pages 17 and 18 of 'The Gentleman Accomptant' (1714).

'Stock in' or 'Stocked in' Phrase used by Malcolm to mean capital paid in to a partnership or the 'Paid up' capital of a partnership. "When I am concerned in a standing Company, I make my Accompt in Company with A.B. &c. ... Debtor for my share stocked in or owing ... ",(Malcolm, 'A New Treatise of Arithmetick and Book-keeping', 1718, p 164); " ... if they stock in Goods ... I make the Accompt Goods Debtor to their Accompt in Company ... " (op cit, p 166).

Subservient Books Term used to describe subsidiary books of account. "Tho' all Merchant-Accompts may be kept by the Waste book, Journal and Ledger alone, yet Men of great Business find it convenient, either for abridging these, or for other Ends, to use some others, generally called Subsidiary or Subservient Books" (Mair, 'Book-keeping Methodiz'd', 1736, appendix, p 1).

Glossary

Supercargoe "Supercargoes are employed by merchants to go voyages, and dispose of cargoes to the best advantage" (Gordon, 'The Universal Accountant', vol I, 1763, p 231).

Suspense (or Suspence) Accompt Goods sent on approval are debited to a Suspense Accompt awaiting the prospective purchaser's decision on whether or not to buy them. When the decision is known, the Suspense Accompt is closed. If he decides to purchase the goods, he (or cash) is debited with their cost, if he decides to return them Goods Accompt is debited (Mair, 'Book-keeping Methodiz'd', 1736, p 4).

Suttle Weight "When Tare and Trett are both allowed, the Tare is first deduced, and the neat Weight is particularly called, in Merchants Stile, Suttle Weight, ... " (Malcolm, A - 'A New Treatise of Arithmetick and Book-keeping', 1718, p 87). See also Gordon, 'The Universal Accountant', vol I, 1763, pp 179-182. "What remains after the tare is taken from the gross, is called Tare-suttle, what remains after the tret is deducted, is called Tret-suttle; and when all deductions are made, the last remainder is called Neat-weight" (Perry, 'The Man of Business', 1774, p 149).

Tack A lease or tenancy of land or the farm or piece of land held on a lease.

Tare " ... an allowance on weighable goods, made by the King to the importer, or by the seller to the buyer, in consideration of the outside package, as cask, bag, chest, wrappers, &c. Concerning which observe, 1. That several sorts of goods have their tares ascertained in a table annexed to the Book of rates; and these tares are constantly observed with respect to imported goods, unless the officers thinking the crown, or the merchant thinking himself wronged, shall desire to have the goods unpacked, and the neat weight taken; which is done by weighing the goods of each cask,&c. or by picking out several casks of each size, and computing the rest according to them. And this is the ordinary method with respect to East-India goods. 2. As to goods whose tares are not ascertained, two land-surveyors in London, and the collector and surveyor in the out-ports, are impowered by the government to adjust them. 3. Sometimes the casks, barrels &c. are weighed beyond sea before the goods are put in them, and the respective weights marked on the casks themselves, or inserted in the merchant's invoice. In which case, if the officers can satisfy themselves, by unpacking and weighing some of the goods, that these invoice-tares are just and true, they commonly esteem them as such nd pass them accordingly. 4. But the unpacking of the goods, and taking the neat weight, being the most just method both for the King and merchant, it is commonly practised in cases where it can be done conveniently, and without detriment to the goods. And this method is always observed with respect to tobacco imported from Virginia and Maryland" (Mair, 'Book-keeping Moderniz'd', 1773, p 619). See also Malcolm, ('A New Treatise of Arithmetick and Book-keeping', 1718, p 87) and Gordon, ('The Universal Accountant', vol I, 1763, pp 178, 182).

Teind Duty In Scotland a tithe duty payable by the land-owner but frequently transferred by him to his tenant as an addition to his rent.

Glossary

Threave An agricultural term. A measure of cut grain, straw etc, consisting of two stooks usually with twelve sheaves in each stook but this varies according to locality. Hamilton uses the term in his specimen field book.

Trett, Tret "Trett is an Allowance for Dust, Waste, Refuse or Inlack of Goods given at so much per hundred Weight; ... " (Malcolm, 'A New Treatise of Arithmetick and Book-keeping', 1718, p 87). More specifically "an allowance in weighable goods of 4 lb. in 104 lb. made by the merchants in London to their own tradesmen and retailers, for break, waste, or dust mixed with the goods" (Mair, 'Book-keeping Methodiz'd', 1736, appendix, p 74). See also Gordon ('The Universal Accountant', vol I, 1763, pp 178, 182).

Trial Balance, Tryall Ballance A test that the accounts are in balance undertaken, in Malcolm's text, after the Profit and Loss Accompt has been prepared but before the outstanding balances are transferred to the Balance Accompt. "You will do best to make this tryall Ballance on a sheet of waste Paper, to try if it proves right ... " ('A New Treatise of Arithmetick and Book-keeping', 1718, p 21). Trial Balance is the more usual spelling but Tryall Ballance is used by Colinson and Malcolm.

Truck Exchange other than wholly for money, see 'barter'. "Q. What if you sell goods in truck for money and other goods? A. The Buying Man Debitor to the goods for all; then the goods you receive in payment, Debitor to him for what they cost, and cash Debitor to him for the money" (Colinson, 'Idea Rationaria', 1683, p 8, Question 26).

Glossary

Unfixt Company, Unfix'd Company "I suppose a very simple Kind of Society, which I call an Unfixt Company; because they have no standing and fixed Stock, but (for Example) buy, from Time to Time, Parcels ... to be disposed of in domestick or foreign Trade; and withdraw their Shares of the Value sold, when they please; by which Means their Stocks or Effects in Company, perpetually vary, according to the value of those different Transactions: And such Partnerships may be enter'd into for one single Parcel of Goods, or Voyage; or they may continue for some Course of Trade" (Malcolm, 'A New Treatise of Arithmetick and Book-keeping', 1718, p 163). In his second book the spelling is changed to 'unfix'd company' ('A Treatise of Book-keeping', 1731, p 65). See 'Fixed Company'.

Usance "Foreign bills are often drawn at usance, at double or treble usance, at half usance, or the like, ... usance signifies the common time allowed for payment by the custom of the places where the bills are transacted" (Hamilton, 'An Introduction to Merchandize', vol I, 1777, p 286).

Usury " ... the gain of any thing above the principal, or that which was lent, exacted in consideration of the loan. 5 per cent. is allowed by law; and more, where the principal is in hazard, as where money is lent on Bottomry" (Mair, 'Book-keeping Methodiz'd', 1736, appendix, p 74). "Anno 12 Car. II. c.13. it was made penal to take above 6 per cent; and anno 12 Annae, c.16. the interest of money was reduced to 5 per cent. from 29th September 1714, and this statute continues in force to this day" (Gordon, 'The Universal Accountant', vol I, 1763, p 353). " ... the law doth not allow money to be put out at compound interest ... " (Gordon, op cit, vol I, 1763, p 368).

Waste Book The Waste-Book is "A Register containing an Inventary of a Merchant's Effects and Debts, with a distinct Record of all his Transactions and Dealings in a Way of Trade, narrated in a plain, simple Stile, and in order of Time as they succeed one another" (Mair, 'Book-keeping Methodiz'd', 1736, p 5). The transactions are transferred to the Journal from the Waste-Book. Malcolm comments on the book's name, "What relation the Word Waste has to the nature of this Book, is neither obvious, nor worth enquiring after" (Malcolm, 'A Treatise of Book-keeping', 1731, p 4). Mair's explanation of the name is as follows: " ... after the Journal is filled up and corrected, the Waste-book is of little further Use; and probably on this Account it has got the Name it bears" (Mair, 'Book-keeping Methodiz'd', 1736, p 7).

Whitsunday 15th May (or, in some parts of Scotland, 28th May), one of the Scottish quarter days. The other quarter days are: Lammas (1 August), Martinmas (11 November) and Candlemas (2 February). Whitsunday and Martinmas are term days when a tenant enters or departs from leased property.

Yoking An agricultural term. "A yoking is the work performed by one man and two horses or cattle ... There are generally two yokings a-day in summer and one in winter" (Hamilton, 'An Introduction to Merchandize', 1788, p 492).

SCOTTISH ACCOUNTING TEXTS FROM 1683 TO 1800

Colinson, Robert
'Idea rationaria, or, The Perfect accomptant, necessary for all merchants and trafficquers, containing the true form of bookkeeping according to the Italian method ... ', Edinburgh: David Lidsay, James Kniblo, Joshua van Solingen and John Colmar. 1683

Newall, W
'The New Merchant's companion being a more exact, quick and easy way for making up of accompts ... ', Glasgow: Donald Govan 1715

Drummond, John
'The Accomptant's pocket companion: a manual instructing merchants, gentlemen of estates and others, to begin their books, carry on their business and make a ballance ... ', Edinburgh: (no printer given). 1718

Lundin, Robert
'The Reason for accompting by debitor and creditor with general rules for attaining to that way of accompting', Edinburgh: (no printer given). 1718

MacGhie, Alexander
'The Principles of bookkeeping explain'd with the chief cases thereof stated and resolved, to which are annexed two setts of books of Fictitious trade, wherein the whole is reduced to practice', Edinburgh: James Watson for the author's relict. 1718
NOTE: Two authorities state that this is the second edition of a work published in 1715 (see p 114) but no trace of an earlier edition has been found.

Scottish Accounting Texts From 1683 to 1800

Malcolm, Alexander
'A New Treatise of Arithmetick and Book-keeping ... ', Edinburgh: printed by John Mosman and William Brown, for John Paton Bookseller and are to be sold at his Shop in the Parliament Closs. 1718

Brodie, Alexander
'A New and Easy Method of Book-Keeping, Or, Instructions for a Methodical Keeping of Merchants Accompts by way of Debitor and Creditor', London: printed for the author. 1722

Hamilton, Robert
'Rental accounts made easy, or, A Clear and distinct method by which persons of estates, ... may ... see what they have received ... and what is yet due ... ', Edinburgh: for the author. 1727

Malcolm, Alexander A
'Treatise of Book-keeping, or, Merchants Accounts; in the Italian Method ... ', London: for J Osborn and T Longman. 1731

Stevenson, William A
'General discourse shewing the usefulness of the Italian method of bookkeeping and the practice of exchange', Edinburgh: R Fleming and Co. 1732

Hamilton, William
'Bookkeeping new modelled, or, A Treatise of merchant's accounts according to the true Italian method of debitor and creditor ... ', Edinburgh: R Fleming for the author. 1735

Lundin, Robert
'The Fundamental principles and reasons for accompting by debitor and creditor ... ', 2nd edition, corrected and enlarged, Edinburgh: (no printer given). 1736

Mair, John
'Book-keeping Methodiz'd', 1st edition, Edinburgh: printed by T and W Ruddimans for the author. 1736

Mair, John
'Book-keeping Methodiz'd', 1st edition, Edinburgh: W Sands, Brymer, A Murray and J Cochran. 1736

Mair, John
'Book-keeping Methodiz'd', 2nd edition, with Additions and Improvements; Dublin: printed by Mary Fuller, at the Globe and Scales in Meath-Street. 1737

Mair, John
'Book-keeping Methodiz'd', 2nd edition, Edinburgh: printed by W Sands, Brymer, A Murray and J Cochran, Sold by W Sands. 1741

Mair, John
'Book-keeping Methodiz'd', 2nd edition, Edinburgh: printed for, and sold by W Sands in the Parliament-close; and by Mess. Midwinter, Innys, Rivington, Knapton, Longman, Manby, Hitch, Astley, Oswald, Hodges, and Davidson, at London. 1741

Mair, John
'Book-keeping Methodiz'd', 2nd edition, printed by Isaac Jackson; Dublin. 1742

Malcolm, Alexander
'A Treatise of Book-keeping, or, Merchants Accounts; in the Italian Method ... ', 2nd edition, London: D.Browne. 1743

Mair, John
'Book-keeping Methodiz'd', 2nd edition, Dublin: printed by Isaac Jackson, at the Globe in Meath street. 1748

Mair, John
'Book-keeping Methodiz'd', 3rd edition, with additions and improvements, Edinburgh: printed by W Sands, A Murray, and J Cochran. Sold by W Sands, and A Kincaid, Edinburgh, and other Booksellers in Town and Country. 1749

Mair, John
'Book-keeping Methodiz'd', the last edition, with additions and improvements; Dublin: printed and sold by Isaac Jackson at the Globe and Bible in Meath-Street. 1750

Mair, John
'Book-keeping Methodiz'd', 4th edition, Edinburgh: printed by W Sands, A Murray, and J Cochran, For W Sands, and A Kincaid & A Donaldson. 1752

Mair, John
'Book-keeping Methodiz'd', 3rd edition, Dublin. 1754

Mair, John
'Book-keeping Methodiz'd', 4th edition, Dublin. 1754

Mair, John
'Book-keeping Methodiz'd', 5th edition with many Additions

and Improvements; Dublin: printed and Sold by I Jackson, at the Globe and Bible in Meath-street. 1754

Stevenson, William
A Serious Advice to Tradesmen. Shewing them the inconveniencies they lye under and needless expence they are put to by not learning Book-Keeping ... ', Edinburgh: R Fleming. 1756

Mair, John
'Book-keeping Methodiz'd', 5th edition, Edinburgh: printed by Sands, Donaldson, Murray, and Cochran, for W Sands, and A Kincaid & A Donaldson. 1757

Mair, John and William Webster
'Essays on bookkeeping ... To which is added a large appendix containing a variety of specimens in company accounts ... and a method of keeping accompts proper for shop-keepers or retailers', by a Teacher of Bookkeeping, Glasgow: for John Orr. 1758

Mair, John
'Book-keeping Methodiz'd', 6th edition, Edinburgh: printed by Sands, Donaldson, Murray, and Cochran, for W Sands, A Kincaid & J Bell, and A Donaldson. 1760

Stevenson, William
'Book-keeping by double entry reduced in its theory to one simple rule', Edinburgh: R Stirling. 1762

Mair, John
'Book-keeping Methodiz'd', 7th edition, Edinburgh: printed

by W Sands, A Murray, and J Cochran, for W Sands, A Kincaid & J Bell, and A Donaldson. 1763

Mair, John
'Book-keeping Methodiz'd', 7th edition, Dublin: printed by H Saunders 1763

Gordon, William
'The Universal Accountant and Complete Merchant', (2 vols), 1st edition, Edinburgh: printed for the author and A Donaldson. 1763/65

Mair, John
'Book-keeping Methodiz'd', 'From the last edition printed at Edinburgh and revised', Dublin: printed and sold by I Jackson, at the Globe in Meath-street. 1764

Stevenson, William
'A Full and Practical Treatise upon Bills of Exchange, Together with An Account of the Nature of the Bank of Amsterdam, and how Payments are made and received in it', Edinburgh: printed by John Robertson, and sold by him and other booksellers. 1764

Gordon, William
'The Universal Accountant and Complete Merchant', (2 vols), 2nd edition, Edinburgh: A Donaldson. 1765

Mair, John
'Book-keeping Methodiz'd', 8th edition, Edinburgh: printed for W Sands, A Murray, and J Cochran, A Kincaid & J Bell, and A Donaldson. 1765

Scottish Accounting Texts From 1683 to 1800

Gordon, William
'The General Counting-House and Man of Business', 1st edition, Edinburgh: printed for A Donaldson and sold at his shops in Edinburgh and London. 1766

Mair, John
'Book-keeping Methodiz'd', 8th edition, Dublin: printed by H Sanders, at the Salmon, in Castle-street. 1767

Gordon, William
'The Universal Accountant and Complete Merchant', (2 vols), 3rd edition, Edinburgh: A.Donaldson. 1770

Gordon, William
'The General Counting-House and Man of Business', 2nd edition, Edinburgh: A.Donaldson & Stanley Crowder. 1770

Gordon, William
'The General Counting-House and Man of Business', 2nd edition, Glasgow: A.Donaldson & Stanley Crowder. 1770

Mair, John
'Book-keeping' section of 'Encyclopaedia Britannica', Edinburgh: printed for A Bell and C Macfarquhar, and sold by Colin Macfarquhar at his printing office in Nicholson Street. 1771

Mair, John
'Book-keeping Methodiz'd', 9th edition, Dublin: printed by H Saunders. 1772

Scottish Accounting Texts From 1683 to 1800

Mair, John
'Book-keeping Methodiz'd', 'From the last edition printed at Edinburgh and revised by John Mair with many additions and improvements', Dublin: printed and sold by R Jackson. 1773

Mair, John
'Book-keeping Moderniz'd', 1st edition, printed for A Kincaid & W Creech and J Bell; Edinburgh. Sold in London by W Johnston, S Crowder and four others. 1773

Perry, William
'The Man of Business and Gentleman's Assistant, containing a Treatise of Practical Arithmetic ... Book-Keeping by Single and Double Entry ... ', Edinburgh: printed for the author by David Willison and sold by J Murray, No 32, Fleet street, London; J Bell, Edinburgh; D Baxter, Glasgow; T Slack and W Charnley, Newcastle; A Graham, Alnwick; J Richardson, Berwick; and G Elliott, Kelso. 1774

Mair, John
'Book-keeping Methodiz'd', (Norwegian translation by Jasper Vande Velde de Fine), Norway. 1775

Gordon, William
'The Universal Accountant and Complete Merchant', (2 vols), 4th edition, Corrected and revised by the author, Edinburgh: printed for Alexander Donaldson, and sold at his Shop (No. 48.) St Paul's Church-Yard, London; and at Edinburgh. 1777

Perry, William
'The Man of Business and Gentleman's Assistant ... ', 2nd

edition with improvements, printed for the author; and sold by J Wilkie. 1777

Perry, William
'The Man of Business and Gentleman's Assistant, containing a treatise of practical arithmetic ... and bookkeeping by single and double entry ... ', 3rd edition with improvements, Edinburgh. 1777

Scruton, James
'The Practical Counting-house, or, Calculation and Accountantship Illustrated ... ', Glasgow: printed for James Duncan, Bookseller, opposite to the Main Guard. 1777

Hamilton, Robert
'An Introduction to Merchandize', (2 vols), 1st edition, Edinburgh: printed for the author; sold by T Cadell, London and John Balfour, Edinburgh. 1777/79

Hamilton, Robert
'Book-keeping' section of 'Encyclopaedia Britannica', 2nd edition, vol 2 Edinburgh: J Balfour et al. 1778

Mair, John
'Book-keeping Moderniz'd', 2nd edition, Edinburgh: printed for John Bell and William Creech, and sold by T Cadell, E & C Dilly, and Richardson & Urquhart. 1778

Rose, John
'The Transactions of the British Farmer Accountant Adapted to the four seasons of the year wherein The Gentlemen

Farmers have a Plan of Books entirely new, and suitable to their occupation', Edinburgh: published by Peter Williamson. C1780

Perry, William
'The Man of Business and Gentleman's Assistant: Containing a Treatise of Practical Arithmetic ... Book-Keeping by Single and Double Entry', 4th edition with improvements, Edinburgh: printed for W Anderson, sold by him and C Eliot. 1780

Mair, John
'Book-keeping Moderniz'd', 3rd edition, Edinburgh: printed for John Bell and William Creech. 1784

Mair, John
'Book-keeping Moderniz'd', 4th edition, Edinburgh: printed for John Bell and William Creech, and sold by T Longman, G G J and J Robinson, T Cadell, C Dilly, and Richardson & Urquhart. 1786

Gordon, William
'The Universal Accountant and Complete Merchant', (2 vols), 5th edition (new modelled), (2 vols), Edinburgh: printed for A & J Donaldson & C.Elliott, and sold in London by C Elliot and T Kay and Co. 1787

Hamilton, Robert
'An Introduction to Merchandize', (1 vol), 2nd edition, corrected and revised, Edinburgh: printed for Charles Elliot; and London: for C Elliot, T Kay, and Co, opposite Somerset House, Strand. 1788

Scottish Accounting Texts From 1683 to 1800

Hamilton, Robert
'A Short System of Arithmetic and Bookkeeping with a Supplement containing answers to the Arithmetical Questions', 1st edition, London: C Elliott & T Kay; and Edinburgh: C Elliott. 1788

Mair, John
'Book-keeping Moderniz'd', 5th edition, Edinburgh: printed for Bell & Bradfute, and William Creech; and sold by T Longman, G G J & J Robinson, T Cadell, and C Dilly, London. 1789

Young, David
'The Farmer's account-book of expenditure and produce for each day, month and year .. ', Edinburgh: for the author. 1790

Mair, John
'Book-keeping Moderniz'd', 6th edition, Edinburgh: Bell and Bradfute, and William Creech. 1793

Mair, John
'Book-keeping epitomized or a compendium of Mair's methodical treatise of merchants-accompts', by the Rev John Shaw, Leeds: printed for J Binns; and London: J Johnson, Ogilvy and Speare, and Vernor and Hood. 1794

Gordon, William
'The Universal Accountant and Complete Merchant', (2 vols), 6th edition, Dublin: printed by T.Henshall. 1796

Hamilton, Robert
'A Short System of Arithmetic and Bookkeeping with a Supplement containing answers to the Arithmetical Questions', 2nd edition, Edinburgh. 1796

Hamilton, Robert
'An Introduction to Merchandize', 3rd edition, Edinburgh: printed by and for J Hunter; Bell & Bradfute, J Dickson, W Creech, J Fairbairn, A Guthrie, P Hill, and Manners and Miller; Glasgow: J & M Robertson; Aberdeen: A Brown; Perth: T Hill; and Leith: W Coke. 1797

Hamilton, Robert
'Book-keeping' section of 'Encyclopaedia Britannica', 3rd edition, vol 3, Edinburgh: Bell and Macfarquhar. 1797

Mair, John
'Book-keeping Moderniz'd', 7th edition, Edinburgh: printed for Bell & Bradfute, and William Creech; and sold by T N Longman, G G J & J Robinson, Cadell & Davies, and C Dilly, London. 1797

Buchanan, Colin
'The Writingmaster and Accountant's Assistant', Glasgow: printed for the author by R Chapman and sold by G G & J Robinson, Caddel & Davis, Vernor & Hood, and J Johnson, London; W Creech, and Bell & Bradfute, Edinburgh; J & A Duncan, Dunlop & Wilson, Brash & Reid, D Niven, A Cameron, and J Murdoch, Glasgow. 1798

Scottish Accounting Texts From 1683 to 1800

Hamilton, Robert
'A Short System of Arithmetic and Bookkeeping with a Supplement containing answers to the Arithmetical Questions', 3rd edition, Edinburgh: printed by and for J Hunter, Bell & Bradfute, J Dickson, W Creech, J Fairbairn (& 3 others in Edinburgh, 1 in Glasgow, 2 in Perth and 1 in Leith). 1798

Hamilton, Robert
'An Introduction to Merchandize', 4th edition, corrected and revised; Edinburgh: printed by and for J Hunter; London: for G G and J Robinson, and T Kay; Edinburgh: W Creech, J Fairbairn, A Guthrie, P Hill, and Manners and Miller; Glasgow: J and M Robertson; Aberdeen: A Brown; Perth: T Hill; and Leith: W Coke. 1799

Mair, John
'Book-keeping Moderniz'd', 8th edition, Edinburgh: Bell & Bradfute, and William Creech. 1800

CHAPTER 1

THE ECONOMIC, SOCIAL AND CULTURAL BACKGROUND OF EIGHTEENTH CENTURY SCOTLAND

NOTES AND REFERENCES

(1) The first printed book on what is now known as the 'double entry system' of book-keeping, was written by an Italian monk and university professor, Luca Pacioli, in 1494. Because Pacioli's book was so influential in spreading a knowledge of the system throughout Europe and because he was describing practices which were in use in Italy, the system became known as the Italian Method.

(2) J Crawford (President of the Institute of Chartered Accountants of Scotland) in his foreword to Pryce-Jones, J and R H Parker, 'Accounting in Scotland', Institute of Chartered Accountants of Scotland, 1974.

(3) Morrison, J, 'The Elements of Book Keeping by Single and Double Entry', London: Longman, Hurst, Rees, Orme and Brown, 1813, p 2.

(4) The first accounting book written by an American did not appear until 1789, for most of the century the book-keeping texts used in America were British and, to a large extent, Scottish (Sheldahl, T K, 'America's Earliest Recorded Text in Accounting: Sarjeant's 1789 Book', The Accounting Historian's Journal, Fall 1985, pp 1-42).

(5) It is not possible to prove the truth of this assertion but the textbook authors believed it to be true so that Colinson considered that a wider dissemination of the 'Art of Book keeping' will " ... tend more to the improvement of Commerce if rightly practised, then all the projects ever yet set on foot" (Colinson, R, 'Idea Rationaria', Edinburgh, 1683, Dedication to the Merchants in Edinburgh). Later he says that " ... its beyond all peradventure, that an accurate Methode and exact Form hath alwayes been the principal cause of the rise, progresse and Advance of Trade in every Kingdom and State, where it hath been observed and Encouraged" (ibid, p 1). The claim seems reasonable in that the demand for accountancy training was increasing throughout the century and businesses did emphasise the importance of book-keeping's role in their financial control systems; see, for example, chapter 7 of 'Presbyteries and Profits' (Marshall, G, Oxford: Clarendon Press, 1980).

(6) See: Scott, W R, 'The Records of a Scottish Cloth Manufactory at New Mills, Haddingtonshire 1681-1703', Edinburgh: Scottish Historical Society, 1905, Marshall, G, op cit, chapter 7. The manufactory's

accounting system included, for example, separate accounts for the dyehouse (Scott, W R, op cit, p 183) and the presshouse (Scott, W R, op cit, p 291).

(7) Hamilton, R, 'An Introduction to Merchandize' (2 vols), Edinburgh, 1777/79. The accounting material is in volume 2 which was published in 1779.

(8) Kelly explains this by noting the fact that many of the 18th century writers (both Scottish and English) were " ... Schoolmasters, or Teachers. And though their profession might have rendered them well qualified for explaining the Principles of Book-keeping, it was not likely to afford opportunities of deducing their Theories from Practice. The works themselves evidently shew that those writers, in general, followed each others plans, and took their documents from Books more than from real Business." (Kelly, P, 'The Elements of Book-keeping, comprising a System of Merchants' Accounts, founded on Real Business, and Adapted to Modern Practice', London: J Johnson and Co, 4th Edition, 1811, p v). Although a number of the writers, particularly at the beginning of the 18th century, did have practical accounting experience, there is some truth in Kelly's assertions.

(9) In 1695 the Scottish parliament had passed an act giving extensive powers to The Company of Scotland Trading to Africa and the Indies. A major objective of this Company was to establish a Scottish colony (New Caledonia) on the narrow isthmus which links North and South America (the Isthmus of Darien). Although the enterprise was actively discouraged by the King, it went ahead and the first group of 1,200 colonists arrived in Darien in November 1698. Others followed but the adventure was a complete failure, 2,000 lives were lost and the money cost of 300,000 Scots pounds was a considerable drain on the nation's cash resources. The causes of failure were the inhospitable climate and the consequent deaths from malaria, the hostility of the Spaniards and the lack of English support because of their wish for peace with Spain. There was considerable Scottish resentment at the absence of English backing.

(10) The Catholic Highlanders had risen in support of James but, despite their success at Killiecrankie (1689), they were ultimately defeated.

(11) Durie, A J, 'The Scottish Linen Industry', Edinburgh: J Donald, 1979, p 8.

(12) Carstairs, A M, 'Some Economic Aspects of the Union of Parliaments', quoted by Marshall, G, op cit, p 263.

(13) Smout, T C, 'A History of the Scottish People 1560-1830', London: Collins, (second edition) 1970, p 242.

Notes and References - Chapter 1

(14) Werner Sombart (1863-1941) was a German economist, historian and sociologist.

(15) Sombart, W, 'The Quintessence of Capitalism' (translated and edited by M Epstein), London: Fisher Unwin, 1915, p 148.

(16) Sombart defines 'capitalism' thus: "By 'capitalism' we mean a particular economic system, recognizable as an organization of trade, consisting invariably of two collaborating sections of population, the owners of the means of production, who also manage them, and the propertyless workers, bound to the markets which they serve; which displays the two dominant principles of wealth creation and economic rationalism." (quoted in Most, K S, 'Sombart on Accounting History', printed in Coffman, E (editor), 'Academy of Accounting Historians Working Papers Series', volume 2, 1979, Working Paper No 35, p 245).

(17) Colinson, R, op cit, p 1.

(18) Marshall, G, op cit, pp 284-319.

(19) See for example: Poggi, G, 'Calvinism and the Capitalist Spirit - Max Weber's Protestant Ethic', London: The Macmillan Press Ltd, 1983.

(20) Max Weber (1864-1920) was a German sociologist and political economist. He wrote, among many other works, 'The Protestant Ethic and the Spirit of Capitalism' (London, 1971).

(21) Marshall, G, op cit, p 5.

(22) Poggi, G, op cit, p 56 and pp 64-66.

(23) "Rejecting monasticism Calvin dignified ordinary economic activities by designating them as 'callings', as tasks set directly by God." (Parsons, T, 'Jean Calvin (1509-1564)', article in Seligman, E (editor), 'Encyclopaedia of the Social Sciences', London: Macmillan and Co Ltd, 1930, volume 3, p 152).

(24) Marshall, G, op cit, p 261.

(25) Marshall, G, op cit, chapter 7.

(26) This is considered more fully in chapter 8, pp 164-166.

(27) Colinson, R, op cit, 'Dedication to the Merchants in Edinburgh'.

(28) " ... Calvin took Augustine as the foundation of Protestantism next to the Bible itself" and " ... Augustine praised labour as a means towards moral perfection; interest charges on money were not allowed under his system, but trade could be carried on, if selling was done honestly and a 'just price' was charged and paid" (Carter, J and P H Muir, 'Printing and the Mind of Man', Karl Pressler, 2nd edition, 1983, pp 2/3). Calvin did not disapprove of moderate interest charges.

(29) Parsons, T, op cit.

(30) Three of the writers that we are considering had strong connections with the Kirk. Hamilton's grandfather and two of his uncles had been moderators of the General Assembly, Mair had considered the church as a career and Malcolm did become a clergyman (although in this he followed his father's example by moving to the Church of England).

(31) Colinson, R, op cit, 'Dedication to the Merchants in Edinburgh'.

(32) During the 18th century there was commonly no such separation of business and private affairs in the books of a merchant trading on his own account (with no partners).

(33) 'Der Moderne Kapitalismus', 1902, quoted from translation provided in 'Sombart on Accounting History', Most, K S, op cit, pp 252/3.

(34) Yamey, B S, 'Accounting and the Rise of Capitalism: Further Notes on a Theme by Sombart'; Journal of Accounting Research, Autumn, 1964. For other views on the issue see: Strachan, J L, 'A Synthesis of and Inquiry into the Contribution of Double-Entry Book-keeping to Capitalism', Working Paper No 43, 'The Academy of Accounting Historians Working Papers Series', volume 3, 1984; Winjum, J O, 'The Role of Accounting in the Economic Development of England: 1500-1750', Center for International Education and Research in Accounting, University of Illinois, 1972, chapters 2 and 3; Lister, R J, 'Werner Sombart's 'Der Moderne Kapitalismus': An Apotheosis of Double-Entry Accounting?', Accounting and Business Research, Summer, 1985.

(35) The union of the crowns had taken place in 1603, the 1707 treaty was a union of the parliaments. Under the 1707 Act of Union the Scottish Parliament was dissolved and provision was made for Scottish members in the English Parliament. The United Kingdom of Great Britain was set up but the Scots were to retain their separate legal system and their Kirk. There was to be free trade between Scotland and England and her colonies.

(36) For example: the export duty on linen (1711), the malt tax (1713 and 1725) and the increased salt tax which had "a calamitous effect on the fishing industry" (Dickson, T (editor), 'Scottish Capitalism', London: Lawrence and Wishart, 1980, p 89).

(37) Smout says that "The short-term impact of the Union on Scottish internal and external trade remains uncertain" (Smout, T C, 'Where had the Scottish economy got to by the third quarter of the eighteenth century?', printed in Hont, I and M Ignatieff (editors), 'Wealth and

Virtue', Cambridge University Press, 1983, p 48).

(38) The Hanse towns were " ... certain free towns in Germany, in number twenty-seven, as Hamburg, Lubeck, Magdenberg, &c joined in a league offensive and defensive against all enemies". (Mair, J, 'Book-keeping Methodiz'd', 1736).

(39) Childs, J, 'A Discourse About Trade', London: printed by A Sowle, 1689, preface (B4)

(40) "Trade to Holland, the main market for Scots goods, was canalised through the staple port of Veere, where the Conservator ... resided and acted as commercial agent and also on occasions as ambassador of his country. ... the system was continued ... until it was interrupted by the Anglo-Dutch Wars and the War with France at the end of the seventeenth century". (Hamilton, H, 'An Economic History of Scotland in the Eighteenth Century', Oxford: Clarendon Press, 1963, pp 252/3). Mair defined a 'staple' as "a city or town appointed by the government, a public mart for merchants to bring goods to for sale" (Mair, J, op cit).

(41) Davidson, J and A Gray, 'The Scottish Staple at Veere', London: Longmans, Green, and Co, 1909.

(42) Gibson, J, 'The History of Glasgow from the earliest accounts to the present time; with an Account of the Rise, Progress, and Present State of the Different Branches of Commerce and Manufactures now Carried on in the City of Glasgow', Glasgow: printed by R Chapman and A Duncan for the Author, 1777, pp 205/6.

(43) Campbell, R H, 'Scotland Since 1707', Oxford: Basil Blackwell, 1971, p 62.

(44) Views have changed in this area, in 1921 Mackinnon stated that there was " ... no appreciable advance in agriculture during the first half of the 18th century" (Mackinnon, J, 'The Social and Industrial History of Scotland from the Union to the Present Time', London: Longmans, Green and Co, 1921, p 3).

(45) Hamilton, H, 'Economic Growth in Scotland 1720-1770', Scottish Journal of Political Economy, 1959, p 90.

(46) Smith, A, 'The Wealth of Nations', 4th edition, London: Strahan, A and T Cadell, 1786, vol I, book I, pp 348/349. Smout examines the evidence for Smith's claim and concludes that it is somewhat overstated (Smout, T C, op cit, 1985, pp 54/55).

(47) Flinn provides figures, based on the hearth tax statistics, of between 766,000 and 862,000 but his calculations exclude Caithness, Kirkcudbright, Ross and Sutherland where the figures are regarded as being too suspect (Flinn, M, 'Scottish Population History from the 17th Century to the 1930's', Cambridge University Press, 1977, pp 198/9). Lythe and Butt say

that estimates ranging from 800,000 to 1,250,000 have been given by various authorities (Lythe, S G E and J Butt, 'An Economic History of Scotland 1100-1939', Glasgow: Blackie, 1975, p 3) but they accept 1,000,000 as being a reasonable guess (p 87).

(48) This figure comes from a survey undertaken by Dr Alexander Webster. Smout (op cit, 1970) discusses Webster's work in chapter XI.

(49) Scruton, J, 'The Practical Counting House', Glasgow, 1777, p 2.

(50) Price, J M, 'The Rise of Glasgow in the Chesapeake Tobacco Trade, 1707-1775', printed in 'Studies in Scottish Business History', edited by Payne, P, London: Cass and Co Ltd, 1967, p 299.

(51) See chapter 12.

(52) See chapter 13.

(53) Macpherson, D, 'Annals of Commerce, Manufactures, Fisheries and Navigation ... ', London and Edinburgh, vol IV, 1805, pp 34/5. In a footnote Macpherson notes that "So strong is the prejudice in favour of town-made goods, that the Glasgow calico printers are obliged, in compliance with the desire of their customers, to use the harmless deception of marking their goods, as if printed in London ... ".

(54) Cotton spinning in Scotland began on a large scale basis when the New Lanark Mills went into production in 1786. Initially flax was too sticky for processing on the machines but drawings and descriptions of flax machines, operated by water power, appeared in the Scots Magazine, vol XXVIII, 1766, pp 77-80, 120, 175/6, with four plates.

(55) Hamilton, H, 'The Founding of the Carron Ironworks', The Scottish History Review, XXV, 185, 1928; Campbell, R H, 'Carron Company', Edinburgh, 1961.

(56) Dickson, T, op cit, p 94.

(57) Stewart, D, 'Dissertation: Exhibiting the Progress of Metaphysical, Ethical and Political Philosophy', vol 1 of the 'Collected Works', edited by Sir W Hamilton, Edinburgh: Thomas Constable and Co, 2nd edition, 1854, p 551.

(58) MacCormick, N, 'Law and Enlightenment', printed in 'The Origins and Nature of the Scottish Enlightenment', edited by Campbell, R H and A Skinner, J Donald, 1982, p 151. Stair's 'Institutions' has been described as "an original amalgam of Roman law, feudal law and native customary law, systematised by resort to the law of nature and the Bible, and illuminated by many flashes of ideal metaphysic". (Cooper, 'Scottish Legal Tradition' quoted by Walker, D, 'The Scottish Legal System',Edinburgh: W Green and Son Ltd, 4th edition,

1976, pp 121/2).

(59) Lieberman, D, 'The Legal Needs of a Commercial Society: the Jurisprudence of Lord Kames', in 'Wealth and Virtue', edited by Hont, I and M Ignatieff, Cambridge University Press, 1983, p 203.

(60) Lieberman, D, op cit, p 205.

(61) Campbell, R H, 1971, op cit, pp 28/9.

(62) Sen, S R, 'The Economics of Sir James Steuart', The London School of Economics and Political Science, 1957, p 2.

(63) Chitnis, A C, 'The Scottish Enlightenment, A Social History', London, Croom Helm, 1976, p 9.

(64) Printing and the Mind of Man Exhibition Catalogue, Indiana University, Bloomington, 1973.

(65) Hume, D, Essay 'Of Refinement in the Arts' in 'Essays Moral, Political and Literary', Oxford University Press, 1963, p 301. Adam Smith, however, related improvements in the arts and sciences to a prior improvement in trade and material prosperity; he said: "Opulence and Commerce commonly precede the improvement of arts and refinement of every sort" and " ... what all the violence of the feudal instititions could never have effected, the silent and insensible operation of foreign commerce and manufactures gradually brought about" ('Wealth of Nations', III, IV, paragraph 10).

(66) Young, D, Introduction to 'Edinburgh in the Age of Reason', Edinburgh: The University Press, 1967, p 11. Chitnis has a contrary view, he says: "The Scottish Enlightenment had little to say of a technical nature to an industrial society. Such Scottish technical contributions as did emerge from the eighteenth and early-nineteenth centuries (Watt and Telford to name but two) were not strictly part of the Scottish Enlightenment". (Chitnis, A C, op cit, pp 240/241).

(67) Arnot, H, 'The History of Edinburgh', Edinburgh: W Creech, 1779, p 438

(68) Arnot, H, op cit, pp 438-441.

(69) Jones, P, 'The Scottish Professoriate and the Polite Academy, 1740-46', printed in 'Wealth and Virtue', edited by Hont, I and M Ignatieff, Cambridge University Press, 1983, p 92.

(70) Bremner, D, 'The Industries of Scotland', 1869, reprinted Devon: David and Charles, 1969, p 500.

(71) MacDougall, W, 'Gavin Hamilton, John Balfour and Patrick Neill: A Study of Publishing in Edinburgh in the Eighteenth Century', Ph D thesis, University of Edinburgh, 1974.

(72) Chitnis, A, op cit, p 38.

(73) Yamey, B S, H C Edey and H W Thomson, 'Accounting in England and Scotland: 1543-1800', London: Sweet and

Maxwell, 1963, p 170.

(74) The first printed exposition of the double entry system is included in this work in a section entitled 'Particularis de Computis et Scripturis.' A translation of this, and a reproduction of the original, are contained in Brown, R G and K S Johnston, 'Paciolo on Accounting', McGraw-Hill, 1963.

CHAPTER 2

AUTHORS, TEACHERS AND PRACTITIONERS

NOTES AND REFERENCES

(1) Childs, C, 'A Discourse about Trade', London: printed by A Sowle, 1689, pp 4/5.

(2) Sombart, W, 'Der Moderne Kapitalismus', 1902, quoted from translation provided in 'Sombart on Accounting History', Most, K S, 'The Academy of Accounting Historians Working Papers Series', volume 2, Edited by Coffman, E N, 1979, Working Paper No 35 , p 258. This figure can be substantiated by reference to: Haan, D Bierens de, 'Bibliographie Neerlandaise Historique - Scientifique des Ouvrages Importants dont les Auteurs son nes aux 16e, 17e et 18e Siecle, sur les Sciences Mathematiques et Physiques, avec leurs Applications', Nieuwkoop, B De Graaf, 1960 (1st edition 1883). See also: 'Historical Accounting Literature', Mansell, 1975 and Hagers, J, 'Bouwstoffen voor de Geschiedenis van het Boekhouden in de Nederlanden', Rotterdam: G Delwel & Co, 1903, reprinted in Parker, R H, 'Bibliographies for Accounting Historians', New York: Arno Press, 1980 .

(3) Parker, R H, 'The First Scottish Book on Accounting', The Accountant's Magazine, v 78, 1974, pp 358-361.

(4) Devine, T M, 'The Merchant Class of the Larger Scottish Towns in the Later Seventeenth and Early Eighteenth Centuries', printed in 'Scottish Urban History', edited by Gordon, G and B Dicks, Aberdeen University Press, 1983, p 95.

(5) "To Cipher - To practice arithmetick" (Johnson, S, 'A Dictionary of the English Language', London: W Strahan, 1755). More specifically ciphering means 'computing with Arabic numbers'.

(6) Devine, T M, op cit, p 95.

(7) Brown, R, 'History of Accounting and Accountants', Edinburgh: T C and E C Jack, 1905, p 183.

(8) Nish, I H, 'The Life and Times of George Watson 1654-1723', printed in 'George Watson's College - History and Record 1724-1970', Edited by Waugh, H L, George Watson's College, 1970, p 4. Watson's mercantile exercise books dating from this period are in the possession of the Edinburgh Merchant Company. A Trial Balance from one of these books is illustrated in Richard Brown's History (op cit) facing p 184 and an extract from the text is given at pp 156/7.

(9) Lectures in Scottish Universities were in Latin until the middle of the century.

(10) The Grammar schools were coming under pressure to introduce a more practical curriculum. "About the

middle of the 18th century there was, in many quarters, a desire for schools with a more liberal and practical curriculum than that in use in the old grammar schools. "Academies" was the name chosen for such institutions. The academies were meant to supplement grammar schools by introducing commercial and science subjects, but in many cases they superseded them or became their rivals." (Kerr, J, 'Scottish Education, School and University from early times to 1908', Cambridge: University Press, 1913, p 162).

(11) Lord Cooper, Watson's College Founder's Day Oration, 1945. This was Watson's only direction as to the education that was to be provided for his scholars. George Watson's Hospital, is now George Watson's College, Edinburgh.

(12) Magnusson, M, 'The Clacken and the Slate', London: Collins, 1974, pp 24/25.

(13) Edinburgh Evening Courant, No 189, 28-30 August 1706.

(14) Marshall, G, 'Presbyteries and Profits', Oxford: Clarendon Press, 1980, chapter 7.

(15) Scott, W R, 'The Records of a Scottish Cloth Manufactory at New Mills, Haddingtonshire 1681-1703', Edinburgh: Scottish History Society, 1905.

(16) Scott, W R, op cit p 33.

(17) Bywater, M F and B S Yamey, 'Historical Accounting Literature: A Companion Guide', London: Scolar Press, 1982, p 131.

(18) Minutes of the Town Council, 15 June, 1705. In 1702 John Spottiswoode (later to become Keeper of the Advocates' Library) had drawn up a plan for a systematic study of Scotland's products and trade. One of the main provisions of the plan was the appointment of a professor of Trade who was to "teach ev'ry thing that relates to the mystery of trade, and what has been written & discover'd concerning it" (National Library of Scotland, MS 2934, pp 123-124, quoted by McElroy, D D, 'Scotland's Age of Improvement - A Survey of Eighteenth-Century Literary Clubs and Societies', Washington State University Press, 1969, p 31).

(19) Edinburgh Evening Courant, No 58, 12-15 October 1705 (and several subsequent issues). The term 'Book-holding', used in this advertisement, is a literal translation of the Dutch 'boekhouden'.

(20) The description is on the title page of his book 'Book-Keeping by Double Entry', Edinburgh, 1762.

(21) Stevenson's lobbying was successful as he later describes himself as "teacher of book-keeping, authorised by Act of Council of the City of Edinburgh" when he published his text-book 'Book-keeping by Double Entry' in 1763. See Murray, D, 'Chapters in the

History of Bookkeeping, Accountancy and Commercial Arithmetic', Glasgow: Jackson, Wylie and Co, 1930, pp 45/6.

(22) Gordon, W, 'The Universal Accountant', volume I, Edinburgh: for the Author and A Donaldson, 1763, p 2.

(23) Law, A, 'Education in Edinburgh in the Eighteenth Century', University of London Press, 1965, p 169.

(24) The Caledonian Mercury, No 7169, 2 July 1768.

(25) Ferguson, T, 'Dawn of Scottish Welfare', London: Thomas Nelson and Sons Ltd, 1968, p 70.

(26) The basic list is that of Edinburgh teachers contained in Law, A, 'Teachers in Edinburgh in the Eighteenth Century', Book of the Old Edinburgh Club, vol XXXII, 1966. This has been augmented by information gleaned from various sources. See also the section on 'Arithmetic, Mathematics, Book-keeping, and Writing in Education' in Law's book 'Edinburgh in the Eighteenth Century', University of London Press, 1965, pp 168-173.

(27) Murray, D, op cit, pp 104/5; Forrester, D A R, 'Whether Malcolm's is Best or Old Charge and Discharge', The Accounting Historians' Journal, Fall 1978, p 57.

(28) This document is Saltoun ms 17594, item 80, National Library of Scotland. Another document indicates that the two pupils mentioned were: Mr Gordon and John Borthwick (item 82). Murray gives James Gordon as the accountant to the British Linen Hall; see Williamson's 'Directory for the City of Edinburgh', 1773-74 and 1775-76.

(29) There were five universities in Scotland compared to two in England.

(30) Arnot, H, 'The History of Edinburgh', Edinburgh: W Creech, 1779.

(31) Sinclair, J, 'The Statistical Account of Scotland', Edinburgh: W Creech, 1793, vol 6, p 589.

(32) "The old English universities have not the same function as the Scotch and Irish universities. The former teach men how to spend a thousand a year with dignity and intelligence, while the latter aim at showing men how to make a thousand a year under the same conditions." (Playfair, Sir L, 'Universities in their Relation to Professional Education', essay in 'Subjects of Social Welfare', London: Cassell, 1889, p 376). Playfair goes on to say: "My object is to see universities assume their old function of being the great liberalising power of the professions" (p 378).

(33) Gordon, W, op cit, vol II, pp 14/15.

(34) Lockhart, J G, 'Peter's Letters to his Kinsfolk', Edinburgh, '2nd edition', 1819, vol III, p 208.

(35) "The founders (of the SSC) are described in the street directory of the time as 'writers'. Writers to the

Signet were separately designated. There are some 230 names of writers in the 1784-1785 directory of whom sixty-three have been traced as joining the SSC Society in the early days." (Barclay, J B, 'The SSC Story, 1784-1984', Edinburgh, 1984, p 10).

(36) Mair, J, 'Book-keeping Methodiz'd', 1765, Introduction, p ix.

(37) Stevenson, W, 'A General Discourse shewing the usefulness of the Italian Method', 1732, p 14.

(38) Stewart, J C, 'Pioneers of a Profession', Institute of Chartered Accountants of Scotland, 1977, p 6.

(39) Paton, G C H, 'The Eighteenth Century and Later', printed in 'An Introduction to Scottish Legal History', Edinburgh: The Stair Society, 1958, p 52.

(40) Lockhart, J G, op cit, vol III, pp 208/209.

(41) Smith, J I, 'The Rise of Modern Scots Law 1660-1707', in 'An Introduction to Scottish Legal History', Edinburgh: The Stair Society, 1958, p 48.

(42) Murray, D, op cit, pp 66/67. See also A C Littleton's 'Note on Scottish Bankruptcy Statutes' in his 'Accounting Evolution to 1900', Academy of Accounting Historians, University of Alabama Press, 1981, pp 285/6.

(43) Paton, G C H, op cit, p 57.

(44) S.30. See Gibb, A D, 'Insolvency' in 'An Introduction to Scottish Legal History', Edinburgh: The Stair Society, 1958, p 226.

(45) Gibb, A D, op cit, p 226.

(46) Grant, I D, 'Landlords and Land Management in North East Scotland 1750-1850', Ph D Thesis, University of Edinburgh, 1978, vol 1, p 34.

(47) Another example is provided by the tutors of Sir James Macdonald of Macdonald. "The tutors' accounts were kept by John Mackenzie, a writer to the signet (solicitor) in Edinburgh, who was employed 'not only in quality of Tutor, but also as Writer Cashier and agent for the pupill and to fitt the factors account and to keep all their affairs in order'. He was instructed 'to preserve all the vouchers of the factors and his own accounts and clearances so as to prevent any confusion; to keep a book wherein he is to ingross a full rentall of the estate and all the accounts already fitted ... ; and another book, in which he is to ingross, first, a full list of an account of all Sir Alexander Macdonald's debts with a column for the several periods from which interest was due thereon'. For his pains John Mackenzie received 'a salary of thirty pounds sterling a year'." (Moss, M, 'Forgotten Ledgers, Law and the Business Historian', paper presented at the Sixth Annual Congress of the European Accounting

Association, University of Glasgow, 1983).
(48) Grant, I D, op cit, p 215.
(49) An Act of the Town Council of Edinburgh Appointing a voluntary Contribution toward the support of the Charity-Warehouse, 18 January 1758.
(50) Act of Edinburgh Town Council, op cit.
(51) Murray, D, op cit, p 97.
(52) Murray, D, op cit.
(53) Brown, R, 'Lists of Deceased Scottish Accountants with Notes, Edinburgh', appendix II of 'History of Accounting and Accountants', Edinburgh: T C and E C Jack, 1905, pp 361-381.
(54) David Murray could not identify an earlier professional accountant in Glagow (op cit, p 108).
(55) Glasgow Mercury, 13 August 1778.
(56) Glasgow Mercury, 30 September 1784. Richard Smellie is not on the list of accountants in Tait's Directory for 1783-84 but in 1785 he was appointed as accountant to the Forth and Clyde Navigation (Forrester, D A R, 'The Great Canal that linked Edinburgh, Glasgow and London', Strathclyde Convergencies, 1980, pp 10/11).
(57) Stevenson, W, 'A Serious Advice to Tradesmen', Edinburgh, 1756, p 11.
(58) Stevenson, W, op cit, p 28.
(59) Stevenson emphasises this point and gives reasons for his views because he says "I would not have any surprized that I rank it (book-keeping) among the Mathematical Studies." (Stevenson, W, op cit, p 2).
(60) This follows the pattern set by Pacioli in 1494. Pacioli says that, after access to cash, "The second thing necessary in business is to be a good accountant and a ready mathematician." (Brown, R G and K S Johnston, 'Paciolo on Accounting', McGraw-Hill, 1963, p 25).
(61) In Williamson's 'Edinburgh Directory' for 1773-74 a number of individuals, described as accomptants, are listed under the heading of 'writers' (ie lawyers). A Bourdeaux directory, 'Almanac de Commerce ... pour ... Bordeaux' (1787) similarly lists 9 accountants as "Ecrivains Teneurs de Livres."
(62) The Society of Accountants in Edinburgh and The Institute of Accountants and Actuaries in Glasgow were both formed in 1853, the Society of Accountants in Aberdeen was founded in 1866. The identification of accountancy with the legal profession continued even after the Scottish professional accountancy bodies were established so that, for example, 'The Scottish Law List' for 1866 (Ravenscroft, E, published by W Patterson, Edinburgh) has a section which lists the members of the Society of Accountants in Edinburgh.

CHAPTER 3

ALEXANDER MALCOLM

NOTES AND REFERENCES

(1) This is the title of a sketch of Malcolm (drawn by his friend Alexander Hamilton) which is contained in 'The Tuesday Club Record Book'. This book is preserved by the Maryland Historical Society at Baltimore. The Tuesday Club was founded in Annapolis in 1745, by Hamilton with the purpose of providing facilities for its members to "meet, converse, laugh, drink, differ, argue, pun, sing, dance and fiddle together" (Sadie, S (editor), 'The New Grove Dictionary of Music and Musicians', London: Macmillan Ltd, 1980, volume 11).

(2) He was baptised on 25 December, 1685. Some authorities give his date of birth as 1687 but this seems to be a confusion with his brother's birth.

(3) Scott, H, 'Fasti Ecclesiae Scoticanae', Edinburgh: Oliver and Boyd, New Edition, 1915, volume I.

(4) Jean Reith was the second wife of Alexander (senior); there were 7 children by his first marriage to Janet Mason. (Lloyd, M, 'Alexander Malcolm, Writer on Mathematics and Music', Scottish Notes and Queries, December 1928, p 34).

(5) Gilbert Burnet (1643-1715) was born in Edinburgh. At the time of Malcolm's visit to him he was Bishop of Salisbury.

(6) Alexander later dedicated one of his books to the Directors of the Royal Academy of Music by name.

(7) No record of his attendance can be traced in the University of Edinburgh archives. Johnstone assumes that he was a student at Marischal College, Aberdeen, but this seems to be based on the assumption that he grew up in Aberdeen (Johnstone, K, 'The Family of Malcolm in Aberdeenshire', Scottish Notes and Queries, July 1904, p 8). Bywater and Yamey state that he was a graduate of the University of Edinburgh but they give no authority for this claim (Bywater, M F and B S Yamey, 'Historic Accounting Literature: A Companion Guide', London: Scolar Press, 1982, p 157). The fact that Malcolm's name has not been traced in the university's records is no proof that he did not attend as there are many gaps in the registers. Malcolm certainly knew the Principal of the university and Professor Charles Macky; there is a letter from him to Macky dated 22 July 1741 in the Manuscript Collection at the University of Edinburgh (La. II. 91).

(8) "We really know very little about this club apart from Mallet's mentioning it in a letter to John Ker, Professor of Greek in Kings College." (McElroy, D D, 'A

Century of Scottish Clubs', pp 40-2, 40-3).

(9) James Thomson (1700-1748), author of 'The Seasons', was apparently regarded by Malcolm as 'the jest of our club' (McKillop, A D, 'James Thomson (1700-1748) Letters and Documents', University of Kansas Press, 1958, pp 34/35).

(10) David Mallet (1705-1765), poet and playwright.

(11) North wrote on a variety of subjects including: 'etimology', 'the Boroscope', fish and fishponds, architecture and natural philosophy.

(12) Edinburgh Evening Courant, 6 November 1721.

(13) Malcolm's interests again run parallel to those of Roger North. North wrote a number of (unpublished) essays on music including a historical essay 'Memoires of Musick'. In this connection Wilson notes that "A long and well-written essay on 'the Ancient Musick' forms the last chapter of Alexander Malcolm's Treatise of Musick (Edinburgh, 1721), though North does not show knowledge of Malcolm's book." (Wilson, J, 'Roger North on Music', Novello and Co Ltd, 1959, p 278).

(14) Maurer, M, 'Alexander Malcolm in America', Music and Letters, vol 33, No 3, July 1952, pp 226, 231.

(15) Sadie, S, op cit.

(16) The Malcolm family may have originated from the Aberdeen area (Johnstone, K, op cit).

(17) Alexander, 1724; Elizabeth, 1727; Quinton, 1729 and Gilbert, 1731; the dates given are baptismal dates (Lloyd, M, op cit, p 235).

(18) De Morgan, A, 'Arithmetical Books from the Invention of Printing to the Present Time', London: Taylor and Walton, 1847, London: reprinted by H K Elliott Ltd , 1967, p 66.

(19) De Morgan, A, op cit, p 67.

(20) Forrester, D A R, 'Whether Malcolm's is Best or Old Charge & Discharge', The Accounting Historians Journal, Fall 1978, pp 51-61.

(21) The New Grove Dictionary (op cit) says that he was a accompanied by 'his two sons' but at a later date all his children seem to be in America, (Lloyd, M, op cit, p 236).

(22) Pratt, D J, 'Annals of Public Education in the State of New York from 1626 to 1746', Albany: The Argus Company, 1872, pp 124-133.

(23) Malcolm had known Charles Macky (or Mackie) when the latter was a student but, at the time of writing this letter, Macky had become the first Professor of History at the University of Edinburgh (Sharp, L W, 'Charles Mackie, The First Professor of History at Edinburgh University', The Scottish Historical Review, April 1962, pp 23-45).

(24) Letter dated 3 July 1738 in Manuscript Collection at the University of Edinburgh (La. II. 91).
(25) He was ordained in London by the Bishop of London.
(26) Letter dated 22 July 1741 in Manuscript Collection at the University of Edinburgh (La. II. 91).
(27) Lloyd, M, op cit.
(28) Alexander Hamilton was the author of 'Itinerarium', which was written in 1744, when he made a tour through the northern colonies; this was published privately in 1907, and more recently by the University of North Carolina Press in 1948.
(29) It seems likely that Malcolm would also have known Robert's father, Gavin Hamilton, as he had been connected with the Athenian Society.
(30) Fletcher, C, 'King William's School Survives the Revolution', Maryland Historical Magazine, vol 81, no 3 Fall 1986, pp 210-221.

CHAPTER 4

JOHN MAIR (1702/3-1769)

NOTES AND REFERENCES

(1) This description of Mair is given by J Morrison in his book 'The Elements of Book-keeping by Single and Double Entry', 1813, p 2.
(2) Quoted from the Introduction to Mair, A, 'A Brief Explication of the Assembly's Shorter Catechism', New Edition, Montrose: Smith and Co, 1830, p iv. Scott also describes the father as a 'manufacturer' (Scott, H, 'Fasti Ecclesiae Scoticanae', vol V, Edinburgh: Oliver and Boyd, 1925, pp 71/2).
(3) 'The Statistical Account of Scotland', (edited by Sinclair, J), Edinburgh: W Creech, 1793, vol V, number IX, p 170, section on Portmoak written by Rev Mr Andrew Grant.
(4) Alexander was born in 1709.
(5) University records show that John belonged to the class of students known as 'ternars' which indicates that he was of artisan, tenant farming or merchant background.
(6) Quoted from the Introduction to Mair, A, op cit, p iv.
(7) Alexander died in 1751 from a "nervous fever" contracted after a dispute connected with his opposition to patronage in the church (Scott, H, op cit, vol IV). In 1752 John Mair published his brother's 'Brief Explication of the Assembly's Shorter Catechism' (Edinburgh: Printed by Sands, Murray and Cochran) and in 1768 (the year before his death) he published a Synod Sermon that Alexander had preached. Volume V of 'Fasti Ecclesiae Scoticanae' (1925) makes reference to a Thomas Mair (born 1701, died 1768) who was a son of a William Mair, manufacturer, Strathmiglo. Thomas Mair was educated at the University of Edinburgh and ordained in 1725. He became minister of the Scottish Church at Rotterdam in 1733 but was excommunicated in 1757. If this was another brother of John, his absence from the family details recorded in the Introduction to Alexander's 'Brief Explication' may be due to this excommunication.
(8) From a letter to Ayr Town Council, November, 1727.
(9) McClelland, J, 'Schools' chapter 14 of Dunlop, A O, 'The Royal Burgh of Ayr - 750 Years of History', Oliver and Boyd, 1953.
(10) Graham, H G, 'The Social Life of Scotland in the Eighteenth Century, London: Adam and Charles Black, 1909, p 427.
(11) No DCCXCVIII, p 2232.
(12) Ayr Town Council Minutes, 18 November 1746.
(13) Taylor, A L, 'The Grammar School of Ayr 1746-96',

Collections of the Ayrshire Archaeological and Natural History Society, vol 7, 1966, pp 58-89.
(14) Paterson, J, 'History of the County of Ayr', Ayr, J Dick, vol 1, 1847.
(15) Boyd, W, 'Education in Ayrshire Through Seven Centuries', University of London Press, 1961, p 76.
(16) Boyd, W, op cit, pp 76/77.
(17) Ayr Grammar School had included book-keeping in its curriculum since 1721.
(18) Boyd, W, op cit, p 77.
(19) Taylor, A L, op cit, p 62.
(20) See Sutherland, D J S, 'John Mair - The Pioneer of Science Teaching in Scotland', The Scottish Educational Journal, 4 July, 1952, p 422.
(21) Presumably sterling.
(22) Sievwright, W, 'Greyfriars' Burying-ground, Perth, its epitaphs and inscriptions', Perth: A Wright, 1893.
(23) Holmes, W, 'Accounting and Accountants in Massachusetts', Massachusetts CPA Review, January, February 1975, p 20.
(24) Sheldahl, T K, 'America's Earliest Recorded Text in Accounting: Sarjeant's 1789 Book', The Accounting Historian's Journal, vol 12, no 2, Fall, 1985, p 7. See also Chandler, A D, 'The Visible Hand: The Managerial Revolution in American Business', Cambridge Mass, 1977, p 521, note 57.
(25) 'Accounting in England and Scotland, 1543-1800', London: Sweet and Maxwell, p 172. The quotation is from Cronhelm, F W, 'Double Entry by Single', London, 1818, p xiii.
(26) 'Essays on Book-keeping', Glasgow, 1758, Preface.
(27) Webster, W, 'An Essay on Book-keeping', London, 1719.
(28) 'Accounting in England and Scotland, 1543-1800', London: Sweet and Maxwell, p 172.
(29) Leeds: for J Binns, J Johnson, Ogilvy and Speare, and Vernor and Hood, 1794.
(30) London, 1760, pp 339-400. These questions are from book III, pp 165-177.
(31) Mitchell, W, 'A New and Complete System of Book-Keeping by an Improved Method of Double Entry ... The Whole in Dollars and Cents', Philadelphia: Printed by Bioren & Madan. The claim that this was the first accounting text to be written by an American author has been challenged by Sheldahl (Sheldahl, T K, op cit, pp 1-42).
(32) Kelly, P, 'The Elements of Book-Keeping ... ', London: J Johnson and Co, fourth Edition, 1811, p iv.
(33) Carter, F Hayne, 'Practical Book-Keeping adapted to Commercial and Judicial Accounting ... ', Edinburgh and

Glasgow: John Menzies and Co, Second Edition, 1874, p 4.

(34) This is Mair's description of the Italian Method in the preface to 'Book-keeping Methodiz'd'.

CHAPTER 5

WILLIAM GORDON (1720/1-1793)

NOTES AND REFERENCES

(1) This description of Gordon is given by J Morrison in his book 'The Elements of Book-keeping by Single and Double Entry', 1813, p 2.

(2) Scottish Notes and Queries, Second Series, vi, 1905, p 145 and Aberdeen Journal Notes and Queries, vol 1, 1908, p 107. The story is repeated in Murray's 'Chapters in the History of Bookkeeping, Accountancy and Commercial Arithmetic', Glasgow: Jackson, Wylie and Co, 1930.

(3) Quoted by Hibbert, C in 'King Mob', Longmans Green, 1958.

(4) Edinburgh Magazine, December 1793, vol II (New Series), p 507.

(5) Miss Joanna Gordon, Historian of the House of Gordon, in correspondence with the author.

(6) Gordon Castle Muniments, Scottish Record Office, GD44, Bundle 23.

(7) See chapter 14, p 289.

(8) Letter dated 3 January 1781 from Thomas Grahame to Charles Gordon, acting for the Duke, Gordon Castle Muniments, Scottish Record Office, GD44, Bundle 23.

(9) Mr G A Gordon (an authority on the history of the House of Gordon) suggests that William could well have been an illegitimate son of either the First or Second Duke.

(10) 'Fasti Academiae Mariscallanae, Aberdonensis 1593-1860 - Selections from the Records of Marischal College and University', vol II, edited by Anderson P J, Aberdeen: New Spalding Club, 1898, p 309.

(11) Charles Gordon of Terpersie was executed after the '45 Rebellion. Several Gordons with the Christian name William are listed in 'A List of Persons concerned with the Rebellion transmitted to the Commissioners of Excise by the Several Supervisors in Scotland in obedience to a general letter of the 7th May 1746', Edinburgh: Scottish Historical Society, 1890.

(12) Sutherland, D J S, 'The History of Milne's, Institution, Fochabers', The Scottish Educational Journal, August 23, 1946, pp 464/5.

(13) Sinclair, J, (editor) 'The Statistical Account of Scotland', Edinburgh: W Creech, 1795, Vol 14, p 265.

(14) A bol is a dry measure equal to 8857 cubic inches. A Parliamentary commission of 1661 had recommended that there should be national Scottish standards for weights and measures. Although the commission's recommendations were generally adhered to, some irregularity existed between commodities in dry measure.

(15) Sincair, J. op cit, p 270.
(16) Saltoun MSS, National Library of Scotland, MS 17564, no 132.
(17) Kirk Session Records, August 20, 27, October 8, December 10, 1755.
(18) Hutchison, A F, 'History of the High School of Stirling', Stirling, 1904, pp 157-158.
(19) Hutchison, A F, op cit, p 158.
(20) Scruton had moved to Glasgow from London in 1749.
(21) Murray, D, op cit, pp 34-37.
(22) This and similar titles, such as 'The Young Man's Best Companion', were very popular in the 18th and 19th centuries. Some of these compendiums of practical knowledge, including the most popular, 'The Instructor: or Young Man's Best Companion' (attributed to George Fisher, 'Accomptant'), had sections on book-keeping but this is not a topic covered in Gordon's text. The 1765 (4th) edition of Gordon's 'Every Young Man's Companion' contains a curious and varied collection of topics such as: Instructions in the Art of Penmanship, Of the Care of Forming the Manners, Directions for Writing Letters, Practical Arithmetic and Geometry, Of Artificial Fireworks (how to prepare various kinds), Shorthand (a section copied from the Alphabet of Reason, 1763), Mystery of Freemasonry Explained, The Common Notion of Spirits, Apparitions, and Witches; their Power and Feats Exposed.
(23) Chauncey Lee acknowledges that the book-keeping section of his work is "a compendium of the Italian mode of Book-keeping agreeably to Gordon's system of accomptantship" (p xxxii of Introduction).
(24) 'The Practical Counting House; or, Calculation and Accountantship Illustrated', Glasgow, 1777.
(25) Murray, D, op cit, p 36.
(26) Gordon Castle Muniments, Scottish Record Office, GD44, Bundle 23 (SRO GD44/42/1/23).
(27) The Tolbooth contained " ... the Justice-court-Hall, within which is the Entry of a large Turn-pike or Stair-case ascending to the Town-council-Hall, above which there was the Dean of Gild's Old Hall; but now this is turned into two Prison Houses for Prisoners of Note and Distinction ... " there were also " ... Five large Rooms appointed for common Prisoners ... " (M'Ure, J, 'A View of the City of Glasgow', Glasgow, 1736, pp 255/6).
(28) Scottish Record Office, CS 25/7 Dec 1782.
(29) Lillie, J A, 'The Mercantile Law of Scotland', 6th edition, W Green and Son, 1965, p 266. See also Brown, R, 'History of the Law of Debtor and Creditor with special reference to Cessio Bonorum', Address to

Annual Summer Conference of the Scottish Institute of Accountants, 1898, Glasgow, 1898.

(30) Scottish Record Office, Edinburgh, West Register House, CS25/7 Dec 1782/Gordon His Creditors.

(31) 20 September, 1764.

(32) Murray, D, op cit, p 40; Glasgow Mercury, 29 May, 1783; Glasgow Journal, 5 June, 1783. John Tait's 'Directory for the City of Glasgow from the 15th May 1783, to the 15th May 1784' lists "Nicol's Accademy, high street" (p 53).

(33) Murray, D, op cit, p 36; Glasgow Journal, 2 October, 1783.

(34) Gordon is still listed in Tait's Directory (1783/84) as resident in Glasgow and operating as a 'teacher of the mathematicks' (p 34).

(35) Caledonian Mercury, 30 September, 1786 and 24 October, 1789. The locations given for him in the Edinburgh Directories are: Allan's Close (Williamson's Directory, 1788/90); Chalmers Close (Aitchison's Directory, 1793/94; Williamson's Directory, 1794/96). These may be the addresses of his private accommodation.

(36) Williamson's Edinburgh Directory, 1794/96. Paton had been appointed 'writing master to the High School' in 1790 but he was dismissed from this post in 1793. He is described as a 'writing master and accomptant' in Aitchison's Directory for 1793/94. The Commercial Academy continued to operate after Gordon's death.

(37) Scot's Magazine, December 1793, Vol 55, p 621; Edinburgh Magazine, December 1793, vol II (New Series), p 507. It might be noted that 'Musgrave's Obituary' mistakenly identifies our William Gordon with an Edinburgh bookseller of the same name whose death in October 1793 is reported in the Gentleman's Magazine of October, 1793 at p 960 ('Musgrave's Obituary Prior to 1800 (as far as relates to England, Scotland and Ireland)', vol III, Sir W Musgrave, Edited by Sir G J Armytage, Harleian Society, London, 1900).

(38) Gordon Castle Muniments, Scottish Record Office, GD44, Bundle 23.

(39) Letter from Thomas Grahame dated 3 January 1781, Scottish Record Office, GD44, Bundle 23.

(40) Scottish Notes and Queries, Second Series, vi, 1905, p 145.

(41) Scottish Notes and Queries ibid and C Rogers, 'History of The Christie Family', 1878.

(42) There is a letter from the Duke of Gordon to William Gordon junior giving his version of the story of the loan to his father, February 1794, Gordon Castle Muniments, Scottish Record Office, GD44, Bundle 23.

(43) There is a begging letter from Mrs Maxwell Gordon to

the Duke in Bundle 23 of the Gordon Castle Muniments (Scottish Record Office).

(44) William Laing opened an academy for classical education in the New Town, Edinburgh. Aitchison's Edinburgh Directory for July 1797 to July 1798 gives Laing's address as 10 East Rose Street.

CHAPTER 6

ROBERT HAMILTON (1743-1829)

NOTES AND REFERENCES

(1) This description of Hamilton is given by J Morrison in his book 'The Elements of Book-keeping by Single and Double Entry', 1813, p 2.

(2) Pilrig House featured in Stevenson's 'Catriona' ("I came in view of Pilrig, a pleasant gabled house set by the walkside among some brave young woods.") and in 'Kidnapped'. It has recently been restored, for a description and sketch of the house see Tranter, N, 'The Fortified House in Scotland', vol 1, Edinburgh and London: Oliver and Boyd, 1962, p 86.

(3) See: McDougall, W, 'Gavin Hamilton, John Balfour and Patrick Neill: A Study of Publishing in Edinburgh in the 18th Century', Doctoral Dissertation, University of Edinburgh, 1974. Gavin Hamilton also showed bravery during the Porteous Riots, when he was almost brained by an axe blow, and during the famine of 1740 when he helped to quell a meal riot at the Water of Leith.

(4) During the occupation of Edinburgh by the Jacobites "Mrs Hamilton, who was sister to James Balfour, then proprietor of Pilrig, took refuge with her children at his house, where many of Mr Balfour's near relations went: the situation of Pilrig being peculiarly fortunate, in lying under the defence of the Fox sloop-of-war, which guarded the coast, it was a safer place than Edinburgh, and she remained there, till the Whigs got possession of the city again. She walked down Leith Walk, with her nursery maid and children, among whom was the late Dr Hamilton ... then two years old, when, at the same time, the Castle was firing cannon over their heads, upon a party of Highlanders, who were passing on that part of the Easter-road that comes out from the south-side of the Calton Hill". (extract from a 'Memoir on Gavin Hamilton' by Miss Betty Hamilton, printed in Balfour-Melville, B, 'The Balfours of Pilrig', Edinburgh, 1907).

(5) Chambers, R (editor), 'A Biographical Dictionary of Eminent Scotsmen', Edinburgh: Blackie and Son, 1875.

(6) Ramsay, J, 'Dr. Robert Hamilton' in 'Select Writings', Aberdeen: J R Smith, 1871, pp 126-133.

(7) The Speculative Society was the " ... most famous and the most successful debating society of the century" (McElroy, D D, 'A Century of Scottish Clubs', Edinburgh 1969, vol I, p 188-6). The club was satirised by Lockhart in 'Peter's Letters to his Kinsfolk' (Edinburgh, '2nd edition', 1819, pp 268-280).

(8) The Newtonian was established by a group of young men

who had completed their university education. " ... members took turns delivering discourses at their weekly Saturday meetings, after which a previously-announced subject was discussed. They called themselves 'Newtonians' because of their interest in natural philosophy but gradually they extended their debates to include miscellaneous subjects, though the discourses 'were always confined to natural science'" (McElroy, D D, op cit, vol I, pp 186-6, 186-7). Hamilton describes the club in a letter to Alexander Smellie (the editor of the 1st edition of the 'Encyclopaedia Britannica') (Kerr, R, 'Memoirs of the Life, Writings, and Correspondence of William Smellie', 1811, Letter 8).

(9) Marischal College was one of the two universities at Aberdeen.

(10) This important enterprise had been carried on by Gavin Hamilton in partnership with his brother-in-law, John Balfour, until 1762 when the partnership was dissolved. Thomson says that, after 1762, the business was carried on by Balfour but this seems to be incorrect although it was subsequently sold to him after Gavin Hamilton's death (Thomson, A G, 'The Paper Industry in Scotland', Edinburgh: Scottish Academic Press, 1974, p 95).

(11) Hamilton, E, 'Short Memoir of Gavin Hamilton, Publisher and Bookseller in Edinburgh in the Eighteenth Century', Aberdeen: printed for private circulation, 1840.

(12) Hamilton Collection at University of Aberdeen, Miscellaneous Papers 36, 83/84.

(13) Campbell, R H, 'Scotland Since 1707', Oxford: Basil Blackwell, 1971, p 10.

(14) Both of Mair's accounting works were in Hamilton's library, Miscellaneous Papers 36, University of Aberdeen Library.

(15) 'Fasti Academiae Mariscallanae, Aberdonensis', vol I, Aberdeen: New Spalding Club, 1889, p 448.

(16) Sage, D, 'Memorabilia Domestica, or, Parish Life in the North of Scotland', Wick: W Rae, 1889, p 199.

(17) 'A Short System of Arithmetic and Bookkeeping', Edinburgh, 1788.

(18) Thomson, R, 'A Key to Hamilton's Arithmetic, containing solutions of all the unwrought questions in that work, commencing with simple proportion', Edinburgh: Printed by, and for J Robertson, No 30 Nicolson Street, 1811. Thomson is described as an 'Accountant' on the title page of this work.

(19) A quotation will give the flavour of this work. " ... war is the absurdest and most destructive of human measures, ... it brings much evil upon the conquering as well as upon the vanquished nation, ... its objects

are often frivolous, seldom attained, and, when attained, seldom advantageous, ... heavy burthens are its constant attendant, and these not confined to the present age, but entailed upon posterity". ('Reflections on Peace and War', pp 58/9).

(20) First edition published in 1813. See M'Culloch, J R, 'A Select Collection of Scarce and Valuable Tracts and Other Publications on the National Debt and Sinking Fund', London: Lord Overstone, 1857 and Hirst, F W, 'The Political Economy of War', Dent, 1915.

(21) His father had been treasurer of the Edinburgh Infirmary.

(22) M'Culloch, who had republished his work on the Redemption of the National Debt, was not enthusiastic about this volume. He says: "In 1830, after his death, his family published a treatise of his, entitled 'The Progress of Society', which embraces a wide range of interesting topics, but it is feebly written, and might without injury to his fame or to the public interests have been allowed to continue in manuscript." (M'Culloch, J R, 'The Literature of Political Economy', London: Longman, Brown, Green, and Longmans, 1845, p 337).

(23) Camic, C, 'Experience and Enlightenment, Socialization for Cultural Change in Eighteenth Century Scotland', Edinburgh University Press, 1983, pp 243-256.

(24) Hamilton's record of his personal 'Nett Stock' survives. This shows a steady increase from less than £300 in the early 1790s to over £3,500 in the mid 1820s (Miscellaneous Papers 36, Hamilton Collection, University of Aberdeen).

(25) Cronhelm, F W, 'Double Entry by Single, A New Method of Book-keeping', London: Longman, Hurst, Rees, Orme and Brown, 1818.

(26) 'Dictionary of National Biography', Smith, Elder and Co, 1908, vol VIII, p 1091.

(27) Morrison, J, 'The Elements of Book-keeping', London: Phillips, 1813 edition, p ii.

(28) Morrison, J, 'The Elements of Book-keeping', London: Phillips, 1810 and 'A Complete Treatise on Practical Book-keeping', A Constable, 1810.

(29) 9th edition, 1880, vol XI, p 416.

CHAPTER 7

A SURVEY OF SCOTTISH ACCOUNTING TEXTS UP TO THE END OF THE EIGHTEENTH CENTURY

NOTES AND REFERENCES

7.1 Introduction

(1) Pryce-Jones, J and R H Parker, 'Accounting in Scotland - A Historical Bibliography', The Institute of Chartered Accountants of Scotland, second edition, 1976. This bibliography is a valuable source of information on 'Scottish' accounting texts up to 1920.

(2) Newall's 'The Merchant's Companion: Being a more Exact, Quick and Easy Way, for making up of Accompts' (1715) and Buchanan's 'The Writingmaster and Accountant's Assistant' (1798).

(3) The exception is Newall's 'Merchant's Companion'. An accountant whose books of interest tables were regularly reprinted was John Thomson. The first edition of his 'Tables of Interest' (Edinburgh: Sands, Murray and Cochran) appeared in 1768; the 11th edition (London: James Duncan) was published in 1837.

7.2 Idea Rationaria
Robert Colinson, 1683

(1) Hugh Oldcastle, 'A briefe instruction and maner how to keepe bookes of Accompts', 1543.

(2) Parker, R H, 'The First Scottish Book on Accounting', The Accountant's Magazine, vol 78, 1974, pp 358-361.

(3) "Little is known about Colinson except that both of the laudatory verses at the beginning of the book refer to him as 'Captain' and his own claim to have spent twenty-five years in commerce as 'student and practitioner'". (Bywater, M F and B S Yamey, 'Accounting Literature: A Companion Guide', London: Scolar Press, 1982, p 131). Murray states that he was a teacher of book-keeping in Edinburgh for some time before 1683 ('Chapters in the History of Bookkeeping, Accountancy and Commercial Arithmetic', Glasgow: Jackson, Wylie and Co, 1930, p 43) and it has been noted (p 23) that in 1682/3 he seems to have acted as advisor to The New Mills Cloth Manufactury. Dr Forrester, of the University of Strathclyde, has found evidence that Colinson was the chamberlain (steward) to the 4th Earl of Winton and that he died in 1692.

(4) At the end of the 17th century Campheer's (or Veere's) dominance of the Scottish trade with Holland was being strongly challenged by Amsterdam and Rotterdam.

(5) Although addressed to the 'Merchants of Edinburgh', there is no mention of The Company of Merchants of the

City of Edinburgh which had received its charter two years earlier (in 1681).

(6) p 5.

(7) Colinson says that he has chosen to use English money, it " ... being most universally known in these 3 Kingdoms, for the use of such, who desire to be informed" (Waste Book A, January 1682).

(8) Parker, R H, op cit.

(9) The example includes: Insurance, Loans, Bills of Exchange, Custom Duty, the use of Factors, Wagers etc.

7.3 The Merchant's Companion
W Newall, 1715

(1) Article XVI of Treaty.

(2) One hundred years later James Lang's Burgess Certificate (issued in 1817 when he became a Burgess and Guild Brother of the Burgh of Glasgow) contained the clause: "And how oft as I shall happen to break any part of this my oath, I oblige me to pay, to the common affairs of this burgh the sum of One hundred pounds Scots money, ... "(Adam, J S, 'A Fell Fine Baker, The Story of United Biscuits', Hutchinson Benham Ltd, 1974, pp 28/9).

7.4 The Accomptant's Pocket-Companion
John Drummond, 1718

(1) pp 3/4.

(2) p 21.

7.5 The Reason of Accompting by Debitor and Creditor
Robert Lundin, 1718

(1) p 3.

(2) Jackson, J G C, 'The History of Methods of Exposition of Double-entry Book-keeping in England' printed in Littleton, A C and B S Yamey, 'Studies in the History of Accounting', Sweet and Maxwell, 1956, pp 303-305.

(3) p 3.

(4) "Advertisement. Writing in all Hands, Arithmetick, Vulgar and Decimal, and Book-keeping, are carefully taught by William Humphrey and Robert Lundin, in the Middle of Cant's Closs."

7.6 A New Treatise of Arithmetick and Book-keeping
Alexander Malcolm, 1st Edition, 1718

(1) John Hay, one of the Baillies, was an accountant.

(2) The contents are arranged as follows: Arithmetick, pp 1-112; Instructions for Book-keeping, pp 113-194; Accounting illustration, 126 (unnumbered) pages; Appendices: I 'Of Arithmetick', pp 1-27; II 'Of Book-

keeping', pp 28-51.
(3) For definitions of 'alligation', 'fellowship', 'tare' and 'trett' see the Glossary.
(4) Preface.
(5) Malcolm's attempt to identify the fundamental principles of accounting might be compared with the continuing efforts of accounting researchers to provide a conceptual framework for the discipline.
(6) p 163.
(7) This book was published anonymously in 1714, the author describing himself as 'a Person of Honour'. Roger North (1653-1734) was the brother of Sir Dudley North and Dudley may well have written the manuscript on which the book was based (Bywater, M F and B S Yamey, 'Historic Accounting Literature: A Companion Guide', London: Scolar Press, 1982, pp 148-151).
(8) Bywater and Yamey, ibid, p 148.
(9) North, R, 'The Gentleman Accomptant', 1714, p 243.
(10) pp 113/4.
(11) p 115.
(12) p 121.
(13) p 121.
(14) pp 121-123.
(15) Malcolm adopted the term 'mediate accompts' from Roger North who uses it on pages 15 and 17; other writers, eg Stephenson (1762), use the term 'fictitious'.
(16) p 116.
(17) p 126.
(18) Proper trade is trade on one's own account rather than through the use of an agent or factor.
(19) 'Company accompts' = partnership accounts.
(20) pp 163-177; 188-192.
(21) p 132.
(22) p 132.
(23) Colinson, R, 'Idea Rationaria', 1683, p 5; North, R, op cit, p 25.
(24) Appendix II Of Book-keeping, pp 28-51.

7.7 <u>The Principles of Book-keeping Explain'd</u>
<u>Alexander Macghie, 1718</u>

(1) Brown, R, 'A History of Accounting and Accountants', Edinburgh: T C & E C Jack, 1905, p 352; Murray, D, op cit, p 44. Both authorities state that the earlier edition is octavo whereas the 1718 '2nd' edition is quarto. There seems to be a reference on page 11 of 'The Principles of Book-keeping Explain'd' to another book by Macghie; 'Vulgar Arithmetick'. No copy of such a book has been located.
(2) p 2.

Notes and References - Chapter 7

(3) Although Macghie's book was published after the union of the Scottish and English parliaments (which standardised the currency in Great Britain), the examples he provides relate to dates which preceded the Treaty of 1707. Transactions were frequently quoted in Scots currency long after 1707.

(4) p 3.

(5) p 52.

7.8 A New and Easy Method of Book-keeping Alexander Brodie, 1722

(1) A more extensive treatment might have been expected but Brodie explains that he has avoided this because there are liable to be changes in the regulations. He also claims (in a Note following the List of Subscribers) that the " ... Instructions and schemes already sent to the Collectors, Comptrollers, and other Officers, are so exact, that no Loss or Damage can accrue to the Merchants thereby".

(2) This title page is the work of George Bickham (d 1769), a writing master and engraver, who was the most famous penman of the time. In 1743 Bickham published 'The Universal Penman'. The catalogue of the Antiquarian Collection of the Institute of Chartered Accountants of Scotland ('An Accountant's Book Collection 1494-1930', 3rd edition, 1976) states that the publisher of Brodie's book is George 'Buckham' but Brodie published the book himself and'Buckham' seems to be a misreading of 'Bickham'.

(3) "Charles Snell (1670-1733), 'accomptant,' was a famous teacher of writing and accounts in Foster Lane, London, during the latter part of the seventeenth and early part of the eighteenth century." (Murray, D, 'Chapters in the History of Bookkeeping, Accountancy and Commercial Arithmetic', Glasgow: Jackson, Wylie and Co, 1930, p 18).

(4) p 9.

(5) p 1.

(6) p 2.

(7) p 2.

(8) p iv of Preface.

(9) There is some confusion in the dates used in the examples. Part I deals with the period from 7 June 1720 to 23 August 1720 but the last page of the Waste Book, erroneously, gives the year as 1721. Part II carries on the example by commencing at 24 August 1721 (the incorrect date) and carries on to 24 October 1721. Brodie's book is marred by a number of errors, possibly printing errors, which make it difficult to follow

through his examples.

(10) Some interesting comments on marine insurance are provided. He notes that there is " ... now a Company established by Law, who have given good Security for the performance of their Contracts, the Insuring of Ships and Goods will no doubt henceforward meet with the greater Incouragement ... Tho while this Busines was only in the Hands of private Persons, it was liable to very great Discompts on the one side, and on the other to fraudulent Practices, which could not bear the Light; and therefore such Accompts were seldom Posted under their proper Title, because the Owners had Insured at several Places on the same Ship and Goods; and oftentimes pretending Accidents where there were none" (p 6).

(11) p 6. The recording of these transactions might have given useful information on contemporary practice in valuing unsold speculative investments but there seem to be a number of errors in Brodie's treatment (or the printer's type-setting) so that it has not been possible to determine the valuation basis used. Brodie optimistically states that "Some Errors having escaped the Press, thro' Inadvertency, the Learner may easily adjust them ... " but this is not as easy as he assumes.

7.10 A Treatise of Book-keeping
Alexander Malcolm, 1731

(1) A New Treatise of Arithmetick and Book-keeping, 1718.

(2) This definition (and the book's title) use the spelling 'accounts' rather than 'accompts' used in Malcolm's earlier book (1718). 'Accounts' is the spelling adopted throughout the new book, except in the Appendix which is, almost word for word, a copy of the appendix in the earlier work. The Appendix uses 'accompt'.

(3) p 5.

(4) p 35.

(5) pp 1-5 (new numbering).

(6) Proper Trade on pp 37-59, Factorage on pp 59-64 and Company Accounts on pp 64-77.

(7) p 38.

(8) pp 77-87.

(9) p 77.

(10) The Waste Book is given on pp 91-114, the Journal Book on pp 115-148 and the Leger Book on 36 un-numbered pages.

(11) The combined Waste Book and Journal is illustrated on pp 1-20 (new numbering) and the Leger is given on 20 pages (these are un-numbered).
(12) pp 7-34 (new numbering).

7.11 A General Discourse Shewing the Usefulness of the Italian Method of Book-keeping
William Stevenson, 1732
(1) p 8.

7.12 Book-keeping New Modelled
William Hamilton, 1735
(1) Murray, D, op cit, p 47. Murray provides details of a fire alarm that Hamilton invented: "In 1740 'he invented a machine, for effectually preventing the breaking of houses; which being plac'd behind the door or window, instantly rings a bell, fires a pistol and lights a candle, on the least attempt to force up either door or window.' This machine was 'highly approved by the Curious.' (Caledonian Mercury, 23 December, 1740)."
(2) Hamilton is quoting from Roberts, L, 'The Merchants Mappe of Commerce', London, 1638, p 36.
(3) Similar claims are made by North, R, op cit and Gordon, W, 'General Counting-House and Man of Business', 1766 (when introducing his section on Estate Accounting).
(4) There is an echo of Malcolm in this section. Hamilton says "... you are to proceed by making a record of your Transactions, the subject of which consists in Men, Money and Goods ... " (p 4). Malcolm said "Men, Goods and Money, are the essential Subjects of Merchants Accompts" ('A New Treatise of Arithmetick and Book-keeping', 1718, p 115).
(5) The first 40 pages (approximately a quarter of the book) contain explanatory material. The illustrative examples deal with: Domestick Accounts, Factorage and Foreign Trade and Company Accounts.
(6) The accounts deal with irregular time periods: the first illustration is concerned with an accounting period from June 1 to August 23, 1734; the second covers the period September 9 to December 31, 1734 and the third covers January 2 to June 18, 1735. The preparation of annual accounts is not considered.

7.13 Book-keeping Methodiz'd
John Mair, 1736

(1) The later book was 'Book-keeping Moderniz'd', it was first published in 1773.
(2) pp 233-270.
(3) pp 235-331. This section is based on material in William Weston's 'The Complete Merchant's Clerk: or British and American Counting House' (1754).
(4) pp 369-398.
(5) 'Dictionary of National Biography', Smith, Elder and Co, 1908.
(6) North wrote 'The Gentleman Accomptant' (1714).
(7) Yamey, B S, 'The Functional Development of Double-entry Bookkeeping', The Accountant, 2 November 1940, p 342, reprinted in 'The Development of Double Entry - Selected Essays', Edited by Nobes, C, New York: Garland Publishing Inc, 1984, p 142.
(8) p 4.
(9) Thus the title page of the 1737 Dublin edition changes the description of the contents of chapter III of the Appendix from 'Precedents of Merchants Writings, peculiar to England, Scotland, and common to both' to 'Precedents of Merchants Writings, peculiar to England, Scotland, and common to Great Britain and Ireland' but there is no change in the text itself. The 1748 Dublin edition does not contain the section on 'Of Monies and Exchanges'.
(10) pp 249-265.
(11) William Jackson advertised on page 248 of the Dublin edition of Mair that he taught "the Art of Book keeping and Accounts, according to the present Practice of the most eminent merchants ... at the Green Door in College-Street, near College Green, Dublin". He was probably a relative of the book's publisher, I Jackson, and there is an announcement of his 'forthcoming' book, 'A New Treatise of Book-keeping, or, the Method of stating Merchant-Accounts; after the true Italian Form of Debtor and Creditor', at page 266. This book does not seem to have been published until 1785 when it appeared as 'Book-keeping in the true Italian form of debtor and creditor ... exemplified, from the precepts of the late ingenious D Dowling ... ' Some later editions were published in America where the book was popular.
(12) pp 179-416

7.14 A Serious Advice to Tradesmen
William Stevenson, 1756

(1) pp 1/2.
(2) p 9.

(3) p 11.
(4) p 11.
(5) In fact the city had appointed a burghal accountant to the official post of Professor of Book-keeping in 1705, but presumably this position had lapsed.
(6) pp 16-18.
(7) See the title page of his 'Book-keeping by Double Entry', 1762.

7.15 Essays on Book-keeping
William Webster and 'A Teacher of Book-keeping', 1758

(1) In the University of Glasgow Library there are two copies of this book. That at Mu30, g5 has a red and black title page. The copy held by the Mitchell Library, Glasgow (at D 114019) and the original of the photocopy held by The Institute of Chartered Accountants in England and Wales also have red and black title pages.
(2) The copy held by the University of Glasgow at BG56 m2 has a title page printed in black alone.
(3) Murray, D, op cit, p 337.
(4) These pages are in the 'black' University of Glasgow copy (bound between pages 120 and 121) and in the Mitchell Library 'red and black' copy (bound between pages 136 and 137). The other two copies of the book that were examined do not have the extra material.
(5) This book was very popular. Its 15th edition was published in 1772 and there was another edition in 1779 (Brown, R, 'A History of Accounting and Accountants', 1905).
(6) Murray, D, op cit, p 337.
(7) The book contains one more question which the 'Teacher of Book-keeping' has not taken from Mair.
(8) Mair does give solutions to questions III and IV in his second book-keeping text, 'Book-keeping Moderniz'd'.

7.16 Book-keeping by Double Entry
William Stevenson, 1762

(1) This was a common 'inferiority complex' of educated Scots in the 18th century. "They regarded the Scots they spoke in daily life as an inferior form of English, though some conceded the strength and vigour of early Scots and the appropriateness of modern Scots for pastoral poetry. They tried hard to avoid what they called 'Scotticisms' in their writings." (Daiches, D, 'Homage to Scotland's Conservative Radicals', The Weekend Scotsman, July 19, 1986). The year before Stevenson's book was published the Select Society of Edinburgh introduced lectures on English

elocution because: " ... gentlemen educated in Scotland have long been sensible of the disadvantages under which they labour, from their imperfect knowledge of the ENGLISH TONGUE ... " (Scots Magazine, vol XXIII, 1761, pp 440/1)

(2) pp 1-18.

(3) p 3.

(4) Formal headings of this type were rare in the 18th century texts. The English writer Roger North had used 'Laus Deo' at the start of his Journal (1714, op cit, p 164) and Macghie (1718, op cit) had opened his Waste-Book with a short Latin prayer but the majority of writers considered this an anachronism.

7.17 <u>The Universal Accountant and Complete Merchant William Gordon, 1st edition, 1763</u>

(1) Vol I, Essay, p 1.

(2) ibid, p 2.

(3) ibid, p 16.

(4) Volume II, pp 14/15.

(5) Part I, pp 1-71; part II, pp 72-104; part III, pp 105-151; part IV, pp 152-408.

(6) pp 178-408.

(7) Tare and Trett, 178-182; Computation of Customs, Bounties, 182-188; Rule of Mixtures, 188-195; Warehouse and Shop Computations, 195-202; Barter Computations, 202-204; Partnership Computations, 204-211; Bankruptcy Computations, 211-218; Stock Jobbing, 218-231; Factorage, 231-235; Insurance, 235-288; Computations in Exchange, 283, 235; Arbitration of Exchanges, 336-350; Comparisons of Weights and Measures, 350-352; Simple Interest, 352-367; Compound Interest, 368-370; Purchasing Freehold or Real Estates (with tables of Terminal Value, Present Value, Annuity Terminal Value, Annuity Present Value, Annuity Purchaseable for £1, for rates of interest of 3, 3½, 4, 4½ and 5% and from 1 to 40 years), 370-387; Annuities on Lives, 387-401; Mensuration of Surfaces and Solids, 401-408.

(8) Mortimer's book is the best known guide to stock market practices in the 18th century. The book went through no less than 13 editions between 1761 and 1810. Mortimer (1730-1810) was a prolific writer. This book is based on his own experiences on the Stock Exchange where he states that, in 1756, he "lost a genteel fortune."

(9) 'Bookkeeping Methodiz'd' (8th edition) deals with 'How the balances are collected, the ledger closed, and a new Inventory formed' at pp 92-95.

7.18 <u>A Full and Practical Treatise upon Bills of Exchange</u>
<u>William Stevenson, 1764</u>
(1) This text, 'Book-keeping by Double Entry' (1762) was considered in 7.16.
(2) pp 214-232.
(3) p 214.
(4) pp 215-216.
(5) ie He writes out a cheque.
(6) ie transfer.
(7) pp 218-220.
(8) p 218.

7.19 <u>The General Counting-House and Man of Business</u>
<u>William Gordon, 1st edition, 1766</u>
(1) His first book-keeping publication was 'The Universal Accountant' (first edition, 1763). This has been discussed at 7.17.
(2) 'The Universal Accountant' was a two volume work but the book-keeping material was confined to the second volume. Volume I was concerned with arithmetic, algebra and business mathematics.
(3) Given the progress of banking in 18th century Scotland, it is surprising that none of the Scottish texts covered 'bankers' accounts'. This did feature in some of the English books, eg Dodson, J, 'The Accountant, or the Method of Book-keeping deduced from clear principles', London, 1750.
(4) Although there was general agreement on the importance of the Waste-Book, Mair and Hamilton also considered modified systems for shopkeepers that did not require this book.
(5) Mair's 'method of keeping accompts proper for Shopkeepers or Retailers' did make use of a Cash Book ('Book-keeping Methodiz'd', 1765, pp 369-370).

7.20 <u>Book-keeping Moderniz'd</u>
<u>John Mair, 1st edition, 1773</u>
(1) Preface, p v.
(2) p 44.
(3) The example is on pp 251-311.
(4) pp 82-250.
(5) p 67.

7.21 <u>The Man of Business, and Gentleman's Assistant</u>
<u>William Perry, 1st edition, 1774</u>
(1) This description appears on the title page of one of his other books 'The Only Sure Guide to the English Tongue', Edinburgh, 1776.
(2) pp 1-174.

(3) pp 175-180
(4) Perry uses this term; it does not appear to have been used by any other 18th century Scottish writer.
(5) In this section the alphabet is given with 26 letters rather than 24 as with earlier writers.
(6) These alterations may have been introduced in the second edition but no copy of this has been located.

7.22 An Introduction to Merchandize
Robert Hamilton, 1st Edition, 1777/79

(1) Part V, chapter III, section 8.
(2) The editor claims in the 'Advertisement' that " ... he has been favoured with the advice of its very respectable Author, with whose approbation this new Edition is published".

7.23 The Practical Counting House
James Scruton, 1777

(1) "6 February 1750. Considering that (blank) Scruton, writing master, late of London, being recommended to the provost, when at London about the towns affairs in Spring last, by several gentlemen, as a fitt person for teaching of writing, arithmetick, and bookkeeping in the city, for the benefite of the inhabitants, and that at the provosts desire he has come here and taken up his residence and school since Whitsunday last, the magistrats and council, for his encouragement, do enact and pay him yearly £25 sterling during his residence and continuing his school here in the place, for the benefite of the inhabitants in teaching of writing, arithmetick and bookkeeping ... " (Extracts from the Records of the Burgh of Glasgow with Charters and other Documents, vol VI, AD 1739-59, Corporation of Glasgow, Glasgow, 1911, p 316).
(2) 'Accountantship' is also used by Scruton's partner, Gordon, in 'The General Counting House and Man of Business' and much earlier by Stephen Monteage (Instructions for Rent Gatherers, 1682/3, p 5). The alternative spelling 'accomptantship' is used by Dafforne in the long title of his 'The Apprentices Time-Entertainer' (see Murray, op cit, p 246).
(3) Smollett, T, Humphrey Clinker, edited by Roscoe, London, 1831, p 281.
(4) The following are examples: John Glasford and Co, pp 60-61; Alexander Speirs, p 75; John M'Call and Co, p 75; Robert Lawson, pp 74-75, 116, 126, Murdoch, Warroch and Co, pp 186-187; Houston's and Co, p 187 James Alston and Co, p 51.
(5) pp 4-14.
(6) pp 15-219.

Notes and References - Chapter 7

7.25 The Writingmaster and Accountant's Assistant
Colin Buchanan, 1798

(1) His book-keeping works are: 'Practical book-keeping being an attempt to assimilate the methods of the school to the practice of the counting house', Edinburgh, 1806, and 'An Engraved system of bookkeeping', Edinburgh, 1808. He also wrote 'Observations on Schools and on Teaching some of the Common Branches of Education (including Bookkeeping)', Edinburgh, 1824.

(2) p 7.

CHAPTER 8

THE NATURE AND OBJECTIVES OF BOOK-KEEPING

NOTES AND REFERENCES

(1) Some English authors did not use this approach, for example both North and Dodson emphasised 'Estate Accounting' (North, R, 'The Gentleman Accomptant', London, 1714; Dodson, J, 'The Accountant, or the Method of Book-keeping deduced from clear principles', London, 1750). The mercantile concentration of the Scottish books may have had greater appeal to potential readers and may have been part of the reason for the success of Mair and Gordon.

(2) For example, among the accounts in Mair's illustrative Ledger A there are accounts for houses, household furniture, lottery tickets and house expenses ('Book-keeping Moderniz'd', Edinburgh: Kincaid, Creech and Bell, 1773, pp 172-245).

(3) Macghie, A, 'The Principles of Book-keeping Explain'd', 1718, p 11.

(4) Colinson, R, 'Idea Rationaria', 1683, p 2, the book was not published.

(5) Malcolm, A, 'A New Treatise of Arithmetick and Book-keeping', 1718, p 124. Colinson compares the ledger to a mirror (p 2) and a similar idea appears in the title of Richard Dafforne's book-keeping book 'The Merchants Mirrour' (London: Nicolas Bourne, 1635).

(6) Malcolm, A, op cit, p 115.

(7) Malcolm, A, 'A Treatise of Book-keeping', 1731, p 3.

(8) Malcolm, Mair, Gordon and Hamilton describe the Italian Method of Book-keeping as an 'art'. Some other writers categorise it as a 'science'. Colinson considered it to be an "honourable and profitable science" (op cit p 1) and Drummond derives its scientific status from its connection with mathematics when he says: "Merchant-Accompts being a Branch of the Mathematicks, are so much improved, that a perfect Knowledge of them is almost become a Science, because every Thing terminates in a clear Demonstration" ('The Accomptant's Pocket-Companion', 1718). Stevenson regards book-keeping as having a place "among the Mathematical Studies", but he considers it as being: "... both a Science and an Art: the Science is the knowledge of Debitor and Creditor; and the Art is to apply them in all kind of business, and to bring the truth of the principles to a demonstration." ('A Serious Advice', 1756, p 2). Although Malcolm considers book-keeping to be an art, he does quote with approval from North who said of the Italian Method that it " ... is so comprehensive, and perfect, as makes it worthy to be

put among the Sciences ... " (North, R, op cit, p 1).

(9) Mair, J, 'Book-keeping Methodiz'd', 1736, p 1.

(10) Mair, J, (1736), op cit, p 6 (emphasis added). Macghie had used the same phrase when he gave book-keeping's objective to be that "the ... merchant may, at any Time, be resolved about ... what he is worth to a Farthing." (op cit, p 1).

(11) Gordon, W, 'The Universal Accountant', vol II, 1745, p 15.

(12) Hamilton, R, 'Introduction to Merchandize', 2nd ed, part IV, p 265 (emphasis added).

(13) MacCormick, N, 'Law and Enlightenment', printed in Campbell, R H, and A Skinner (editors), 'The Origins and Nature of the Scottish Enlightenment', Edinburgh: John Donald, 1982, p 150.

(14) Yamey, B S, H C Edey and H W Thomson, 'Accounting in England and Scotland: 1543-1800', London: Sweet and Maxwell, 1963, pp 170-173.

(15) Colinson, R, 'op cit, Dedication 'To the Merchants in Edinburgh'.

(16) Colinson, R, op cit.

(17) Malcolm, A, (1718), op cit. pp 113/4.

(18) Stevenson, W, 'A General Discourse', 1732, p 19.

(19) North, R, op cit, p 4.

(20) Colinson, R, op cit, p 1.

(21) Malcolm, A, (1731), op cit, p 3.

(22) Malcolm, A, (1731), op cit, p 3.

(23) Stevenson, W, (1732), op cit, p 9.

(24) Differences between a textbook's claimed objectives and the objectives of its intended readership are not particularly unusual. Taxation textbooks provide a modern example where the interests of the readers in tax avoidance are often only acknowledged indirectly by the authors.

(25) Malcolm talks of the relevance of a sound book-keeping system for a trader as "a Man and Christian, to be in Condition at all Times, to satisfie the World of the Honesty and Fairness of his Dealing" (1718, op cit, p 114).

(26) Hont I and M Ignatieff, 'Needs and Justice in the Wealth of Nations: an introductory essay' printed in Hont I and M Ignatieff (editors), 'Wealth and Virtue, The Shaping of Political Economy in the Scottish Enlightenment', Cambridge University Press, 1983, pp 24/5.

(27) The industrial capitalists "... recognized in the self-interest which he put at the centre of human conduct the motive which inspired their everyday business life. And they were delighted to know that their pursuit of profit was now to be regarded as unselfish" (Roll, E,

'A History of Economic Thought', Faber and Faber, 1940, pp 151/2). Smith's views reinforced the Calvinistic justification of capitalism, see chapter 1, pp 5-8.

(28) A list of Hamilton's books made in 1825 shows that he then owned a copy of the 'Wealth of Nations' but this was the 1814 edition (Miscellaneous Papers 36 (147-154), Hamilton Collection, University of Aberdeen). Although there is no record of Hamilton having read the first edition, it would seem more likely that he did, than that he did not.

(29) Yamey, B S, H C Edey and H W Thomson, op cit, p 173.

(30) Presumably the authors considered that their task was to explain the 'Italian Method' and this did not not include Accounts Charge and Discharge.

(31) Smith, A, 'The Wealth of Nations', 4th Edition, London, vol III, 1786, book V, chapter I, p 124.

(32) Malcolm, A, (1718), op cit, p 189.

(33) Malcolm, A, (1718), op cit, 'Appendix of Book-keeping', p 34.

(34) This is quite similar to the original meaning of 'control' which had its origins in medieval treasury accounting practices where a 'counter-roll' was maintained as a check on the record of transactions which were inscribed on the 'roll.' The word subsequently became confused with 'comptrol'.

(35) Malcolm, A, (1718), op cit, 'Appendix of Book-keeping', p 34.

(36) Erskine, J, 'The Principles of the Law of Scotland', Edinburgh: Bell and Bradfute, New Edition, 1809, pp 465/6.

(37) Brodie, A, 'A New and Easy Method of Book-keeping', 1722, p 1.

(38) Mair, J, (1736), op cit, p 9.

(39) Robert Hamilton ('Introduction to Merchandize', vol II, 1779, pp 2/3) and W Perry ('Man of Business, 1774, p 181) consider the waste-book to be more important as legal evidence. Macghie (op cit, p 3) supports Brodie and Mair.

(40) Colinson, R, op cit, p 3.

(41) Mair, J, 'Book-keeping Methodiz'd', 1765, p vii.

(42) Colinson, R, op cit, p 1.

(43) Brodie, A, op cit, p iv of Preface.

(44) Young, D, 'The Farmers Account-Book', c 1789, Introduction.

(45) Mair, J, 'Book-keeping Methodiz'd', 5th Edition, 1757, p 373.

(46) Drummond, J, 'The Accomptant's Pocket-Companion', 1718.

(47) Colinson, R, op cit, p 1.

(48) Advertisement in Edinburgh Evening Courant, Number 58,

12-15 October 1705, text reproduced in Chapter 2, pp 23/4.

(49) Colinson, R, op cit.

(57) This seems to be implied by his thesis that "As market machinery has become less and less effective ... accounting technique has been developed to supplement and supplant it. So pervasive is this increasing dependence upon accounts that it suggests an organization of economic institutions around accounts comparable to the earlier organization around the market." ('The Cultural Significance of Accounts', Scholars Book Co, Kansas, 1973, p 283).

(51) Williams, P F, 'The Legitimate Concern with Fairness', Accounting, Organizations and Society, 1987, pp 169-189.

CHAPTER 9

THE BOOKS OF ACCOUNT AND THE CANONICAL SYSTEM

NOTES AND REFERENCES

(1) For example part IV of Hamilton's 'Introduction to Merchandize' (Vol II, 1779) has a 29-page chapter (chapter I) devoted to 'General Principles and Rules'. The contents of this chapter are: a one-page introduction, 18 1/2 pages describing the three principal books and 9 1/2 pages on Posting and Balancing the Ledger.

(2) The alternative name of 'Memorial Book' is mentioned by Malcolm ('A Treatise of Book-keeping', 1731, p 4).

(3) Hamilton, R, op cit, p 2.

(4) Malcolm, A, 'A New Treatise of Arithmetick and Book-keeping', 1718, p 114.

(5) Brodie, A, 'A New and Easy Method of Book-keeping', 1722, p 1.

(6) Brodie, A, op cit, p 1.

(7) Mair, J, 'Book-keeping Methodiz'd', 1749, appendix, chapter VIII; Gordon, W, 'The General Counting-House', 1766, pp 422-462; Hamilton, R, op cit, vol II, part V, chapter IV.

(8) Brodie, A, op cit, p 1.

(9) Hamilton, R, op cit, p 8.

(10) Malcolm, A, (1731), op cit, p 32.

(11) Malcolm, A, 'A New Treatise of Arithmetick and Book-keeping', 1718, p 129. The text continues: " ... where I suppose there may be sundry Debtors and sundry Creditors ... there would be a greater Difficulty to express this Case neatly, and with a distinct Connection of the Debtors and Creditors, in the Journal: But we may always shun this, by dividing the Transaction into two Parts, wherein we shall have one Debtor and sundry Creditors, or contrarily ... ".

(12) Malcolm, A, (1718), op cit, p 126. Perry claims that "There is no necessity to keep a journal ... except where merchants deal in a great variety of articles, their trade considerable, and their entries in the waste-book pretty long" (Perry, W, 'The Man of Business', 1774, note on p 3 of illustrative Waste Book).

(13) Macghie, A, 'The Principles of Book-keeping Explain'd', 1718, p 3.

(14) Colinson, R, 'Idea Rationaria', 1683, p 3.

(15) Hamilton, R, op cit, vol II, p 2.

(16) "If any dispute arise in trade, this book is produced as the principal voucher; and therefore merchants cannot be too particular in their records" (Perry, W, op cit, p 181).

(17) Hamilton, R, op cit, vol II, pp 2/3.

(18) Malcolm, A, (1718), op cit, p 158. The quotation shows the word "narration" being used in a technical sense. The marginal journal is illustrated in Malcolm's 1731 book at p 31.
(19) Malcolm, A, (1731), op cit, p 32. North had given 'foul journal' as an alternative name for the Waste-Book (North, R, 'The Gentleman Accomptant', 1714, p 29).
(20) Hamilton, W, 'Book-keeping New Modelled', 1735.
(21) Mair, J, 'Book-keeping Methodiz'd', 1736, pp 11/12.
(22) Mair, J, 'Book-keeping Moderniz'd', 1773, pp 12/13.
(23) Scruton, J, 'The Practical Counting House', 1777.
(24) Hamilton, R, op cit, vol II, p 242. This criticism is muted in later editions.
(25) Colinson, R, op cit, p 2.
(26) Malcolm, A, (1731), op cit, p 6.
(27) Malcolm, A, (1718), op cit, p 116. This emphasis on the 'leger' as the "principal Book of Accounts" is continued in 'A Treatise of Book-keeping', 1731, p 5.
(28) Jackson, J G C, 'The History of Methods of Exposition of Double-Entry Book-keeping in England', Printed in Littleton, A C and B S Yamey, 'Studies in the History of Accounting', London: Sweet and Maxwell, 1956, pp 288-312.
(29) Lundin, R, 'The Reason of Accompting by Debitor and Creditor', 1718, p 3. Scruton described the ledger as "the principal book of accounts" (op cit, p 4) and Macghie said "The Ledger is the Perfection of all the other Books" (op cit).
(30) Drummond, J, 'The Accomptant's Pocket Companion', 1718, p 14.
(31) Malcolm, A, (1718), op cit, p 154.
(32) Malcolm, A, (1718), op cit, p 158.
(33) Mair, J, (1736), op cit, appendix, p 1. Mair makes the point that "Merchants in England that have Cash keepers, must beware to write any thing in the Cash book themselves; for if they do, the Cash keeper is no more accountable for what is stated in the Book: And therefore the Master, in case of Money delivered to him, in the Cash keeper's Absence, must keep it till he come home; and then deliver it to him, and see him enter it in the Book himself." (ibid p 2). In later editions the words "in England" are omitted.
(34) Brodie, A, op cit, p 14.
(35) Malcolm, A, (1718), op cit, p 154.
(36) Macghie, A, op cit.
(37) Perry, W, op cit, p 183.
(38) Booth, B, 'A Complete System of Book-keeping', London, 1789, p 8.
(39) Hamilton, R, op cit, vol II, p 246.

(40) Hamilton, R, op cit, vol II, p 243.
(41) Colinson, R, op cit, p 3.
(42) Scruton, J, op cit, p 7. Robert Hamilton also mentions this book (op cit, vol II, p 229).
(43) Perry, W, op cit, p 183.
(44) Mair, J, op cit, p 11.
(45) Hamilton, R, op cit, vol II, p 234.
(46) Scruton, J, op cit, p 5. Macghie also mentions an Invoyce Book (op cit).
(47) Malcolm, A, (1718), op cit, p 158.
(48) Booth, B, op cit, p 8.
(49) Perry, W, op cit, pp 182/3.
(50) Malcolm, A, (1718), op cit, pp 155/6.
(51) Mair, J, (1736), op cit, appendix, p 3.
(52) Scruton, J, op cit, p 6.
(53) Mair, J, (1736), op cit, appendix, p 3.
(54) Mair, J, (1736), op cit, appendix, p 3.
(55) Drummond, J, op cit, p 5.
(56) Scruton, J, op cit, p 7.
(57) Drummond, J, op cit, p 4.
(58) Brodie, A, op cit, p 8.
(59) Macghie, A, op cit; Malcolm, A, (1718), op cit, p 63.
(60) Perry, W, op cit, pp 182/183.
(61) Mair, J, (1736), op cit, appendix, pp 4-6. 'Factory' means relating to the trader's factors.
(62) Scruton, J, op cit, p 6.
(63) Scruton, J, op cit, p 6.
(64) Scruton, J, op cit, p 6.
(65) Mair, J, (1736), op cit, appendix, pp 7/9.
(66) Scruton, J, op cit, p 6. Hamilton describes such a book (op cit, vol II, pp 229/230).
(67) Malcolm, A, (1718), op cit, pp 154/155.
(68) Malcolm, A, (1731), op cit, p 54.
(69) Macghie, A, op cit.
(70) Mair, J, (1736), op cit, appendix, p 4; Perry, W, op cit.
(71) Malcolm, A, (1718), op cit.
(72) Mair, J, (1736), op cit, appendix, p 12.
(73) Scruton, J, op cit, p 6.
(74) Mair, J, (1736), op cit, appendix, p 12.
(75) Mair, J, (1736), op cit, appendix, p 12.
(76) Gordon, W, op cit, pp 7/8.
(77) An example of such a Month Book, is provided by Gordon at p 350.
(78) Colinson, R, op cit, p 2.
(79) Malcolm, A, (1718), op cit, pp 156/157; (1731), op cit, p 64.
(80) Scruton, J, op cit, p 5.
(81) Perry, W, op cit, p 183. Scruton also describes a Bill Book (op cit, p 6).

Notes and References - Chapter 9

(82) Mair, J, (1736), op cit, appendix, p 9; (1773), op cit, pp 336/337.
(83) Hamilton, R, op cit, vol II, pp 231/232.
(84) North, R, op cit, p 2.
(85) See Yamey's comments on Stephens' book in Yamey, B S, H C Edey and H W Thomson, 'Accounting in England and Scotland: 1543-1800', London: Sweet and Maxwell, 1963, p 178.

CHAPTER 10

BALANCING THE BOOKS

NOTES AND REFERENCES

(1) There were other reasons. Under the heading of 'Leagers-Conclusion, or Ballancing of the Leager', the 17th century English writer, Dafforne, lists the following reasons for making a 'Generall Ballance': "1. When the Journall, and Leager are full written; so that there must be New-bookes: 2. When a Merchant ceaseth from Trading: 3. When the Book-Owner departeth this world:" (Dafforne, R, 'The Merchants Mirrour', 1635, p 46). It should be noted that Estate and Farm Accounts would normally have been prepared at regular annual intervals, often from Martinmas to Martinmas.

(2) Malcolm, A, 'A New Treatise of Arithmetick and Book-keeping', 1718, p 178; Macghie, A, 'The Principles of Book-keeping Explain'd', 1718, p 52.

(3) An exception is Malcolm who acknowledges the possibility that a partner might require a copy of the state of his account (op cit, p 189).

(4) Hamilton, R 'Introduction to Merchandize', vol II, 1779, pp 84/85.

(5) Winjum, J O, 'The Role of Accounting in the Economic Development of England 1500-1750', University of Illinois, 1972.

(6) Yamey, B S, 'The Development of Company Accounting Conventions', The Three Banks Review, September, 1960, pp 22-37.

(7) Mair, J, 'Book-keeping Methodiz'd', 1736, p 89. The context of these quotes is given on pp 209/210.

(8) Malcolm A, op cit, Preface.

(9) Macghie, A, op cit, p 52.

(10) Malcolm A, op cit, p 133.

(11) William Hamilton confirms this role for the Profit and Loss Account when he gives, as one of the objectives of book-keeping, the provision of information to the merchant on " ... what he has gained or lost by every Subject ... ".('Book-keeping New Modelled', 1735, p 1). Another writer who adopts this position is Stevenson. When a transfer is made to Profit and Loss, from a ledger account, Stevenson regards such an account as representing a 'branch' of the merchant's trade and therefore the Profit and Loss Account is primarily viewed as a record of the gains and losses arising from the various branches of trade rather than being a list of income and expenditure. The only expenses appearing in the Profit and Loss Account might be expenses that it was not convenient (or meaningful) to allocate to a specific 'branch of trade'. ('Book-Keeping by Double

Entry', 1762, p 13).
(12) ie factor's wages.
(13) Macghie, A, op cit, p 14.
(14) ie 'drawings'.
(15) Although this list of categories of expense and income might seem to be more in line with what is now dealt with in the income statement, Macghie's specimen profit and loss accompts are not particularly informative as to the sources of income and the types of expense because the detail is only shown in the journal. Macghie is, of course, not catering for absentee owners whose only source of information, on the profitability of their investment, is the income statement, but for a merchant who would always have recourse to the journal if he needed information on the makeup of a figure appearing in his profit and loss account.
(16) Gordon, W, 'The General Counting-House', 1766, p 424.
(17) Gordon, W, ibid.
(18) Edwards, R, 'Some Notes on the Early Literature and Development of Cost Accounting in Great Britain', The Accountant, 7 August 1937, p 193.
(19) Yamey, B S, 'Common Costs and Business Decisions: An Historical Note', The Accounting Historian, Winter 1975, p 1.
(20) Hamilton, R, op cit, vol II, part IV, chapter I, section 107.
(21) Hamilton, R, op cit.
(22) Malcolm, A, 'A Treatise of Book-keeping', 1731, p 47.
(23) Thomas, A L, 'The Allocation Problem in Financial Accounting Theory', American Accounting Association, 1969; 'The Allocation Problem', Part Two, American Accounting Association, 1974; Wells, M C, 'Accounting for Common Costs', University of Illinois, 1978.
(24) Malcolm, A, (1731), op cit, p 49.
(25) Malcolm, A, (1731), op cit.
(26) In particular chapters 16 and 17.
(27) This will be considered in chapter 14.
(28) Hamilton, R, op cit, pp 491/492.
(29) Or indeed interest payable.
(30) Malcolm, A, (1731), op cit, p 51.
(31) Malcolm, A, (1718), op cit, p 155. It is the trader's personal expenses that are being considered.
(32) Malcolm, A, (1731), op cit, p 43 and p 55.
(33) Hamilton, W, op cit, p 8.
(34) Mair, J, (1736), op cit, p 89.
(35) Malcolm, A, (1718), p 133.
(36) Gordon, W, op cit, p 422.
(37) Yamey, B S, 'The Functional Development of Double-Entry Bookkeeping', The Accountant, 2 November 1940, p 336 (reprinted in Nobes, C. (editor), 'The Development of

Double Entry', Garland Publishing Co, 1984, p 136).

(38) Colinson, R, op cit, Waste-Book and Journal for July 1, 1682.

(39) Brodie, A, 'A New and Easy Method of Book-keeping', 1722.

(40) In this respect 18th century practice contradicts Sombart's view that: "The Method of double-entry book-keeping actualizes the complete separation of the funds used in profit making and the funds used for everyday life." (Sombart, W, 'Medieval Enterprise', printed in 'Enterprise and Secular Change', edited by Lane, F C, London, p 38).

(41) Colinson, R, op cit, p 5.

(42) Colinson dismisses a Dutch method of concealing the Stock balance by merging the Stock and Cash Accounts.

(43) Mair, J, 'Book-keeping Methodiz'd', 5th Edinburgh edition, 1757, p 24. This note does not appear in earlier editions. Mair's second book adds 'furniture' to the list of household items. ('Book-keeping Moderniz'd', 1773, p 25).

(44) "When you receive Money, in Legacy or Compliment, or with an Apprentice, or as gained on a Wager, or by Exchange of Money, &c. for which nothing goes out, enter Cash Dr. to Profit and Loss, or to Stock." (Mair, J, (1736), op cit, pp 29/30, emphasis added). Note that Mair is not making the distiction between private transactions and business transactions but between normal business exchange transactions and receipts "for which nothing goes out".

(45) Mair, J, (1773), op cit, pp 30/31.

(46) Malcolm, A, (1731), p 106.

(47) Malcolm, A, (1718), p 143.

(48) Gordon, W, (1766), pp 424/5.

(49) Malcolm, A, (1718), p 139. Malcolm dismisses the possibility of any profit arising from a 'gain' in the weight or volume of merchandise by saying that this cannot arise "if every Body has Justice done to them".

(50) Colinson, R, Journal entries 2 January and 1 July 1682; Malcolm, A, (1718), p 184; (1731), p 89; Macghie, A, p 49; Brodie, A, p 3; Stevenson, W, (1762); Gordon, W, (1766), pp 424/425; Perry, W, 'The Man of Business', 1774, folio 2 of illustrative double entry ledger and Scruton, J, 'The Practical Counting House', 1777, p 12.

(51) Yamey, B S, 'Cost, Market or Something Else: Asset Valuation in some Early Treatises', printed in 'External Finanial Reporting', Edited by Carsberg, B and S Dev, Prentice-Hall International, 1984, p 176.

(52) Malcolm, A, (1731), op cit, p 89.

(53) Malcolm, A, (1731), op cit, p 89.

Notes and References - Chapter 10

(54) Drummond, J, 'The Accomptant's Pocket Companion', 1718, p 3.
(55) Hamilton, R, 'Introduction to Merchandize', 1788, p 285 (emphasis added). In the 1820 edition this (and much else of Hamilton's writing) disappears and unsold goods are valued at cost (p 395). This is the work of Elias Johnston who rewrote the book-keeping section of the 'New Modelled' book.
(56) 'Back to an Age of Falling Prices', The Economist, July 13, 1974, pp 62/63.
(57) 'Inflation Accounting', Report of the Inflation Accounting Committee, London: HMSO, 1975.
(58) Bonbright, J C, 'Valuation of Property', The Michie Co, Virginia, 1965 reprint.
(59) Baxter, W T, 'Depreciation', Sweet and Maxwell, 1971.
(60) Bonbright, J C, 'Valuation of Property', The Michie Co, Virginia, 1965 reprint, p 71.
(61) Hamilton, R, (1788), op cit, p 285; Gordon, W, op cit, in section on 'The Retailer's Counting-House'.
(62) Malcolm, A, (1731), op cit, pp 52-53. Yamey, B S, H C Edey and H W Thomson reproduce illustrations of the use of the two methods. ('Accounting in England and Scotland: 1543-1800', Sweet and Maxwell, 1963, Plates X and XI).
(63) Hamilton, R, (1788), op cit, part IV, chapter II, p 334.
(64) It has previously been noted that 'asset' is absent from the 18th century book-keeping vocabulary.
(65) Malcolm, A, (1731), op cit, p 90. Mair (1773) values two houses at 'prime cost' in an illustrative example (op cit, pp 198, 214).
(66) Yamey, B S, 'The Development of Accounting Conventions', The Three Banks Review, September 1960, pp 22-37. Only Malcolm's method 3 would answer Yamey's criticism.
(67) Drummond, J, op cit, p 3.
(68) Yamey, B S, (1960), op cit, pp 22-37.
(69) Pollard, S, 'The Genesis of Modern Management', Arnold, 1965.
(70) Malcolm, A, (1718), op cit, p 178.
(71) Malcolm, A, (1731), op cit.
(72) "Storekeepers generally balance their Books once a-year: On which Occasion they make out two fair Copies of the whole Books; one of which they send home to Britain for the Use of their Employers, and the other they retain in the Store." (Mair, J, 'Book-keeping Methodiz'd', 1749, p 254).
(73) Mair, J, 'Book-keeping Methodiz'd', 5th edition, 1757, chapter VIII of the appendix.
(74) Gordon, W, 'The Universal Accountant', vol II, 1765,

p 50.

(75) Mair, J, 'Book-keeping Moderniz'd', 1773, p 67. If Mair was here copying Gordon it is only right to note that Gordon had earlier copied extensively from Mair.

(76) Hamilton, R, (1788), op cit, part IV, chapter I, section 46, p 284.

(77) Stevenson, W, op cit.

(78) Watanabe, I, 'The Development of Working Sheet', Osaka Keida: Ronshu, No 157, January 1984.

(79) 'Vierde Stuck Der Wisconstighe Ghedachtnissen Vande Weeghconst', Leyden, 1605-8.

(80) Gordon could be added to this list. (Gordon, W, 1765, op cit, vol II, p 56).

(81) For example see: Mair, J, 'Book-keeping Methodiz'd', 1749, p 254.

(82) Partnership accounting is considered in chapter 11.

(83) Yamey, B S, (1960), op cit, pp 22-37.

(84) Hamilton, R, 'Introduction to Merchandize', p 287.

CHAPTER 11

ACCOUNTING FOR PARTNERSHIPS

NOTES AND REFERENCES

(1) Towards the end of the 17th century Colinson was well aware of the capital intensive nature of manufactories. He said: "There are two things, which are supposed to be the product of this Countrey, the Manufactories and the fishing trade; which are not to be done with one mans stock, but by many: so men are obliged to joyn in Partnership." (Colinson, R, 'Idea Rationaria', 1683, p 1).
(2) Colinson, R, op cit.
(3) Colinson, R, op cit.
(4) Partnership Act, 1890, section 1 (1).
(5) Stair, James Viscount of, 'Institutions of the Laws of Scotland', vol 1, Bell and Bradfute, 1832, p 140.
(6) Forbes, W, 'The Institutes of the Law of Scotland', vol I, Edinburgh, 1722, p 184.
(7) Hamilton, R, 'Introduction to Merchandize', vol II, 1779, p 326.
(8) 'or Capital' is added in 1773 edition, p 50.
(9) Mair, J, 'Book-keeping Methodiz'd', 1736, p 46.
(10) Mair, J, op cit, p 46.
(11) Macghie, A, 'The Principles of Book-keeping', 1718, p 9: note that there is a similar passage at p 55. The factor's 'provision' is his recompense for acting as a factor.
(12) Macghie, A, op cit, p 55.
(13) Mair, J, 'Book-keeping Moderniz'd', 1773, p 57.
(14) Bell, G J, 'Commentaries on the Municipal and Mercantile Law of Scotland, considered in relation to the subject of Bankruptcy', Edinburgh, 1804, vol II, Introduction to Book VIII, p 495.
(15) 'Fixt' is used in 'A New Treatise of Arithmetick and Book-keeping', 1718 and 'Fix'd' in 'A Treatise of Book-keeping', 1731.
(16) Malcolm, A, (1718), op cit, p 163; (1731), op cit, p 65.
(17) Malcolm, A, (1718), p 163; similar in 1731 book, p 65.
(18) Mair, J, (1736), op cit, p 50.
(19) Mair, J, (1736), op cit, p 46.
(20) Hamilton, R, op cit, vol II, p 80.
(21) The partnership name.
(22) Altered in later editions to "The capital is specified ... ".
(23) Hamilton, R, op cit, vol II, pp 326-328.
(24) Malcolm, A, (1718), op cit, p 163.
(25) Mortimer makes such a distinction between 'copartnership' and 'company'. "A number of merchants

uniting, and applying to the government for an exclusive charter, to prevent others from engaging in the same commerce, and for a power to raise money by an open subscription, in order to form their STOCK, or CAPITAL, are generally denominated COMPANIES. A conjunction of three or four persons, who jointly contribute different or equal sums, towards forming a general STOCK to trade with, is called a COPARTNERSHIP ... ". (Mortimer, 'Every Man His Own Broker', 5th Edition, London, 1762, p 7.).

(26) Lorimer, J, 'A Hand-Book of the Law of Scotland', Edinburgh: T and T Clark, 1859, p 288.

(27) Stevenson V MacNair, 1757, Morison, 14,467, 14,560.

(28) The Arran Fishing Company had about 40 shareholders (partners).

(29) DuBois, A B, 'The English Business Company after the Bubble Act 1720-1800', New York, pp 224/225.

(30) "The judgement, as reported by Lord Kilkerran, found, that the parties are not liable beyond their subscriptions ... ". (Bell, G J, 'Commentaries on the Laws of Scotland and n the Principles of Mercantile Jurisprudence', 5th Edition, Edinburgh, 1826, vol II, 1826, p 628).

(31) Bell, G J, op cit, p 627.

(32) Quoted in Malcolm, C A, 'The History of the British Linen Bank', Edinburgh: Constable, 1950, pp 7/8.

(33) The company was the British Linen Company, which was later to become the British Linen Bank. Malcolm, C A, op cit, pp 516/517.

(34) Bell suggested that the distinction between this and the Arran Fishing Company case was that 'Ayr Bank' was the colloquial name of the bank, whereas its real name did identify some of the partners. (Bell, G J, op cit, p 628). J M'Laren, the editor of the 7th edition, (a reprint of the fifth edition) expresses his disagreement with Bell on this point (7th edition, 1870, vol II, pp 516/517).

(35) "In the well-known case of the Douglas Bank, all the partners were held to be responsible as individuals, notwithstanding that the bank, though trading under the personal firm of Douglas, Heron, and Co, could not possibly be viewed as a partnership proper. The whole subject was thus again thrown loose, and the consequence was the introduction of the English doctrines, first by implication, and latterly by express enactment." (Lorimer, J, op cit, p 289).

(36) Scott, W R, 'The Records of a Scottish Cloth Manufactory at New Mills, Haddingtonshire, 1681-1703', Edinburgh: Scottish Historical Society, 1905, p xc. 'by and attour' = 'in addition to'.

(37) Partnership Act, 1890, section 24 (1).
(38) Forbes, W, op cit, p 184.
(39) See for example: Gordon, W, 'The Universal Accountant', vol I, 1763, pp 204-210; Malcolm, A, (1718), op cit, pp 68-71 and 'A New System of Arithmetick', 1730, pp 549-556. The standard method involved weighting the capital by the time that it had been invested and then apportioning the profit on the basis of the weighted capitals.
(40) Malcolm, A, (1731), op cit, p 65. In his earlier book (1718, p 163) the wording is "my share of Stock ... is to be under the Direction of another Partner".
(41) Malcolm, A, (1718), op cit, pp 163/164; (1731), op cit, p 65. Mair agrees with this (1765, pp 49/50).
(42) It is relevant to note here that the introduction of any additional capital is referred to by Malcolm as a 'Purchase' of Stock.
(43) Hamilton, R, op cit, vol II, p 80.
(44) Malcolm, A, (1718), op cit, pp 164/165; (1731) op cit, p 66.
(45) Mair, J, (1736) op cit, p 50.
(46) Hamilton, R, op cit, vol II, p 81.
(47) Malcolm, A, (1731), op cit, p 65; In his 1718 book the corresponding wording is: "When I am Partner, and entrusted with the Direction and Management." (p 163).
(48) See Murray, D, 'Chapters in the History of Book-keeping, Accountancy and Commercial Arithmetic', Glasgow: Jackson, Wylie and Co, 1930, pp 13-15.
(49) Malcolm, A, (1718), op cit, pp 165-170; (1731), op cit, pp 67-71.
(50) Hamilton, R, op cit, vol II, p 81.
(51) Hamilton, R, op cit, vol II, p 84.
(52) Hamilton, R, op cit, vol II, pp 84/85.
(53) Malcolm, A, (1718), op cit, p 173.
(54) Malcolm, A, (1731), op cit, p 74.
(55) Hamilton, R, op cit, vol II, p 85.
(56) Malcolm, A, (1718), op cit, pp 170-173; (1731), op cit, pp 71-74. Mair, J, (1736), p 63; Hamilton, R, op cit, vol II, p 85.
(57) Malcolm, A, (1718), op cit, p 173; similar in 1731 book, op cit, p 74.
(58) Malcolm, A, (1718), op cit, p 173; (1731), op cit, p 74.
(59) Mair, J, op cit, 1736, p 63.
(60) Malcolm, A, (1718), op cit, p 174; (1731), op cit, p 75.
(61) Malcolm, A, (1718), op cit, p 174; (1731), op cit, p 75.
(62) The official title of the South Sea Company was 'The Governor and Company of Merchants of Great Britain

trading to the South Sea and other parts of America and for encouraging the Fishery'.

(63) Campbell, R H, 'The Law and the Joint-Stock Company in Scotland', printed in 'Studies in Scottish Business History', edited by Payne, P L, London: Frank Cass and Co Ltd, 1967. Bell's view (op cit) was that the Arran Fishing Company decision meant that either the Bubble Act had been overlooked or else that it was considered that it did not apply to Scotland.

(64) Malcolm, A, (1718), op cit, p 175.

(65) Malcolm, A, (1731), op cit, p 76.

(66) Campbell, R H, op cit.

(67) The Bubble Act also seems to have been ineffectual in England.

(68) Malcolm, A, (1718), op cit, p 189.

CHAPTER 12

ACCOUNTING FOR THE TOBACCO TRADE

NOTES AND REFRENCES

(1) Mair, J, 'Accounting Methodiz'd', Edinburgh 3rd Edition, 1749, pp 233-270. From the Edinburgh 5th Edition (1757) this became chapter VII.
(2) Hamilton, H, 'An Economic History of Scotland in the Eighteenth Century', Clarendon Press, Oxford, 1963, p 259.
(3) Price, J M, 'The Rise of Glasgow in the Chesapeake Tobacco Trade 1707-1775', William and Mary Quarterly, 3rd Series, vol XL, April 1954, reprinted in Payne, B L (editor), 'Studies in Scottish Business History', London: Cass and Co, 1967, pp 299-318.
(4) Mair, J, (1749), op cit, p 235.
(5) See ledger account on pp 60/61.
(6) Devine, T M, 'The Tobacco Lords, A Study of the Tobacco Merchants of Glasgow and their Trading Activities c 1740-90', Edinburgh: John Donald, 1975.
(7) It was also used by certain English 'outports'.
(8) Smith, A, 'Wealth of Nations'.
(9) Scruton, J, 'The Practical Counting House', 1777, pp 116, 125, 126, 251, 268, 269. Note: The pages that should bear the numbers 268 and 269 are erroneously printed as 168 and 169. Another 'character' from Scruton's example is William Christie of Stirling, this is one of the in-laws of Scruton's partner, William Gordon. William Christie and Company were woollen cloth manufacturers.
(10) Devine, T M, op cit, p 9.
(11) Scruton, J, op cit, p 321.
(12) Gibson, J, 'The History of Glasgow, from the Earliest Accounts to the Present Time', Glasgow, 1777, p 206 and p 212.
(13) Mair, J, (1749), op cit, p 234.
(14) Pares, R, 'Merchants and Planters', Economic History Society, Cambridge University Press, 1960, p 49.
(15) Mair, J, (1749), op cit, p 234.
(16) Mair, J, (1749), op cit, p 237.
(17) Smith, A, 'Wealth of Nations'.
(18) Devine, T M (editor), 'A Scottish Firm in Virginia, W Cunninghame and Co, 1767-1777', Edinburgh: Scottish History Society, 1984, p 26.
(19) See Baxter, W T, 'The House of Hancock, Business in Boston 1724-1775', Harvard University Press, Massachusetts, 1945.
(20) Mair, J, (1749), op cit, p 255.
(21) Maurer, M, 'Alexander Malcolm in America, Music and Letters', vol 33, No 3, July 1952, p 228.

(22) Mair, J, (1749), op cit, p 255.
(23) Mair, J, (1749), op cit, p 253.
(24) Mair, J, (1749), op cit, pp 253/4.
(25) Mair, J, (1749), op cit, p 254. Although the books were commonly 'balanced' annually, Mair states that it was not usual to 'draw out a Balance-accompt' more frequently than once in three or four years.
(26) This phrase is used by Scruton in the example in his 'The Practical Counting House' (1777, p 174). Mair says that a fair copy of all the year's transactions, transcribed from the store's books, is sent to the employer but some storekeepers send only an accompt-current.

CHAPTER 13

ACCOUNTING FOR THE SUGAR TRADE

NOTES AND REFERENCES

(1) The new material on the sugar trade is contained in chapter VI of the appendix and it continues as such in later editions and in 'Book-keeping Moderniz'd' (1st edition 1773). The only changes noted are in the dates used in the illustrative examples and the spelling of 'accompt' in 'Methodiz'd' (pp 246/247) which becomes 'account' in 'Moderniz'd' (pp 409/410).

(2) Gordon, W, 'The General Counting-House and Man of Business', 1766, pp 379-421.

(3) The book, which was published in London by R Griffiths in 1754, went to two more editions, 1761 and 1781. William Weston describes himself on its title page as "some years a practitioner in Real Business, and now Master of the French School, in Queen Street, near the Seven-Dials". In 1765 he wrote another book on 'Specimens of abbreviated numbers, or an Introduction to an entire new species of Arithmetic'. See: Hodgson, R A, 'An Early Accounting Textbook', Accountancy, June 1956, pp 222/3.

(4) Aykroyd, W R, 'Sweet Malefactor, Sugar, Slavery and Human Society', London: Heinemann, 1967, p 31.

(5) Beer, G, 'The Origins of the British Colonial System, 1587-1660', Clouchester, Mass: Peter Smith, 1959, p 412.

(6) Mair, J, 'Book-keeping Methodiz'd', 1765, p 235.

(7) Woodruff, W, 'Impact of Western Man', New York: St Martin's Press, 1967, p 265.

(8) Pares, R, 'Merchants and Planters', Economic History Society, Cambridge University Press, 1960, p 23.

(9) The cane from the fields was crushed and the juice was crystallized, by evaporation, in the Boiling House. The resulting sugar was then scooped from the coolers into 56 pound earthenware 'potts'. The residue of liquid molasses were drained off and "the potts ... stood over stone troughs in the curing house, where after 48 hours they were tapped and left draining and maturing for several weeks before being weighed, carted, and shipped." (Craton, M and J Walvin, 'A Jamaican Plantation, The History of Worthy Park 1670-1970', London: W H Allen, 1970, p 110).

(10) Mair, J, 'Book-keeping Methodiz'd', 1757, pp 330/331.

(11) Weston, W, op cit, p 25 of section dealing with 'Book-keeping in a Wharf or Plantation'.

(12) Weston, W, op cit, p 24 of section dealing with 'Book-keeping in a Wharf or Plantation'.

(13) Weston, W, op cit, p 25 of section dealing with 'Book-

keeping in a Wharf or Plantation'. Mair took over the term 'Double Entry' into his text.
(14) Pares, R, op cit, p 38.
(15) Craton, M and J Walvin, op cit, pp 145-147. Burns, reluctantly planning to emmigrate to Jamaica as a book-keeper, foresaw the possibility of becoming " ... a victim to that inhospitable clime gone to the world of Spirits".(letter to Dr John Moore, August 1787)
(16) Mair, J, (1757), op cit, p 236.
(17) Gordon, W, op cit, p 379.
(18) Weston, W, op cit, part II, p 5.
(19) Weston, W, op cit, part II, pp 5-7.
(20) Mair, J, (1757), op cit, pp 255-257.
(21) Mair, J, (1757), op cit, p 236. The word 'factory' is being used to describe the factors' trading establishment. This seems to be an extension of the legal definition of 'factory' as: "authority granted to a person to act on behalf of another". (Robinson, M (editor), 'The Concise Scots Dictionary', Aberdeen University Press, 1985). The word 'manufactory' would be used for a factory in the modern sense.
(22) Pares, R, 'A West-India Fortune', London: Longmans, Green and Co, 1950, chapter 3.
(23) Pares, R, (1950), op cit, p 32.
(24) Pares, R, (1950), op cit, pp 35/36.
(25) Weston, W, op cit, part II, p 12.
(26) Mair, J, (1757), op cit, p 237.
(27) Quoted in Pares, R, (1950), op cit, p 34.
(28) Mair, J, (1757), op cit, p 244.
(29) Gordon, W, op cit, p 378.
(30) Mair, J, (1757), op cit, p 245.
(31) Mair, J, (1757), op cit, p 245.
(32) Gordon, W, op cit, p 380.
(33) Mair, J, (1757), op cit, p 246.
(34) Mair, J, (1757), op cit, p 248.
(35) Mair, J, (1757), op cit, p 255.
(36) Mair, J, (1757), op cit, p 231; 'Book-keeping Modern-iz'd', 1773, p 394.
(37) Mair, J, (1757), op cit, p 240.
(38) Mair, J, (1757), op cit, p 268.
(39) Mair, J, (1757), op cit, p 240.
(40) Pares, R, (1960), op cit, p 38.
(41) Scruton, J, op cit, p 322. Hamilton gives another list: "They receive from Britain manufactures and utensils of every kind, lime, bricks, beer, French wines, and East India commodities, from Ireland, linen, beef, pork, and other provisions ... ". ('Introduction to Merchandize', 1779, volume II, p 296)
(42) Mair, J, (1757), op cit, p 254.
(43) Mair, J, (1757), op cit, p 255.

CHAPTER 14

ESTATE ACCOUNTS

NOTES AND REFERENCES

(1) This phrase is used by Malcolm ('A New Treatise of Arithmetick and Book-keeping', 1718) at p 34 and elsewhere. North, whose book-keeping text was written around estate accounting, says "It is to be considered That Persons of Quality and Fortune have as many Branches in their accomptable Business, as most traders have; for they are concerned with Rents, Pensions, Interest Money, House-keeping, Bailiffs, Managery of Land, Building, Repairs, Pleasures, Extravagances, &c." (North, R, 'The Gentleman Accomptant', London, 1714, p 87).

(2) Mair, J. says that the accounting records would be the same whether they are kept by a 'chamberlain' or the estate owner himself. (Book-keeping Moderniz'd', 1773, p 577).

(3) Pollard, S, 'The Genesis of Modern Management', Harvard University Press, 1965, chapter 6.

(4) Mair states "The method of keeping accounts of a land-estate, and those in mercantile affairs, being founded on the same principles, ... every occurence in the one .(is). stated and conducted in the same manner as a similar case in the other" (op cit, p 576).

(5) Malcolm even retains the spelling of 'accompt' in the appendix to the 1731 text whereas elsewhere he changes to 'account'.

(6) The second book is 'The General Counting-House and Man of Business', 1766. The material referred to is in pp 462-487.

(7) Brodie similarly states his belief that estate owners will find it a pleasing diversion to keep their books in the manner that he suggests; he includes a short section on estate accounts in his 'New and Easy Method of Book-Keeping' (1722).

(8) 1st edition, 1773, pp 576-606.

(9) Mair, J, op cit, p 577.

(10) 'Introduction to Merchandize', 1777/79, vol II, chapter VI of part V.

(11) North's book is 'The Gentleman Accomptant', (London, 1714).

(12). Scottish Record Office, Edinburgh, GD 44/51/405/58.

(13) Whitsun is one of the Scottish quarter days. Although the date of Whitsun is not fixed, a Scottish act of 1693 (Act anent the Term of Whitsunday) had fixed it at 15 May for some tenancy purposes. (Erskine, J, 'The Principles of the Law of Scotland', Edinburgh: Bell and Bradfute, A New Edition 1809, p 192).

Notes and References - Chapter 14

(14) Note the distinction; 1st January was recognised as New Year's Day in Scotland from 1600 but in England it was 25 March (Lady Day) until changed in 1751, by the Calendar (New Style) Act, 1750. The English writer Roger North, writing in 1714, writes the year of transactions occurring between 1 January 1708 and 24 March 1708 as 1708/9 (see illustrative journal in 'The Gentleman Accomptant', pp 164 and 170).

(15) Martinmas (one of the Scottish quarter days) is 11 November. Malcolm's later book (1731) adds here "for Estates in Scotland, and Christmas for England". Candlemass (two lines on) is another quarter day, it is 2 February.

(16) 'due' in 'A Treatise of Book-Keeping, 1731.

(17) Malcolm, A, (1718), op cit, appendix, p 9.

(18) Virtually the same material is also in the appendix to his second book-keeping book (1731).

(19) 'Stewards' added in the version appearing in 1731 book.

(20) Malcolm, A, (1718), op cit, appendix, p 35. The text is virtually unchanged in Malcolm's later book (1731), appendix, p 15.

(21) Malcolm, A, (1718), op cit, appendix, p 35; (1731), op cit, appendix, p 16.

(22) Malcolm, A, (1718), op cit, appendix, p 35; (1731), op cit, appendix, p 16.

(23) " ... it is to be considered, that a Gentleman, who receives and spends, shall have most of his Business run through his Cash". (North, R, op cit, p 89).

(24) North disapproves of those who by-pass the Waste-Book and write cash transactions directly into the Cash Book (North, R, op cit, pp 90/91).

(25).Scottish Record Office, Edinburgh, GD 44/51/405/58.

(26) Malcolm, A, (1718), op cit, appendix, p 35; (1731), op cit, appendix, pp 16/17.

(27) Malcolm, A, (1718), op cit, appendix, p 36; (1731), op cit, appendix, p 17.

(28) Malcolm, A, (1718), op cit, appendix, p 38; (1731), op cit, appendix, p 20.

(29) North, R, op cit, pp 91/93.

(30) Malcolm A, (1731), op cit, appendix, p 17 but substantially the same in 1718 book, appendix, p 36.

(31) North, R, op cit, pp 98/99.

(32) Malcolm, A, (1731), op cit, appendix, p 17 but substantially the same in 1718 book p 36. Note that in this quotation Malcolm appears to be using 'Stock' to refer to the specific holdings of an asset rather than as 'Capital'.

(33) This appears in his second book on book-keeping, 'The General Counting-House and Man of Business', 1766, pp 461-487.

(34) Malcolm, A, (1718), op cit, appendix, p 45; (1731), op cit, appendix, p 27.
(35) Malcolm, A, (1718), op cit, appendix, p 39.
(36) Malcolm, A, (1718), op cit, appendix, p 40.
(37) Malcolm, A, (1731), op cit, appendix, p 21.
(38) Mair, J, 'Book-keeping Moderniz'd', 1773, p 576.
(39) Malcolm, A, (1718), op cit, appendix, p 37; (1731), op cit, appendix, p 18.
(40) " ... the interest of money was reduced to 5 per cent. from the 29th of September 1714, and this statute continues in force to this day". (Gordon, W, 'The Universal Accountant', vol I, 1763, pp 352/353). In 1777 Scruton uses 4% (25 years purchase) for valuing two estates ('The Practical Counting House', p 16 and p 24) and 6.66% (15 years purchase) for valuing a house (ibid, p 24).
(41) The records would be similar if the landowner were to be managing his own estate and collecting his own rents.
(42) Malcolm, A, (1718), op cit, appendix, pp 36/37; 1731, appendix, pp 17/18.
(43) William Lorimer discusses this (Scottish Record Office, GD 248/38/1, pp 5-7 and 16/17). There are examples of victual rent well into the 19th century. On the Gordon Castle Huntly Estate from Crop 1840 the victual was sold to the tenants. (Scottish Record Office, CR 8/65, Records from the Fochabers Estate Office).
(44) Malcolm, A, (1718), op cit, appendix, p 36; (1731), op cit, appendix, pp 17/18.
(45) Mair, J, (1773), op cit, p. 578; Gordon, W, (1766), op cit, p 462.
(46) Stevenson, W, 'Book-keeping by Double Entry', 1762, Illustrative example dated 1 November 1760 in Estate Waste-book.
(47) Malcolm, A, (1718), op cit, appendix, p 37; (1731), op cit, appendix, p 18.
(48) Stevenson, W, op cit, Illustrative Waste Book entry, 15 January 1761.
(49) Malcolm, A, (1718), op cit, appendix, p 37; (1731), op cit, appendix, p 18.
(50) Malcolm, A, (1718), op cit, appendix, p 37; (1731), op cit, appendix, p 18.
(51) 'teinds' = 'tithes'.
(52) Malcolm, A, (1718), op cit, appendix, p 37; (1731), op cit, appendix, p 18.
(53) Shortly after the American war, David Young (who published 'The Farmer's Account-book' in 1790) stated as his opinion that, with all the improvement that had taken place, infield was still not one tenth of outfield and that not one twentieth part of the infield

was in sown grasses.

(54) Baxter, W T, 'The Account Charge and Discharge', The Accounting Historians Journal, Spring 1980, p 69.

(55) Chatfield, M, 'A History of Accounting Thought', Revised Edition, R E Krieger, New York, 1977, p 25.

(56) Jones, R H, 'Accounting in English Local Government from the Middle Ages to c 1835', pp 197-209, Accounting and Business research, Number 59, Summer 1985. See also: Brown, R, 'History of Accounting and Accountants', Edinburgh: T C and E C Jack, 1905, pp 41-73 and Littleton, A C, 'Accounting Evolution to 1900', New York: The American Institute Publishing Co, p 123 (reprinted by University of Alabama Press, 1981).

(57) North, R, op cit, p 248.

(58) Lisle, G, 'Charge and Discharge Accounts', article in 'Encyclopaedia of Accounting', edited by G Lisle, vol II, William Green and Sons, Edinburgh, 1903, p 75.

(59) Hamilton, R, op cit, vol I, pp 350.

(60) Brodie, A, op cit.

(61) Brodie, A, op cit.

(62) 'cautioner' is a Scots law term meaning 'one who becomes security for another'.

(63) Hamilton, R, op cit, vol I, pp 350/351.

(64) North, R, op cit, p 248. North goes on to say that although the 'Chequer Way' is simple to describe " ... when the rolls are produced, and the Marginal Ligatures, Distinctions, and Continuando's (like to old Genealogies) are observed, one would undertake as soon to resolve an Accompt out of a set of regular Books, as from them" (ibid, pp 248/249).

(65) 'Charge and Discharge' is particularly entrenched in Scottish trust accounting.

(66) Hamilton, R, op cit, vol I, p 350.

(67) Malcolm, A, (1718), op cit, appendix, p 36.

(68) Hamilton, R, 'Introduction to Merchandize', 2nd edition, 1788, part V, chapter VI, 31, pp 490/491.

(69) For comparison purposes see Mason, P, 'Illustrations of the Early Treatment of Depreciation', The Accounting Review, September 1933, pp 209-218. Arthur Young, the agricultural writer, also appreciated the need to charge depreciation, he says: "At the end of every year an account must be taken of all the stock, the implements of all kinds valued, and carried to the new year's account accordingly: and as the article of wear and tear includes everything relative to implements, the annual valuation will throw into that account the decrease of value ... ".(Young, A, 'Rural Oeconomy', London: T Becket, 1770, p 214).

(70) Lockhart, J G, 'Peter's Letters to His Kinsfolk', Edinburgh, 1819, vol III, p 212.

Notes and References - Chapter 14

(71) Brown, R, 'History of Accounting and Accountants', Edinburgh: T C and E C Jack, 1905, pp 71/72.
(72) Grant, I D, 'Landlords and Land Management in North East Scotland 1750-1850', Doctoral Dissertation, University of Edinburgh, 1978, vol 1, p 13.
(73) Gordon, G, 'The Last Dukes of Gordon and their Consorts 1743-1864 : A Revealing Study', Taylor and Henderson, Aberdeen, N D.
(74) Pollard, S, op cit, chapter 6, p 210.
(75) Malcolm, A, (1718), op cit, appendix p 42. This is not repeated in his 1731 book.

CHAPTER 15

FARM ACCOUNTS

NOTES AND REFERENCES

(1) Run-rig was a system in which land leased by joint tenants was allocated periodically in strips to the individual lessees, often the allocation was changed annually by lot to achieve some sort of fairness among the tenants.
(2) Act anent inclosing of Ground, 1669.
(3) Act concerning the Dividing of Commonties, 1695.
(4) Act anent lands lying Run rig, 1695.
(5) Young, A, 'Introduction to The Farmer's Kalendar', Robinson and Roberts, 1771. Young also gives accounting advice in 'Rural Oeconomy', London: T Becket, 1770, pp 201-216.
(6) Although there were many similarities in their careers, David Young does not appear to have been a relative of Arthur Young. Both published books with the title 'The Farmer's Calendar'.
(7) Hamilton, R, 'Introduction to Merchandize', volume II, part V, chapter VII, 1779.
(8) Hamilton, R, 'Introduction to Merchandize', 1788, pp 491/492. Paragraph 31 (referred to in the last sentence) is concerned with making a depreciation charge, this has been considered in chapter 14. Arthur Young was also aware of the need to charge depreciation, he says: "The sinking of a horse's value is as much a part of the expence of tillage, as the reparation of a plough." (Young, A, 1770, op cit, p 214).
(9) Specialised account books for farmers began to appear in the 19th century but the only other example of a Scottish 18th century book of this type seems to be 'The Transactions of the British Farmer Accountant Adapted to the four Seasons of the year wherein The Gentlemen Farmers have a Plan of Books, entirely new, and suitable to their occupation' by John Rose, Accomptant, published by Peter Williamson, Edinburgh. This book was advertised in several volumes of Williamson's 'Directory of the city of Edinburgh, Canongate, Leith and Suburbs' which was published annually by Peter Williamson from 1774 to 1781. No copy of this has been located.
(10) Tables 34 and 35.
(11) Tables 32 and 33.
(12) Hamilton, R, (1788), op cit, p 285.
(13) Hamilton, R, (1788), op cit, p 492.
(14) This definition is clarified by Alexander Taylor who says: "One man and two horses engaged together for five

hours make one yoking." (Taylor, A, 'The Farmer's Guide and Agriculturist's Companion; Being a New, Clear, and Comprehensive System of Farm Book-keeping', Edinburgh, 1827, p 25).

(15) Hamilton, R, (1788), op cit, p 500.

(16) The original table is in £. s. d. with several other errors apart from the printing error of £100 specifically noted.

(17) Sir John Sinclair (1754-1835) enouraged the formation of this Board which operated from 1793 to 1822. It operated under a Royal Charter with an annual grant made by Parliament.

(18) Arthur Young (1741-1820) contributed to the success of the programme of Agricultural Surveys undertaken by the Board of Agriculture. His voluminous writings show a down-to-earth 'cost benefit' approach to agricultural experiments.

(19) Young, A, (1770), op cit, p 202.

CHAPTER 16

ROBERT HAMILTON AND THE ORIGINS OF COST ACCOUNTING

NOTES AND REFERENCES

(1) In Scotland the Profit and Loss Account of the British Linen Company for the 15 months to January 1748 (Saltoun Collection, National Library of Scotland, MS 17594, item 52) shows an analysis of the gains from each of the various branches of business. This suggests the use of some form of process costing. The details from this are reproduced in chapter 17, pp 353/4. See also: Kendrick, N, 'Josiah Wedgewood and Cost Accounting in the Industrial Revolution', Economic History Review, vol 23, 1970, pp 45-67; Pollard, S, 'The Genesis of Modern Management', Harvard University Press, 1965, chapter 6; Roll, E, 'An Early Experiment in Industrial Organisation; Stone, W E, 'An Early English Cotton Mill Cost Accounting System : Charlton Mills, 1810 - 1889', Accounting and Business Research, No 10, Spring 1973, pp 71-78.

(2) Edwards, R S, 'Some Notes on the Early Literature and Development of Cost Accounting in Great Britain', The Accountant, 7, 14, 21, 28 August; 4, 11 September 1937; pp 193-195, 225-231, 253-255, 283-287, 313-216, 343/4.

(3) Pollard, S, op cit, p 215.

(4) Dodson, J, 'The Accountant, or, the Method of Book-keeping', London: printed for J Nourse, 1750, pp Y8-Aa8 (17 pp).

(5) Thompson, W, 'The Accomptant's Oracle', York: N Nickson for the author, vol II, 1777, pp 243-253. The page numbers are, in fact, printed as 243-153 as the printer has misnumbered pp 249-253.

(6) In the first five editions.

(7) Hamilton, R, 'Introduction to Merchandize', vol II, 1779, section 152.

(8) Hamilton, R, op cit, pp 269/70.

(9) "The specimen I shall give is in the thread-hosiery branch; and altho' I am not acquainted with all the various branches of it, nor with the particular prices paid to workmen for each, yet mistakes or ignorance in those things can in no measure affect the general plan" (Thompson, W, op cit, p 243).

(10) For example in section 159, p 269.

(11) In 1778 Hamilton's article on 'Book-keeping' appeared in the second edition of the 'Encylopaedia Britannica', this was largely from the accounting material in vol II of 'An Introduction to Merchandize' which was not published until the following year.

(12). Scott, J, 'Parish of Perth', chapter XIX of Sinclair, J, (editor), 'The Statistical Account of Scotland',

Edinburgh: printed by W. Creech, 1796, p 513.

(13) John Mair's patron, Charles, Lord Cathcart, was one of the 21 Commissioners of this board from 1755.

(14) Walton, P, 'The Story of Textiles', 1936.

(15) Smout, T C, 'A History of the Scottish People 1560-1830', London: Collins, 2nd ed, 1970, p 244. See also: Lord Kames, 'Progress of Flax-Husbandry in Scotland, The Scots Magazine, vol XXVIII, Jan 1766, pp 15-22.

(16) Edinburgh: John Donald, 1979.

(17) Butt, J, 'The Industrial Archaeology of Scotland', Newton Abbot: David and Charles, 1967, p 142.

(18) In addition to being a major element of Perth's linen industry, the Sandeman family were also responsible for Sandeman Port and the Sandemanians, a Protestant sect.

(19) Saltoun MSS 17564, items 254 and 255, National Library of Scotland.

(20) Freudenberger, H and F Redlich, 'The Industrial Development of Europe: Reality, Symbols, Images', Kyklos, XVII, 1964; Chapman, D, 'The Textile Factory Before Arkwright: A Typology of Factory Development', Business History Review, Winter 1974, pp 451-477.

(21) Chapman, D, op cit.

(22). Pollard, S, op cit, pp 34/5. Smout, however, notes that "Almost the whole of Smith's discussion of industrial work and payment in Book I (of the 'Wealth of Nations') relates to the domestic system and could have been drawn from his observations of the linen trade." (Smout, T C, 'Where had the Scottish economy got to by the third quarter of the eighteenth century?', printed in Hont, I and M Ignatieff (editors), 'Wealth and Virtue', Cambridge University Press, 1983, p 63.

(23) Johnson, H T, 'The Role of Accounting History in the Education of Prospective Accountants', Arthur Young Lecture No 6, University of Glasgow, 1984.

(24) Hamilton, R, op cit, section 152, p 264.

(25) Sutcliffe, P and C Burrows, 'Accounting for Labour Costs and Performance: The Objectives of North, Hamilton, Battersby and Garcke and Fells', paper presented at the University of Tasmania at Meetings of the AAANZ and Accounting History Committee, 1984.

(26) Johnson, H T, op cit.

(27) Hamilton, R, op cit, section 157, p 268.

(28) Chapman, D, op cit.

(29) Hamilton, R, op cit, section 154, p 265.

(30) Wells, M C, 'Accounting for Common Costs', University of Illinois, 1978.

(31) Monteage, S, 'Debtor and Creditor Made Easie', London: Ben Billingsley, 1675.

(32) Young, A, 'Rural Oeconomy or Essays on the Practical

Parts of Husbandry', London: T Becket, 1770, pp:210-214; The Farmer's Kalendar', London: Robinson and Roberts, 1771, Introduction.
(33) Young, A, 1770, op cit, p 206
(34) Hamilton, R, op cit, pp 275/6.
(35) Wells, M C, op cit, p 48.
(36) Wells, M C, op cit, p 46.
(37) Hamilton, R, op cit, section 157, p 268.
(38) Hamilton, R, op cit, section 158, p 268.
(39) Saltoun Collection, National Library of Scotland, MS 17594, item 52.
(40) This company later became The British Linen Bank.
(41) Malcolm, C A, 'The History of the British Linen Bank', Edinburgh: T and A Constable Ltd, 1950, pp 237-240.
(42) Rimmer, W G, 'Marshalls of Leeds Flax-Spinners 1788-1886', Cambridge: University Press, 1960, pp 121/2.
(43) Littleton, A C, 'Accounting Evolution to 1900', New York: American Institute Publishing Co, 1933, pp 338/339 (reprinted by University of Alabama Press, 1981).
(44) Norton, G P, 'Textile Manufacturers' Book-keeping', Huddersfield: A Jubb; London: Hamilton, Adams and Co, 1889, p 226. Norton, an English Chartered Accountant, was a founder of the accountancy firm of Armitage and Norton. Garner discusses Norton's method in chapter VII ('Evolution of the Accounting for Interdepartmental Transfers of Product') of his 'Evolution of Cost Accounting to 1925' (University of Alabama Press, 1925)
(45) Littleton, A C, op cit, p 340.
(46) Pollard, S, op cit, p 223.
(47).Young, A, 'The Farmer's Guide in Hiring and Stocking Farms', London: W Strahan and W Nicoll, Salisbury: B Collins; Edinburgh: J Balfour, 1770, pp 77/8; 1771, op cit, Introduction.
(48) Yamey, B S, 'Common Costs and Business Decisions: An Historical Note', The Accounting Historian, Winter 1975.
(49) Hamilton, R, op cit, part IV, chap I, section 107.
(50) Hamilton, R, op cit, part V, chap V, section 154.
(51) Hamilton, R, op cit, part V, chap V, section 158.
(52) Hamilton, R, op cit, part IV, chap I, section 107; Malcolm, A, 'A Treatise of Book-keeping', 1731, p 47; Scruton, J, 'The Practical Counting House', 1777, illustrative journal entry, p 108.
(53) Wells, M C, op cit.
(54) Chatfield, M, 'A History of Accounting Thought', New York: Krieger, 1977, p 102.
(55) Crossman, P, 'The Genesis of Cost Control', The Accounting Review, October 1953, pp 522-527.
(56) Garner, S P, op cit, pp 39-41.
(57) Edwards, R S, 'A Survey of French Contributions to the

Study of Cost Accounting during the 19th century', The Accounting Research Association, published as a supplement to The Accountant, 26 June 1937.

(58) In contrast to Hamilton, Norton considers that the cost accounts should be memorandum records outside the double entry system. He says: "In the first place, accounts of Manufacturing Departments should be entirely supplemental to the Trading Account, and they should neither interfere with, nor form part of the ordinary book-keeping" ('Textile Manufacturers' Book-keeping', A Jubb, Huddersfield and Hamilton, Adams and Co, London, 1889, p 219).

APPENDIX

(1) This refers to a section on 'Goods on Consignment'.

(2) This section seems to confirm that Hamilton is describing a system which is in use.

CHAPTER 17

ROBERT HAMILTON AND RESIDUAL INCOME

NOTES AND REFERENCES

(1) Pollard, S, 'The Genesis of Modern Management', Arnold, 1965, p 212.

(2) Accounts were usually classified into personal, real, and fictitious.

(3) Or if the books became too full to take any further records.

(4) See British Linen Company profit and loss account on p 353.

(5) Scott, W R (Editor), 'The Records of a Scottish Cloth Manufactory at New Mills, Haddingtonshire, 1681-1713', Edinburgh: Scottish Historical Society, 1905, pp lxxxiv-lxxxix).

(6) Young, A, 'Rural Oeconomy or Essays on the Practical Parts of Husbandry', London: T Becket, 1770, vol I, pp 324, 340; vol II, pp 18, 25 etc. Young considers that " ... no less profit than 20 per cent should be thought, in agriculture, great, or even sufficient. There are no insurances in farming".(op cit, vol I, p 342).

(7) Edwards, B, 'The History, Civil and Commercial, of the British Colonies in the West Indies', London: J Stockdale, 1793, pp 255, 260.

(8) Ashton, T S and J Sykes, 'The Coal Industry of the Eighteenth Century', Manchester University Press, 1929, pp 245/246.

(9) Edwards, B, op cit.

(10) Edwards, B, op cit, p 260.

(11) Craton, M and J Walvin, 'A Jamaican Plantation, The History of Worthy Park, 1670-1970', London: W H Allen, 1970, p 57.

(12) Bursal provides details which suggest that there may have been earlier advocates of residual income in Germany (Bursal, N, 'The Use of Interest as an Element of Cost in Germany in the 16th and 17th Centuries', The Accounting Historians Journal, Spring 1986, pp 63-70).

(13) See references in Mepham, M J, 'The Residual Income Debate', Journal of Business Finance and Accounting, Summer, 1980, pp 183-199.

(14) Anthony, R N, J Dearden and R F Vancil, 'Management Control Systems: Cases and Readings', Irwin, 1965, Case 3-2; Solomons, D, 'Evaluating Divisional Performance by Return on Investment and Residual Income' in 'Divisional Performance: Measurement and Control' New York: Financial Executives Research Foundation, 1965.

(15) Kaplan, R S, 'The Evolution of Management Accounting', The Accounting Review, July 1984, pp 390-418).

(16) Pollard, S, 'Capital Accounting in the Industrial Revolution', Yorkshire Bulletin of Economic and Social Research, November 1963, pp 75-91.
(17) Moss, M, 'Forgotten Ledgers, Law and the Business Historian', paper presented at the Sixth Annual Congress of the European Accounting Association', University of Glasgow, 1983.
(18) Smith, A, 'The Wealth of Nations', vol II, 4th edition, 1786, book II, chapter IV, p 43.
(19) Smith, A, op cit.
(20) Gordon, W, 'The Universal Accountant', vol I, 1763, pp 352/3.
(21) Malcolm, A, 'A Treatise of Book-keeping', 1731, p 51.
(22) Knight, F H, Article on 'Interest' in Seligman, E R A (editor) 'Encyclopaedia of the Social Sciences', London: Macmillan and Co, 1932, vol 8, pp 131-144.
(23) Hamilton, R, "Introduction to Merchandize', 1779, vol II, part V, chap III, section 8.
(24) Letter dated 3 March 1766, Monymusk Papers, Monymusk House, Uniform Box G, bundle 29 (Archieston), quoted by Durie, A J, 'The Markets for Scottish Linen 1730-1775', The Scottish Historical Review, April 1973.
(25) Fussell, G E, (editor), 'Robert Loder's Farm Accounts 1610-1620', London: Royal Historical Society, Camden 3rd Series, 1936; Yamey, B S, 'Some Topics in the History of Financial Accounting in England 1500-1900', printed in Baxter, W T and S Davidson, 'Studies in Accounting Theory', London: Sweet and Maxwell, 1962, pp 14-43. Loder's appreciation of the nature of interest seems more advanced than the views of economists at the time. At the end of the 17th century the English economist Nicolas Barbon (c 1640-1698) recogised that: " Interest, is the rent of Stock, and is the same as the Rent of Land ... for the Money borrowed is laid out to buy Goods ... no Man takes up Money at Interest to lay it by him, and lose the Interest of it" ('Discourse of Trade', 1690). There may be a hint of interest viewed as an opportunity cost in this quotation but there is room for doubt.
(26) Parker, R H, 'Management Accounting: an Historical Perspective', London, Macmillan and Co 1969.
(27) "I have calculated a great number of estimates to show the most beneficial manner of disposing any sum from £50 to £20,000 in agriculture ... " (Young, A, 'The Farmer's Guide in Hiring and Stocking Farms', London: W Strahan, 1770, p vi). This treatise is filled with Youngs's estimated accounts. See also his article 'On the Profit of a Farm' in his 'Annals of Agriculture', Bury St Edmunds: printed for the Editor, 1788, pp 235-244.

(28) Young, A, 'The Farmer's Guide in Hiring and Stocking Farms', London: W Strahan, 1770, vol I, p 129.
(29) Hamilton, R, op cit, part V, chap III, section 8, emphasis added.
(30) 'The Wealth of Nations', volume II, book IV, chapter V, p 263 in 1786 edition. A similar point is made in Smith's comment on bounties paid to the fishing industry, p 283.
(31) 'The Wealth of Nations', book I, chapter VI (emphasis added).
(32) Note that Hamilton also regards profit as being, in part, a reward for risk bearing, ie "the compensation for his hazard".
(33) Hamilton, R, op cit, part V, chap III, section 8.
(34) Hamilton, R, op cit, part V, chap III, section 13.
(35) Hamilton, R, op cit, part V, chap III, section 13.
(36) Anthony, R N, 'Accounting for the Cost of Interest', D C Heath, 1975, p 9. See also the following publications by Anthony: 'Accounting for the Cost of Equity', Harvard Business Review', November/December 1973, pp 88-102; 'Recognising the Cost of Interest on Equity', Harvard Business Review, January/February 1982, pp 91-96; 'Equity Interest, its time has come', Journal of Accountancy, December 1982, pp 76-93; 'Tell It Like It Was: A Conceptual Framework for Financial Accounting', Irwin, 1983.
(37) Pollard, S, 1963, op cit, p 80.
(38) Molleson, J A, 'Books and Book-Keeping', Lecture given to the Chartered Accountants Students' Society of Edinburgh, 23 March 1887.
(39) Figures to the right of the pence in the credit column are sixteenths of a penny.
(40) The final item on the credit side is intriguing.
(41) Saltoun MS 17594, item 52 (National Library of Scotland).
(42) Stone, W E, 'An Early English Cotton Mill Cost Accounting System: Charlton Mills, 1810-1889', Accounting and Business Research, Winter 1973, pp 71-78.
(43) Norton, G P, 'Textile Manufacturers' Book-keeping', 3rd Edition, 1894, reprinted by Arno Press, 1976, p 79.
(44) Norton, G P, op cit.
(45) Young, A, 1788, op cit, pp 235-244.
(46) Modern discounted cash flow approaches to investment appraisal commonly suggest that, when an investment proposal is being assessed, its anticipated cash flows should be discounted (at the cost of capital rate) and totalled to establish their present value. If the net present value of the cash flows is positive, the project is considered acceptable. An alternative to calculating the project's net present value is the

calculation of its annual value. The annual value is ex ante residual income. See Mepham, M J, op cit, on this point. Malcolm, Mair, Gordon and Hamilton include 'compound interest' in their mathematical writings and they are aware of the use of discounting procedures to calculate the present value of a stream of future cash flows. The topic is not, however, considered to be part of accounting although it does feature, obliquely, in a few cases where it is suggested that estates can be valued at so many years purchase of their annual rents.

(47) "The expence of making a navigable canal of 27 miles in length is estimated at £1250 per mile for digging; `150 per perpendicular foot for lockage, the ascent from the entrance, at either extremity, to the canal of partition being 147 feet; purchase of 418 acres of land, at £20 per acre, and for extra expences, £9790. 20,000 tons of merchandize annually pass the canal, and pay lockage duty at the rate of 2d. per ton each mile. The annual expence for repairs and collection is £660. Required how much per cent of the original cost the undertakers will draw per annum? (Hamilton, R, 'A Short System of Arithmetic and Bookkeeping', 1788, Problem XCIII).

(48) If the straight line approach has been used this implies that the looms will have a life of 22 years. The theoretically correct approach is to use the sinking fund depreciation method; with a 5% interest rate the charge would be about right if the asset's life is 15 years but it is very unlikely that this method would have been used.

(49) A further sheet gives "Calculation of the Cost of 100 Looms for Weaving Edinburgs & Sheeting". The total cost of the looms is estimated at £201 5 -, so that interest is being charged at 5%.

(50) The Account Charge and Discharge system was not completely supplanted by the Italian Method and the terms 'charge' and 'discharge' were frequently used as synonyms for debit and credit.

CHAPTER 18

SUMMARY

NOTES AND REFERENCES

(1) Nobes, C, 'The Development of Double Entry', Garland Publishing Inc, New York, 1984.

(2) Yamey, B S, H C Edey and H W Thomson, 'Accounting in England and Scotland: 1543-1800', London: Sweet and Maxwell, 1963, pp 170-173.

(3) Mair was also the pioneer of science education in Scotland (Sutherland, D J S, 'John Mair, The Pioneer of Science Teaching in Scotland', The Scottish Educational Journal, 4 July, 1952, p 422).

(4) Stevenson, W, 'A Serious Advice to Tradesmen shewing them the inconveniences they lye under ... by not learning Book-keeping', Edinburgh, 1756, p 1.

(5) North, R, 'The Gentleman Accomptant', London, 1714; Dodson, J, 'The Accountant, or, the Method of Book-keeping deduced from Clear Principles', London, 1750.

(6) Gordon, W, 'The Universal Accountant', 1765, vol II, p 15.

(7) Stevenson was one of the most enthusiastic in extolling the virtues of this 'universally necessary' art ('A General Discourse Shewing the Usefulness of the Italian Method of Book-keeping, Edinburgh, 1732).

(8) Morrison, J, 'The Elements of Book Keeping by Single and Double Entry', London: Longman, Hurst, Rees, Orme and Brown, 1813, Preface.

(9) North, R, op cit, 1714, p 89.

(10) Winjum, J O, 'The Role of Accounting in the Economic Development of England: 1500-1750', Center for International Education and Research in Accounting, University of Illinois, 1972.

(11) Malcolm, A, 'A New Treatise of Arithmetick and Book-keeping, 1718, Appendix, p 40; A Treatise of Book-keeping, 1731, Appendix, p 21.

(12) Hamilton, R, 'Introduction to Merchandize', 2nd edition, 1788, part V, chapter VI, section 31, pp 490/491.

(13) Malcolm, A, 1731, op cit, p 47.

(14) Hamilton, R, 'Introduction to Merchandize', vol II, 1779, part IV, chapter I, section 107.

(15) This might be regarded as an example of the use of opportunity cost.

(16) Gordon, W, 'The General Counting-House and Man of Business', 1766, pp 463-487.

(17) Hamilton, R, 1779, op cit, part V, chapter V, section 154.

(18) Gordon, W, 'The Universal Accountant', vol II, 1765, p 50.

(19) Littleton, A C, 'Accounting Evolution to 1900', New York: The American Institute Publishing Co, p 150 (reprinted by University of Alabama Press, 1981).

(20) Malcolm, A, 1718, op cit, p 189.

(21) Colinson, R 'Idea Rationaria', 1683, Dedication to 'the Merchants of Edinburgh'.

(22) Littleton, A C and V K Zimmerman, 'Accounting Theory: Continuity and Change', Englewood Cliffs: Prentice-Hall, 1962, pp 263/264.

(23) Marshall, G. 'Presbyteries and Profits', Oxford: Clarendon Press, 1980. Marshall describes, for example, how Sir John Clerk of Penicuik set out to use his accounting system to improve the profitability of his colliery: "In order that the profitability of the colliery might be continuously assessed, both costs and output had to be calculable, reasonably consistent, indeed predictable. A series of control measures were implemented by Sir John in order to achieve this end. As regards costs, strict accounting procedures were to be observed in order to maintain the highest possible degree of control over the colliery's business, and to prevent any loss of cash or materials through pilfering. Colliery officials were to inventory and keep track of all coal and other materials pertaining to the mine and the books were to be balanced and cleared with Sir John on a regular basis." (p 243). Sir John's records could have been maintained without using the Italian Method but the textbook writers emphasised the considerable advantages of using that system.

(24) Gordon, W, 1765, op cit, p 4.

(25) Smith, A, 'The Wealth of Nations',1786 edition, vol II, book IV, chapter V, p 263.

(26) Metcalfe, C H, 'Cost of Manufacturers and the Administration of Workshops, Public and Private', New York: Wiley and Sons, 1885; Garcke, E and J M Fells, 'Factory Accounts', London: Crosby Lockwood and Co, 1887; Norton, G P 'Textile Manufacturers' Bookkeeping for the Counting House, Mill and Warehouse', Huddersfield: Alfred Jubb, 1889.

(27) Sir Walter Scott, writing in 1820, refered to accountancy as a branch of legal practice (quoted in Brown, R, 'A History of Accounting and Accountants', Edinburgh: T C and E C Jack, 1905, p 197).

(28) Hume, D, 'A Treatise of Human Nature', 1st edition 1739, reprinted Oxford: Clarendon Press, 1975, p 273.

(29) Malcolm, A, 1718, op cit, pp 113/4.

(30) Gordon, W, 1765, op cit, p 12.

(31) Sombart, W, 'Der Modern Kapitalismus', 5th edition 1902. The translation is that provided by Lister, R J, 'Werner Sombart's Der moderne Kapitalismus': An

Apotheosis of Double-Entry Accounting?', Accounting and Business Research, Summer 1985, pp 229-231.

(32) Malcolm, A, 1731, op cit, preface.

(33) Hatfield, H R, 'An Historical Defense of Book-keeping', printed in Baxter, W T and S Davidson, 'Studies in Accounting Theory', London: Sweet and Maxwell, 1962, p 12.

(34) Camic lists both Robert and his father (Gavin) among 375 18th century Scottish 'intellectual achievers' (Camic, C, 'Experience and Enlightenment, Socialization for Cultural Change in Eighteeenth Century Scotland', Edinburgh: University Press, 1983, pp 243-256).

INDEX

Note: A listing of the references for William Gordon, Robert Hamilton, Alexander Malcolm and John Mair would be lengthy and not particularly helpful for the reader. For these writers the Table of Contents and the Index entries for the required subject matter should be consulted .

Accounting Books Published by Garland

NEW BOOKS

- *Altman, Edward I., *The Prediction of Corporate Bankruptcy: A Discriminant Analysis.*
  New York, 1988.

- Ashton, Robert H., ed. *The Evolution of Accounting Behavior Research: An Overview.*
  New York, 1984.

- Ashton, Robert H., ed. *Some Early Contributions to the Study of Audit Judgement.*
  New York, 1984.

- *Bodenhorn, Diran. *Economic Accounting.*
  New York, 1988.

---

* Included in the Garland series Foundations of Accounting
† Included in the Academy of Accounting Historians, Classics Series, Gary John Previt, ed.

■ *Bougen, Philip D. *Accounting and Industrial Relations: Some Historical Evidence on Their Interaction.*
New York, 1988.

■ Brief, Richard P., ed. *Corporate Financial Reporting and Analysis in the Early 1900s.*
New York, 1986.

■ Brief, Richard P., ed. *Depreciation and Capital Maintenance.*
New York, 1984.

■ Brief, Richard P., ed. *Estimating the Economic Rate of Return from Accounting Data.*
New York, 1986.

■ Brief, Richard P., ed. *Four Classics on the Theory of Double-Entry Bookkeeping.*
New York, 1982.

■ Chambers, R. J., and G. W. Dean, eds. *Chambers on Accounting.*
New York, 1986.
Volume I: Accounting, Management and Finance.
Volume II: Accounting Practice and Education.
Volume III: Accounting Theory and Research.
Volume IV: Price Variation Accounting.
Volume V: Continuously Contemporary Accounting.

■ *Clark, John B. (with a new introduction by Donald Dewey). *Capital and Its Earnings.*
New York, 1988.

▪ Clarke, F. L. *The Tangled Web of Price Variation Accounting: The Development of Ideas Underlying Professional Prescriptions in Six Countries.*
New York, 1982.

▪ Coopers & Lybrand. *The Early History of Coopers & Lybrand.*
New York, 1984.

▪ Craswell, Allen. *Audit Qualifications in Australia 1950 to 1979.*
New York, 1986.

▪ Dean, G. W., and M. C. Wells, eds. *The Case for Continuously Contemporary Accounting.*
New York, 1984.

▪ Dean, G. W. , and M. C. Wells, eds. *Forerunners of Realizable Values Accounting in Financial Reporting.*
New York, 1982.

▪ Edey, Harold C. *Accounting Queries.*
New York, 1982.

▪ Edwards, J. R., ed. *Legal Regulation of British Company Accounts 1836-1900.*
New York, 1986.

▪ Edwards, J. R. ed. *Reporting Fixed Assets in Nineteenth-Century Company Accounts.*
New York, 1986.

▪ Edwards, J. R., ed. *Studies of Company Records: 1830-1974.*
New York, 1984.

▪ Fabricant, Solomon. *Studies in Social and Private Accounting.*
New York, 1982.

▪ Gaffikin, Michael, and Michael Aitkin, eds. *The Development of Accounting Theory: Significant Contributors to Accounting Thought in the 20th Century.*
New York, 1982.

▪ Hawawini, Gabriel A., ed. *Bond Duration and Immunization: Early Developments and Recent Contributions.*
New York, 1982.

▪ Hawawini, Gabriel A., and Pierre A. Michel, eds. *European Equity Markets: Risk, Return, and Efficiency.*
New York, 1984.

▪ Hawawini, Gabriel A., and Pierre Michel. *Mandatory Financial Information and Capital Market Equilibrium in Belgium.*
New York, 1986.

▪ Hawkins, David F. *Corporate Financial Disclosure, 1900-1933: A Study of Management Inertia within a Rapidly Changing Environment.*
New York, 1986.

▪ *Hopwood, Anthony G. *Accounting from the Outside: The Collected Papers of Anthony G. Hopwood.*
New York, 1988.

▪ Johnson, H. Thomas. *A New Approach to Management Accounting History.*
New York, 1986.

■ Kinney, William R., ed. *Fifty Years of Statistical Auditing.*
New York, 1986.

■ Klemstine, Charles E., and Michael W. Maher. *Management Accounting Research: A Review and Annotated Bibliography.*
New York, 1984.

■ *Langenderfer, Harold Q., and Grover L. Porter, eds. *Rational Accounting Concepts: The Writings of Willard Graham.*
New York, 1988.

■ *Lee, T. A., ed. *The Evolution of Audit Thought and Practice.*
New York, 1988.

■ Lee, T. A., ed. *A Scottish Contribution to Accounting History.*
New York, 1986.

■ Lee, T. A. *Towards a Theory and Practice of Cash Flow Accounting.*
New York, 1986.

■ Lee, T. A., ed. *Transactions of the Chartered Accountants Students' Societies of Edinburgh and Glasgow: A Selection of Writings, 1886-1958.*
New York, 1984.

■ *Loft, Anne. *Understanding Accounting in Its Social and Historical Context: The Case of Cost Accounting in Britain, 1914-1925.*
New York, 1988.

▪ McKinnon, Jill L.. *The Historical Development and Operational Form of Corporate Reporting Regulation in Japan.*
New York, 1986.

▪ *McMickle, Peter L., and Paul H. Jensen, eds. *The Auditor's Guide of 1869: A Review and Computer Enhancement of Recently Discovered Old Microfilm of America's First Book on Auditing by H. J. Mettenheimer.*
New York, 1988.

▪ *McMickle, Peter L., and Paul H. Jensen, eds. *The Birth of American Accountancy: A Bibliographic Analysis of Works on Accounting Published in America through 1820.*
New York, 1988.

▪ *Mepham, M.-J. *Accounting in Eighteenth-Century Scotland.*
New York, 1988.

▪ *Mills, Patti A., trans. *The Legal Literature of Accounting: On Accounts by Diego del Castillo.*
New York, 1988.

▪ *Murphy, George J. *The Evolution of Canadian Corporate Reporting Practices: 1900-1970.*
New York, 1988.

▪ *Mumford, Michael J., ed. *Edward Stamp—Later Papers.*
New York, 1988.

▪ Nobes, Christopher, ed. *The Development of Double Entry: Selected Essays.*
New York, 1984.

- Nobes, Christopher. *Issues in International Accounting.*
New York, 1986.

- Parker, Lee D. *Developing Control Concepts in the 20th Century.*
New York, 1986.

- *Parker, Lee D., ed. *Financial Reporting to Employees: From Past to Present.*
New York, 1988.

- *Parker, Lee D., and O. Finley Graves, eds. *Methodology and Method in History: A Bibliography.*
New York, 1988.

- Parker, R. H. *Papers on Accounting History.*
New York, 1984.

- Previts, Gary John, and Alfred R. Roberts, eds. *Federal Securities Law and Accounting 1933-1970: Selected Addresses.*
New York, 1986.

- *Reid, Jean Margo, ed. *Law and Accounting: Nineteenth-Century American Legal Cases.*
New York, 1988.

- *Sheldahl, Terry K., ed. *Accounting Literature in the United States before Mitchell and Jones (1796): Contributions by Four English Writers, through American Editions, and Two Pioneer Local Authors.*
New York, 1988.

▪ Sheldahl, Terry K. *Beta Alpha Psi, from Alpha to Omega: Pursuing a Vision of Professional Education for Accountants, 1919-1945.*
New York, 1982.

▪ Sheldahl, Terry K. *Beta Alpha Psi, from Omega to Zeta Omega: The Making of a Comprehensive Accounting Fraternity, 1946-1984.*
New York, 1986.

▪ *Sheldahl, Terry K., ed. *Education for the Mercantile Countinghouse: Critical and Constructive Essays by Nine British Writers, 1716-1794.*
New York, 1988.

▪ Solomons, David. *Collected Papers on Accounting and Accounting Education (in two volumes).*
New York, 1984.

▪ Sprague, Charles F. *The General Principles of the Science of Accounts and the Accountancy of Investment.*
New York, 1984.

▪ Stamp, Edward. *Edward Stamp—Later Papers. See* Michael J. Mumford.

▪ Stamp, Edward. *Selected Papers on Accounting, Auditing, and Professional Problems.*
New York, 1984.

▪ *Staubus, George J. *Activity Costing for Decisions: Cost Accounting in the Decision Usefulness Framework.*
New York, 1988.

▪ Storrar, Colin, ed. *The Accountant's Magazine—An Anthology.*
New York, 1986.

▪ Tantral, Panadda. *Accounting Literature in Non-Accounting Journals: An Annotated Bibliography.*
New York, 1984.

▪ *Vangermeersch, Richard G. *Alexander Hamilton Church: A Man of Ideas for All Seasons.*
New York, 1988.

▪ Vangermeersch, Richard, ed. *The Contributions of Alexander Hamilton Church to Accounting and Management.*
New York, 1986.

▪ Vangermeersch, Richard, ed. *Financial Accounting Milestones in the Annual Reports of the United States Steel Corporation—The First Seven Decades.*
New York, 1986.

▪ *Walker, Stephen P. *The Society of Accountants in Edinburgh, 1854-1914: A Study of Recruitment to a New Profession.*
New York, 1988.

▪ Whitmore, John. *Factory Accounts.*
New York, 1984.

▪ *Whittred, Greg. *The Evolution of Consolidated Financial Reporting in Australia: An Evaluation of an Alternative Hypothesis.*
New York, 1988.

▪ Yamey, Basil S. *Further Essays on the History of Accounting.*
New York, 1982.

▪ Zeff, Stephen A., ed. *The Accounting Postulates and Principles Controversy of the 1960s.*
New York, 1982.

▪ Zeff, Stephen A., ed. *Accounting Principles Through the Years: The Views of Professional and Academic Leaders 1938-1954.*
New York, 1982.

▪ Zeff, Stephen A., and Maurice Moonitz, eds. *Sourcebook on Accounting Principles and Auditing Procedures: 1917-1953 (in two volumes).*
New York, 1984.

▪ *Zeff, Stephen a., ed. *The U. S. Accounting Profession in the 1890s and Early 1900s.*
New York, 1988.

REPRINTED TITLES

▪ *American Institute of Accountants. *Accountants Index, 1920* (in two volumes).
New York, 1921 (Garland reprint, 1988).

▪ American Institute of Accountants. *Fiftieth Anniversary Celebration.*
Chicago, 1937 (Garland reprint, 1982).

▪ American Institute of Accountants. *Library Catalogue.*
New York, 1919 (Garland reprint, 1982).

▪ Arthur Andersen Company. *The First Fifty Years 1913-1963.*
Chicago, 1963 (Garland reprint, 1984).

▪ Bevis, Herman W. *Corporate Financial Reporting in a Competitive Economy.*
New York, 1965 (Garland reprint, 1986).

▪ Bonini,. Charles P., Robert K. Jaedicke, and Harvey M. Wagner, eds. *Management Controls: New Directions in Basic Research.*
New York, 1964 (Garland reprint, 1986).

▪ **The Book-Keeper and the American Counting Room.*
New York, 1880-1884 (Garland reprint, 1988).

▪ Bray, F. Sewell. *Four Essays in Accounting Theory.* London, 1953. *Bound with* Institute of Chartered Accountants in England and Wales and the National Institute of Economic and Social Research. *Some Accounting Terms and Concepts.*
Cambridge, 1951 (Garland reprint, 1982).

▪ Brown, R. Gene, and Kenneth S. Johnston. *Paciolo on Accounting.*
New York, 1963 (Garland reprint, 1984).

▪ Carey, John L., and William O. Doherty, eds. *Ethical Standards of the Accounting Profession.*
New York, 1966 (Garland reprint, 1986).

▪ Chambers, R. J. *Accounting in Disarray.*
Melbourne, 1973 (Garland reprint, 1982).

▪ Cooper, Ernest. *Fifty-seven years in an Accountant's Office.* *See* Sir Russell Kettle.

▪ Couchman, Charles B. *The Balance-Sheet.*
New York, 1924 (Garland reprint, 1982).

▪ Couper, Charles Tennant. *Report of the Trial ... Against the Directors and Manager of the City of Glasgow Bank.*
Edinburgh, 1879 (Garland reprint, 1984).

▪ Cutforth, Arthur E. *Audits.*
London, 1906 (Garland reprint, 1982).

▪ Cutforth, Arthur E. *Methods of Amalgamation.*
London, 1926 (Garland reprint, 1982).

▪ Deinzer, Harvey T. *Development of Accounting Thought.*
New York, 1965 (Garland reprint, 1984).

▪ De Paula, F.R.M. *The Principles of Auditing.*
London, 1915 (Garland reprint, 1984).

▪ Dickerson, R. W. *Accountants and the Law of Negligence.*
Toronto, 1966 (Garland reprint, 1982).

▪ Dodson, James. *The Accountant, or, the Method of Bookkeeping Deduced from Clear Principles, and Illustrated by a Variety of Examples.*
London, 1750 (Garland reprint, 1984).

▪ Dyer, S. *A Common Sense Method of Double Entry Bookkeeping, on First Principles, as Suggested by De Morgan. Part I, Theoretical.*
London, 1897 (Garland reprint, 1984).

▪ *† Edwards, James Don. *History of Public Accounting in the United States.*
East Lansing, 1960 (Garland reprint, 1988).

▪ *† Edwards, James Don, and Robert F. Salmonson. *Contributions of Four Accounting Pioneers: Kohler, Littleton, May, Paton.*
East Lancing, 1961 (Garland reprint, 1988).

▪ *The Fifth International Congress on Accounting, 1938 [Kongress-Archiv 1938 des V. Internationalen Prüfungs- und Treuhand-Kongresses].*
Berlin, 1938 (Garland reprint, 1986).

■ Finney, A. H. *Consolidated Statements.*
New York, 1922 (Garland reprint, 1982).

■ Fisher, Irving. *The Rate of Interest.*
New York, 1907 (Garland reprint, 1982).

■ Florence, P. Sargant. *Economics of Fatigue and Unrest and the Efficiency of Labour in English and American Industry.*
London, 1923 (Garland reprint, 1984).

■ *Fourth International Congress on Accounting 1933.*
London, 1933 (Garland reprint, 1982).

■ Foye, Arthur B. *Haskins & Sells: Our First Seventy-Five Years.*
New York, 1970 (Garland reprint, 1984).

■ *† Garner, Paul S. *Evolution of Cost Accounting to 1925.*
University, Alabama, 1925 (Garland reprint, 1988).

■ Garnsey, Sir Gilbert. *Holding Companies and Their Published Accounts.* London, 1923. *Bound with* Sir Gilbert Garnsey. *Limitations of a Balance Sheet.*
London, 1928 (Garland reprint, 1982).

■ Garrett, A. A. *The History of the Society of Incorporated Accountants, 1885-1957.*
Oxford, 1961 (Garland reprint, 1984).

■ Gilman, Stephen. *Accounting Concepts of Profit.*
New York, 1939 (Garland reprint, 1982).

- Gordon, William. *The Universal Accountant, and Complete Merchant* ... [Volume II].
  Edinburgh, 1765 (Garland reprint, 1986).

- Green, Wilmer. *History and Survey of Accountancy.*
  Brooklyn, 1930 (Garland reprint, 1986).

- Hamilton, Robert. *An Introduction to Merchandise, Parts IV and V (Italian Bookkeeping and Practical Bookkeeping).*
  Edinburgh, 1788 (Garland reprint, 1982).

- Hatton, Edward. *The Merchant's Magazine; or, Tradesman's Treasury.* London, 1695 (Garland reprint, 1982).
Hills, George S. *The Law of Accounting and Financial Statements.*
  Boston, 1957 (Garland reprint, 1982).

- *A History of Cooper Brothers & Co. 1854 to 1954.*
  London, 1954 (Garland reprint, 1986).

- Hofstede, Geert. *The Game of Budget Control.*
  Assen, 1967 (Garland reprint, 1984).

- Howitt, Sir Harold. *The History of the Institute of Chartered Accountants in England and Wales 1880-1965, and of Its Founder Accountancy Bodies 1870-1880.*
  London, 1966 (Garland reprint, 1984).

- Institute of Chartered Accountants in England and Wales and The National Institute of Social and Economic Research. *Some Accounting Terms and Concepts.* *See* F. Sewell Bray.

■ Institute of Chartered Accountants of Scotland. *History of the Chartered Accountants of Scotland from the Earliest Times to 1954.*
Edinburgh, 1954 (Garland reprint, 1984).

■ *International Congress on Accounting 1929.*
New York, 1930 (Garland reprint, 1982).

■ Jaedicke, Robert K., Yuji Ijiri, and Oswald Nielsen, eds. *Research in Accounting Measurement.*
American Accounting Association,
1966 (Garland reprint, 1986).

■ Keats, Charles. *Magnificent Masquerade.*
New York, 1964 (Garland reprint, 1982).

■ Kettle, Sir Russell. *Deloitte & Co. 1854-1956.* Oxford, 1958. *Bound with* Ernest Cooper. *Fifty-seven Years in an Accountant's Office.*
London, 1921 (Garland reprint, 1982).

■ Kitchen, J., and R. H. Parker. *Accounting Thought and Education: Six English Pioneers.*
London, 1980 (Garland reprint, 1984).

■ Lacey, Kenneth. *Profit Measurement and Price Changes.*
London, 1952 (Garland reprint, 1982).

■ Lee, Chauncey. *The American Accomptant.*
Lansingburgh, 1797 (Garland reprint, 1982).

■ Lee, T. A., and R. H. Parker. *The Evolution of Corporate Financial Reporting.*
Middlesex, 1979 (Garland reprint, 1984).

■ *† Littleton, A. C.. *Accounting Evolution to 1900.*
New York, 1933 (Garland reprint, 1988).

■ Malcolm, Alexander. *The Treatise of Book-Keeping, or, Merchants Accounts; In the Italian Method of Debtor and Creditor; Wherein the Fundamental Principles of That Curious and Approved Method Are Clearly and Fully Explained and Demonstrated ... To Which Are Added, Instructions for Gentlemen of Land Estates, and Their Stewards or Factors: With Directions Also for Retailers, and Other More Private Persons.*
London, 1731 (Garland reprint, 1986).

■ Meij, J. L., ed. *Depreciation and Replacement Policy.*
Chicago, 1961 (Garland reprint, 1986).

■ Newlove, George Hills. *Consolidated Balance Sheets.*
New York, 1926 (Garland reprint, 1982).

■ North, Roger. *The Gentleman Accomptant; or, An Essay to Unfold the Mystery of Accompts; By Way of Debtor and Creditor, Commonly Called Merchants Accompts, and Applying the Same to the Concerns of the Nobility and Gentry of England.*
London 1714 (Garland reprint, 1986).

■ **Proceedings of the Seventh International Congress of Accountants.* Amsterdam, 1957 (Garland reprint, 1988).

■ Pryce-Jones, Janet E., and R. H. Parker. *Accounting in Scotland: A Historical Bibliography.*
Edinburgh, 1976 (Garland reprint, 1984).

■ *Reynolds, W. B., and F. W. Thornton. *Duties of a Junior Accountant* [three editions].
New York, 1917, 1933, 1953
(Garland reprint, 1988).

■ Robinson, H. W. *A History of Accountants in Ireland.*
Dublin, 1964 (Garland edition, 1984).

■ Robson, T. B. *Consolidated and Other Group Accounts.*
London, 1950 (Garland reprint, 1982).

■ Rorem, C. Rufus. *Accounting Method.*
Chicago, 1928 (Garland reprint, 1982).

■ Saliers, Earl A., ed. *Accountants' Handbook.*
New York, 1923 (Garland reprint, 1986).

■ Samuel, Horace B. *Shareholder's Money.*
London, 1933 (Garland reprint, 1982).

■ *The Securitites and Exchange Commission in the Matter of McKesson & Robbins, Inc. Report on Investigation.*
Washington, D. C., 1940 (Garland reprint, 1982).

■ *The Securities and Exchange Commission in the Matter of McKesson & Robbins, Inc. Testimony of Expert Witnesses.*
Washington, D. C., 1939 (Garland reprint, 1982).

■ Shaplen, Roger. *Kreuger: Genius and Swindler.*
New York, 1960 (Garland reprint, 1986).

■ Singer, H. W. *Standardized Accountancy in Germany. (With a new appendix.)*
Cambridge, 1943 (Garland reprint, 1982).

■ *The Sixth International Congress on Accounting.*
London, 1952 (Garland reprint, 1984).

■ Stewart, Jas. C. (with a new introductory note by T. A. Lee). *Pioneers of a Profession: Chartered Accountants to 1879.*
Edinburgh, 1977 (Garland reprint, 1986).

■ Thompson, Wardbaugh. *The Accomptant's Oracle: or, a Key to Science, Being a Compleat Practical System of Book-keeping.*
York, 1777 (Garland reprint, 1984).

■ *Thornton, F. W. *Duties of the Senior Accountant.* New York, 1932. *Bound with.* John C. Martin. *Duties of Junior and Senior Accountants, Supplement of the CPA Handbook.*
New York, 1953 (Garland reprint, 1988).

■ Vatter, William J. *Managerial Accounting.*
New York, 1950 (Garland reprint, 1986).

■ Woolf, Arthur H. *A Short History of Accountants and Accountancy.*
London, 1912 (Garland reprint, 1986).

■ Yamey, B. S., H. C. Edey, and Hugh W. Thomson. *Accounting in England and Scotland: 1543-1800.*
London, 1963 (Garland reprint, 1982).